THE GREAT RUSSIAN REVOLUTION

A RECENT PHOTOGRAPH OF VICTOR CHERNOV

Courtesy of Boris M. Joffe

THE GREAT RUSSIAN REVOLUTION

BY

VICTOR CHERNOV

TRANSLATED AND ABRIDGED BY

PHILIP E. MOSELY

... by Viktor Mikhaĭlovich Chernov

NEW YORK / RUSSELL & RUSSELL

1966

REISSUED, 1966, BY RUSSELL & RUSSELL
BY ARRANGEMENT WITH PHILLIP E. MOSELY
L.C. CATALOG CARD NO: 66—13165
PRINTED IN THE UNITED STATES OF AMERICA

CONTENTS

ILLUSTRATIONS

THE GREAT RUSSIAN REVOLUTION

CHAPTER ONE

THE COLLAPSE OF A DYNASTY

THAT tragic couple—Nicholas II and Alexandra Feodorovna—seemed to have been created at history's special command to end their dynasty.

It was as if some evil fate impended over that man and his family from the very beginning. So true was this that when, at the very climax of the World War, the Tsar took it into his head to remove Grand Duke Nicholas Nikolayevich and take his place as commander in chief, almost all his associates were horror stricken. They realized his complete unsuitability for such a task, his absolute incompetence in military matters. Above all, they feared the effect on the soldiers and the country. A low-voiced rumor was continually repeated about the ill-starred Emperor, whose presence would not bring good fortune to the troops.

The character of Nicholas II had taken final form beneath the relentless pressure of his destiny—a destiny by no means accidental. The poet Alexander Blok wrote of him: "Stubborn but will-less, nervous but deadened to everything, with no trust left in people, worried and cautious in words, he was not master of himself." Rasputin said, "There is something missing inside."

To adversity he opposed a kind of stubborn passivity, as if he wished to escape from life. His reactions to events were languid and, so to speak, automatic. He seemed not a man but a poor copy of one. At crucial moments power in his hands was "not power, but its pale shadow."

The depression of Nicholas II's inner life evidently dated from his childhood, spent under the severe authority of his father. Alexander III was rough hewn, inflexible, fully capable of bending another's will by the ponderous despotism of his own character. Nicholas' weak, almost feminine nature adapted itself quickly to his father's tyrannical will. He became obedient and fawning. Within the family these qualities won him the nickname of "Nicky-ducky."

The memory of Alexander II, annihilated by the terrorists' bomb, was strong in the imperial family. Surrounding himself with concentric circles of secret police, Alexander III lived like a recluse, like a hunted wolf snarling at his pursuers, "like the prisoner of war of the Russian Revolution in his palace of Gatchina," as Marx dubbed him. This enchanted circle, with its musty atmosphere, had a depressing influence on the young Grand Duke. Even his opportunity of temporary escape—his journey to the Far East and to Japan—brought him no luck. Through some absurdity of fate he found his way into a temple strictly forbidden to foreigners and from the sword of a plain Japanese samurai received a terrible blow on the head, a symbol of the even more severe blow which tiny Japan was to deal to the Tsar's military prestige in the Far East, and, indeed, throughout the world.

But Nicholas still had to undergo a second dose of "home-arrest." Among the "human documents" of that troubled time is the naïve little letter of a private in the palace guard, written to his family after the murder of the minister Sipyagin by a revolutionary. "The minister was buried on Thursday, but the poor Emperor went only to the church, not to the cemetery. His life is worse than ours. The Emperor is afraid of every little thing, and mostly sits in the Winter Palace, just like someone under arrest. His only amusement is playing with his dogs; he unleashes five of them, sometimes eight, and runs along the garden with them, they jump up on him; occasionally he runs along the roof or plays ball with his brother; such is their unfortunate situation."

It most certainly was not a pleasant life. On his own estate Livadia in the Crimea he lived a shut-in existence, as if besieged in a fortress. The inhabitants were strictly forbidden to approach the imperial residence; cordons and pickets were everywhere, troops and police, official and secret, in uniform and in mufti. And during his journeys across Russia a line of soldiers was always posted along the railroad. Constant reconnaissances and inspections were carried out. In towns, attics and cellars along the Emperor's route were boarded up. Plumbing and drainage were inspected because of the danger of mines. Windows and balconies could be approached only by special permit. Tickets were issued granting people the right to stand on the sidewalks. It was all very boring!

In this twilight existence there was one moment of exhilarating triumph. After the death of his gloomy, tyrannical father, from a "poor, terrified young man," as Leo Tolstoy once called him, Nicholas was suddenly elevated to omnipotent dominion over one fifth of the entire globe. That was enough to turn any head. He was Tsar. His subjects, wearied of Alexander III's bleak rule, expected better things of him. Had not Nicholas himself felt that heavy paternal hand just as his subjects had? All that was alive in the country eagerly sought hints of a milder rule to come.

Russian society of that time was not difficult to please. Two or three August marginalia, "favorable," "consoling," on the governors' reports, opposite accounts of the expansion of the school network; two or three trips away from the palace without secret service guard; a ukaze assigning fifty thousand rubles to assist needy authors—these were enough to make hearts swell with hope. But trips without a guard at once aroused alarm, and the cordon was doubled around "that incautious young man." The money assigned to assist authors was added to the "reptilian," that is, the corruption, fund. As for the Emperor's marginalia, the censorship, not daring to conceal them, forbade comment on them.

Feeling the welcoming and expectant glances of his subjects concentrated upon him, Nicholas could consider himself happy, and happy people are not unwilling to make others happy. Witte confirms this. "When Emperor Nicholas II ascended the throne, a spirit of good will radiated from him, if one may put it so. Sincerely and with all his heart he wished happiness and peace to all Russia, to all the nationalities in Russia, to all his subjects, for the Emperor undoubtedly had a very kind heart, and if other traits of his character cropped up in later years, that was because the Emperor had to endure a very great deal." Even the opposition papers published outside Russia were not irreconcilable toward the young Tsar. After vainly waiting seven years for a glimmering of better things, the liberal paper, *Liberation,* refused to give up hope. "The Tsar himself is good and passionately anxious to make Russia happy," it insisted. It is pleasant to believe what one desires deeply, and the rumor, once started, of the young Tsar's personal kindness and "good will" maintained itself by tradition. Even a terrorist like Eugene Shauman, assassin of the Governor General of Finland, could write: "Your Majesty! I sacrifice my life, attempting to convince you, Majesty, of the bad condition of affairs in Russia. Knowing the kind heart and noble intentions of Your Majesty, I beseech you, Majesty, to examine the situation carefully . . . With the deepest and most loyal respect, I remain the faithful subject of Your Imperial Majesty, the Most Powerful and Most Merciful Emperor, Eugene Shauman."

The moment when he ascended the throne was the best in Nicholas' life. But there was a fly even in this ointment. The Moscow coronation ceremonies, during which the imperial presents and refreshments were to be distributed to the populace, were organized with Asiatic carelessness and drew a tremendous mob of people to Hodynka Field. The ground was full of old ditches and holes carelessly boarded over. There was a panic and when it was past these holes were crammed with the bodies of people trampled to death.

Where stood the laden table, now stands the coffin;
Where shouts of banqueting resounded,
The burial faces moan;
Pale death looks out on all . . .

Popular superstition took this catastrophe as an ill omen for the reign. And now the young Tsar showed for the first time that astonishing insensibility which was to surprise his people so often. Not wishing the coronation ceremonies to be broken off, Nicholas set an example of imperturbability. Although the bodies of a huge number of victims—the exact figure has never been published—were still unburied, he honored with his presence the luxurious ball given by a foreign embassy.

One other mishap cast a shadow over the young Tsar's ascension to the throne. While receiving a zemstvo delegation, which in its address of loyalty hinted at the need for liberal reforms in government, the Tsar did not follow the words of his prepared speech, which declared impossible of satisfaction these "baseless aspirations"—for a constitution. This in itself would have been a sufficiently abrupt refusal. Instead, by a slip of the tongue, he uttered the sharper, directly insulting words, "*senseless* aspirations," and in embarrassment, left the room hastily. The foreign correspondents of the time referred to his "boyish lack of ease, his shuffling gait, his shy glances"; for them he was "a manikin Tsar," who left an "almost sickly impression, but seemed at the same time strong because of this very hysteria and automatism."

Plainly "Monomakh's cap" was far too heavy for the head to which it had fallen. Nicholas bent low beneath its burden; all his life he tried to straighten up and not let people see that he was ill at ease. He tried to spur himself with the persistent notion that he was not a mere mortal, but God's anointed; that a special blessing of heaven rested on him, invisibly guiding him along the true path without the effort of his own will. Thus he moved along his path of life, a half smile, incomprehensible, "mysterious," as many said, hovering over his lips, his glance never pausing for long at a visitor's eyes, but slipping slowly over the face, or staring into the distance.

These traits were intensified throughout Nicholas' life. Count Kokovtsev shuddered on seeing him in January, 1917. "His face was terribly thin, sunken, and furrowed with tiny wrinkles. His eyes . . . had lost all color, and roved helplessly from one object to another." At important moments of their conversation the Tsar "fell into an absolutely incomprehensible, helpless state. A strange smile, expressionless, somehow ill, I would even say almost unconscious, never left his face, and he kept looking at me, perplexed, as if seeking support and anxious for me to remind him of something that had absolutely disappeared from his memory." After his audience, Count Kokovtsev went as far as to say to Dr. Botkin, "Do you not see the state the Emperor is in? Why, he is on the verge of mental collapse, if not already in its grip." Botkin's reply was an eloquent silence.

The abrupt close of the young Tsar's first appearance before the delegation of his subjects was indeed accidental. He himself probably suffered more than anyone else. He disliked violent scenes. Whenever a person fell into disfavor, Nicholas preferred to arrange his disgrace behind his back, without ceasing to be outwardly "invariably well disposed." In general, he held to those manners which, from childhood, had made him "a model boy," the personification of good breeding. He was even said to remind people of Alexander I, who had been a "*grand charmeur.*" "I do not know anyone," says one minister, "who, on first being presented, was not charmed by the Emperor; he charms by his sincere manner, his kindly treatment, and especially by his astonishing good breeding; in all my life I have never met a man with more cultivated manners than the Emperor."

Nicholas II should have been born not an emperor but an average country gentleman, with a fortune sufficient for a peaceful life in quiet times remote from social disturbances. As General Danilov put it: "A life without responsibility and without sadness, it seems to me, would have better suited the inner tendency of the last Russian monarch." Instead, history cast on his clumsy shoulders a great burden, that of being the chief figure in the final and tragic chapter in the history of a three-hundred-year-old dynasty.

Nicholas inherited from his ancestors the traditions of a foreign policy of conquest. In his fantasies and plans for the future he generously compensated himself for his failures in the present. The confidant of his intimate thoughts, General Kuropatkin, wrote in his diary: "I told Witte that our Emperor had grandiose plans in his head: to take Manchuria for Russia, to set about the annexation of Korea to Russia. He wishes to take Persia, to seize not only the Bosphorus, but also the Dardanelles. He dreams of bringing Tibet under his authority." Hence, the Tsar's ideas of foreign policy: "The quarrel of Serbia and Bulgaria is useful for us." It was advantageous "to excite the Tibetans against the English." It was beneficial "to create a strip of wild and almost impassable land to separate the Russian and Japanese spheres of influence." It was advantageous "to hire the hun-huz bandits"; it was especially profitable to entice the Japanese into Korea, for "it was better to fight them on the Korean mainland." But, since his ministers could not approve such risky adventures, the Tsar turned against them: "He still thinks he is right, that he understands better than we Russia's needs and advantages. Therefore the Emperor deceives us." Hence, any casual favorite, ready to approve anything, "seems to the Tsar to understand his ideas better than we, his ministers."[1]

And the greatest of his servants, like Witte, could only note their thoughts and regrets. "I am sorry for the Tsar. Sorry for Russia. Poor, unfortunate Emperor. What did he receive, and what will he leave behind? And he is, to be sure, a kind and clever man, but without a will, and through this trait of his character his faults as a statesman have developed; that is, his faults as a ruler, and especially as an absolute and unlimited ruler: God and I."[2]

A Social Revolutionary press once played the Tsar a

cruel joke. From the *Government Herald* and other official sources it carefully collected all his speeches, which were chiefly toasts. They were not very numerous and consisted mainly of a banal repetition of his address to the troops, on May 21, 1896: "I drink a goblet of wine to the health of the troops. Your health, gentlemen!" The monotony and paucity of their subject-matter made a resounding political scandal out of the publication of the book. The censor hastened to confiscate the entire edition under the pretext that the Emperor's speeches could be published only by special permission of the "august orator."

The Tsar left behind one other type of literature: his comments on the reports of governors, governor generals, and ministers, his own resolutions on events or on petitions sent to him, and his telegrams to various persons and institutions. No malignant pamphlet could create an impression like that left by these "flourishes of the Tsar's pen."

The Council of State presents for the ruler's examination a proposal to abolish corporal punishment in Russia. He comments: "Reëxamine this question." The Council of State again proposes it. Nicholas notes: "When I want to, I will abolish it." Seventy-eight leading authors present a petition asking the Tsar to do away with the arbitrary action of the censorship and "bring literature under the protection of the law." Nicholas' note: "Leave this without effect." In 1896, four years after the famine which had shaken the peasants' economy to its foundations, the representatives of the nobility are presented to the Tsar. He says: "I know of the difficult times experienced by the nobility. You may be certain, I shall not forget its needs." On the page of the Russian census, answering the question as to his class or estate, Nicholas writes: "The first nobleman," and to the question as to profession, "Master of the Russian land." On the draft of a law for restricting the residence right of Jews, he writes: "Jews who abandon the pale of settlement annually fill whole towns of Siberia with their repulsive faces. This intolerable situation must be changed." On a report of the evil-doing of Count Podgorichani, captain of cavalry in the *gendarmerie*, during the Jewish pogrom in Belostok, the Emperor notes: "What concern is that of mine?" On numerous reports dealing with torture in prisons, with the execution of rebellious prisoners, with the burning of entire villages during agrarian disturbances, he comments as follows: "Hurrah, my fine fellows!" "Fine fellows, these convoying troops, they didn't lose their heads." "The Tsar's thanks to these fine fellows." On a report concerning the appearance of agitators in the barracks, he writes: "I hope that they were immediately shot." On a report on the conviction of the organizers of pogroms: "Grant them pardon." Countless such marginal notes revolutionized this or that part of the population more than a score of agitators could have done.

All this was capped by the Tsar's attitude toward the Black Hundreds' "Union of the Russian People," which Count Witte called "hooligans and thieves" and even Stolypin denounced as "a criminal gang." The Tsar proclaimed this union his "reliable support," rewarded its activities with his gratitude, and began to wear the pin of an honorary member. Despite all his devotion to the dynasty, Count Witte could not stand this. In his memoirs there escape from his pen words like "the squalor of political thought and the sickliness of soul of the autocrat Emperor."

The Emperor's diaries over several years have been published. A diary is of course a most intimate form of literature; alone with his soul, a man confides to paper his most sacred and personal thoughts and feelings. This "human document" in the case of the Tsar leaves an astounding impression of absolute woodenness. On the most commonplace days of his life and on days of the greatest shocks, joys, or losses, the diary is equally monotonous, petty, and empty. With the accuracy and indifference of a clock he notes walks, hunting, tea drinking, someone's visit, the death of a person who must have been close to him or the marriage of another.

This is not a diary, but "an official register." It is a rare record of complete psychical automatism. It is as if nothing could touch the man deeply. Everything slipped over his moral epidermis. Even on the day of his abdication the Tsar noted with care: "Read the life of Julius Cæsar and played dominoes."

General Danilov saw the Tsar at close range during the bitter days of universal disturbance after the Far Eastern disaster, and again during the even more tragic March days of 1917, before the abdication. He was astounded at his "cold, stony calm," which contrasted with the general depression. "What is this, I asked myself; is it a tremendous, almost incredible restraint, achieved by training, faith in divine predestination, or lack of intelligence?" He was inclined to explain it by "some special, Oriental fatalism, native, however, to all the Russian people."

Witte wrote similarly. "The Emperor, by nature, is an indifferent optimist. Such people experience a feeling of fear only while the storm is right before their eyes; and as soon as it has passed, that feeling goes instantly. Their sensitiveness to phenomena at even a very short distance is deadened . . . It must be noticed that the Emperor has a feminine character; someone remarked that by a trick of nature just before birth he was equipped with attributes distinguishing man from woman. Every person who has to make reports to him, especially if appointed by him, at first enjoys his special favor, which frequently goes beyond the limits of moderation; sooner or later this favor gives way to indifference, sometimes, and not infrequently, to a kind of bitterness due to resentment at having once loved, for, if the feeling had passed, its object must have been unworthy."

Witte also notes an interesting story concerning that "element of personal rivalry" which always disturbed the relations between Nicholas and William II of Germany. Everyone, including even the minister of the court, Fredericks, "was somewhat embarrassed that the Tsar did not have an imposing imperial appearance, because of his short stature, on account of which he had to refuse to wear certain German uniforms which made him appear even smaller." In general:

> William, as a personality, evidently stood out, or at least was considered by the public opinion, not only of Russia, but of the world, higher than he. William was, physically, much more the Emperor than he. Nicholas II, who was vain in certain ways, was vexed by this. I remember that after his first meeting with William certain post cards appeared, representing the two Emperors with William's hand on the Emperor's shoulders, as if embracing him. The Emperor came just below William's shoulder. All these cards were ordered confiscated at once.

This episode was symbolic. Nicholas II did not like to have big people around him. More than once he had to have recourse at critical moments to the services of Count Witte, who stood, politically, head and shoulders above the mass of courtiers and career seekers. More than once Witte saved a seemingly hopeless situation. But in his heart the Tsar could never forgive him for having been inevitable and irreplaceable at certain moments. The Tsar continually suspected Witte, and quite unjustly, of slowly but surely preparing to become president of the Russian Republic. Only in extremity, only with reluctance, would he have recourse to Witte, and invariably rewarded his services—after granting outward marks of distinction—with the blackest ingratitude. The Tsar preferred ministers whom he could change like his gloves, replacing one by another without affecting the administrative routine. Characteristically in the very last years and months of the Tsarist régime this shifting of ministers grew so that Purishkevich—that *enfant terrible* of the Right wing in the Imperial Duma—protested indignantly and publicly against the "ministerial leapfrog."

No wonder everyone with a heart, who had devoted his strength and even life to the service of the throne, was left with a feeling of profound bitterness against his ruler. When the murder of the minister Bogolepov opened a new era of terrorist activity, a militant figure was needed as Minister of Home Affairs. The Tsar asked the advice of the spiritual head of the reactionary clique, Pobedonostsev, as to his choice between Sipyagin and Plehve. Pobedonostsev replied that there was no difference, the one was a fool, the other a scoundrel. The Tsar appointed the first, then the second; both were removed by the Militant Organization of the party of Social Revolutionaries. Of the two, Sipyagin was in truth not very able, an ultra-reactionary and a nobleman to his very marrow, but utterly devoted to the Emperor. Not long before his death he told Witte "frankly and with great bitterness that the Emperor could not be trusted, and worst of all, was untruthful and deceitful. In despair he told this to his wife as well." After Sipyagin's death special messengers appeared, to take his "diary" for the Tsar's inspection. When it was returned to the widow of the assassinated minister, the most important part was missing. According to Count Sheremetiev, the Tsar, after destroying it in person, "condescended" to cast the shadow of suspicion upon his messenger, Adjutant General Hesse.

Gratitude was a feeling for which the Russian Tsar was too highly placed. At least, such was the conviction of the Empress, who, immediately after Stolypin's death, read a lesson to Count Kokovtsev. "You attach too much importance to Stolypin. We must not regret so strongly those who are no more. Each carries out his rôle, and if someone is missing among us, that is because he has fulfilled his rôle and had nothing more to accomplish."

The most important recent memoirs—Count Kokovtsev's two volumes—tell how even Witte, a man of enormous self-assurance and irresistible drive, was brought to the point of contemplating suicide.

When Prince Svyatopolk-Mirsky tried gentle methods of government in order to reconcile the country with its ruler, he failed because, behind his back, and to his own surprise, his entire policy was blown sky high by a whole series of the most reactionary appointments. On resigning he declared with bitterness: "The Emperor cannot be trusted in anything he says, for tomorrow he rejects what he approves today." His place was taken by Trepov, a straightforward, coarse, and self-confident officer whose "dashing appearance, terrifying eyes, and direct and soldierly speech" so impressed the Tsar that for a time he became practically a dictator. The Tsar resolved to rid himself of this "most loyal and devoted servant" by some artful design, and became entangled in it himself. Witte refers vaguely to "the tragic situation of this man, ignorant but honest and devoted to the Tsar, during the last weeks before his death." Witte himself noted bitterly: "As for the Emperor's assurances, I already knew then that he could not be trusted. He should not trust himself, for a directionless man cannot direct himself; he is driven by the winds that blow, unfortunately, for the most part from unclean sources."

Recently General Mosolov, who, as vice minister of the court, had the best possible opportunity of observing the Tsar at close hand, has attempted to rehabilitate him. According to him, the Tsar was not false by nature. He was unusually shy, shy through sickly vanity, through fear of lowering his dignity. Hence he avoided arguments in which he might not have the upper hand, was extremely reserved, and liked to listen to everyone, while keeping his own opinions to himself. He did not resist ministers who tried to convince or influence him. They withdrew, sure of their success, later to be disappointed. After a gracious audience they might be retired unexpectedly. Mosolov attributes this to the Tsar's extraordinary "training." Words were not worth arguing about. According to Mosolov, Nicholas had undergone this schooling as a lad at the hands of his tutor, Adjutant General Danilovich, nicknamed by the pupils of his corps "the Jesuit."

The notes of Grand Duke Nicholas Mikhailovich Romanov, the only intelligent man in the dynasty, and a historian by profession, have recently been published. It is astounding to read his almost unprintable expressions about the Empress and his curt opinion of the Tsar. "But what sort of a man is he! He is repulsive to me, and yet I love him, for he is not naturally a bad sort, and is the son of his father and mother. Perhaps I love him by reflection, but what a vile little soul he is!"[3]

From a whole series of documents, but chiefly from the "Notes" of Grand Duke Nicholas Mikhailovich, we know that Rasputin's assassins were regarded literally as heroes by a great many persons of the court circles and even of the imperial family, and evoked "the wildest enthusiasm." Even the Grand Duke, in his heart horrified by this murder and its details that included homosexual relations between one of the murderers and Rasputin, nevertheless sympathized with it and was all but willing to take part in it himself. "Everything they accomplished," he noted, "although it has cleared the air, is but a half measure, since Alexandra Feodorovna [the Empress] and Protopopov must absolutely be gotten out of the way. So you see, schemes of murders again flash into my mind . . . for otherwise it may be worse than it has been. Countess Bobrinsky, Misha Shakhovskoy frighten me, arouse me, and beg me to act; but how? with whom? It is unthinkable alone . . . And after their departure and Purishkevich's I do not see or know any others who could carry it out." And later, referring to his sympathy for the assassins, he added: "I could not show anything but heartfelt sympathy, and the regret that they did not carry through the job of extermination."

In the highest circles in Petersburg the members of Lord Milner's mission frequently heard frank talk of the possible assassination of the Tsar and Tsaritsa. The present British Ambassador in Paris, Sir George Clerk, wrote: "Each of us has to hear of the inevitability of the most serious events, the only question being as to who should be removed: the Emperor, the Empress, Protopopov, or all three."[4]

But there were many people, even of the extreme Right, who had long since dreamed of removing the Tsar for the monarchy's sake. Professor Nikolsky, an active leader of the reactionary "Union of the Russian People," in his secret diary summarized in April, 1905, his impression gained from frequent audiences with the Tsar:

> Shall I admit it, under vow of secrecy? I think that the Tsar is organically incapable of understanding. He is worse than untalented. He is, may God forgive me, a complete nonentity. If that is so, his reign will not soon be atoned for. Oh, God, can we have merited that our fidelity be so hopeless?
>
> If we could hope that he would commit suicide, that would be at least a chance. But not he! What have we lived to see! I have little faith in the immediate future. A *single* assassination is too little now to clear the air. We need something Serbian . . .*
>
> The dynasty would be the only victim. But where can we get a new one? In a word, the end, the end. Miracles do not happen. An end to that Russia which I served, which I loved, in which I believed. I shall not see her resurrection: the night will be long. The agony may be prolonged, but what is the use?

When even extreme Right-wing monarchists came to opinions like these, the monarchy and the dynasty were very close to having no support at all.

The unfortunate Tsar reaped what he had sown. At the critical moment, when the revolution had already cast down his throne, he felt a yawning abyss around him. He noted in his diary: "My abdication is needed . . . I have agreed . . . At one o'clock in the morning I left Pskov with a heavy feeling: all around is treason, cowardice, deception."

If the "feminine" traits in the Tsar's character are admitted almost unanimously, the male rôle in the imperial couple falls to the Empress Alexandra Feodorovna. The living evidence is her correspondence.

* A reference to the plot of May 29, 1903, in Belgrade, which removed Alexander I and Queen Draga at one blow, and substituted the Karageorgevich dynasty for the Obrenovich.

"Dearest," she writes playfully to her husband, "do not laugh at your stupid old wifey, but she has on invisible trousers." With her ambition to become the "guardian angel" and "aid in everything" for her husband, at every step she teaches him "to be more the autocrat," "to be stern, to be more determined and self-confident," "to show his energetic, confident sides," to display the "ruler's will." The best compliment for any of her candidates as minister was the recommendation: "He is a man, not a petticoat." The others she always overwhelmed with ridicule: "That Voeikov is a coward and a fool . . . I told him that all the ministers were '*des poltrons*' . . . I assure you, I am yearning to show these cowards my own immortal trousers." She treats no better even experienced generals, military "big-wigs" at headquarters, for their tendency to half measures. "Only cowards could have proposed that to you . . . I see that my black trousers are needed at headquarters—all that is too disgusting, the idiots."

"No one liked the Tsaritsa," writes Zinaida Gippius, the poetess, "even long ago, when she was the youthful fiancée of the heir to the throne. Her sharp face, beautiful, but ill-tempered and depressed, with thin, tightly pressed lips, did not please; her German, angular height did not please." Probably, her suspicious attitude toward those who surrounded her was not liked. In her letters to her husband she lets herself go, and calls them all "milksops," "fools," "cowards," "scoundrels," and "idiots." No one has described more ruthlessly the circles immediately surrounding the imperial throne.

A poor German princess had once been the Autocrat of All the Russias—Catherine II. Why should not this woman, who felt herself more of a man than most of those around her, aspire to something similar, though behind the back of a man small in every way in comparison with her? She tries by every means to inspire in her husband this idea: Your enemies are those who "fear that I interfere too much in affairs of state" . . . "that shows that whoever is devoted to you in the true sense of the word, will seek me." Finally, her aim achieved, she exults: "How splendid that you have given me the Supreme Council . . . Imagine me meeting with all the ministers . . . Since the time of Catherine no Empress has received in person and alone."

To such a proud nature, so fond of power, so contemptuous of people, fate had sent as her life companion a man of minute ability, irresolute, a perpetual failure, depressed and secretly embittered by his failures; a man mistrustful of everyone, tortured by vulnerable vanity and by an organic lack of self-confidence; a man who sought support outside himself, but at the same time was painfully envious of whoever was capable of furnishing it and never pardoned superiority; a man grudging, double-dealing, stubborn, unfortunate, and childishly self-pitying. A vain and masterful woman, she resolved at any cost to raise her husband to a fitting height. To achieve this she set in action all the resources of her ingenious and restless mind. Though at first she was indifferent, and even felt a certain repulsion for her husband, she finally managed to fall passionately in love with him, with her own unsuccessful creation, her own grown-up imperial pupil, like a mother, who, after having suffered difficult birth-pangs, begins to love her fragile, defective child with a painfully intense love, to love in it the personification of her own suffering, that great price which its birth has cost her. This half-maternal love, magnified by a wife's feeling for her husband, was transformed into burning dislike of all who might outshine her spiritual offspring, crush him by their superiority, or keep him in leading strings.

A doctor treating nervous patients by suggestion might envy the art with which the Empress works on her husband in her letters: she instructs and encourages, she flatters his vanity, kindles his suspicions, lovingly chides him, she beseeches and hypnotizes by verbal passes, stubbornly driving her point home. He is, she says, too kind and gentle, he is so charmingly modest, but people are bad, they abuse his kindness. He must hold them in obedience by his mind and his experience; he has these, if only he did not fear to display them. The love of those who surround him is not enough, they must fear him, nay, tremble before their Tsar. He must show his iron will by carrying out his decisions even against universal opinion and desire. He must learn to command without asking whether the thing is possible or not. "Use your broom . . . Show them your fist, punish them, be the master and ruler, you are the autocrat, they dare not forget that, but when they forget, as now, then woe be unto them."

Yes, she wanted to be her husband's good genius, and was his evil genius, for she mercilessly drove from him all who had the slightest degree of independence. She tolerated only those who could and would play the rôle of ugly girls around a doubtful "beauty." The Emperor's will—at bottom, the will which she breathed into him—had to be sensed, whatever spheres of life it touched. She wished to command even in the ecclesiastical sphere; frequently church questions were decided by imperial command, in flagrant violation of canonical rules. She even wished to influence military operations, and suggested measures to her husband. She nursed a painful hate for the Grand Duke Nicholas Nikolayevich because of his supposed popularity as commander in chief, for she felt that this popularity had been "stolen" from the Tsar, who should have been commander in chief himself. William II's feverish activity at the front gave her no rest. Nicholas Nikolayevich, especially after his manifesto to the Poles, she suspected of a secret desire to secure after the war "the Polish or Galician throne." Later she suspected him of much worse: He "receives endless rewards . . . and gratitude." At every step he forgets that "he has absolutely no right to give orders before asking your permission." He "decides everything, appoints, removes." "The ministers go off to him with their reports, as if he were already Emperor." "He is trying to play your rôle," "is usurping your rights," "wishes to be your mentor." He and his "treacherous headquarters" are depriving the Tsar of "the first place."

First she instigates the Tsar, behind the back of the commander in chief, to arrange an unexpected trip to the front, to publish a manifesto to the army without mentioning the commander in chief. Later she talks of the Tsar's replacing his uncle as supreme commander. Still later when Nicholas Nikolayevich had been shipped off to honorable exile in the Caucasus, the Tsaritsa keeps track of his intercepted letters, suggests to the Tsar that "all kinds of bad elements gather around uncle and try to use him as a banner," that he had taken to the Caucasus a suspiciously numerous suite, that he would "continue to brew his mess," that the Synod was working for him, and during the three fast days, at the prayers for the Tsar, "a thousand portraits of N. were distributed to the crowd," that in the surroundings of the former commander in chief there was talk of committing the Tsaritsa to a convent by force and like plans. They must be watched, "people must be sent" "to sniff the air," "they are now dangerous enemies," "this is becoming treason." That was to be all, for the time being. But, "after the war is over, you must punish them—why should they remain at liberty and in pleasant posts, when they had everything ready to dethrone you and lock me up in a convent?"

But the fiercest thunder and lightning from the Empress' pen struck the Imperial Duma, its leading parties, and all public organizations which interfered in matters which must and could be decided only by the autocrat, on whom rests God's blessing. "Do not assemble the Duma," "dissolve the Duma immediately," do not believe them when they try to "scare" you by "black forebodings"; "a few strikes are nothing, for they can and must be crushed." To the Empress the chief foes seem to be, not the revolutionaries, but parties and people like the Right-wing Constitutional Democrats, the Octobrists, Guchkov, Rodzianko, Miliukov, anxious to serve as buffers between the throne and the exasperated country, anxious to draw the Tsar into constitutional paths in order to forestall the revolution. One letter hastens after the other: "You should get rid of Guchkov, but how?—that is the question. This is wartime, could he not be seized in some way, in order to lock him up?" Or even simpler: "Oh, could not Guchkov be hanged?" Then, "Why is Miliukov at liberty?" Hearing the Tsaritsa's threats, even Rodzianko, president of the Duma with its Right majority, prepared to go into exile.

All this is, in truth, "in the manly fashion." Now there begins a part all too "womanly." A figure, fatal for the dynasty, makes his appearance—Rasputin.

THE relations between the Tsaritsa and Rasputin were long the subject of a "scandalous chronicle." After the fall of the dynasty they were particularly relished by the "yellow" press, which knows no pity for the defeated, especially when they are former idols.

Food for scandalous rumors was furnished by Rasputin himself by hints, repulsive silences, and drunken boasts. There is no need to repeat them. They would only obscure the true meaning of that tragi-comedy which was heightened by Rasputin's appearance in the imperial apartments.

We shall stick to severely tested facts.

We have the Synod's "Report on Rasputin." As early as 1902, after a communication from the priest in the village of Pokrovskoye, the Tobolsk district commissioner reported to the governor the suspicious conduct of a peasant of that village, Gregory Rasputin. He referred to certain nocturnal assemblages in a specially arranged, windowless building, supposedly a "bathhouse." The governor passed on the question to the local archbishop, Anthony. The latter sent one of his missionaries to make a detailed investigation, supplemented by searching Rasputin's hut. His report was handed for examination to a specialist on sects, the inspector of the Tobolsk Ecclesiastical Academy, Berezkin. He established

Rasputin's undoubted membership in the *Khlysty*, one of the most obscure mystical sects, in which religious exaltation leads to neurotic orgies. This sect, at least in some branches, is noted for abrupt transition from torture and subjection of the flesh to sensual outbursts. As leader of a Khlyst commune or "ship," Rasputin had established absolute power, particularly over the feminine members, who saw in their subjection to his caprice a mystical communion with the spiritual principle pervading him. "Some of the details referred to in the report," asserts Rodzianko, who examined the Synod's report, "were so immoral and repulsive that they could not be read without abhorrence." The ecclesiastical authority decided to carry out supplementary researches and then to refer the case to the state's attorney.

Meanwhile, profiting by the delay in the ecclesiastical investigation, Rasputin had attracted the attention of a well-known Black Hundreds agitator, Dean Vostorgov, and reached St. Petersburg. He returned with money and presents "as souvenirs" from various highly placed personages, with signatures, with a medallion portrait of the Empress, and so forth. The investigation met with a stumbling block. Shortly an order arrived from the Synod, backed by the imperial command: from Archbishop of Tobolsk, the Right Reverend Anthony was raised to be Archbishop of Tver and Kashin. It turned out that he had been offered the choice either of putting an end to the Rasputin investigation and then of being promoted to be Archbishop of Tver, or "retiring." Anthony, as a practical man, preferred advancement to retirement.

At that time a demagogic Black Hundreds group had been formed in the heart of the Orthodox Church. It filled its sermons with politics of a strongly reactionary trend. Among its leaders, besides Dean Vostorgov, were Hieromonach Iliodor, a passionate, masterful preacher, whose burning eyes and fiery eloquence made him the idol of the common people and especially of the women in Tsaritsyn; Father Gapon, who began his career under the patronage of the secret police, but whose unbalanced, adventurous soul, to everyone's surprise, afterwards drew him into the path of revolution; Iliodor's patron, Hermogen, the influential Bishop of Saratov; a turbulent monk, Varnava, who rose from an ordinary market gardener to a bishop, and many others. At that time the reactionary party was eager for people from among the "common lot." It was seeking fusion with the "land." It dreamed of organizing the union "of the Tsar with his people," ignoring "the educated freethinkers and petty politicians."

The sly Rasputin, catching the spirit of the times, hastened to swim with the stream. Half-literate and profoundly ignorant, he made no attempt to acquire polish. He did not change his rough peasant manners. He realized that they were the key to his career. At first he acted with caution, observed, took aim, sought to discover how he could most brilliantly and surely make his way in the world. He was a muzhik, greedy for life, thick-set, athletic in build, unbelievably strong and enduring, especially in drinking bouts and orgies of the flesh. He quickly perceived that the upper crust of St. Petersburg was teeming with bored, sated women, psychopathic and hysterical. Many, suffering from the scantiness of their spiritual life, were ready to surrender their will to any fashionable prophet and miracle worker. Others were greedy for adventure, for excitement of any kind. For ladies languishing in inactivity, only something especially perverse could have flavor. When they called Rasputin "an unappetizing muzhik," they felt an unhealthy attraction. "*Le laid, c'est le beau.*" And Rasputin cleverly beclouded their weakness in a fog of mysticism. He provided a mixture of sexual with religious hysteria. Merely touching him or his clothing had a mysterious influence, sometimes curing ills, sometimes bringing happiness and success. That most intimate contact with him which would have been natural in marriage must do more, must transport one to higher spheres and absolutely "renew" one. It was a marriage "in the spirit," the most genuine "mystery." Rasputin had a genuine harem through which he passed as many as possible of the insistent and curious women who besieged him. He contrived to keep this harem with its permanent and shifting membership fascinated by his hypnotic eloquence and religious foolery. His eloquence was out of the ordinary. Evidently it was disconnected, unexpected, primitive. It had to be. Once simple fishermen had been summoned by Christ to shame by their simplicity the vanity of pagan, philosophical education and science. So Rasputin's clumsy words must hide a higher, god-inspired wisdom.

Gradually Rasputin, like a Pythias in bark shoes, the young miracle worker from the common people, made his way in the salons of St. Petersburg. There had been fashionable "women's prophets" before him, more or less pretentious "venerable" men and women. Near-by, in Kronstadt was Father John, who, although less of an adventurer, had likewise appeared at the right moment and been advertised over all Russia as a "sainted man." Always surrounded by a crowd of feminine adorers, he was incapable of using them, like Rasputin, in a manner befitting a baudyhouse. The poetess Gippius describes a similar person, almost identical with Rasputin, "the little father of Chemryak," Shchetinin. Finally, according to her, Varnava was a "younger brother" of Rasputin, "a cheap edition." And even the last Tsarist metropolitan, Pitirim, was of the same type, although more cautious, more decorous, more hampered by his lofty title.

Like many of his peers, Rasputin would probably have flashed across the Petersburg horizon like a bright meteor and fallen in some too filthy affair, had he not discovered new and dazzling possibilities. They led directly to the imperial apartments.

Alexandra Feodorovna, as Empress, had a special mission: to provide an heir for the dynasty. But one confinement after another ended with the birth of a daughter. For the Empress each fresh confinement was a tragedy of expectation, alarms, hopes, disappointments, and hopelessness. She had suffered one miscarriage and the illusion of false confinement. Her psychic equilibrium was gone. Out of this grew her hysterical religiosity, her eagerness for a miracle, the superstitious searching for a miracle worker. From time immemorial the retinue of the Moscovite Tsaritsas had swarmed with all types of "venerables," Bible-searchers, phantasts, and pious charlatans, "God's fools," and religious eccentrics. The Empress threw herself into the arms of these religious madmen who seemed so exotic to her, and of the epileptic Darya Osipova, who treated women whose "babies would not stay," and she embraced the tongue-tied God's fool, Mitya. With this motley crowd she mingled miracle workers imported from abroad—some sort of semi-Mason from Lyons, the semi-spiritualist Philippe, and his pupil, the well-known charlatan Papuce.

At that very time the highest church authorities were holding secret conferences. They were afraid that the times of sectarianism and of Masonic influence at the court were returning, and that the influence of the Orthodox faith would suffer. Then Bishop Theofan was promoted to be the spiritual advisor of the imperial couple. By all description he was a man not of this world, with a pure and Christianly submissive soul and as sound a faith. But it occurred to him that the best way to counteract the unhealthy inclinations of the Empress' feminine mysticism was to bring her into contact with the strong, simple faith of the common people. The bishop's intelligence was not equal to his godliness. He discovered the personification of the peasants' religious primitivism in Gregory Rasputin.

Rasputin became the "imperial lamp tender," in charge of the lamps ever burning before the icons, and guardian of the imperial collection of rare icons painted by the old masters. This new position caused numerous protests from women who had been corrupted by him and then freed from his hypnotic fascination to be hopelessly entangled in police, administrative, and judicial red tape.

At last the Tsaritsa gave birth to a son. But this great joy was poisoned from the beginning. The child was incurably ill with hæmophilia, a disease in which the slightest cuts bring the danger of hemorrhages. Medical science was helpless. The only salvation was a miracle. Rasputin offered that miracle. The Tsaritsa grasped at it.

Rasputin, like the majority of his kind, was an unconscious magnetizer. His power of suggestion was complained of by women who, despite the remnants of their own will, despite inner suffering, did whatever he wished. Superior people, highly willed natures, like Stolypin, felt that force in him. On one occasion, after Stolypin had sent for Rasputin to frighten him and expel him from Petersburg, he related his experience to Rodzianko. "His whitish eyes ran over me, he uttered mysterious and disconnected expressions from the Scriptures, moved his arms in a strange way, and I felt an insuperable repulsion to that horrible being rise in me. But I realized that the man had great hypnotic power and was producing on me a strong psychic impression, true, one of repulsion. Mastering myself, I shouted at him . . ." Rodzianko describes his encounter with this coarse muzhik Cagliostro in almost the same terms:

> Rasputin turned his face toward me and his eyes began to move over me: at first over the face, then over the region of the heart, and again over the eyes. This lasted several seconds. Personally I am not in the least subject to the influence of hypnosis—I have tested it many times—but this time I experienced a tremendous and incomprehensible force. I felt a purely animal rage rising in me, blood rushed to my heart, and I realized I was approaching a state of genuine madness. In turn I began to stare straight into Rasputin's eyes and felt as if my eyes were bursting from their orbits.

The Empress looked into those whitish eyes with a hope,

at first timid, but later more and more fervent. Rasputin cleverly chose to appear after medical aid had been rendered to the child and improvement was to be expected. The improvement was ascribed entirely to him. The imperial surgeon Feodorov was once horrified at finding the bandages and other material, which he had prepared for the sick child in the operating room, covered with some filthy article of a man's clothing. It had been taken from his own body by Rasputin, so that the forthcoming operation might be blessed from on high.

He knew how to amuse and enliven the little boy. And above all, he was able to calm the mother completely. Her hysterical attacks were ended by his power of suggestion.

For the mother all life was contained in that sickly, tiny heir to the dynastic power, not merely her son, but an incarnation of imperial existence. Her husband was also in a sense her spiritual child, for whom she was constantly alarmed and sick at heart. Both these loves, fused into a single love, both these creatures, bound together through her and indebted to her for so much, were one with her. If they were taken away, nothing would remain in her. Such a feeling does not admit of any immoral connection with Rasputin, a connection that the salons believed in and which popular rumor willingly maintained. Rasputin himself did not dare to reach so high. Even in the imperial apartments a restless profligate, he was satisfied with seducing a person of his own rank, the nurse of the imperial children, who was put out of sight in time and from somewhere wailed that the imperial children should be snatched "from the claws of that devil."

Toward the Tsaritsa Rasputin acted so that she might believe in his purity and saintliness. For her he was the man sent by Providence, a guardian angel for her beloved child—indeed, for that other child, adult and crowned, toward whom Rasputin affected an anxious, paternal love. Once the Tsar and the Tsaritsa together had read a mystical book, *Les Amis de Dieu*. It said that sometimes "God's people" appear, sent from above to guide rulers on earth and to intercede for them in heaven. Such was the spiritualist, Philippe. He had presented to the Tsaritsa an image with little bells; their ringing would warn her against dangerous people, hostile to the throne. Rasputin went further. He presented the Tsaritsa with an image of Nicholas the Miracle Worker to hold in her hand before every important conference. Another gift was a stick from New Athos, which represented a fish holding a bird; this was to be held with another stick blessed by the touch of the spiritualist Philippe. Rasputin made a present of his own comb. The Emperor was to comb his hair several times before important conferences, and clarity of penetration would then come of itself. The Empress also had a large collection of little images, given by him, each with its special fetish power, and amulets, including a lily of the valley, a crust, and a little bottle "as if containing Madeira wine," not ordinary but miraculous wine.

The Empress, whom the courtiers called "the brilliant woman" and compared to Catherine II, who had received a superior education, spoke several languages, was in touch with the cream of modern literature and art, absorbed from Monsieur Philippe and Rasputin faith in all this nonsense, together with a belief in lucky and unlucky days, auspices, dreams, particularly the dreams and visions of Rasputin himself, with whom every act had to be planned, even an offensive at the front.

In the Rasputin episode there was something terrifying. But it was not because "the wife of Cæsar, duty-bound to stand above all suspicion," made a scandalous and filthy adventurer her intimate. It was because she and the Tsar and the crowds of ministers and princes of the church, who displayed this spiritual poverty and low level of moral consciousness, held in their hands, at the most critical moment of world history, the fate of a colossal country, stretching from the polar ice to the sun-scorched wilderness of Central Asia and from the Baltic to the Pacific.

CHAPTER TWO

RASPUTIN'S FOLLOWERS AND THE SEPARATE PEACE

RASPUTIN has attained an unexampled degree of real influence. The Tsaritsa believes in him and hangs upon his every word. She in turn inspires her husband's policy. What does Rasputin himself want? What policy does he lay down for the government? He has no policy, in the higher sense of the word. He merely wishes to overthrow whoever dislikes him and to elevate those who protect him or seek his favor. The Grand Duke Nicholas Nikolayevich views his escapades sternly. Through the Tsaritsa Rasputin has him replaced by the Tsar as head of the army, an action which disturbs the Entente Powers and delights the Germans.

There are spiritual leaders of the church anxious to excommunicate Rasputin as one accursed and profligate. He secures "august commands," by which these leaders are exiled, in violation of all canonical rules, through a mere report of the Procurator of the Holy Synod, "the black-coat administrator of priestly frocks." There is the Imperial Duma. Its helplessness, contrasted with the omnipotence of an obscure adventurer, more and more arouses public opinion. Rasputin incites the Tsar against the Duma and ruthlessly works for complete annihilation of that dim shadow of constitutionalism, spared, in the interest of Tsarism itself, by Stolypin's counterrevolution.

As these audacious tests of Rasputin's influence succeed, his house and various private compartments in the aristocratic dives where his Homeric orgies take place are thronged by a motley mob of petitioners, schemers, career seekers, adventurers, spies, brokers, and obscure speculators, and, finally, by men covetous of ministerial portfolios. They all need Rasputin's recommendation, a little word dropped at the right moment, and his illiterate notes to highly placed personages. They are all eager to arrange their affairs great and small through him. They all bring their contributions, of course only for Rasputin's charities! They all have something to whisper to him, they try to worm something out of him and urge him to do something. The sly comedian does not listen to everyone. Little by little he picks out "suitable" persons, faithful to him. He gradually creates a peculiar, half-political, half-speculative "joint-stock company," a compact band of followers. In that group Rasputin is Tsar and God. Its members are bound together by an unwritten bond of joint responsibility; they coöperate in helping one another to the top and in clearing all obstacles from their oracle's path. This clique is dreaded by everyone. Some people at most dare intrigue against it behind stage, but usually they play its game or come to sinister agreements with it.

The game of "ministerial leapfrog" goes merrily on. One caliph for an hour replaces another. The agile acrobats clamber to the top over other people's backs, offer one another their support, swarm past, shove those who stumble, stumble in turn and fall. Some of the more decent conservatives, like Rodzianko, try to arouse the Tsar to the horror of the situation. The Tsar, quite sincerely, does not understand. Some of the Grand Dukes begin to fear that he is moving to his own fall, even more that his fall will sweep them all away. The Tsar becomes angry. In the Duma even such rabidly reactionary monarchists as Purishkevich begin to fume. The Tsar stiffens. The Duma's warrant is signed. The last buffer between the government and the silently agitated country may be destroyed any day.

To cap all, in the army, in the rear, through drawing rooms and peasant huts, everywhere creeps that hissing word "Treason." It is heard after defeat. It appears as the inevitable concomitant of demoralization. The target for suspicion is there. It invites attack. The "German," the Empress, is intriguing for "her people," she is preparing to betray the Allied cause and make a separate peace. Through the Tsaritsa the enemy learns the most important secrets of the defense. Her Rasputin circle is deliberately disorganizing the administration. Without hesitancy Rodzianko asserted, even many years later, that "the Rasputin circle undoubtedly was influenced by the enemy, and served Germany's interests."

What truth there was in these suspicions we know now, or at least practically know.[1]

In August, 1916, in a personal letter to the Tsar, the King of England referred to the great activity of German agents in Russia. Not denying their existence, and promising "to deal with them," Nicholas II replied: "I regard as a more serious phenomenon, one requiring constant struggle, the influence of certain banks, which before the war were in German hands, and whose influence is felt strongly, but invisibly, especially in the slow execution of orders for war materials, ammunition, etc."

Although Russian capitalism, and, particularly, financial capitalism was, in a sense, the daughter of Entente capitalism, still, German capitalism had its own sphere of control. The participation of German capital was especially strong in the Petrograd International Bank (Director A. I. Vyshnegradsky), which belonged to the Disconto-Gesellschaft, and in the Russian Bank for Foreign Trade, which was dependent on the Deutsche Bank in Berlin; finally, the Russo-Asiatic Bank (under the management of A. I. Putilov, with Vyshnegradsky participating in the management) had far-reaching connections with the German banking house of Warburg & Co. and with Krupp. Of these three banks the first two controlled the greater part of Russian metallurgy (the textile industry belonged to the Entente sphere). In addition, Siemens & Halske had established an important electro-technical corporation with its Petersburg branch, the Electrical Society of 1886. With the Allgemeine Elektrizitätsgesellschaft (Rathenau), which penetrated Russia later, it had set up the Russian Electrical Syndicate, which covered the entire country with electric construction on a definite plan. Such was the powerful position of German capital in prewar Russia. Its creepers stretched out to various political groups, to influential people in government and society. To it led the threads of numerous intrigues, which tried to undermine sympathy for the Entente and worked for Germany and a separate peace.

According to William II's memoirs, he was later informed by his Ambassador, Mirbach, of a memorandum handed to the Tsar in 1914 by Count Kokovtsev, former Minister of Finance, a man of great authority in Russian banking circles. In it he argued against war and for close contact with Germany. He predicted that the war "would be a failure and would lead the dynasty to ruin." Helferich, one of the most active leaders in the Deutsche Bank, describes the steps taken on the very eve of war by the "Russian peace party" headed by Kokovtsev. To exert a peaceful influence on Germany's financial circles, it sent a special emissary, L. F. Davydov, prominent in the Russian Bank for Foreign Trade. Once war had actually broken out, these circles had to be outwardly silent, while waiting for a favorable opportunity to hasten its end and to join hands.

Probably the chief agent in this work was the well-known financier, Manus. According to Paléologue he "was in constant touch with Stockholm . . . that is, with Berlin," and "was the principal distributor of German subsidies in Russia." Every week Manus entertained Rasputin and a number of other persons connected with the lady in waiting, Vyrubova, and through her, with the Empress.

In accord with the general rule for confiscation of German enterprises, the Moscow City Duma had long and vainly striven for the confiscation of the Electrical Society of 1886. This enterprise, now camouflaged as Swiss, was defended by Rasputin's well-known follower, Prince Andronnikov. Finally the Society was not closed, but at the end of 1916 received the government's guarantee of a 4,000,000 ruble bank loan. A great sensation was caused in the Duma by the speech of a deputy of the Right, Hvostov, against "German preponderance" and the unslackening but secret influence of German capital in Russian life. Hvostov threatened fresh disclosures, particularly in the matter of the electrical industry. The disclosures were not made. Andronnikov, through Rasputin, Vyrubova, and the Empress, made Hvostov minister. "The purpose," Hvostov afterwards told the investigating commission, "was to bring me into the center of the government, to avoid speeches about German capital, and especially about the electrical enterprises." Hvostov now brought in his relative, Tatishchev, as Minister of Finance. This cost Tatishchev a 100,000-ruble gift to Rasputin, according to his accomplice, the former director of the department of police, Beletsky. Later Tatishchev was investigated and accused of furnishing "aid and comfort to the enemy." But by giving Rasputin's placeman, Protopopov, 100,000 rubles to buy flour for certain problematical "shops of the Society for the Struggle against the High Cost of Living," Tatishchev secured from Protopopov the appointment of his guardian angel, Beletsky, "to watch the progress of the investigation."

Perhaps the most sinister member of the Rasputin circle was Manasevich-Manuilov. The reports of Isvolsky, former Minister of Foreign Affairs, show that this man had acted as agent of the German Ambassador, Pourtalès, in an unsuccessful attempt to buy for 800 rubles a leading journalist of the *Novoye Vremya.* When he was arraigned for blackmail and bribery, at the Tsaritsa's request the Tsar himself ordered the case dropped. Under pretext that "the witnesses did not appear," the case was removed from the docket and never restored.

AGAINST this background of German intrigue and governmental disintegration history draws the fantastic pattern of court intrigue for a separate peace and the maneuvers of an astoundingly audacious espionage.

The steps in favor of a separate peace ran along two parallel lines: industrial-financial and dynastic-diplomatic.

Let us begin with the first. At the beginning of June, 1915, the director of the Deutsche Bank, Monkewitz, appears in Stockholm. He meets a Russian businessman, "a wealthy Russian-Polish Jew," with connections in Berlin (perhaps Manus). Through the latter Monkewitz expresses to the Russian envoy the wish "that two persons might meet as soon as possible in Moscow or in Copenhagen, very secretly, from the German side someone like Bodelsohn* or Warburg,† and from the Russian side a prominent financier . . ." (the name is lacking), in order to carry on private negotiations for peace, "without compromising the official diplomacy of the two countries." The Russian Minister at once reported this to the Minister of Foreign Affairs, Sazonov, adding that the communication had the earmarks of a "direct offer" of separate peace, and that "these proposals are rather serious, for a person like the director of the Deutsche Bank, Monkewitz, would not be acting on his own." The names of the "businessman" and "prominent financier" from the Russian side are still unknown, but they undoubtedly belonged to those commercial and financial spheres which before the war were controlled by German capital.

Sazonov was resolutely hostile to the idea of a separate peace. It was only a year later that Monkewitz' project seemed about to be realized. Meanwhile, in late March, 1916, at the home of the German Envoy in Stockholm, Herr von Lüzius, a conversation took place between Stinnes and the Japanese Envoy. Stinnes proposed that "influential representatives of Russia, Japan, and Germany meet to exchange opinions on peace conditions." Stinnes, the head of the German electrical trusts, was closely connected with Russia

* Swedish, pro-German financier.

† Hamburg banker, connected with A. I. Putilov, used for diplomatic missions.

through their branches, and through the International Bank (A. I. Vyshnegradsky).

And then, in Stockholm, supposedly by accident, a meeting actually took place between the German banker Warburg and a member of the Russian "parliamentary delegation" returning from London, the vice president of the Duma, Protopopov. Protopopov was also president of the Council of the Metal-Working Industry, controlled by banks dependent on German syndicates. With Protopopov were the "important financier" and oil baron, Polyak, and the Swedish banker, Ashberg. Warburg tried to convince his interlocutors that England had always deceived her allies, would do the same now, and would alone derive advantage from the war. For Russia it was better to exchange friendship with England for friendship with Germany. He outlined the "natural" conditions of a separate peace: Poland would be restored from the lands belonging to the Russian crown within its ethnographical boundaries, Courland would go to Germany, Russia would be rewarded by the Bukovina, part of Galicia, and the Straits, provided she took them from the Turks by force of arms. The play on Nicholas II's vanity runs like a red thread through Warburg's arguments: "England wants to dominate and to bind the will of the Russian Tsar, by forbidding him to conclude a separate peace."* The conversation did not go further, at least, according to Protopopov.

On returning to Petrograd, Protopopov told Miliukov of his interview with Warburg, and asked his advice about reporting it to the Tsar. Miliukov "took fright and thought this proposal might be taken seriously." He urged Protopopov "not to ascribe especial significance" to this Stockholm episode and to regard it "as a tourist's incident." Pro-

* It must not be forgotten that in the work of instigation against England Warburg had powerful allies. On June 5, 1916, the Empress wrote to her husband about Vyrubova: "She forget to tell you, that our Friend [Rasputin] says its good for us that Kitchener died [*sic!!*] as later on he might have done Russia harm and that no harm papers were lost with him. You see he always fears about England at the end of the war when the peace-negotiations begin."

topopov listened to his advice and did just the opposite, "he attributed very great significance to it, and thus gained in the opinion of the Emperor." Indeed, in a letter of Nicholas II to his wife of July 20, 1916, there is an obscure reference to Protopopov: "He was abroad with the other members of the Duma and told me many interesting things"; he "pleased me very much."

The Warburg interview opened up a career for Protopopov and made him acceptable as minister. Above all, it won him the favor of Rasputin and the Empress. They now began a persistent campaign, so mysterious that in their correspondence Protopopov was given the conspirator's nickname of "Kalinin." At last their goal was achieved, and the Empress wrote her husband: "God bless your new choice of Protopopov—our Friend says you have done a very wise act in naming him." Protopopov at once began negotiations with the banking, commercial, and industrial groups on which he had relied in his upward progress. In agreement with the government he wished to introduce into the next Duma a compact group of their representatives, of fifty to eighty members: "The branches of the private banks in the provinces would serve as their electoral cells" (there were about twelve hundred of these); several private banks had already offered to set up a campaign fund of two million rubles, to purchase the requisite electoral qualifications* for their candidates and "perhaps, to buy votes."

Protopopov now entered the central core of the reactionary clique, which was working through Rasputin. On the eve of the February Revolution the Empress wrote to the Tsar about her intimate, a prominent follower of Rasputin, N. N. Sablin: "He is dining tonight with Maklakov, Kalinin, Rimsky-Korsakov, and others at Bordukov's." Bordukov was the go-between between Protopopov and Tatishchev in passing those 100,000 rubles for the famous "flour." Rimsky-Korsakov was one of the leaders of the Black Hundreds organization,

* To be eligible for election they must, for example, own property.

"The Union of the Russian People," which during the war turned Germanophil. Maklakov, according to the French press, had before the end of 1914, together with Shcheglovitov and Baron Taube, presented to Nicholas a memorandum on the necessity for stopping the war. At the beginning of February, 1917, in transparent form he reported to the Tsar that the government must "restore order in the state, *at whatever cost*, and be certain of the victory over the foe *within*, who long since has become both more dangerous and more relentless than the *foreign enemy*."

This makes plain the tactics of the Rasputin clique, beginning with its struggle to remove Grand Duke Nicholas Nikolayevich from the high command. Granted the suspicious and embittered Alexandra Feodorovna had in truth persuaded herself that Nicholas Nikolayevich was attempting to win a certain military popularity in order to take the throne of her luckless husband. But Rasputin's whispered hints were, of course, dictated by real interests of equally real economic groups. In his *Memoirs*, concerning the steps toward a separate peace with Russia in the spring of 1915, the German former Crown Prince notes: "The chief difficulty lay in the fact that Grand Duke Nicholas Nikolayevich was still in power." In truth, so long as he remained commander in chief, the slogan of "war to the victorious end" could not be modified, and the partisans of a separate peace had to overthrow him first, whatever the cost. Rodzianko, in his desperate efforts to deter the Tsar from taking the high command, spoke plainly: "The people will explain your step as suggested by the Germans who surround you and who, in the minds of the people, are linked with our enemies and with treason to Russia's cause." Yakhontov's protocol notes of the secret meetings of the Council of Ministers show that it was being anxiously debated whether the Grand Duke Nicholas Nikolayevich would submit to the Tsar's decision, or by imperious orders from headquarters raise the question of a dynastic overturn. After a sharp conflict with the president of the Council, eight ministers besought the Tsar not to remove Nicholas Nikolayevich. They tried to frighten him with the danger of "serious consequences" for him and the dynasty, and reënforced that petition with a request for their own retirement.

The German military authorities were so well informed of this disorder at the top of the Russian Government that they attempted to force events by issuing a forged manifesto of the Tsar to his soldiers. It was carefully collected and concealed from the public by the Russian Government.

"SOLDIERS!

"*In the most difficult moment of his life your Tsar appeals to you, his soldiers.*

"*This unfortunate war came about against my will: it was caused by the intrigues of Grand Duke Nicholas Nikolayevich and his partisans, who wished to put me aside, in order to occupy the throne. On no conditions would I have consented to declare this war if I had foreseen its unfortunate result for Mother Russia, but my wily relative and his perfidious generals are preventing me from making use of the power given me by God, and, fearing for my life, I am compelled to execute all that they demand of me.*

"*Soldiers! Refuse to obey your perfidious generals, turn your weapons against all those who menace the life and liberty of your Tsar, the safety and security of your beloved country.*

"*Your unfortunate Tsar,* NICHOLAS."[2]

The further campaign of the party of the Empress and Rasputin was waged steadily against the eight ministers who had resisted the removal of the commander in chief, and one after the other they were discharged. At last Sazonov's turn came. The British Ambassador, Buchanan, abandoned his watchful waiting. In a secret telegram he begged the Tsar "to weigh the serious consequences which the retirement of M. Sazonov would have for the important diplomatic negotiations now going on, and for the even more important negotiations which will certainly arise as the war continues."

But the question was already settled, not only of Sazonov's retirement, but his replacement by Stürmer. There had been long discussion as to whether it was worthwhile "to risk his German name," or first allow him to exchange it, as he himself had for a time suggested, for the ancient and noble Russian name of Panin. These negotiations were carried on like a conspiracy. "I want his appointment, if it takes place, to resound like a thunderclap," Nicholas wrote his wife. And so it was. The former German Crown Prince writes:

> A favorable moment for concluding peace with Russia came in the late summer of 1916, when Russia's military situation was very bad. At that very time the Tsar appointed Stürmer as head of the ministry, and the latter was undoubtedly well disposed to us. That appointment I regarded as an indisputable sign of a desire to open negotiations for peace.

Stürmer immediately crossed the *t*'s and dotted the *i*'s. He began in every way to delay publishing the agreement with England concerning Constantinople, and the manifesto on Poland. He did so at the Tsar's express command. These acts would have been most unfavorable in concluding a separate peace. According to Bethmann-Hollweg, German political circles were strongly of the opinion, which he did not share, that a separate peace with Russia was now to be regarded "as a matter of course," and that this chance could be let slip only "by the most clumsy diplomacy."

German diplomacy, however, did prove to be "clumsy." Unlike Stürmer, the German Government proclaimed the organization of a Polish kingdom under a German protectorate. Erzberger called this "a positive political catastrophe," undermining "the only chance for peace."

But on the Russian side matters were not regarded as beyond repair. The Empress and Rasputin's followers were working to create an energetic government which would free itself of the Ententophil supervision of the Duma parties. Dissolution of the Imperial Duma, announcement of a radical revision of the fundamental laws and reduction of the Duma to a purely advisory rôle, proclamation in the capitals and larger cities of martial law or even of siege law, closing of all Left newspapers, militarization of all war industries, such was the vigorous program of a memorandum originating in the circle of Senator Rimsky-Korsakov, to which the ministers Maklakov and Stürmer belonged, and with which Protopopov was in agreement. The members of this "energetic" government were to "prove by oath to their monarch their willingness to succumb in the coming struggle, to indicate their successors beforehand, and to receive full power from the monarch."

On February 1, the Ataman of the Cossacks, Grubbe, presented to the Tsar a plan of struggle against "the serious violations of order" which "cannot fail to accompany the demobilization of an enormous army," and which "may grow into insurrection." The chief rôle in the work of pacification he assigned to the Cossacks.

Quietly but in deadly earnest Tsarism was preparing to end the struggle on the front and transfer it to the rear. Yet its supporters became indignant when Lenin openly preached "the transformation of the World War into civil war."

The parties of the Duma had a foreboding of the plans of the reactionary party for a separate peace. On behalf of the Moscow All-Russian Conference of Presidents of Zemstvo Administrations, Prince Lvov declared: "Tormenting, horrible suspicions of treason, of secret forces working for Germany and striving to prepare a shameful peace by destroying the people's unity and sowing dissension, have now passed into clear realization that the enemy's hand is secretly influencing the direction of the state." The Chief Committee of the Union of Cities publicly accused certain influences hostile to Russia of deliberate sabotage of the national defense. It is plain what name all these leaders and organizations dared not utter. But this name was at the tongue tip of the army leaders. Later, in the spring of 1917, General Denikin "put that tormenting question" to the chief of staff, Alexeyev. The latter "answered vaguely and reluctantly: 'In sorting the Empress' papers they had found a map with the detailed location of the troops of the entire front, of which only two copies were prepared, one for me and one for the Emperor. That depressed me. There is no saying who might have used it.' Not one word more. He changed the subject."[3]

The hypothesis of "betrayal to Germany" by the Empress cannot be accepted. The "Muraviev Commission," appointed by the Provisional Government, with the participation of representatives of the Soviets, failed to corroborate it. The published correspondence of Alexandra Feodorovna with Nicholas, in our opinion, forbids that possibility. Of course, the Empress' "heart was torn" at the thought that her husband, her son, she herself were on the Russian side, while her father, brother, sister, all of her native Hesse were in the opposite camp. She would not have been human had she not from time to time cursed this war with all her heart. For this only the most hardened chauvinist could condemn her. The Empress was, and remained, to a considerable degree German in feeling. But that did not mean that she was ever on William's side in spirit. To be exact, she did not pity Germany, which for her was a pretty abstract conception, but rather her own "tiny country," her own Hesse, toward which William, with his ideas of Pan-German domination of the world, seemed to her cruelly to blame. As a German she was profoundly provincial. Her heart went out to all those Hesses, Mecklenburg-Strelitzes, and Mecklenburg-Schwerins, Schwarzburg-Sonderhausens and Schwarzburg-Rudolstadts, to the small principalities and dukedoms, whose ruling houses supplied brides like herself for the marriage market of all crowned Europe. Her feelings as little prevented her from wishing for Nicky's triumph over William and Francis Joseph as they had kept a former princess of

Anhalt-Zerbst, renamed Catherine II, from carrying on a most aggressive foreign policy against Russia's western neighbors. "All her blood boils at the thought of the malignant joy in Germany" at every Russian failure. She was revolted by the thought that after the Russian evacuation of Galicia the triumphant William would perhaps spend the night "in that same bed of old Francis Joseph" in which Nicholas had slept at Lemberg. She was exultant when told that at the occupation of Constantinople by the Russian troops the regiment bearing her name would enter first. "Oh, what a day that will be when evensong will again be sung in St. Sophia!" She felt that from his grave Nicholas I was blessing his great grandson for avenging Austria's treachery to him and uniting the ancient Slav lands beneath his scepter.

The Empress is Pan-Slav, not Pan-German. But a peculiar Pan-Slav. She is merely a patriot of the dynasty which she has joined. Panslavism is to her a means for expanding the bounds of its power; "expanding their dominions was always the most pleasant occupation of rulers." It is by no means due to love for the Slavs. "Oh, I wish those Balkans states would drop through the earth," she writes frankly to her husband. "Russia has always been a loving mother to them, and then they treacherously turn against her." During Serbia's tragic days she edifyingly declares that "this is a punishment to the country for having murdered its king and queen." On the occupation of Cetinje by the Austrians she rejoices: "Now the king and his sons and his dark daughters up here [she is referring to the Princesses Stana and Militsa, married to two Russian Grand Dukes and hostile to Rasputin] who so madly wanted this war will pay for all their transgressions against God and against you since they have opposed our Friend, in spite of knowing who he is."

On the whole the Empress did not love or sympathize with anyone. Her heart was too narrow for that. For her the Italians were "detestable egoists," the French not above concluding a separate peace behind Russia's back and at her expense. With England's selfish policy Russia would face "terrible complications" in concluding peace.

Fiat dynastia—pereat mundus!

RASPUTIN'S "pacifism" was of longer standing and more calculating. The recollections of the French Ambassador, Paléologue, quote that violent supporter of Rasputin, Vyrubova: "If the venerable man had been here, we would not have had the war. I do not know what he would have done, what he would have advised, but God would have inspired him . . . Oh, it is a great misfortune that he was not among us and could not enlighten the Emperor." After his return to Petrograd Rasputin "spoke of the war only in ambiguous and apocalyptic terms, showing that he did not approve of it and foresaw great misfortunes." After military defeats the Tsaritsa liked to remind the Tsar of Rasputin's farsightedness. "Our Friend has always been against this war, saying that the Balkans were not worth fighting about and that Serbia would be just as ungrateful as Bulgaria."

However, all this may be regarded as narrowly egoistic nationalism, and nothing more. The Empress occasionally inclines to Rasputin's view, during military failures. After military successes she seems inspired, and dreams of crowning with laurels her hapless husband, "born, truly on the day of Job the Long Suffering." Had she been from the very beginning opposed to the war with Germany for Germany's sake, she would certainly have acted differently, she would have utilized a succession of openings.

On September 10, 1914, Paléologue received a call from Witte, just back from Biarritz. "He told me this war was madness . . . It could only be ruinous for Russia. Only France and England could expect to gain by victory . . . No serious people here take any more interest in those restless and vainglorious Balkans, where there is nothing Slav, and which are inhabited by Turks baptized by mistake."

Witte was not attracted by the prospect of uniting all Poland under the Russian scepter, for Poland would offer more trouble united than divided. The conquest of the Dardanelles was even more risky; they would be too difficult to defend, and would require double protection against all kinds of appetites. If the Entente won, "the republic will be proclaimed throughout central Europe, and that will be the end of Russia's imperial era. As for the consequences of defeat, I prefer not to speak of them."

Of the statesmen of that time only Witte had the manliness to state publicly: "My practical conclusion is that we must liquidate this mad adventure as quickly as possible."

Paléologue dreaded lest the first military failures bring to the fore Witte, "this man who realizes that his strength is not utilized and who is devoured by ambition, resentment, and hauteur." Had the Tsaritsa been secretly Germanophil, she would have hastened to bury her old grudges against Witte and to use him. But she was intoxicated by the patriotic manifestations. Paléologue watched: "The Tsar's face was beaming. The Empress' entire form expressed a joyous ecstasy." "The Empress scarcely replies, but her tense smile and the strange gleam of her yearning, magnetic, and ardent glance expresses her inner enthusiasm." He is not mistaken. The Tsaritsa's letters to her husband breathe her pleasure. "This is a healthful war in the moral sense . . . It has raised the morale, cleansed many stagnant minds, united feelings."

The idea of a separate peace is accepted by the Tsaritsa later, when the delusive mirage of victory has slipped away, leaving behind disappointment and loss of faith. The correspondence of the imperial couple illustrates clearly the German soundings for peace with Russia.

One proposal was made through a lady in waiting, Mme. Vasilchikov.[4] Related to the Austrian aristocracy and overtaken in Austria by the outbreak of war, she was visited by three persons from court circles of Vienna and Berlin, unconnected with official diplomacy. Later with the consent of

William II she was summoned to Berlin to see the Minister of Foreign Affairs, Von Jagow. She was to report in Russia that "neither in Austria nor in Germany is there any hatred for Russia," but "there is tremendous hatred for England." A large party favored peace, a lasting peace with Russia, "the friendship of the three Emperors, *l'Alliance des trois empereurs*." In this alliance the Tsar was given an honorable mission in the Far East. "There is the frightful yellow race and only Russia is a wall against it." As for the Dardanelles, "the Russian Tsar has only to wish it and their passage will be free." In her next letter she writes: "I have been asked to inform Your Majesty that from a very secret source it is known that England intends to keep Constantinople and to create a new Gibraltar at the Dardanelles, and that secret negotiations are now going on between England and Japan to leave Manchuria to the latter."

The first Vasilchikov efforts met no response. The Entente, not bound to Turkey, as Germany was, could promise more. On March 3, 1915, Nicholas himself informed Paléologue that he had determined to make "a radical solution of the problem of Constantinople and the Straits." That sounded very much like an ultimatum. A week after Sazonov had presented the Allies with a memorandum in this spirit, England gave her consent, while reserving suitable compensation. France delayed her answer by more than ten days. At that time the German Minister in Stockholm, Von Lüzius, gave the Swedish press a rumor about secret negotiations between France and England "to prevent Constantinople from passing into Russian hands." France's consent was now received. However, the suspicion planted by Mme. Vasilchikov did not wither. In November, 1915, at the Allied military conference in Chantilly, the Russian representative advised the Allies to liquidate the Gallipoli expedition. A secret telegram to General Alexeyev gave the unstated motive of this advice: the danger "of the creation of a permanent English port, of a new Gibraltar, at the entrance to the

Mediterranean Sea." Such a complete and literal coincidence with Mme. Vasilchikov's letter is hardly an accident.

Meanwhile Mme. Vasilchikov was pounding away at the same weak spot. Quoting Von Jagow, she informed the Tsar that England, "despite all her promises," had resolved not to give Russia Constantinople and the Straits, and that after the war Germany expected England to make some "proposals to use her forces against Russia." Germany preferred an agreement now with Russia, for she "needs a strong and monarchic Russia, and both reigning houses must support their old monarchic and friendly traditions." "The continuation of the war [by Russia] was in Germany viewed as a danger to the dynasty."[5]

In her letter of May 14 Mme. Vasilchikov offered to report "in person" all she had heard, and requested "every facility for her journey to Tsarskoye Selo." Although her arrival at the Russian boundary led General Bonch-Bruyevich to ask General Alexeyev whether she could be admitted, and whether she should not be subject to search and arrest, as coming with the consent of the enemy,[6] she was admitted. In Petrograd special quarters were prepared for her. She was received in Tsarskoye Selo, and brought the Tsaritsa letters from her relatives in Hesse.

Mme. Vasilchikov was not equal to a secret mission. She imagined herself practically a diplomat and wrote Sazonov and other ministers, and even Rodzianko. Her mission was compromised. To hush up the political scandal she was deprived of the title of lady in waiting and exiled to her sister's estate in Chernigov guberniya.

Alexandra Feodorovna had earlier taken advantage of a trip to Germany by an unnamed "American from the Y.M.C.A.," to instruct him to see Prince Max of Baden and Princess Victoria, and to talk over an apparently innocuous question, the agreement on the treatment of prisoners. In Germany great importance was attached to this initiative of a former princess of Hesse in reëstablishing the first direct contact between the dynasties of the two warring states. The Tsaritsa forwarded to her husband letters from the American, from "Max" and from "Vicky." "Please do not tell," she asks him, "where these letters are from (you may tell only Nikolasha [Grand Duke Nicholas Nikolayevich] about Max, as he is looking after our prisoners), they sent the letters to Anna [Vyrubova] through the Swedes,* but not through the lady in waiting [Mme. Vasilchikov], because *no one must know of this, not even their mission.* I do not know why they are so much afraid. I openly telegraphed Vicky, thanking her for her letter and asking her to thank Max in my name for all that he is doing for our prisoners." The naïveness of this letter is not entirely genuine, for in the beginning of the letter the Tsaritsa herself asks her husband "not to tell anyone." In other cases she is also greatly alarmed by fear of publicity. For example, in informing him that "Mita Benkendorf told at Paul's [Grand Duke Paul Alexandrovich], that Masha [Vasilchikov] had brought letters from Ernie [the Tsaritsa's brother, Grand Duke of Hesse], Ania said she knew nothing, and Paul said it was true—who told him?" And the Tsaritsa intends, on seeing Paul, to "explain things to him which are as clear as day."

Through the Empress' brother, Grand Duke of Hesse, the most serious attempt was made to establish contact between the reigning families regarding peace. On April 17 the Tsaritsa wrote her husband that she had received "a long, dear letter from Ernie." After hinting at the unlikelihood of Russian military success the Grand Duke informed her that "in Germany there is no real hatred against Russia." He would like to find "a way out of this dilemma," and assumed that "someone ought to begin to make a bridge for discussion." But who could better begin this than he himself, since his own sister was the wife of the Russian Emperor? He had resolved on "quite privately sending a man of confidence to

* In a personal letter to Nicholas II, Gustav V had offered his services as mediator.

Stockholm," in order to meet a confidant of Nicholas, sent in the same "private" fashion, ignoring the ministers and the diplomatic corps. The Tsaritsa writes that he had already "sent a gentleman to be there on the 28," and to return a week later. But matters took an unfavorable turn. "That is two days ago, and I only heard today" (April 17, Old Style, is April 30, New Style). Only five days were left and the Tsar was far away, at headquarters. "So I at once wrote an answer (all through Daisy [Swedish Crown Princess Marguerite]) and sent it the gentleman telling him you are not yet back, so he better not wait—and that tho' one longs for peace, the time has not yet come." "I wanted to get all done before you return, as I know it would be unpleasant for you. W. [William] knows of course absolutely nothing about this."

Here the naïveté is obviously acted. Whoever could believe that under German ideas of order a Grand Duke of Hesse, without William II's knowledge, could send a confidential emissary to negotiate with the personal plenipotentiary of the Russian Emperor? The affair is, indeed, "as clear as day." Grand Duke Paul Alexandrovich, an intimate of the French Ambassador, was told by the Tsaritsa that Nicholas "even in his sleep has no idea of peace, and knows it would mean revolution here." Paul Alexandrovich not only was aware of the correspondence with Ernie, but said he had heard of the "insane German conditions." For all these reasons, aside from the fact that it was too late, the Tsaritsa could act only as she did. Still, the ice had been broken. From now on the German side was informed that, although "the moment had not yet come," "everyone was eager for peace."

Thus we now know all the intermediaries in the secret negotiations for peace. For the Germans they were the "Swedes"; i.e., members of the Swedish royal family; no one else could have gone over the heads of the Swedish mission in Petrograd. For the Tsaritsa they were "Anna," "Mary," "Daisy," and an unidentified American from the Y.M.C.A.

In the Tsaritsa's correspondence with the Tsar there is one other side, no less important than the question of peace. More than once, donning her "invisible trousers" and even tucking them into equally invisible boots, she suggests concrete military plans. Nicholas should "send a few Cossack regiments along the bank," or "move up our cavalry a little to the north, in the direction of Libau." She mentions even the corresponding army detachments—let us not forget General Alexeyev's story of the very secret map, with the disposition of the Russian troops. She discusses whether the movements of the guards have been executed, "to the south of Keller," how and by whom the rear has been reënforced in such and such a place, elsewhere, how the left flank has been reënforced, where the artillery has been sent, and so forth. The question arises: whence all these strategic inspirations? Her correspondence settles this question. The Tsaritsa needs to know everything "for our Friend, who can aid." She scolds when "they begin a movement without asking him. He always thinks things over and decides when the right moment has come for the offensive." Or, in other cases, when it must be stopped. In one letter the Empress insists that "Brusilov be ordered immediately to stop his southern offensive." Rasputin not only reflects. He also receives strategic inspirations from on high. One letter of the Empress is most remarkable:

I must pass on to you the following request from our Friend, suggested to him by a nocturnal vision. He asks you to order an offensive near Riga. He says it is essential . . . Just now that will take them by surprise, and we shall succeed in making them retreat. He says that it is most essential *right now,* and asks you *seriously* to order our troops to advance. He says that we *can* and *must* attack, and for me to write you that immediately.

Who knows in what low resort Rasputin had that "nocturnal vision"? Perhaps he was surrounded by suspected spies, frequently noticed about him? Hvostov tells how Rasputin, on going to Tsarskoye Selo, was instructed by Dmitry

Rubinstein, the Germanophil banker and speculator, to find out whether there would be an offensive. Rubinstein said he needed to know whether to buy timber in Minsk province. Rasputin found out. Then in letters to her husband the Tsaritsa wonders how "people abroad know things that can be known only by well-informed men at headquarters." The picture is horrible, even if appearances made Rasputin no spy, but merely the unwitting agent of German espionage. While one warring country applies all the resources of military science and technique, all the exertion of experience and genius, the other side risks the fate of hundreds of thousands of people on the drunken dream of an ignorant, lascivious "fool of God"!

All limits had been passed. After this it is not surprising that Grand Duke Dmitry Pavlovich proved to be involved in Rasputin's murder, organized by Purishkevich for love of country and dynasty. The Tsaritsa was preparing to square accounts after the war with Nicholas Nikolayevich, with the "black daughters" (the Montenegrin princesses), and with other relatives whom she suspected of planning to depose her husband and to commit her to a convent. But they too were not napping. Even in the atmosphere of palaces and drawing rooms the accumulation of electricity was felt. The Grand Duchess Maria Pavlovna, widow of Grand Duke Vladimir, late one night so mysteriously and insistently summoned the president of the Imperial Duma, Rodzianko, that it seemed to him "like a conspiracy." The next day at luncheon the Grand Duchess

began to speak of the internal situation, the government's incapacity, Protopopov, and the Empress. At that name she became more excited and said that the Empress was ruining the country, that, because of her, danger to the Tsar and the entire imperial family was growing, that such a state of things could be tolerated no longer, that it must be changed, destroyed, set aside . . .

Wishing to clear up more exactly what she meant, I asked: "What do you mean, set aside?"

"Indeed, I do not know . . . Something must be undertaken, invented . . . You yourself understand . . . The Duma must do something . . . She must be destroyed . . ."

"Who?"

"The Empress."

"Your Highness," I said, "permit me to consider this conversation of ours as never having occurred . . . Otherwise, my oath of allegiance would compel me to go to the Emperor and report . . ."

Rodzianko says that for a long time the Grand Duchess could not make up her mind to approach the real aim of her interview, and that finally Grand Duke Cyril Vladimirovich persuaded her. He has since proclaimed himself, in a special manifesto, Emperor of All the Russias, Cyril I, and declared that he will rule with the "soviets." During the revolution he placed his military detachment at the disposal of the Imperial Duma, and adorned his uniform with the red kerchief of the revolution.

The tragic end of the Russian Louis XVI and Marie Antoinette was approaching. The Russian Orléans were already coming forward. They had their own "Cyril Égalité."

This was the inward collapse of the dynasty. Its outward downfall was not far behind.

One last attempt at salvation was possible. The country could be taken by surprise by making a separate peace and proclaiming an energetic reactionary dictatorship.

This seemed already on the way. On February 4, 1917, the Russian Ambassador in Christiania, Gulkevich, was visited by the Bulgarian Minister to Berlin, Rizov. He was asked to telegraph to Petrograd "Germany's desire to conclude a separate peace with Russia on extraordinarily favorable terms." Rizov said he was acting on his own, but, as Gulkevich testifies, he "did not leave the slightest doubt but that he was acting on German instructions." Gulkevich, for form's sake, refused, but naturally telegraphed Petrograd immediately. In reply he was ordered, if Rizov took new steps, "to listen attentively to all he has to say and to secure a more exact formulation of the conditions."

Count Czernin in his memoirs speaks of "an authorized representative of one of the neutral countries" who approached him "for one of the enemy countries without the others' knowledge." The Count "did not doubt for a moment but that Russia was meant." Czernin made the same proposal as "Ernie" previously, to dispatch confidential agents to a neutral state. It was already too late. Instead of "the confidential agent" he received the news of the revolution in Petrograd.

CHAPTER THREE

THE DUMA OPPOSITION

IN his *History of the Second Russian Revolution* Miliukov, the leader of the Cadet or bourgeois liberal party, offers a rather original interpretation of the February upheaval. In his opinion, it began as a street movement, absolutely elemental in force, "formless and objectless." At this point a new and a decisive factor intervened. "The intervention of the Imperial Duma furnished a rallying point to the street movement, gave it a banner and a slogan, and thus transformed an insurrection into a revolution which overthrew the old régime and dynasty."

Miliukov states that "much had already been accomplished by the Duma toward the success of this movement through its activity during the war and, especially, during the Progressive Bloc."

Miliukov's version is less accepted in Russia than beyond her boundaries. The tone for foreign conceptions of what had happened in Russia was set by information furnished by Miliukov as first Minister of Foreign Affairs in the Provisional Revolutionary Government. In his radiogram of March 3, he depicted the course of the revolution even more simply: "On the evening of February 28 the President of the Imperial Duma received the Tsar's ukaze postponing its meeting till April. On the same morning the rank and file of the Volynian and Lithuanian regiments had gone down to the street, and organized demonstrations in favor of the Imperial Duma. By evening excitement among the troops and the population had grown to a very alarming degree. The Executive Committee of the Imperial Duma decided to take over the functions of the executive power. During the next few days disorders spread from the capital to its suburbs and danger grew ominously. To prevent complete anarchy the Provisional Government undertook to restore military authority. It succeeded in stopping street excesses and restoring order."

Revolutionary circles of the Left repudiate Miliukov's version. Even the President of the Duma, Rodzianko, protested repeatedly against "accepting on faith the far from incontestable assertion that the Fourth Imperial Duma had prepared, created, inspired and embodied the coup d'état of February 27 and the revolution."

In order to test the theses of the disputing parties by the facts, we must examine more closely the mood of the Duma and its parties from the outbreak of war to February, 1917.

As soon as the war broke out, the Duma fraction of the Constitutional Democratic party (Cadets), led by Miliukov, declared roundly that "although the fraction has not modified its view of the necessity for reforming Russia," still, "at this minute another task, formidable and splendid, faces us . . . We are fighting to free our fatherland of foreign invasion, we are all united in this struggle: we set no conditions or demands, we simply place on the scales our firm will to overcome the enemy."

Earlier, during the struggle against revolution and the victory over it, the government had answered the opposition parties with the famous formula: "First, tranquilization, then reforms." Now outdoing the government, the opposition itself hastened to declare: "First, victory against the Austro-Germans, then reforms." The opposition signed its complete political abdication for the duration of the war.

Of course, it did so in the vain expectation that the government would appreciate the magnitude of this abdication and respond by a reconciliation with the opposition parties and by drawing them into the responsible work of the state, to organize all the country's forces and resources under the slogan of "Everything for the war! Everything for victory!"

In other words they believed that the government itself would organize what was called in Germany the *Burgfrieden* and in France the *union sacrée*.

Guchkov, a leader of the Octobrists, a party of semi-opposition at most (during Stolypin's time it was ironically dubbed by Cadet circles "the party of the latest government decree"), declared: "All party friction must disappear. The Duma's work must be carried on through the union of all political groups. Moreover, union between the national representative body and the government is essential, and, hence, the head of this government should be a man enjoying the confidence of the broad masses and of the national representative body."

The Progressists and Cadets agreed to furl their opposition banners. They figured that after the war the influence of the various parties would be directly proportioned to their working ability, to their importance in organizing national defense. "He who knows how to work will be master of the country." The Cadet party, which contained a very large number of highly educated people—professors, writers, lawyers, doctors, engineers, leaders in zemstvo and city self-government—seemed to have more chance than any other of penetrating the apparatus of administration and making itself irreplaceable and so irremovable. Hence its tactic of "enveloping" the government, its aim of gradually making the government the prisoner of moderate democracy.

But the government easily saw through this plan, and made up its mind that if it gave the opposition "devil" an inch, it would take an ell. One minister, Maklakov, declared: "Even under pretense of supplying boots to the soldiers you will carry on revolution." Therefore, only under the pressure of terrible failures at the front would the governing circles stretch out a hand to the so-called "civic" organizations: the Unions of Zemstvos and Cities and the War Industries committees. The danger past, the government immediately thrust them aside.

So matters went—until failure became catastrophe.

Sentiment in the country changed sharply. At the beginning of the war, despite the dull uncomprehension and occasional murmur of the masses, the entire "superstructure" of society had created an atmosphere of universal enthusiasm. But the hopeless inability of a stupid government to use it in building an organization for national defense turned the energy of enthusiasm to indignation against the existing régime.

Shulgin, a member of the Nationalist group, tells of a vice minister describing a trip to the south:

You know, Kiev is rather reactionary . . . And, do you know, I was stopped by the best-intentioned people there: "When are you going to drive *them* out?" They mean the government. And, you know it has become even worse since Rasputin was killed. Formerly, they piled all the blame on him . . . But now they have realized that it was not Rasputin. He has been killed, but nothing has changed. And now all the arrows fly right at the mark, without straying in Rasputin's direction.

The Moscow secret police reported Miliukov's impression of the older capital: "I would never have believed, if I had not heard it with my own ears, that Moscow had begun to speak such a language. I have known Moscow for several decades, and if, twenty years ago, I had been told that such a catastrophe would occur in Moscow sentiment, I should have called it a stupid joke. The most inert, most unenlightened people talk like revolutionaries."

At the Zemstvo Congress delegates Ivanenkov, Makarov, and Beschinsky confirmed a similar change in such a traditionally monarchist stratum as the Cossack communities. A report of the Moscow department of secret police for February 19, 1916, speaks of the growth "to a horrifying degree" "of universal and profound irritation against the person of His Majesty the Emperor, now reigning," and "with great sorrow states" that "if it were to resist all cases of impudent and open *lèse-majesté*, the number of cases under Article 103 would become unprecedented." A similar report of the Petrograd secret police refers to anti-government excitement "literally in all strata of society, including those which formerly never expressed any dissatisfaction, such as various circles of officers of the imperial guards."

The Duma's tactics were twofold: it was emboldened by the upper-class fronde and restrained by its glimpse of the revolutionary seething among the lower classes.

The Imperial Duma contained all the "statesmanship" of censitary,* propertied, privileged Russia. The alarming conditions consolidated its various factions politically. From Left to Right, the Cadets, the Progressists, the Zemstvo Octobrists, the Right-wing "Union of October 17," the Right "Center," and even the more progressive wing of Nationalists, neighbors of the reactionary Black Hundreds, formed the "Progressive Bloc."

Rodzianko, an Octobrist, describes the political significance of the Bloc. "The Party of Popular Liberty [Cadets] had been most subjected to preëlection persecution, and was obviously inclined to join the extreme Left. The danger of revolutionary feeling in the very heart of the Duma was growing, not by days, but by hours. This menaced the Duma's very existence, and might lead to revolutionary disorders in the country." To avoid this, "the influential Cadet party had to be brought into an agreement, and its alliance with the socialist groups forestalled," while attracting as many as possible from the militant, extreme Right wing, which was ready to explode the Duma from within by irritating it and supporting all the ministers' anti-Duma "words and deeds." Rodzianko praises the Progressive Bloc for "destroying the already formed [?] agreement between the Party of Popular Liberty and the socialist and revolutionary circles."[1]

* Elected under property suffrage.

The nationalist Shulgin, unable to defend the government, saw a single loophole:

Recognizing the growing discontent to be just, we must try to guide it into the mildest, most acceptable forms. . . . In other words, to substitute for the discontent of the masses, which might easily lead to revolution, the discontent of the Duma . . . Thus the Progressive Bloc was created. By this step we bound the Cadets to a minimum program . . . So to speak, we released them from revolutionary ideology and reduced matters to trifles . . . It seemed to me as if we were like a chain of soldiers advancing arm in arm . . . Of course, we are pushed from behind and compelled to advance. But we resist. We stick together and do not let the mob break through . . . Thus, we go on resisting, but we have been pushed from behind for a year and a half . . . God knows, if we had not formed that chain, perhaps the mob would have broken through long ago.[2]

"It was not for the sake of revolution," declared Guchkov, "that we summoned the government to meet the demands of society, but to strengthen the government for the defense of the fatherland against revolution and anarchy."

Within the Cadet party, membership in this "chain" aroused great friction. The Left wing of the party, according to the police records, "disapproved of the Bloc from the first. It asserted that the Bloc was compromising the party, for it had not compelled its Right members to adapt themselves to the Cadets, but, on the contrary, had adapted itself to its Right members by rejecting the main Cadet demands." This was perfectly natural. The law of all opposition blocs is that their program can be drawn up only "by removing from brackets the common political denominator" of the groups to be united. In other words, they adopt the program of the least oppositional party in the bloc. The leader of the Left-wing Cadets, Mandelstam, declared:

The tactics of the Right wing of the Cadet party, led by Miliukov, threaten to compromise the party beyond repair among the broad democratic circles of the population, and among the liberal intelligentsia. . . . Miliukov's terrible mistake lies in not realizing the fruitlessness of this game, in trying to inspire the bureaucracy with confidence in the Cadet party, in trying to get something from it by bargaining. Instead, he is losing trust and prestige among the broad democratic circles . . . In the near future events will move so fast that all the demands of the Progressive Bloc will seem mere childish lisping . . . Whoever sees the wave of popular wrath rising higher and higher, understands clearly that the Cadet party must not form a bloc with the Right but with the Left, must go arm in arm with the democratic parties. If we do not do so, events will pass us by, we shall lose the leading rôle in them. Let us be frank: in our circle many people are frightened by the specter of revolution, and see in it only another Pugachev revolt. But these very fears must dictate a policy diametrically opposed to Miliukov's. If we do not want the people's coming punishment of a criminal government to turn into disorganization, chaos, senseless insurrection, we cannot ignore the popular movement, we must strive to lead it. . . . Otherwise, the Cadet party, compromised in the eyes of the people, risks being stranded once and for all on the side of the moderate, antipopular political parties. That would be a misfortune for our party—the party of the Russian intelligentsia—and for the people.[3]

How did Miliukov, the leader of the Right-center majority of the party, defend his tactics?

People who spread such slogans are playing with fire. Evidently, they fail to consider the frightful strain under which all Russia is now living, and the consequences of that strain. It is quite probable that the government does not realize what is going on in the depths of Russia. But we sensitive and intelligent observers plainly see that we are walking over a volcano, that a slight jar is sufficient to throw everything into movement and confusion. All Russia is one huge inflamed wound, all pain, all sorrow, all suffering . . . The strain has reached its highest point, a careless match would cause a terrible conflagration. And may God preserve us from witnessing that conflagration. It would not be a revolution, it would be that awful "Russian revolt, senseless and merciless," which made Pushkin quiver. It would be that bacchanalia of the rabble, which we have just witnessed in Moscow.* It would be a new wave of that muddy filth from the depths which ruined the beautiful sprouts of the 1905 Revolution. No matter what the government, good or bad, a strong government is more necessary now than ever before.[4]

To Miliukov revolution was a sinister, treacherous element which only most dangerous illusion could hope to guide into proper channels. Russia was ripe for revolt, not for revolution. A change of tactic would, therefore, be fatal. Miliukov appealed to his party:

For God's sake, do not yield to the government's provocation. It is striving with might and main for a separate peace with Germany, it is trying to provoke complications within the country. . . . By pointing to the growth of the revolutionary movement in Russia the government would explain to its Allies the impossibility of going on with the campaign. It would lay the responsibility for failure at the door of the revolutionary and opposition circles . . . Do not succumb to this provocation. We have one thing to do: to endure patiently, to swallow the bitterest pills, not to increase but to restrain popular agitation; the government's position at the approaching day of reckoning will be hopeless, and the triumph of Russian liberalism will be complete and absolute.[5]

The "Right-center" elements of the Cadet party were sure of success. During the peace congress the government "can not do without the Duma." It would need "to strengthen" all its demands and solicitations "by reference to Russian public opinion, personified by the people's representatives." A conflict with the Imperial Duma just before or during the congress would weaken Russia's international position. Secondly, after the war the interest alone on its debt would require a half billion rubles, plus restoration of the ruined fortresses and construction of new ones, enlargement of the

* A chaotic pogrom of shops belonging to proprietors with German names turned into the plundering and wrecking of stores in general.

railroad system, expenses of demobilization, and so forth. In case of conflict with the Duma, "the government will not get a single kopeck abroad." One other circumstance must be reckoned with:

Unquestionably an ominous movement of the people is to be expected after the war . . . In its struggle the government will find itself helpless . . . At the last minute it must reach out to us, and then our job will be, not to strike the last blow at the government, which would mean supporting anarchy, but to give fresh content to the government . . . To encourage the leaders of anarchic revolution for the sake of fighting the government would mean risking all our political achievements since 1905.[6]

Rodzianko was later quite correct in asserting that "Miliukov in nearly all questions backed the Octobrists, even against the Progressists" (the Progressists were to the Left of the Octobrists, but to the Right of the Cadets). Shulgin assured the ministers that they should not fear the Cadets. "Why, they know that the Girondists' heads ended in the same basket as the Monarchists' . . . They are afraid of revolution. For three years they have been shouting, 'Everything for the war!' And that will be held against them in case of revolution."

And even the "danger from the Left," as personified by the Cadets, did not particularly alarm the Right-wing Monarchist circles. A memorandum, drawn up in the reactionary circle of Rimsky-Korsakov, appraised Miliukov's party as follows:

The strongest and most active of them [the moderate liberal elements] is the party of the Cadets, which leads all the rest. But if we look at it closely, we must admit that this party is strong only in its weakness. Democratic in name, but purely bourgeois in composition, with no basis of its own, it had to accept the slogans of popular rights and denial of property forced upon it from the Left. Although it contains a considerable number of so-called zemstvo leaders and landowners, the Cadet party made its first point the alienation of the land, the complete ruination of its own members. Of course its leaders were not sincere and did not strive very hard for this. They were quite willing to drop the point from the program of the Progressive Bloc, created and led by them. But is that not the best proof that they do not believe in their independent existence and seek for outside sympathies through concessions and sacrifices? Without this sympathy from the Left, without these trumps drawn from a pack of cards not their own, the Cadets are only a numerous society of liberal lawyers, professors, and officials of various ministries, and nothing more.[7]

When the Council of Ministers brought up the question of an agreement with the Progressive Bloc, two opinions clashed. One group would not consent at any price to forgive Miliukov for the Cadets' old attempt to block Stolypin's foreign loan after the dispersal of the First Duma. "Miliukov, no matter how he may change his skin, will always be a revolutionary in my eyes, until he apologizes for his actions abroad."* Others insisted on a sober appraisal of the situation, without resentment. Sazonov asserted: "If everything is arranged decently and an opening offered, the Cadets will be the first to come to an agreement. Miliukov is a thoroughgoing bourgeois and dreads a social revolution worst of all. The majority of the Cadets are trembling for their capital."[8]

In the autumn of 1915 Miliukov's calculations that the government would be stranded, with no escape but to invite members of the Progressive Bloc into the government, seemed close to realization. The front was passing through days of catastrophe. Panic seized masses of soldiers and their commanding officers. Headquarters insisted on evacuating Kiev. The abandonment of Petrograd was discussed. In the rear the situation was no better. The Minister of Internal Affairs, Prince Shcherbatov, reported his absolute helplessness, "the complete disorganization of local service," the multiple authorities and the resultant lack of authority, "the unimagi-

* Not Miliukov, but Prince Paul Dolgorukov and V. A. Maklakov, tried to prevent the loan in France; they were disavowed by their party.

nable confusion in the provinces," the ruining of the apparatus of the ministry of Home Affairs by the panicky and dictatorial orders issued by the military authorities, including even ensigns and barrack commanders. "At the front we are beaten by the Germans, in the rear lieutenants are dealing the final blows," concluded Krivoshein. The Minister of War reported that "at headquarters disorder is increasing every day, no one wants to do anything, no orders are issued." "The entire life of the country is being disorganized, the government apparatus is decomposing, everywhere there is chaos and discontent." The Council of Ministers at times realized that Russia was on the verge of bankruptcy. The Comptroller of State remarked bitterly that the country and army placed no confidence in the government, and if they still had any hope, it was only in the Duma and the War Industries committees. The Tsar too paid no attention to the Council of Ministers, and heeded only the placeman of the Empress and Rasputin, the decrepit and cynical bureaucrat, Goremykin. "The government has no confidence even from him who is the source of governmental power," declared Prince Shcherbatov, and no one contradicted him. The general feeling was summarized by Sazonov. "The government is dangling in mid-air with no support from below or above."[9]

Under such conditions there were only three possible ways out: to make concessions to organized society, find a second Stolypin and intrust him with dictatorial powers, or, finally, conclude a separate peace and thus escape the clutches of the crisis. But the people close to the Tsar still thought a separate peace would provoke an immediate revolution. A second Stolypin was not to be found. The upper stratum of the bureaucracy had degenerated as rapidly as the dynasty. Surrender to organized society was an impossibility because of the ambition of the camarilla of courtiers, the religious and dynastic Messianism of the Tsar and the Empress, and the hatred of society which had eaten into the heart and blood of the higher bureaucracy.

However, negotiations with the Progressive Bloc were begun. For the government they were conducted by the Comptroller of State, Haritonov, assisted by Ministers A. A. Hvostov, Prince Shcherbatov, and Prince Shakhovskoy, and for the Bloc by Miliukov, Yefremov, Shidlovsky, and Dmitriukov. At a secret session of the Council of Ministers it was reported that "in the main the program of the Progressive Bloc is acceptable and differs from the government's view only in certain questions." No wonder, for the Bloc did not even demand a ministry responsible to the Duma. It left the appointment of the individual ministers as a prerogative of the monarch, and was anxious only for a personal composition of the ministry to assure the confidence of the broad groups of society; i.e., a ministry formed from the Bloc. In concrete questions in which the Duma requested a more liberal policy, it would be difficult to invent more cautious and elastic formulæ. The ministers themselves laughed at the phrase regarding the Jewish question: "entering upon the path of a gradual weakening of restrictions."

Yet an agreement with organized society always struck a blank wall in the Tsar.

Goremykin, strong in the support of the Tsaritsa and Rasputin, at the decisive moment broke off negotiations by drawing from his pocket the imperial ukaze for the Duma's dissolution. To the warnings of his excited colleagues he replied with contempt: "Whether the Duma dissolves with a scandal or without is a matter of indifference." "To annoy the Emperor by talking of the danger of disorders I consider impossible, for I do not share those fears." "All this has been invented by Rodzianko to scare us." "The Duma will be dissolved on the appointed day, and no blood will flow." "Miliukov may talk whatever nonsense he likes. I believe so strongly in the Russian people and in their patriotism that I cannot even admit the thought that they would answer their Tsar by disorders, especially in wartime. If individual bands of intriguers begin to misbehave, the police will take care of them and there is no need to pay attention to them." Thus reasoned his successors as well.

There was no lack of dramatic scenes. The president of the Duma, Rodzianko, made a special visit to the Council of Ministers and tried to persuade the head of the government not to play with fire when the fate of Russia and the dynasty was at stake. He met such conceited, bureaucratic imperturbability that, "looking absolutely mad, without saying good-bye, forgetting his cane, he rushed to the door with the hopeless words, 'I am beginning to believe those who say that there is no government in Russia.' " Ten ministers sent the Tsar a collective declaration of their disagreement with the premier and of their disbelief in the possibility of continuing their work. They received a reprimand with the order to remain at their posts—only to be retired later one by one. On the other hand, the Empress' favor was given to Hvostov, the only minister who took Goremykin's side against the rest and proposed a very simple recipe for the Duma: "They must simply be driven out."

"Drive them all out . . . the police will suffice." Guchkov exclaimed, "The deluge is approaching, and a pitiful, miry government is preparing to encounter this cataclysm with the same measures by which they protect themselves from a good drenching rain: they put on their rubbers and open their umbrellas." Even Buchanan, the British Ambassador, began to realize that "the revolution, I fear, is inevitable."

The same fear haunted the leading circles of the Duma. In the same month of August, 1916, Guchkov wrote General Alexeyev: "Our weapons are double edged and because of the excitement of the masses, especially the workers, they may be the first spark of a conflagration, the dimensions of which cannot be foreseen or localized."

The same doubts begin to assail Shulgin.

Russia's irritation has, to be sure . . . been diverted successfully to that safety valve called the Imperial Duma. . . . We have succeeded in substituting for "revolution"; i.e., blood and destruction, "resolution"; i.e., a verbal reprimand to the government. But . . . in moments of doubt, I sometimes begin to feel that, instead of firemen, trying to put out the revolution, we are, against our will, becoming its instigators.

The Imperial Duma began more and more to dread the tenseness of the popular sympathies which were drawn to it. It was not far wrong.

On January 24, 1917, the Workers' Group of the Central War Industry Committee, taking note of the government's obvious hostility to the workers, appealed to the people:

The working class and democracy must not wait any longer. Every day of neglect is dangerous. The resolute elimination of the autocratic régime and the complete democratization of the country is now the task which demands immediate solution, a question of life and death for the working class and democracy . . . At the opening of the Duma we must prepare a universal demonstration. Let all working-class Petrograd, factory by factory and district by district, at the opening of the Duma, march in a comradely spirit to the Tauride Palace, to state the fundamental demands of labor and democracy. The entire country and army must hear the voice of the working class: only the establishment of a Provisional Government, relying on the people organized for struggle, can lead the country out of its blind alley and fatal ruin, strengthen political liberty and guide it to a peace on conditions acceptable to the Russian proletariat and to the proletariat of other countries.

The Workers' Group represented the extreme Right of the labor and socialist movement. It was composed of so-called "defensive war men," firmly resolved, despite accusations of "social treason," to coöperate loyally with the class of merchants and manufacturers in the national defense. The Group itself was hard pressed by the feeling of the masses, which were becoming more and more hostile to the war. Its attempt to call a demonstration for the day of the Duma's opening was intended to avoid a complete rupture between the Duma and the masses, by pressing the Duma to more decisive action and accustoming the workers to let the Duma lead the popular movement. In a word, the extreme Right wing of the Socialists was trying to achieve what the Left wing of the Cadets desired.

The government's reply was the immediate disbanding of the Workers' Group and mass arrests among workers, trade-union leaders, and others.

On the morning of January 29, the Central War Industries Committee held a special meeting with representatives of the Zemstvo and City Unions and of the Progressive Bloc. There was one member from the Workers' Group—Obrosimov. Supposedly he had escaped arrest by accident. Actually he had been left at liberty intentionally, as a police agent and provocator. His speech was to furnish the police with material to accuse the group of preparing an armed insurrection under pretext of peaceful demonstration. But even before Obrosimov spoke, according to the report of the Petrograd secret police,

> the deputy of the Imperial Duma, Miliukov, obviously excited, pointed out that the Duma was now the center of the attention of the entire country, that only the Duma must and could dictate to the country the conditions of the struggle against the government, that it alone must unify this entire struggle and offer suitable slogans. Aside from the Duma no one, not a single class of the population, not a single group of society was entitled to advance its own slogans and independently commence or wage that struggle. Therefore, the policy of the Workers' Group and of labor was absolutely incomprehensible to him, Miliukov, and he did not see how to harmonize that with the situation which had arisen.

The report adds that "those present, having expected to hear a fiery speech from Miliukov, were positively downcast by this statement." The leader of the Social Democratic fraction in the Duma, Chkheidze, felt compelled to state that "under such conditions Miliukov was running the risk of being outstripped by events one fine day, since, if things continued in this way, the workers alone might unexpectedly find themselves leading political action and events." The government's measures were "a blow at labor, but remember," and Chkheidze raised his voice in warning, "the workers' downfall will be followed by your own."

Thus, only three weeks before the outbreak of the revolution, a fresh crack appeared between the Cadet wing of the Progressive Bloc and the labor movement. A week later it widened still farther. On February 9, foreseeing the demonstration at the opening of the Duma, the district military commander, Habalov, issued a declaration that no "true son of the fatherland" would "betray his brothers," and hence none would heed the appeal "to go in a mass to the Tauride Palace to present political demands." "Do not listen to the criminal instigators who urge you to commit treason." On the following day the newspaper *Rech* published a letter from Miliukov to the editor. Shulgin remarks that "strangely enough, these two documents were not unlike." Miliukov also warned the workers not to respond to the summons to demonstrate. The workers were especially excited by a reference to "pernicious and dangerous advice" which "evidently proceeds from the most sinister source." "To follow this advice means to play into the hands of the enemy."

Habalov's declaration had provoked a turbulent explosion of indignation among the working class. They were greatly excited by the arrest of the Workers' Group and by rumors that the pretext for arrest had been arranged through a most shameless act of provocation.* To this was now added an attempt to vilify the moral and political reputation of the victims of this sinister police intrigue. It is easy to understand the bad impression left by Miliukov's letter under these circumstances. It was deepened by speeches in the Duma, hint-

* The Minister of Internal Affairs, Protopopov, later questioned on this subject, confirmed the fact that Obrosimov, to avoid the spread of rumors among the men arrested, had had to be tried along with the Workers' Group, after which a fictitious escape from prison was promised him by the government.

ing that the very idea of the demonstration had perhaps been palmed off on the workers through police provocation. A Social Democratic deputy, Skobelev, protested to the Duma against the "insinuation that the labor movement was working for the foreign enemy and that an act of police provocation was the origin of that movement."

It must be mentioned at this point that the appeal of the Workers' Group had absolutely nothing in common with the tendencies of Bolshevism. On the contrary, the Bolsheviks were hostile to any attempt to link the labor movement to the Duma. According to the secret police, they "regarded the Workers' Group as a politically impure organization, and did not recognize the Imperial Duma. Instead, they passed a resolution not to support the demonstration of the group, but to set going a movement of the proletariat by their own forces, fixing the demonstration for February 10, the anniversary of the trial of the former members of the Bolshevist faction in the Duma. For that day a general strike was proposed." The Petrograd Committee of Bolsheviks on February 7 issued a proclamation to this effect. But at that time the Bolsheviks were too weak to succeed in such an attempt. Their own organ, *Pravda*, had to admit that "because of disagreements among the radical groups, the day was unsuccessful as regards the demonstration." No general strike came of it. There was only a partial interruption of work at several factories, at different times of the day, to organize informal meetings with speeches and resolutions. But by the opposition of the Bolsheviks and the admonitions of the Cadets the February 14 demonstration was badly undermined. In all, about sixty enterprises, with several tens of thousands of workers, went on strike. In three or four parts of the city the police had to disperse demonstrators. As Goremykin had said, the police were still "adequate." During these events two Left deputies, Chkheidze and Kerensky, attacked the Progressive Bloc and the Cadets. They accused them of "lack of will to act," of dread of the revolution, and tried to prove that there was no escape except through revolution. "The government in the most fatal manner is striving to hurl itself over the precipice, and it is more sensible to break with it in time than for others to be dragged with it into the chasm."[10]

But the opposition leaders in the Duma remained true to themselves. Their stakes were on another card. They still hoped to wrench the government from the reactionary clique, and they regarded with complacency their service in helping to restrain the workers from their street demonstration. It seemed to them evidence of their influence among the workers. They were all the more surprised by the street movement which flared up less than a week later in Petrograd, this time beyond restraint, and which grew into revolution.

The revolutionary failures of February 10 and 14 convinced the political police of their own strength and of the workers' helplessness. At first they rejoiced in the confusion of the Duma opposition. A memorandum of the Petrograd secret police says:

> The inclination of the underground socialist organizations to transform a peaceful demonstration of the people into violent, revolutionary action, terrifies the "claimants of power" to the utmost, and compels them ruefully to ask if they have not seasoned things too highly, if they do not resemble the witch in the Bible, and if, without expecting it, they have not evoked, not the obedient "phantom of revolution" to scare the recalcitrant government, but the evil spirit of revolution, which in its march of destruction is preparing to destroy the government . . . and to devour them.[11]

The secret police were having a hearty laugh.

Yes, of course there was something comical in the position of the leaders of the Progressive Bloc. One of them, Shulgin, later wrote in all sincerity:

> I had a fellow feeling for them, my comrades in the Bloc, and for myself. We were born and brought up to praise or blame the government under its protecting wing . . . At most we could

have passed painlessly from a deputy's chair to the ministerial bench . . . Provided the imperial sentinel guarded us . . . But faced by the possible downfall of the government, by a bottomless pit, our heads whirled and our hearts were numbed.[12]

The secret police laughed heartily—but they had not long to laugh.

BECAUSE of their fear of revolution, because of their desire to forestall it, the opposition circles were bound to bring forth, and did bring forth, the idea of a *palace revolution.* A change of monarchs might be the way out of the blind alley, assuming that the new monarch or regent would be inclined to cooperate in the "envelopment" of the government by the liberal elements of society and in the gradual remodeling of absolutism into a régime of constitutional, democratic monarchy.

In his *History* Miliukov asserts that the conviction was widespread in society that after Rasputin's murder

> the next step to be accomplished in the immediate future was a palace revolution with the assistance of officers and troops. . . . Nicholas' successor was to be his son, Alexis, with Grand Duke Michael Alexandrovich as regent during his minority. After General Krymov's suicide it was learned that this comrade of Kornilov's was the self-sacrificing patriot, who, early in 1917, had discussed in his intimate circle the details of the approaching overturn. Its execution was already outlined in February. At the same time another circle, formed around several members of the steering committee of the Progressive Bloc with zemstvo and city leaders, although not exactly informed of the preparations, discussed the rôle of the Duma after the coup d'état. Having canvassed various possibilities, this circle likewise agreed on the regency of Grand Duke Michael Alexandrovich as the best means of establishing a constitutional monarchy. Several members of the First Provisional Government took part in the conferences of this second circle, while some of them were aware of the other's existence.[13]

Kerensky asserts that "during the monarchy's last winter General Krymov, with Guchkov and Tereshchenko, arranged a palace revolution." The police, however, were on the alert. At a secret meeting of the Council of Ministers, on August 4, 1915, Hvostov had spoken of Guchkov's being supported by Left groups because "they thought him capable of leading a battalion to Tsarskoye Selo." In his "absolutely secret" report of January 26, 1917, General Globachev mentions a group, "acting so far in conspirative manner," composed of A. I. Guchkov, Prince Lvov, S. N. Tretyakov, Konovalov, M. M. Fedorov, and several others. "All the hopes of this group are centered on a palace revolution, considered to be inevitable in the near future, and supported by at least one or two favorable military detachments." Drawing on the materials of the investigating commission of the Provisional Government, Blok sketches the following picture:[14] "Guchkov hoped that the army, with few exceptions, would favor the coup d'état, to be accompanied by a terrorist act (like the bodyguards of the eighteenth century or "the student with a bomb"), not elemental or anarchic in character, but rather like the Decembrists' plot. A plan existed for seizing the imperial train between headquarters and Tsarskoye Selo and compelling the Tsar to abdicate. At the same time, with the aid of the troops, the government was to be arrested, and then the coup d'état and the composition of the new government were to be announced."

In his recollections Professor Lomonosov writes: "In the staffs and at headquarters the Tsaritsa was mercilessly cursed, people spoke of locking her up in a convent and even of deposing Nicholas. They talked of this even at the generals' tables. But in such conversations the most probable outcome was always considered a palace revolution, like Paul I's murder." According to Denikin, active steps were to be preceded by a last appeal to the Tsar by one of the Grand Dukes, and if the Tsar refused, "his physical removal" was expected. In regard to the coup d'état Generals Alexeyev, Ruzsky, and Brusilov were sounded out regarding their attitude. Only the first returned a determined "No."[15]

Shulgin "was sounded out" by a certain Cadet, N. (Nekrasov?)

> regarding a thing which everyone was chattering about over coffee in every salon; i.e., a palace revolution. I knew a formless plan existed, but not its participants or its details. Incidentally, I heard of a so-called "sea-plan." The Empress was to be invited on board a cruiser under some pretext, and carried off to England, supposedly at her own wish. By another version, the Emperor was to go too, while the heir was to be proclaimed Emperor. I regarded these conversations as idle chatter.

Finally, there is a more concrete account by Rodzianko of General Krymov's trip from the front to Petrograd early in January, and his report, made at Rodzianko's private apartment.

> Krymov ended approximately as follows: "Feeling in the army is so strong that everyone will welcome with joy the news of the coup d'état. The overturn is inevitable; that is felt at the front. If you resolve on this extreme measure, we will support you. Time is not to be lost."
>
> Krymov fell silent and for several seconds everyone sat perplexed and despondent. The first to break the silence was Shingarev: "The general is right, a coup d'état is essential. But who will make up his mind to do it?"
>
> With bitterness Shidlovsky said: "There is no reason to spare or pity him, when he is ruining Russia."
>
> Many members of the Duma agreed with Shingarev and Shidlovsky. Brusilov's words were quoted: "If I have to choose between the Tsar and Russia, I shall follow Russia."
>
> The most implacable and incisive of all was Tereshchenko, who disturbed me greatly. I interrupted him and said: "You do not consider what will happen after the Tsar's abdication . . . I will never join a coup d'état. I have taken an oath . . . If the army can secure his abdication, let it do so through its com-

manders, but till the last minute I shall act by persuasion, not by force."

The picture of the "plot" is not very imposing. The *military* part of the plot, through Krymov, tells the civilian element: If *you* make up your mind, we will support you. But the civilian part, through Rodzianko, replies: If *you*, the army, can compel the Tsar to abdicate, we will take advantage of that. In a word, there was evidently more talk about a conspiracy than conspiratorial action. They were all sounding each other out. After Rasputin's murder, according to the secret police records, "people have of late talked much and earnestly about a National Party, formed around Purishkevich; this party, it was said, had decided by a palace overturn to save Russia from revolution"; however, the *gendarmerie* admitted that this might be merely the "leisure invention of gossipers." Rodzianko says that "many people were absolutely and sincerely convinced that I was arranging an overturn and that I was assisted by many officers of the guards and by the British Ambassador, Buchanan," in itself an obvious absurdity.

Such was that strange "plot," which was being discussed in the palaces of Grand Dukes and apartments of Duma deputies, in fashionable salons and cabinets of the army commanders, in reports of the political police and secret meetings of the Council of Ministers. "I regarded it as idle chatter," said Shulgin, and he was close to the truth. The last fragment of that plan was a conference between Rodzianko, his assistant Nekrasov, the secretary of the Duma, Dmitriukov, and Deputy Savich, and Grand Duke Michael Alexandrovich, on February 27, when the street movement was growing into a victorious revolution. "It was indicated . . . to the Grand Duke that the situation could still be saved: he must accept immediately the dictatorship of Petrograd, compel the ministers to resign and by direct wire demand a manifesto of His Majesty the Emperor granting a responsible ministry." But even this halfway palace revolution was only talked about: "The Grand Duke's irresoluteness" spoiled everything. Of the entire program he fulfilled only one part: he talked with the Tsar by direct wire and having received a blank refusal, "crossed his useless hands on his empty breast."

CHAPTER FOUR

THE DUMA BENEATH THE STORM OF REVOLUTION

THE Duma, as we have seen, tried in every way to escape the revolution. From the first day of its triumphal march through the streets of Petrograd the revolution "passed by the Duma." The workers who poured onto the street and were gradually drawn into the maelstrom of the movement, like the soldiers, united spontaneously under the two slogans of "Bread!" and "Down with the war!" The latter slogan made the movement not merely alien to the Duma, but positively hostile to it. The Duma knew that the autumn summons of 1916 had already raised the number of recruits to thirteen million, that four million incapacitated men meant twenty million widows, orphans, and old men, taking the average of five persons to a Russian family. It knew that the refugees from the evacuated provinces had increased the heavy burden of unproductive population. It knew that the finances of the country were shattered and could be maintained only through inflation, which disorganized production and exchange. It knew that the equipment of war industry and transport was exhausted, in a word, that Russia's economy was cracking at the seams, straining all social bonds and ominously sharpening all social antagonisms. But till then the Duma had had to deal with only one form of the yearning for peace: with court intrigues for a separate bargain between Nicholas II and William II, which for Russia would have meant the blind alley of reaction and the vassalage of the Russian dynasty of Holstein-Gottorp, renamed Romanov, to the victorious Hohenzollerns. Against this separate bargain the Duma had mobilized public opinion, it had interwoven the slogans of liberalism and patriotism, and it could not destroy with its own hands what it had built with such labor and at such moral and political sacrifice. The mood of the masses made the demand for peace a *revolutionary* slogan, a slogan summoning the workers of the entire world by their united interference to stop the "military amusements" of their rulers. For the Duma this was something new, incomprehensibly Utopian, and unexpected. This movement could not inspire the Duma, but only ignore it.

And the Duma would have been left stranded in its shallow bay, forgotten by all, refusing alliance with the people, rejected by the autocracy, useless to everyone. But at this point the government, little suspecting, hastened to its rescue. Just as the street movement was reaching its height, the government issued a decree dissolving the Duma. The news suddenly swept through the streets of Petrograd: the Duma has refused to disperse! For all those of the discontented who were hesitant or irresolute and for all those who had begun to doubt the stability of the government they were defending, that was the last straw. The former, through herd instinct, joined a movement which even the Duma supported, while the latter, paralyzed by loss of faith, abandoned the sinking ship of state.

Yet the Duma's refusal to disperse was nothing more nor less than an artificial legend. Yes, the Left urged it to refuse. But "by disobeying the monarch the Duma would be unfurling the banner of revolt and would have to head that revolt with all its consequences," writes Shulgin. "Rodzianko and the great majority of us, including the Cadets, were absolutely incapable of that." This became clear at the meeting of the steering committee of the Progressive Bloc, at which "no one proposed anything worthy of attention."

The Duma decided to submit to the imperial ukaze of dissolution, and to recognize that it had ceased to function. However, the members of the Duma agreed not to disperse, but to assemble at once in "private conference." To avoid confusing a private conference of its entire membership with a formal session, they went from the large White Hall to the small, Semicircular Hall. All radical proposals were now rejected by an overwhelming majority. The general equation was hit upon by Miliukov. He recommended caution, warned against any overhasty decision, especially when they did not know whether it was true that the old government had fallen, or how serious this popular movement would be. The "conference" barely had time to select a "Provisional Committee," which later, to lend it greater importance, people began calling the "Provisional [and sometimes even the "Executive"] Committee of the Imperial Duma." This it never was in reality. It was only "the committee of a *private conference.*" It bore the long and awkward title of "Provisional Committee for relations with persons and institutions on the question of restoring public order and quiet in the capital," or something like that.

By then the news had come that, upon learning of the "dispersion" of the Duma and its refusal to submit, crowds of people, thousands, perhaps tens of thousands, were hastening to the Duma. According to Miliukov's story, the Duma had only to furnish the movement "a center, a banner, and a slogan," to make the "formless and objectless" movement a genuine revolution. The members of the Duma, according to Shulgin, were waiting to fulfil this mission, "alarmed, excited, somehow pressing closer together in spirit . . . Even enemies of many years' standing suddenly felt that there was something equally dangerous, ominous, repulsive to all of them . . . That something was . . . the street mob!"

The mob. Oh, yes, of course it was not handsome to look at. Peasants' jackets, army coats, sweat shirts, leather half-coats, caps, greased boots . . . They were odorous, not of scent, but of tar, sheepskin, and toil. The fragrant smoke of Turkish cigarettes and Havana cigars was lost in the thick, biting stench of plebeian cut tobacco. But the mob was not one of gabblers, or lordly politicians, or of effeminate cowards, able only to move from the deputy's chair to the ministerial bench by imperial condescension. For over a week this mob had been fired upon by the machine guns of the police, it had been dispersed by sabers and revolvers, but it had reassembled again and again. It had just proven its ability to sacrifice its life. In the font of revolution it had received a fresh baptism. That "rabble" was a holy rabble, capable of accomplishing immortal deeds. It longed to give itself up to the guidance of someone wise, good, rich in knowledge and experience. But woe to him who tried to deceive it or toss it aside with lordly contempt, like a useless ladder.

How did the Duma greet the crowd?

"I recall," relates Shulgin, "the moment when the blackish-gray sediment, pressing at the doors, like a never-ceasing flood, drowned the Duma. From the first moment of that inundation, repulsion filled my soul . . . I felt in myself helpless and, hence, all the wilder fury. Machine guns!"[1]

If the Duma was unwilling to go to the revolution, the revolution, represented by the people in arms, would come to the Duma. It was visited by the organized representative of the revolution, the Soviet of Workers' Deputies, which had been elected by the factories after February 21 and had also installed itself in the Tauride Palace. The Duma had to make the best of things. The legend of its refusal to obey the ukaze of dissolution had gradually led to an unprecedented and ambiguous situation. Military detachments arrived to certify their abandonment of the Tsar, whom the Duma had resolved loyally to obey even after the order to dissolve. They confirmed their loyalty to the revolution, represented by the Duma, which shuddered inwardly at contact with it. The crowd cheered Rodzianko.

And a moment came when Rodzianko said to himself:

I do not wish to revolt. I am no insurgent, I did not make and do not wish to make a revolution. If it has been made, it is because people did not heed us . . . I am no revolutionary. But, on the other hand . . . Well, there is no government. The ministers have fled. They cannot be found. From all sides people rush to

STREET SCENE IN PETROGRAD, FEBRUARY–MARCH, 1917

Courtesy of the Muzei Revolutsii, U.S.S.R.

DEMONSTRATION IN PETROGRAD, JUNE, 1917

Courtesy of the Muzei Revolutsii, U.S.S.R.

me. What shall I do? Withdraw? Leave Russia without a government?

From the Right, even from the Duma group of Nationalists, people were urging him to make up his mind. "Take power. That is not rebellion. Take it as a loyal subject. There may be two ways out: everything will pass off, the Emperor will appoint a new government, and we will surrender power to it. But if we do not take power, it will be seized by those fellows who have already been electing some scoundrels or other at the factories."

The "revolutionary against his will," the *Kammerherr* of the court, who had just wept bitterly on learning that the Home Minister, Prince Golitsyn, had abandoned the struggle and announced his resignation, tried to take power in order to come to some agreement with the Tsar to cancel the entire revolution.

Nothing could be more eloquent than the documents from General Ruzsky's archives concerning Rodzianko's negotiations with the Tsar and headquarters.

On February 27 Rodzianko telegraphed the commander of the northern front, General Ruzsky, regarding the riots in the capital, the inability of the authorities to restore order, the necessity for the Tsar immediately to form a new ministry under "someone whom the entire country can trust." "Delay is impossible, delay is death." Rodzianko sent the same message to the Tsar, adding, "I pray God that in this hour responsibility will not fall upon the ruler." After reading the telegram, the Tsar said: "Again that fat fellow, Rodzianko, has written me all sorts of nonsense, to which I shall not even reply." Rodzianko sent another telegram: "The situation is becoming worse. Measures must be taken, for tomorrow will be too late. The final hour has arrived, the fate of the fatherland and dynasty is being decided." The Tsar's brother, Michael, likewise appealed to Nicholas II on February 27. The reply was: "Thank you for your advice, but I myself know how I must act." Finally, from Petrograd the Minister of War, Belyayev, who had up to then guaranteed to subdue everything and everyone, reported gloomily that with "the few detachments which are still faithful to their duty" he was unable to do anything, and that "many units are gradually joining the rebels." He demanded the "speedy arrival of an adequate number of really reliable units." General Ruzsky appealed to the Tsar with the respectful suggestion that "measures of repression can only make the situation more acute," for the army at the front "reflects the feeling of the country," which must be satisfied by "immediate measures." In reply, the Tsar sent General Ivanov, the placeman of Rasputin and the Empress, to Petrograd with special powers, with two battalions of St. George soldiers. The northern and western fronts each were ordered to reinforce Ivanov by a machine-gun brigade, two infantry and two cavalry regiments, "the most reliable," commanded by "firm generals."*

The next day, February 28, the chief of staff, General Alexeyev, informed the front commanders that the Tsar (who was alarmed for the Empress and his children and needed her advice) had left for Tsarskoye Selo, and that, although Petrograd seemed entirely or almost entirely in the rebels' power, still it was essential "to preserve the troops' loyalty to their duty and their oath." On the same day Alexeyev hastily dispatched a supplementary telegram. Affairs in Petrograd appeared to him in better light.

A Provisional Government, under Rodzianko's presidency, is meeting at the Imperial Duma. It has invited the commanders of the military detachments to receive necessary orders for the maintenance of order. A proclamation to the people, issued by the Provisional Government, refers to the necessity of monarchy

* "The commander of a St. George battalion, General Pozharsky, assembled his officers on February 27, and said that, once in Petrograd, he would not issue any order to fire into the people, even though it were demanded by General Ivanov" (Blok, *op. cit.,* p. 41). Rodzianko's communication to Ruzsky shows that the first two troop trains, sent from the northern front to Petrograd, revolted, and resolved . . . not to let even the imperial trains go through. Matters were no better in the other detachments.

for Russia, to the need for fresh elections, and for the appointment of a government. I await impatiently His Majesty's arrival in order to report the above with the request to accept these wishes of the people. If this information is exact, the methods of your action are changed, negotiations will lead to pacification.

The information was false. As yet there was no Provisional Government. The good intentions of the Duma leaders were accepted and reported as facts. On March 1 more news arrived. There were disorders in Kronstadt. Rear Admiral Kurosh was helpless, he could "not guarantee a single detachment." Admiral Nepenin was unable to prevent the Baltic Fleet from pronouncing for the Duma. Moscow was gripped by insurrection and the troops were going over to the rebels. Headquarters was now alarmed for the imperial train. The same day, the direct wire from the northern front to headquarters reported that Grand Duke Serge Mikhailovich insisted that the Tsar appoint Rodzianko premier before it was too late. General Alexeyev made bold to address the same proposal to the Tsar, for the "leaders of the Duma, guided by Rodzianko, can still check the universal breakdown, and our work can be carried on with them, while each hour's loss lessens the last chance for preserving and restoring order and favors seizure of power by extreme Left elements." On March 2 he learned that "the garrison of Luga has gone over to the committee," and hence, they must bring General Ivanov's troop trains back to the front. But above all "the entire imperial family is in the hands of the insurgent troops, which have occupied the palace at Tsarskoye Selo." The Tsar telegraphed Ivanov not to take any measures until he had reported in person. Nicholas agreed to send the troops back to the front, and permitted General Ruzsky to open telegraph negotiations with Rodzianko, whom the Tsar himself awaited for a personal audience.

The telephone conversation between Ruzsky and Rodzianko was a curious one. First, Ruzsky asked why Rodzianko had abandoned his trip to Pskov, to negotiate personally with the Tsar. Rodzianko spoke of "the impossibility of leaving the excited popular passions without my personal presence," "since so far they believe *only me* and fulfil *only my* commands."

As a matter of fact, something much more prosaic had happened. The railwaymen refused Rodzianko a train without the special permission of the Executive Committee (of the Soviet of Workers' Deputies). When he appealed to the committee, its Left section replied:

> Rodzianko must not be allowed to go to the Tsar. We do not yet know the intentions of the leading groups of the bourgeoisie, of the Progressive Bloc, and of the Duma Committee, and no one can guarantee them . . . If there is any force on the side of the Tsar, then the "revolutionary" Duma, which "has taken the side of the people," will certainly side with the Tsar against the revolution . . . And what the Tsar alone would be unable to do, he can easily accomplish with the aid of the Duma and Rodzianko, that is, collect and move up troops to establish "order" in Petrograd.[2]

The Executive Committee at first refused Rodzianko his train, but later, after Kerensky's interference, granted it. But it was already too late.

Rodzianko's claim that "they believe only me and fulfil only my commands" was a great distortion of the truth. One query arises: was this a maneuver to strengthen his candidacy for the premiership, or was it mere boasting? In his memoirs he afterwards described his failure to secure a train, and many other occurrences. When a group of Preobrazhensky soldiers brought him the reactionary Tsarist minister, Shcheglovitov, Rodzianko, "dumbfounded by this arbitrary action," invited Shcheglovitov "kindly to step into his study." Astonished by the friendliness of the president of the "revolutionary" Duma toward a leader of the deepest dyed reaction, "the soldiers abruptly refused to release him," and when he "tried to display his authority," the "soldiers drew closer around their prisoner and in the most insolent manner pointed to their rifles." The next day the crew of the Second Fleet asserted bluntly that Rodzianko "must be shot as a bourgeois, and that the sailors would not be sorry to perform this act."

Rodzianko and the other Duma leaders might imagine that they could outwardly lead the revolution and actually catch it in their diplomatic nets. The catch was too big for the fishers.

A select group of the leaders of the Progressive Bloc now assembled secretly without including the newly elected members, Chkheidze, who rejected the invitation, and Kerensky.* Guchkov at once got down to business.

> In this chaos we must above all think of saving the monarchy. Evidently the present monarch must not reign any longer. But can we calmly wait for this revolutionary rabble to destroy the monarchy? That will happen inevitably if we let the initiative slip from our hands . . . Therefore, we must act secretly, swiftly, without asking, without taking anyone's advice. We must confront them with an accomplished fact. We must give Russia a new monarch . . . Under this new banner we must collect everyone we can . . . to resist! We must act swiftly and resolutely!

He proposed to go to the Tsar, to persuade him to abdicate. Shulgin offered to accompany him. Guchkov's motives were simple:

> I knew that if he abdicated into our hands, there would, so to speak, be *no revolution*. The Emperor would abdicate of his own free will, power would pass to a regent, who would appoint a new government. The Imperial Duma, which had submitted to the ukaze of dissolution and had taken power only because the old ministers had fled, would transfer power to the new government. Juridically speaking, there would be no revolution . . .

No sooner said than done. At dawn, when "the revolutionary people were still asleep," Guchkov and Shulgin suc-

* Their groups, the Social Democrats and the Labor Group, were not members of the Progressive Bloc.

ceeded in persuading the stationmaster to give them a train, and went to fetch the "voluntary abdication."

Now General Ruzsky informed Rodzianko of a new favor: the Tsar had first proposed to intrust him with forming a government responsible to himself, but was persuaded to make a fresh concession: the ministry would be responsible to the legislative chambers.

His Majesty and you [answered Rodzianko] evidently do not realize what is going on. One of the most dreadful of revolutions has begun and will not be so easy to combat . . . Such anarchy has developed that the Duma and I could but try to get the movement into our own hands and to guide it . . . Unfortunately, I have been far from successful. The people's passions have flared so high that they can scarcely be restrained. The troops are completely demoralized. Hatred for Her Majesty the Empress has reached an extreme. The dynastic question is acute. To avoid bloodshed, I was obliged to lock up all the ministers, except those of War and Marine, in the fortress of Peter and Paul, and I very much fear the same fate for myself.

Rodzianko has already forgotten his previous assertion: "They believe only me and fulfil only my orders." He has forgotten the unpleasant incident of the soldiers' rifles. His own hatred toward the Tsaritsa for ruining the dynasty, he attributes to the people. He says, not what is true, but what serves his purpose. To General Ruzsky's question as to what he meant in saying that the dynastic problem was acute, he replied, "with pain in his heart": "Hatred for the dynasty has reached an extreme . . . Threatening demands are heard for the Tsar's abdication in his son's favor, with Michael as regent." If this change were made, "the entire people was resolved firmly to carry the war to a victorious conclusion." "With terrible sorrow I report all this to you, but what can one do! Stop sending troops, for they will not act against the people . . . My heart sinks when I see what is going on."

Ruzsky was not convinced, and indeed Rodzianko's words

would hardly convince any one. If "hatred for the dynasty" had reached "an extreme," whence these "threatening demands" for substituting Alexis and Michael for Nicholas? As a matter of fact, the Tsar, the Tsaritsa, Alexis, and Michael were all one to the insurgents. "The horse-radish is no sweeter than the radish," said the soldiers.[3] The dynasty as a whole, and the monarchy, together with the war, were not objects of indifference but of hatred. Either Rodzianko did not realize that, or else felt it unwise to stun the moderately liberal general by such horrors. When asked whether the people would not be appeased by a responsible ministry, Rodzianko replied with a fresh bundle of contradictions: "I myself hang by a hair . . . Anarchy has gone so far that I was compelled last night to appoint a Provisional Government . . . The overturn may be voluntary and absolutely painless for everyone, and then all will be over in a few days; one thing I can say—there will be no bloodshed and no needless victims. *I shall not allow that.*"

Here Rodzianko is an actual dictator, a super-dictator, supposedly "appointing" a Provisional Government (as a matter of fact, he was only a candidate for premier, and as such rejected by the Left, and even by the Cadets), and a man "hanging by a hair." However, even in this "hanging" position he still believes or pretends to believe he can "allow" and "not allow" something.

The military authorities at headquarters and at the various fronts do not know what to do. Headquarters no longer dares hinder the spreading of the news about what has been happening in Petrograd. General Danilov informs General Lukomsky: "Both you and General Alexeyev are well acquainted with the Emperor's character and the difficulty of securing a definite decision; all last evening, till late at night, was spent in persuading him to accept a responsible ministry. His assent was granted only at 2 A.M." Now all this work has been wasted, and he must be brought to a greater decision.

General Alexeyev asks the army commanders for their

opinions. He points out that "the army's existence and the operation of the railroads are in the hands of the Petrograd Provisional Government," that it is better to avoid "the temptation to take part" in this overturn, since that would lead only to the breakdown of the army. "Even at the price of costly concessions" the "independence of Russia and the fate of the dynasty must be saved." The first to respond is Grand Duke Nicholas Nikolayevich. "On bended knee" he appeals to the Tsar by his "sacred love for Russia and the heir." "There is no other way out; crossing yourself with the sign of the cross, transfer your heritage to him." General Brusilov also begs him to avoid "infinite catastrophic consequences," and "to save the dynasty in the person of its lawful heir." General Evert reports that "the army, in its present composition, cannot be relied upon in suppressing internal disorders," that "there are no means for stopping the revolution in the capitals," and that there is nothing to do but accept the proposal of the president of the Duma.

Nicholas II was unable to withstand this cross fire. When he could not break through to his trusted adviser, his wife, and especially when he learned that his son and heir was hostage for the dynasty in the hands of the insurgents, he fell into his characteristic "manikin" state, and with a face of stone prepared his reply to Rodzianko. There was no sacrifice which he would not make for Russia, and therefore he was "willing to abdicate in favor of my son on condition that he remain with me until his majority, with my brother, Michael Alexandrovich, as regent."

In this state Nicholas was found by the Duma envoys, Guchkov and Shulgin. When Guchkov began to explain the necessity of abdication, General Ruzsky whispered, "That matter is decided. Yesterday was the hard day. There was a storm."

Guchkov was astounded at the ease with which Nicholas consented to abdicate. "The scene made a painful impression on him through its commonplaceness, and it occurred to him that he was dealing with an abnormal man, of low consciousness and sensibility." The courtiers murmured that the Tsar had abandoned his throne "as if transferring a squad of soldiers." Shulgin suddenly felt that "this was a mask, not the Emperor's real face, and that his true face had perhaps been glimpsed by very few people, perhaps some had never seen it." The interview was brief. "Quietly, simply and exactly," with "a slightly foreign accent, like that of a Guards officer," Nicholas settled the entire problem.

"I have resolved to abdicate the throne. Until three this afternoon I thought I might abdicate in favor of my son, Alexis. But then I changed my decision in favor of my brother, Michael . . . I hope you will understand a father's feelings . . ."

In the labyrinth of events in which Nicholas wandered so helplessly, an "Ariadne's thread" was probably thrown to him from Tsarskoye Selo. He received three letters from the Empress, dated March 1, 2, and 3. She kept up hope to the last. The essence of the situation seemed clear to her: "Two tendencies, the Duma and the revolutionaries, two serpents, which, I hope, will gnaw off one another's head—that would save the situation." He must be patient and wait. The Empress feared lest in her absence Nicholas be compelled to grant something like a "responsible ministry or constitution." "It is a nightmare to think that, not having the army back of you, you may be compelled to do that." With hypnotic persistence the Tsaritsa continually urges on her husband: "If you are compelled to make concessions, in no case will you be obliged to carry them out, since they are secured by unworthy means." "Such a promise will have no force when power is in your hands again." "If we have to submit to circumstances, God will help us free ourselves from them."

It is difficult to judge how far the last Russian Emperor thought and felt in unison with his political Egeria. In any case she felt no doubt, and regarded his abdication in Michael's favor as a maneuver.

I fully understand your action, my hero! I know that you could not sign anything contrary to your coronation oath. We understand one another to perfection, we do not need words, and, I vow by my life, we shall see you again on your throne, elevated again by your people and your troops to the glory of your realm. You have saved your son, and the country, and your sacred purity and (Judas of a Ruzsky) you will be crowned by God himself on this earth, in your own country.

This indefatigable woman wished, immediately after his abdication, to get her husband to plan his restoration. "I have a feeling that the army will revolt . . . Have you any plans now?" she asks him in feverish impatience.[4]

Meanwhile for Guchkov and Shulgin every minute was dear. They must not come too late. They must bring a new Tsar to Petrograd, to the people. Alexis or Michael, that was a detail. General Danilov called their attention to the fact that abdication in favor of the brother, and disregarding the lawful heir, a minor son, were not provided for by the law of succession. But the delegates reasoned: "Suppose there is some error. Perhaps time can be gained. Michael will rule for a while, and later, when everything has quieted down, it may be discovered that he has no right to reign, and the throne will pass to Alexis Nikolayevich."[5]

In other words, the heir, his father, and his mother were for the time being "out of play." In their place Grand Duke Michael was to face the music. In case of failure he would pay with his head; in case of success, the fruits would revert to another. The crown which Guchkov and Shulgin were bringing Michael was truly a "gift of the Greeks."

In their haste the delegates did not notice the scandalous character of the "historical event" which had just taken place: the Russian throne had been recognized as the *personal property* of each Tsar, with the right to grant it to whomever he wished.

They were anxious, as soon as possible, to confront the revolutionaries "with an accomplished fact." They were afraid they might arrive too late and find a different accomplished fact, the Russian Republic, proclaimed by some "scoundrels."

The delegates returned with a manifesto for Nicholas' abdication in Michael's favor. At the front the preceding manifesto was still being proclaimed, granting a responsible ministry. The telegraph was already spreading the news of "Tsar Alexis." The imperial train moved in a direction opposite to that of the delegates, toward Mohilev, to headquarters. And then—

No one will ever know what feelings were struggling in the soul of Nicholas II, the father, the monarch, and the man, when, in Mohilev, looking at Alexeyev with tired, kindly eyes, he said in a somewhat undecided manner:

"I have changed my mind. Will you kindly send this telegram to Petrograd."

On a sheet of paper, in his clear hand the Emperor had written his consent to Alexis' taking the throne.

Alexeyev did not show any one this telegram "in order not to confuse people's minds." He kept it in his wallet and handed it to me [General Denikin] at the end of May, when he gave up the supreme command.[6]

Guchkov and Shulgin, with no inkling of the Tsar's new change of heart, were racing toward Petrograd. Guchkov, burning to delight the people with their new Tsar, went to a huge workers' meeting in the railway shops. The effect was tremendous: it was immediately moved to arrest the self-appointed negotiator. Only great efforts secured his liberation.

Meanwhile, in their absence, in the Catherine Hall of the Tauride Palace, Miliukov, speaking on the formation of the Provisional Government, tried to carry out the same maneuver. "The old despot, who led Russia to complete ruin, will voluntarily renounce the throne or else be overthrown. Power will pass to a regent, Grand Duke Michael. Alexis will be the heir." Shouts and tumult broke loose. "What, the old dynasty?" Miliukov hastened to correct the bad impression.

Though he himself had no love for that dynasty, he pictured Russia as a parliamentary and constitutional monarchy. Others might favor a republic, but the dispute would finally be settled by the Constituent Assembly, to which both sides would submit in order to avoid civil war. But even the rumor of a provisional restoration of the old dynasty was like the explosion of a bomb. In vain Miliukov tried to explain to the representatives of soviet democracy that the Romanovs were not dangerous, and that, of his candidates for the throne, "one was a sick boy, the other a thoroughly stupid man."[7] "Late that evening the Tauride Palace was entered by a large crowd of extremely excited officers, who declared that they could not return to their troops unless Miliukov retracted his words." The Provisional Committee of Duma members did not require other persuasion. In violation of the truth Miliukov had to declare that "his words about the provisional regency of Grand Duke Michael and Alexis' succession represented merely his personal opinion."[8]

The attempt to save the dynasty was nearing a complete fiasco. The majority of the Progressive Bloc felt that the only thing left was to beat an orderly retreat. On the following day, March 3, the members of the Provisional Committee and of the newly formed Provisional Government assembled at the home of the involuntary claimant to the throne. They had agreed to leave the decision to him, not to argue with each other and not to press him. The Grand Duke was not particularly enchanted by his brother's imperially generous gift. A turbulent exchange of opinions took place after all. Although Miliukov agreed that the Tsar's abdication, not only for himself, but for his son, made the situation very shaky even in a legal sense, he besought Michael to accept the crown. They needed a symbol of power, to which the masses were accustomed; without it the Provisional Government would be "a leaky scow." The attempt, of course, was not without risk for the personal safety of the Grand Duke and all those present, but that had to be accepted. "In addition, outside Petrograd it is fully possible to collect the military force necessary to defend the Grand Duke."[9] The rôles were reversed: the extreme Left member of the Progressive Bloc was now more to the Right than his colleagues, and his attitude fully justified the mistrust of the representatives of the Soviet in refusing trains to the Duma delegates. To save the dynasty he was willing to begin a civil war. Shulgin writes with enthusiasm:

Gray with insomnia, absolutely hoarse from speech-making in barracks and at meetings, he did not speak, he croaked hoarsely, he croaked wise and weighty words . . . the greatest words of his life: "If you refuse, Your Highness, . . . that means ruin. Because Russia will lose its axis. The monarch is the axis . . . the country's only axis. The mass, the Russian mass . . . around what will it assemble? There will be anarchy . . . chaos . . . a bloody mess . . . The monarch is the only, so far the only . . . general concept of power in Russia. If you refuse . . . there will be no oath. But the oath is the only answer which the people can give . . . to us all . . . that which has happened . . . is its sanction, its approval, its consent . . . without which there will be no Russia, no state! There will be nothing."[10]

Only Guchkov backed Miliukov.

For us it was absolutely plain [Rodzianko wrote] that the Grand Duke would not have reigned more than a few hours. Tremendous bloodshed would immediately have taken place within the walls of the capital, and would have marked the beginning of civil war. It was clear to us that the Grand Duke would have been murdered immediately, with all his supporters, for he had no faithful troops at his disposal and therefore could not rely on armed force.

After a general exchange of opinions, the Grand Duke called Rodzianko into another room. "The Grand Duke Michael asked if I could guarantee his life, if he accepted the throne, and I had to reply in the negative, for, I repeat, I had no trustworthy force. Even to get him out of Petrograd secretly appeared impossible: not a single automobile would have been allowed to leave the city, nor a single train."[11]

The Grand Duke withdrew to reflect. Then he returned and began to speak. "Under these conditions I cannot accept the throne because . . ." Without finishing, he burst into tears. Miliukov and Guchkov declared that, after what had happened, they were willing to back the Provisional Government, but refused to remain members of it. The "conspirator" and the "palace revolutionary," Tereshchenko, threatened to shoot himself. Kerensky alone heaved a deep sigh of relief: he had scarcely been able to find soldiers to guard the Grand Duke's house, and every minute dreaded the irruption of some revolutionary military unit. It was over. Michael issued a public manifesto, declaring that "he would accept the power of state" only if it were offered him by the future Constituent Assembly.

And the "revolutionaries against their will" of the Duma parted, finally recognizing the Constituent Assembly as their platform. And yet, as Shulgin said to himself:

> If any one had told me two days before that I would listen to this demand [for the Constituent Assembly], and not object, but even acknowledge that there was no other way out; if he had told me that this very hand would write the abdication of Nicholas II, two days ago I would have called him a madman, and would have thought myself insane. But today I can make no objection. Yes, the Constituent Assembly, on the basis of universal, direct, equal, and secret franchise.

Once again they had to come to an agreement with headquarters. There people had not even heard of a Constituent Assembly. They had begun proclaiming the most gracious manifesto on the responsible ministry. That was followed by a still more gracious manifesto, that of abdication. Tsar Alexis was supposed to have been proclaimed, and finally, on the way from Pskov to Petrograd Shulgin had proclaimed Michael II wherever possible. Now it had to be done over.

Rodzianko again is at one end of the direct line and General Ruzsky at the other. Rodzianko asks Ruzsky not to publish the manifesto transferring imperial power to Michael. "People would have been reconciled to his regency and to the enthronement of the Tsarevich, but his enthronement as Emperor is absolutely inacceptable." "By the greatest labor we have succeeded in keeping the revolutionary movement within bounds of decency, but the situation is not yet normal and civil war is possible." Ruzsky is gloomily ironical. "It is a great pity that the delegates yesterday did not know themselves what they wanted." "The delegates cannot be blamed," answers Rodzianko, and he begins to excuse himself and them by mingling truth with fancy.

> Unexpectedly, there broke out a soldiers' revolt the like of which I have never seen. Not the soldiers of course, but muzhiks from the plow, proclaimed all their muzhik demands. All we could hear in the crowd was "Land and Liberty!" "Down with the dynasty!" "Down with the Romanovs!" "Down with the officers!" and in many detachments they began to beat their officers. They were joined by the workers, and anarchy reached its apogee.

Actually there had been absolutely no change for the worse, but now Rodzianko and the others had begun to grasp the essence of the movement—the "apogee" had been reached by their own fears. Rodzianko outdoes himself. First he frightens his interlocutor: "Proclaiming Michael Emperor would be pouring oil on the fire, and a merciless extermination would begin"; "we would lose all authority, and there would be no one to subdue the popular disturbance." Again he allures him with sweet hope: "The troops, little by little, during the night, are being brought to order . . . the Supreme Council [a nonexistent institution] will act till about the close of the war . . . with the Provisional Government." But the "restoration of the dynasty is not impossible," for "a decisive victory will be certain," with "a wave of patriotic feeling."

Still General Ruzsky wishes to know more exactly how

things stand with the government, and what to do with the Tsar's ukaze appointing Nicholas Nikolayevich commander in chief. Rodzianko says that "there is no objection to publishing this ukaze," that is, to intrusting the army to one of the most influential members of the old dynasty. Indeed, no one could object, for the very existence of this ukaze had been concealed from mutinous Petrograd. As for the formation of a government, he again mentions "the Supreme Council, the responsible ministry, the work of the legislative chambers till the decision of the Constituent Assembly concerning a constitution." Upon Ruzsky's questioning him as to the head of the Supreme Council, Rodzianko corrects himself; he was speaking, really, of the Provisional Committee of the Duma, of which he himself was president.

Thus, after the failure of their attempt to revive the dynasty directly, the leaders of the Duma were still dreaming of keeping the "Provisional Committee" of their private conference as a kind of Supreme Council, the source of all power. They were dreaming of restoring the Tsarist Duma, which had humbly submitted to the ukaze of dissolution, and even the Tsarist State Council, making the Provisional Government of the revolution responsible to all these wrecks of the past.

What did headquarters decide after this exchange of opinions? General Ruzsky proposed two measures: (1) "that from then on only headquarters, not the government, should give the army commanders instructions," and (2) that "to restore calm the commanders must remain at their posts" as "the only authoritative power on the spot to which everyone appealed for assistance." In other words, the front was to be transformed into an independent republic of commanders, while waiting "for the Grand Duke to take over the supreme command."

Even this most intelligent of Tsarist generals imagined in all seriousness that in an era of revolution the army and the country at large could live each its own life. As if modern warfare had not destroyed the self-sufficing army of the barracks, replacing it by "the people in arms," linking the front and rear by thousands of intimate and unbreakable ties. As if the army's spirit could be different from that of the country in a period of great revolution, which is inevitably a tremendous moral revolution!

General Alexeyev immediately concluded from Rodzianko's conversations, and so informed the commanders, that "in the Imperial Duma and its Provisional Committee there is no unanimity: the parties of the Left, strengthened by the Soviet of Workers' Deputies, have acquired great influence" and are putting "powerful pressure" on Rodzianko; "the troops of the Petrograd garrison have been thoroughly propagandized by the Workers' Deputies, and are pernicious and dangerous for everyone, including the moderate elements of the Provisional Committee." General Alexeyev's hostility to these phenomena was shared by the members of the Duma. But Alexeyev noted that "Rodzianko's communication lacked directness and sincerity." He had information of his own regarding the situation in Petrograd. "The situation in Petrograd on March 2 was much calmer," "rumors of butchery of officers by soldiers are arrant nonsense." He even suspected poor Rodzianko of wishing by false information "to incite the representatives of the army to take extreme decisions." His mind was already working toward a meeting of the army commanders, "their collective voice," and the "conditions" to be set by them in order "to influence the course of events." As General Lukomsky asserts, Alexeyev, after dispatching this telegram, said: "I shall never forgive myself for having believed in the sincerity of certain people, for having listened to them and sent the telegram to the army commanders about the Tsar's abdication."

The revolution was already menaced by conflict with the supreme command, which was even more Right in feeling than the Duma Bloc. The Bloc, in turn, followed in the steps of the revolution resisting at every step, gritting its teeth.

Outwardly the Progressive Bloc had succeeded. In the legal sense there was no revolution. The Tsar had abdicated voluntarily in Michael's favor. Michael had abdicated in favor of the Constituent Assembly. There was a Provisional Government—we shall see how and under what conditions it was created—with Prince Lvov as premier. But Guchkov and Shulgin had a ukaze of the Tsar, dated one hour before his abdication, "commanding Prince G. E. Lvov to be president of the Council of Ministers." The same trick was played in appointing Nicholas Nikolayevich commander in chief. But that was not all. Among the papers in General Ruzsky's archives is a telegram to the Tsar from General Alexeyev. "To establish complete order, to preserve the capital from anarchy," Rodzianko asks headquarters "immediately to appoint as commander of the Petrograd military district a brave and energetic general who will be popular and influential among the people." On behalf of the Duma Committee he suggests Lieutenant General Kornilov. Alexeyev considered this expedient to "tranquilize the capitals and establish order among the troops of the garrison." On the telegram Nicholas wrote: "Execute."

In a word, there was nothing left for the revolution to do, for everything had already been thought out and decided behind its back. From now on it was only in the way. Juridically speaking, there had been no revolution. It had been, so to speak, eliminated. There was but a single fear: the revolution might not realize that it had been eliminated. When Shulgin called the attention of Kerensky, Miliukov, Rodzianko, and others to the fact that Lvov had been appointed by a ukaze of the Tsar, they "explained that they knew it, but it must be carefully concealed, in order not to undermine Prince Lvov's position."[12]

The appointment of General Kornilov by the Tsar to fight the revolution and establish order was concealed no less carefully. Only the publication of General Ruzsky's archives has shed complete or almost complete light upon the final phase of events in February, 1917, and enabled us to reconstruct the attempts of the Duma "revolutionaries against their will" to nullify the entire revolution. But it was so mighty and sweeping a force that in passing it knocked down all the little card houses built by the cunning backstage intrigue of petty politicians.

In the beginning the Duma seemed to have succeeded, or almost succeeded, in its plan. The Provisional Government, formed from its members, was recognized by everyone. But here is a characteristic fact. Several Tsarist ministers, come voluntarily to place themselves under arrest, heard the composition of the Provisional Government transmitted by telephone. The first to break the silence was Krivoshein, the "old wolf" of Russian conservatism.

> Without addressing anyone in particular, he said: "This government has one serious . . . very serious defect . . . It is too far to the Right . . . Yes, to the Right. A couple of months ago it would have satisfied everyone. It would have saved the situation. Now it is too moderate. That is its weakness. Right now force is needed . . . Because of this, gentlemen, you will ruin your big child, the revolution, and our common fatherland, Russia."[13]

CHAPTER FIVE

SOVIET DEMOCRACY

IN the Revolution of 1917, as in that of 1905, censitary democracy, based on limited, property suffrage, was opposed by soviet or revolutionary democracy, whose organized ranks had in ordinary times remained underground and naturally constituted a mere skeleton. Work in secret, illegal organizations had created a special type, the "professional revolutionary," with no occupation in life but revolution. He was in his own way a magnificent type of the wandering apostle of socialism and of the knight errant protector of the oppressed and punisher of ravishers. Prison was his university, where at forced leisure he feverishly supplemented his intellectual baggage; the repressions and cruelties of the jailors were a test of endurance and firmness of spirit; escapes were episodes; conspiracy and disguise a habit; hiding from detectives a sport; propaganda and agitation an indispensable necessity. At the London congress of the Social Democratic party (338 present) a questionnaire among the participants showed that they had spent 597 years under the official supervision of the police, in prison, exile and galley labor, had been arraigned 710 times and effected 201 escapes; yet their average age was twenty-eight. An even greater record of persecution was typical of the Social Revolutionaries. At their London conference with 61 present, they totaled 121 years of exile, 104 years of prison, 88 years of galley labor, 228 police raids, 146 arrests. In the secret organizations the professional revolutionaries set the tone. The members of the scattered system of local committees, built up on a more or less strict centralization, looked to them, patterned themselves after them. The mass groups of the provinces, under the influence and leadership of rival revolutionary organizations, remained at bottom chaotically dispersed. Only in periods of great historic events did the picture change. Profiting by the government's helplessness and confusion, this mass periphery of peasants and workers organized, the workers by factories and shops, the peasants by villages and hamlets. Their casually changing representatives were chosen in factory or village, most often by acclamation, with no elaborate election process, and with varying and undefined norms of representation. The duties of the persons elected were just as undefined—they were to consult with persons similarly elected in other factories and districts, to lead to success the cause of the "people," or of the "working class," or, even more narrowly, of the "proletariat." Hence the name of Soviets of Workers' (later, Soldiers', Peasants', Cossacks', etc.) Deputies.

Censitary democracy had lost its Imperial Duma in the heat of revolution, but rallied around the "Provisional Committee," a private conference of its members. It at once experienced strong pressure from the revolutionary mob, from the street. Let us see how this "mob" was composed and how its own spontaneous revolutionary organization took form.

The first factor to be noted is the universally recognized *spontaneity* of the street movement. In Petrograd there were, of course, secret "committees" of all the principal illegal socialist groups. There were no big men in them. Under the blows of government repression they had a constantly shifting membership, and frequently could continue to exist only by enrolling inexperienced youth, which had scarcely grown in strength and experience when it in turn was torn from their ranks, to be replaced with difficulty. Neither these committees, nor the "Workers' Group," nonpartisan in name, but socialist in tint, and connected with the Central War Industries Committee, had sufficient influence to summon the mass of workers to the street. The Bolsheviks tried to promote the slogan of a general strike on the anniversary of the condemnation of their Duma deputies to exile for defeatist agitation. It was a complete fiasco. Not much greater success fell to the Workers' Group with its slogan for a demonstration by the people at the opening of the Imperial Duma.

The Social Revolutionaries did not even attempt such enterprises. Demonstrations by workers alone in wartime seemed to them foredoomed to defeat. The report of the director of the Petrograd Gendarme Department for October, 1916, contained extracts from a report prepared by them for the proposed Moscow conferences of the Workers' Groups of the War Industries Committees:

> The war is daily adding tens of thousands to the opponents of war and militarism. . . . The discord of party programs, lack of proper organization among the several classes of the population, impossibility of carrying on propaganda, etc., compel the Social Revolutionaries to view things differently from the Social Democrats and other Left-wing parties: *in Russia a revolution on the 1905 model is impossible at present, but a combined revolution by the military and working-class masses* is more than possible.
>
> The success of the propaganda of the Social Revolutionaries in the army, concerning which new data are arriving daily, leads us to expect that the revolution will be begun by those soldiers formed from yesterday's workers and by those workers who are subjected to the galley-like rule of the militaristic police state, and driven to work by bullets and bayonets.

The director of the Gendarme Department pessimistically agreed that

> certain facts, such as success in spreading pacifism among the soldiers and the militarized workers, growth of general discontent with the high cost of living and lack of food . . . are true, and the Social Revolutionary agitators correctly realize that the present moment is most favorable for harrowing the soil to receive revolutionary ideas and Utopias.[1]

The ideas of the Social Revolutionaries did not go beyond mere propaganda, or preparatory activity. Immediate transition to insurrection in concrete forms did not yet interest them; "sufficient unto the day is the evil thereof."

Neither the Bolsheviks, nor the Mensheviks, nor the Workers' Group, nor the Social Revolutionaries, either separately or collectively, led the workers of Petrograd on to the street. It was someone mightier than they: Tsar Hunger.

It began with ordinary food riots. The bakeshops lacked sufficient bread. Long queues, at first chiefly of women and boys, took out their resentment on the bakers, suspecting them of hoarding flour for purposes of speculation. The police restored order. They were greeted with hostile shouts. The people demanded "Bread!" Then naturally they began to shout, "Down with the police!" But as soon as the thousand-voiced echo caught this up, there appeared the old slogans, "Down with the autocracy!" and "Down with the war!" "There were disorders, there was still no revolution."[2] There was no leader, but every revolutionary and democratic group, organized or unorganized, rushed headlong into the movement, trying to attract as many people as possible and to inspire it with definite and militant political slogans. On February 23, and especially on the 24, all Petrograd witnessed countless demonstrations and street meetings. During these days, several attempts were made to create interparty centers to make up for the weakness of the several illegal party organizations. Personal conferences were held by leaders of the trade-union movement, of the coöperative, cultural, and educational organizations with deputies of the extreme Left of the Duma and prominent representatives of the revolutionary parties.

At these conferences an old Social Democrat, Cherevanin, first suggested that the Soviet of Workers' Deputies must be organized at once. The idea was already in the air. On the 24 there had been reports of elections to the Soviet in some factories. As soon as the idea of reëstablishing the Soviet was presented and welcomed by the leading groups of the intelligentsia, regardless of party, the movement at once became universal. However, deputies chosen at individual factories still had no common rallying point and did not even know where to assemble. Indeed, there had been no time to deal with that question. Street agitation, meetings, attempts to arrange fraternizing with the troops drew people into a whirlpool of activity and left no time for anything else. It was only on February 27, when certain military units began to pass to the side of the people, as predicted by the Social Revolutionary memorandum, that a crucial event occurred. The recently arrested members of the Workers' Group and many other political prisoners had been freed from prison by the people. Headed by a worker, Kuzma Gvozdev, they appeared at the Tauride Palace. With the socialist deputies in the Duma and other influential members of the labor movement, they formed a provisional Executive Committee of the Soviet of Workers' Deputies, a kind of organizing bureau, which at once informed the wards that on that same evening all the deputies were to assemble for the first meeting of the Petrograd Soviet.

Soviet democracy had set up its organization.

In the question of the rôle of the Soviets in the February Revolution we at once stumble upon two opposite legends.

One, accepted with especial willingness in conservative and bourgeois circles, says that the Petrograd (and later the all-Russian) Soviet was created, for the special purpose of undermining the Provisional Government, by revolutionaries who were afraid to attack it openly and who therefore tried to create their own parallel, backstage government, and by its action to bind the Provisional Government hand and foot and thus set up the system of disintegrating diarchy.

The other legend, less popular, was expressed by the President of the Imperial Duma, Rodzianko. According to his profound conviction, the "Executive Committee of the Soviet of Workers' Deputies had existed without a break, though secretly, since 1905 and had never ceased its agitation."

Both versions are equally remote from the truth. The Petrograd Soviet was certainly not created as a second center of authority to work against the Provisional Government. It arose prior to the Provisional Government, and its elections began previous to the Tsar's ukaze for the dissolution of the Duma, and hence still earlier than the creation of the Duma's own Provisional Committee. Neither was the Soviet a permanent, organic part of the revolutionary world. Both in 1905 and in 1917 it was an organization *ad hoc*, the specific type of organization of a *united socialist and revolutionary front* in a militant period, in the fire and storm of advancing revolution. Unlike all other militant organizations of the working class, it was built not from above but below, by election at factory and shop meetings, and hence in some features was like a "preliminary parliament" of the working class.

As in 1905, the duties of the Soviets were not clearly defined. They were simply rallying points of revolutionary energy. For the Russian workers of 1905 and the spring of 1917 the Soviets were, in a sense, what the revolutionary clubs, particularly the Jacobin Club, had been for the bourgeoisie in the French Revolution. The clubs were improvised organizations due to the absence of stable, well-established, and distinct *parties*. In Russia, true enough, there was no lack of parties. Rather, they were overabundant. But they included only the small world of professional revolutionaries and the "cream" of the working class. For the toilers as a whole they scarcely seemed to exist, or belonged to the sphere of legend. Nor did Russia possess those broad trade-union organizations without which the working class is only "human dust." Hence the Soviets arose as a temporary substitute for the trade-union and political organizations of the working class.

Like the revolutionary clubs of 1789 the Russian Soviets fulfilled a double function: during great events they served as rallying points for the direct initiative of the masses, throwing into the scale their enthusiasm, their blood and lives. In periods of relative stability they were organs of popular control. This right they won by their energy and their ability to gain the support of the masses and to set them in motion.

What passes abroad for the Soviet idea—turning an extensive, logically developed system of Soviets, from the smallest, local bodies to the central ones, into the *formal basis* of the state, transforming them into the unified and sole constitutional mechanism for the normal administration of the country—this idea was absent at the birth of the Soviets. In the history of the Russian Soviets it was an alien idea, introduced from without, the product of foreign importation. It was merely a later refurbishing in Russian style of the main idea of South European anarcho-syndicalism, at best, an unconscious parody of it. It is one thing to construct a working-class state on a firm basis, on labor unions forged by many years of mass struggle and practical activity; it is quite another to build it on improvized half clubs, half parliaments, without experience, without a definite constitution or regular system of elections. Trade-unions have their history, their rich experience and traditions, their life and ethics. The Soviets, like the revolutionary clubs, lacked all that. They had scarcely any "yesterday," only a "today." They were marked by responsiveness and impressionability, and also by instability, diffuseness and chaos. A well-developed trade-union movement can only be *served;* the Soviets were easy to *manage*. Trade-unions are both militant and business organs. The Soviets were exclusively militant, suited in spirit and organization to the exceptional conditions of a revolutionary period when life has torn loose from all bonds. As business organs they were always a negligible quantity. Indeed, they did not lay claim to that rôle. Their only task was to spread the "sacred spirit of revolution" throughout Russia, to remove all obstacles, to crush and destroy in embryo all attempts to rebel against the revolution from the Right, and finally to see to it that the Provisional Government which had issued from the revolution served the revolution in program and personnel. That was all. The Soviets never had a very definite constitution; elections to them were always rather chaotic and unorganized. If there was anything which the Soviet least resembled it was a regular government institution.

All this, in a transitional period, by no means prevented the Soviet from being the only active law-creating force. Let us not forget that the Provisional Committee of a private conference of members of the Imperial Duma in these very days defined its mission as that of *negotiator* between the people and the old government, and was trying, through agreement with the latter and by broad concessions exacted from it, to save what it could of the old order. Let us not forget that censitary democracy plunged into negotiation with the high command, with the Tsar, finally, with his "testamentary heir." It tried all possible combinations, but was forced to recognize that they had failed. Finally it was faced with the dilemma of either taking power "by the grace of the revolution," or standing by while others took it. Soviet democracy was poorly informed of these backstage agreements; much was concealed from it; much it quietly ignored since it did not attach importance to politicians' intrigues.

What *was* Soviet democracy doing? It was not seizing power, nor declaring itself the government. It was acting as an immediate, revolutionary, law-creating force. It was involuntarily performing certain functions of government, as a person might "talk prose." The Provisional Executive Committee of the Soviet of Workers' Deputies, which was simply a self-created organizing bureau, was already functioning as a government in a great many matters, simply because there was no one else to decide them. First, it organized a provisional military staff from a large number of Leftist officers, among whom the Social Revolutionaries Filipovsky and Mstislavsky (Maslovsky) stood out. It organized a provisional food commission, in which an important part fell to the Social Democrats, Grohman, Frankorussky, and others. The military staff attempted to introduce some order and leadership into the torrential movement of the soldiers, sailors, and armed workers, who were filled with great enthusiasm, but were uncoördinated because of the complete lack of organization. It fitted out flying squads of armed men, led, for lack of officers, by casual persons of initiative, sometimes better educated soldiers, sometimes students and other civilians. It sent them to make reconnaissances throughout the city, to seize certain strategic points, railway stations, police stations, secret police headquarters, telegraph, telephone, various barracks, to arrest ministers and other agents of the old government, and clear garrets of police who had barricaded themselves with machine guns, disarm patrolmen, etc. The food commission undertook, not without success, the experiment of fixing prices for certain over-dear articles like butter. It at once took measures to secure a supply of provisions for the military forces which had joined the revolution. Many groups of soldiers which appeared at the Tauride Palace and placed themselves at the command of the revolution had broken away from hesitant or neutral regiments and feared to return to their barracks. Or on returning they found the commanders gone and the supply of provisions cut off. A hungry sea of soldiers without officers and provisions meant danger of looting and anarchy. At the first session of the Soviet one other measure was taken: Petrograd was divided into wards and special revolutionary Soviet commissars were dispatched to them to supervise the election of "ward committees" as the local organs of popular government, and to form an armed working-class militia, made up of one hundred men per thousand of factory personnel. Finally, the Soviet reorganized radically. Having begun as the Soviet of Workers' Deputies, it immediately became such a powerful center of attraction for the military units that it could not hold to its previous form. At the first session the Soviet welcomed a kaleidoscope of delegations from all sorts of military units. They proclaimed their complete solidarity with the working class as represented in the Soviet. Side by side with it they swore to carry through the revolution and to gain every conquest possible for the toiling people. When the revolution and its leader, the Soviet, were joined by the entire Semenov Regiment, whose name had been inscribed in Russia's history for having put down the Moscow insurrection of 1905, universal enthusiasm and faith reached their apogee. It was now determined to transform the Soviet of Workers' Deputies into the Soviet of Workers' and Soldiers' Deputies, by proclaiming the right of each battalion to send one delegate.

Within a few days the Soviet was turned into a gigantic workers' and soldiers' preliminary parliament. Its membership soon reached 2,000, and, by the middle of March, 3,000. Each decision was instantaneously reported to barracks and working-class quarters by a thousand channels. This was a force with which no one could contend.

Small wonder if Rodzianko could not secure a train to go to the Tsar without the Soviet's permission, and Guchkov and Miliukov ran a great risk in attempting to proclaim Michael Tsar against its will, while Michael himself, had he tried to exercise the right delegated to him by Nicholas II, would have been staking his life in rebellious Petrograd, and could scarcely have found means to escape to a less dangerous spot.

Nor was that all. Only the Soviet could stop the general strike, and reopen the factories. It alone could restore streetcar traffic. Controlling the entire printers' union, it alone could permit the appearance of newspapers, of all or some. The Provisional Government had to appeal to the leaders of the Soviet as soon as it was organized and wished to publish its first declaration. When the military units of Petrograd became a component part of organized Soviet democracy, the Soviet was transformed into the only real source of power. At its first session the Soviet resolved that measures be taken immediately to remove all public financial resources from the control of the old government. By virtue of this *Soviet* decision revolutionary sentries occupied and guarded the State Bank, Central and Provincial Treasuries, Mint, Engraving Office, etc.

Here special emphasis must be placed on a very characteristic detail: the declaration of the Soviet read that it "intrusts the Provisional Committee of the Imperial Duma with the immediate execution of the present decree." At that time no one thought of asking: is the Provisional Committee a subordinate organ of the Soviet, to receive instructions from it? The Soviet, as the direct emanation of the masses of soldiers and workers who had made the revolution, was at that time the chief center. To it came owners of printing houses, requesting permission to resume work, in view of the "tranquilization" which had set in. On March 3, a conference of representatives of the Petrograd banks requested the Soviet "to permit the banks to be opened immediately." The former favorite of Nicholas II, the famous ballerina Kseshinskaya, appealed to the Soviet, petitioning it to grant her quarters in her own palace, requisitioned during the revolutionary interregnum and occupied chiefly by Bolshevist organizations. Grand Duke Michael requested the Soviet to grant him a special train from Gatchina to Petrograd. He was told that "because of the high cost of coal citizen Romanov may buy a ticket and travel in an ordinary train on equal terms with other citizens." From morning to night the Soviet was besieged by "a mob of outsiders, of people with business to settle, of soldiers' and workers' deputies, officers, all kinds of businessmen, students, muzhiks with knapsacks and papers in their hands, officials, weeping women."[3] The Executive Committee of the Soviet was appealed to in all kinds of matters, including divorces and legal disputes; it took considerable labor to explain to many naïve visitors that the Soviet's competence was not universal.

A student of the social and economic side of the revolution,

THE FIRST CONGRESS OF THE SOVIETS

Courtesy of the Muzei Revolutsii, U.S.S.R.

Professor G. Shvittau, came to the conclusion that the "Soviet régime" was "completely present in the very first period of the February Revolution," for the Soviet acted earlier and was the real government to a much greater degree than the Provisional Committee of the Duma and the Provisional Government. "It is difficult to speak of diarchy in this period," he asserts; "rather there already existed a single 'Soviet government,' which had not yet formed its ideology and temporarily hid behind a more or less legalized organ of bourgeois-revolutionary government, the Provisional Government."[4] Sukhanov says that "the Soviet apparatus of administration began involuntarily, automatically, against the Soviet's own will, to displace the official governmental machine, which had less and less to do. At that time nothing could be done about this; we had to reconcile ourselves, and take over various functions of administration, while creating and maintaining the fiction that the government was being run from the Marinsky Palace."[5]

CHAPTER SIX

THE POSITION OF THE SOCIALIST PARTIES

WHY, under such conditions, did not Soviet democracy take power into its own hands? Why did it not set up a Provisional Government of its own? The answer to this question, like its meaning, may be twofold. First, how did the leaders of Soviet democracy rationalize their own position? Second, what objective causes suggested this conduct?

Within Soviet democracy there was no unanimity of view. When the first gleams of the still distant revolution flashed across Russia, toward the end of the 1890's, two great political parties took form and divided revolutionary democracy of that day. They were the Social Democrats and the Social Revolutionaries.

Through the fog of the future, each party in its own way tried to make out the mysterious outlines of the approaching revolution, to unriddle its underlying character, historic significance and extent. Each party tried to picture its own historic mission in the concluding phase of the movement in order to advance firmly toward it from the start.

In the beginning Social Democracy, before it divided into Bolsheviks and Mensheviks, derived from prewar orthodox Marxism. It considered that Russia's historical evolution would, by and large, follow the well-beaten track of the Western European countries. This was the path of capitalist development. It would be longer for Russia, a poor agrarian country, whose industrialization was impeded by the presence of powerful international competitors; yet Russia had to be not only industrialized, but transformed from a poor capitalist country into a wealthy one. The mission of Russia's approaching revolution, like the first revolutions of other European states, was merely to clear the way for her capitalist evolution, to free her of all pre-capitalist survivals, of servile, forced labor, of the political absolutism which fettered the initiative and activity of her population. With the fall of autocracy the rule of the bourgeoisie would begin; hence the leading rôle in eliminating absolutism must fall to the bourgeoisie. The proletariat, as the historic heir to the bourgeoisie, must arm itself with patience and first aid the bourgeoisie, the historic heir of absolutism, to claim its inheritance. Thus, the rôle of the proletariat was (1) to support the liberal bourgeoisie against absolutism, (2) to urge it forward in eliminating autocracy completely, instead of patching up some shoddy compromise, (3) in return for its support to gain from the bourgeois revolution full liberty for its own further organization, both political and trade-union, full right to participate in deciding matters of state and in creating legislation which would give the proletariat more and more influence in the factory.

Such was the original, classical view of Social Democracy regarding the coming revolution and the rôle of the proletariat.

The first hidden rock on which it struck in Russia was the agrarian question.

By analogy with industry, the Social Democrats expected the same process of development in agrarian capitalism, but through an even slower and more painful process. They expected the landed gentry to be transformed into modern large-scale landowners, creators of rationalized "grain factories." They expected to see the village broken up, the minority of the peasants transformed into petty capitalists, while the majority would become landless proletarians, the village branch of the industrial working class. But as events progressed, the outlines of the coming agrarian revolution became clearer. The entire toiling peasantry would toss to one side the possession of property by non-toilers, while the embryonic agricultural proletariat strove to become peasants again by partitioning the property of the non-toilers.

The second hidden rock was the political conduct of the bourgeoisie. The farther east in Europe, the more cowardly and fawning the middle class became toward the autocracy, the more suspicious and afraid of the labor movement.

The split between Bolsheviks and Mensheviks was due to the resolute attempt of the former to adjust themselves to these two peculiarities of Russian reality, not foreseen by Marxist doctrine. In its prewar development Bolshevism retained the classical Social Democratic dogma that the Russian Revolution would be directed against absolutism, bureaucracy, nobility, and serfdom, but not against the bourgeoisie. "Revolution in Russia," wrote Lenin in 1907, in a preface to one of Kautsky's pamphlets, "is not socialist, for it can certainly not lead the proletariat to *sole rule* or dictatorship." In other words, it would be only a bourgeois-democratic revolution. But the Russian bourgeoisie was antidemocratic, greedy for compromise with Tsarism because of its own hatred for the labor movement. Therefore, the bourgeois revolution had to be carried out against the bourgeoisie. The working class must carry out that revolution for it. The unreliability of the bourgeoisie as an ally it must remedy by alliance with the peasantry. "The bourgeois revolution, achieved by the proletariat and peasantry despite the instability of the bourgeoisie—that is a main thesis of Bolshevist tactics," Lenin proclaimed at that time. In case of extremity, an allied dictatorship of the proletariat and peasantry was possible, but its mission would be merely to squeeze from the bourgeois-democratic revolution all its revolutionary consequences, and, in no case, to advance to the socialist revolution.

The Mensheviks refused to follow Lenin on this path; they regarded it as a political adventure. From their point of view, a socialist party could suffer no worse misfortune than to achieve power at a time when the country was not prepared for socialism. To be content with bourgeois and liberal reforms while exercising the plenitude of power meant falling into striking contradiction with one's own socialism; no matter how that contradiction might be explained historically, such justification would not be understood by the simple-minded, straightforward masses, uninitiated into scientific doctrine. One would either disappoint the masses and be left isolated, having pleased no one and embittered everyone; or, under pressure of the masses one would go farther than was admissible from a sober analysis of historic possibilities and undertake a fantastic socialist experiment preordained to failure. That meant political bankruptcy and condemning one's own program to failure.

The Bolsheviks were perfectly aware of the force of this argument, which they themselves had often repeated during the unity of "classical" Marxism. A way out of the contradiction was first found during the World War. The spectacle of highly developed German War Socialism, fortified with universal military service, with food, coal, and other dictatorships, with control over industry, including compulsory syndicalization with price-fixing and food-rationing, struck their imagination. If a similar economic system were placed in the hands, not of a bourgeois-military state, as in Germany, but of a "dictatorship of the proletariat and peasantry," and, instead of serving military needs, were turned to the service of peaceful development, it seemed to them the desired socialist Elysium would be attained.

The classical Marxist, Social Democratic theory of revolution was opposed from the very beginning by the Social Revolutionaries.

The Social Revolutionaries maintained that a bourgeois revolution, which would affect the form of government only, without touching social structure and property relationships, and open the way to capitalist hegemony in every field of economic life, was impossible in Russia. There was no bourgeoisie fit for leadership in a revolution of that type, since the Russian bourgeoisie was, by all its antecedents, certain to be an integral part of the alliance of reactionary forces led by the Tsarist government. On the other hand, the Russian Revolution in its agrarian phase was bound, they believed, to deal a radical blow to the institution of private property. The Social Revolutionaries realized that Russia's toiling masses lacked the maturity, and the training in economic self-government, in coöperative association, and in management of autonomous labor organizations requisite to the establishment of a socialist society. Yet, instead of drawing a metaphysical line of demarcation between capitalism and socialism, they visualized a long transition period of "laborism." The alliance of the proletariat with the peasantry could bring about this "populist-labor" revolution, with its thoroughgoing political democracy, gradually filling its forms with a deeper social content. The new order would not be socialism, but the building of a new social-labor legislation within the framework of a money economy. It would represent the gradual development of collective forms of economic activity or of control over economy at the expense of purely individual economy. It would mean the elimination of private agriculture based on Roman law, and its replacement by a régime of equal but individual right to the labor use of the land, now nationalized. It would include the evolution of co-operation, speeded up by the support of the state, the development of municipal and government enterprise, the growth of a system of factory constitutionalism, with the creation of a self-administering industrial republic as its final term. In a word this revolution would mean the gradual expulsion from economic life of personal arbitrary will by organized economic democracy. It must be created, not by ukazes to join collectives, enforced by the prohibition or strangulation of private economic initiative, but through the organic development of social initiative, which must first prove in practice its ability to replace private capital by competing on equal conditions and giving an equal result with smaller expenditure or a better result with the same expenditure. This régime of labor democracy is not socialism. But the path from it to socialism is free of all further catastrophes and revolutions. It is the path of peaceful development, which in economic life combines the individual with the social, not through doctrinaire theories, but through living and developing practical experience.[1]

Finally, to run the gamut of the attempts to divine the riddle of the approaching revolution, we must also note the theory of Parvus and Trotsky, the theory of "permanent revolution," which claimed to be the syncretic total of all the preceding ones, and to "place" each of them in time. According to it, the constantly developing revolution will inevitably commence as a bourgeois-democratic revolution; in logical sequence it will try a whole series of intermediary solutions, all of them self-contradictory and mongrel; by virtue of this contradiction they will not last, and will continually provoke a fresh advance, until the cycle is completed by realization of the maximal program, that of complete, integral socialism.[2]

This illustrates sufficiently the variety of opinion on the historic meaning of the revolution, then prevalent within Soviet democracy. These divergencies were multiplied by disagreement in appraising the World War and the duty of the proletariat in its bloody chaos. In this question the ideas of the revolutionary democratic parties took four entirely different channels.

1. The demand for the earliest possible ending of the war at any price, since the burden of the most dismal peace was a lesser evil than the further growth of mutual national hatred, the deadening of moral consciousness by familiarization with mass destruction of human life, and the mad wastage of mankind's resources, menacing all civilization with eclipse.

2. Intensified refusal to accept the war, sabotaging it from within, disintegrating the apparatus of the war, the army, a policy dictated by the desire for defeat of one's own govern-

ment, as a greater enemy than the foreign foe. The logical consequence of this view was the transformation of the foreign war into civil war.

3. The unreserved "acceptance of the war," for the sake of threatened national interest. This acceptance meant the temporary postponement of all special party and class purposes, in order, for the sake of victory, to unite the efforts of all classes and all parties.

4. The striving for an internal revolutionary overturn during the war, in order immediately to modify the purpose of the war; i.e., its political and international aims: instead of conservative purposes, to set a defensive (or even offensive) revolutionary aim.

But differences over the war did not always coincide with differences of tendency regarding the historic purpose and extent of the revolution. In other words, a single attitude toward the aims of the revolution might be combined with various views of the war, while agreement in evaluating the war might be destroyed by dissension over the purpose of the revolution.

When the question of organizing the government had to be answered on the morrow of autocracy's fall, the Soviet was led by the Social Democrats. The initiative in creating the Petrograd Soviet lay partly with the Menshevist fraction of the Imperial Duma (the Bolshevist fraction had been convicted for "defeatist" activity and exiled to Siberia), and at that, with its more moderate Right wing, the "Workers' Group connected with the Central War Industries Committee." The Social Revolutionaries had boycotted the elections to the Fourth Duma. Certain individuals, influenced by their ideas, had, however, joined the so-called "Labor Group," mildly infused with a semisocialism; such was the leader of this group, Kerensky; such was the old revolutionary, N. V. Chaikovsky, who represented the "Laborites" in the Soviet, and who had evolved far to the Right (toward peaceful development of the coöperative movement and patriotism). Their nearness to the bourgeois camp could only aid the triumph within the Soviet of the "classical" Social Democratic viewpoint, that the leadership of the Russian revolution by the bourgeoisie was inevitable.

A more Leftist Social Democratic group, headed by Steklov and Sukhanov, supported the practical conclusions based on the "classical" point of view, and disagreed with the majority only on the war; it was inclined to "peace at any price" tactics, while most Social Democratic leaders favored either the patriotic acceptance of the war (the "defensists"), or its revolutionary transformation ("revolutionary defensists").

The leading Social Democratic members of the Soviet felt it was natural for Soviet democracy to refuse to set up a Provisional Government, and to leave that to censitary democracy. The view prevailed in the Soviet that the Russian Revolution was a bourgeois revolution, which was to open a long historical period of Russia's capitalist industrialization. The course of events seemed to favor that view. The actual outcome of the disputes over organizing the government could best be rationalized by this theory. However, the further course of the revolution scarcely corroborated it. More important, however, was the fact that at the decisive moment the theories and doctrines of the several factions proved much less of a driving force than was imagined by men who had believed in them fanatically all their lives. The revolutionary situation so strongly determined practical conduct that at times people had no opportunity to notice whether their conduct was in sharp contradiction to the ideas of the revolution which they had entertained when it was a distant "music of the future."

Soviet democracy abandoned the creation of a government to censitary democracy—perhaps without itself realizing this—simply because this was the line of least resistance;

because, otherwise, it would have been confronted by too great difficulties, by external obstacles, even more by profound internal difficulties.

Soviet democracy was wanting in unanimity of program. True, in the camp of censitary democracy, in the Progressive Bloc, all was not well. From the beginning the structure had creaked ominously, and the Tsarist ministers had with malignant joy anticipated its disintegration. However, the bourgeois politicians of that period were more pliant and skilled in political compromise than the leaders of the revolution. Long "underground" existence, exclusion from legal political activity tended to ideological intensity, to relentless logic, bordering on the fanaticism of party dogma. Illegal struggle at all times and among all peoples has been a school of unpractical theorizing, of proud irreconcilability. Only real influence on affairs of state cultivates realization of responsibility and ability to appraise each step by its immediate results.

In the second place, censitary democracy was in possession of its full intellectual and political resources. It had its general staff assembled, the brain of the party. At the decisive moment revolutionary democracy was represented by casual elements, by second-, even fifth-rate forces. Its best men were in Siberia or in even more remote foreign exile. In the absence of their intellectual fathers, inspirers, and commanders, the modest rank-and-file hesitated to shoulder a responsibility which would perhaps have been unbearable even for the leaders.

Thirdly, as between the leaders of revolutionary democracy and those of censitary democracy the latter had one enormous advantage. Their chief figures had big names throughout Russia. In the city dumas, legal, civic, scientific, educational, and other associations, in election meetings, finally at the highest tribunal, the Imperial Duma, the flower of the bourgeois parties had long since gained the eyes and ears of the entire country. The leaders of revolutionary democratic parties, known and treasured in their own narrow circles, hiding beneath pseudonyms, changing names and passports, carefully masking from outsiders their own importance, were, with few exceptions, mysterious strangers, about whom their enemies could spread whatever legends they wished.

Fourthly, the greatest leaders of revolutionary democracy were absolutely ignorant of the technique of government administration and its apparatus. Even many Cadets felt themselves insufficiently prepared in this sphere. Shulgin tells how, when the Progressive Bloc was demanding a "ministry enjoying public confidence," that formula was explained as the transfer of power into nonbureaucratic hands. A Right-wing Cadet, later Ambassador of the Provisional Government in Paris, Maklakov, protested: "Why not bureaucratic hands? Why, I think that it must be transferred to bureaucratic hands, only different ones, cleverer and cleaner . . . But these people 'clothed in public confidence' will not do a thing. Why? Because we do not understand this business. We do not know the technique. And now there is no time to learn."[3] But the Cadets had studied this "technique" in the city dumas and zemstvos, in the four Imperial Dumas, in parliamentary commissions, coöperating with the ministers in drafting the budgets of the ministries and supervising their work. The leaders of revolutionary democracy had studied in prisons and along the weary trek to Siberian exile, as *objects* of governmental administration; "self-government" was familiar to them, through the institution of elected prison elders. The leap from the remote Siberian village or the Genevan colony of exiles straight to the seats of government was like being transferred to a different planet.

Finally, the bourgeois parties had had more than ten years of public existence and stable, legal organization, while the labor, socialist, and revolutionary parties were almost always confined to skeleton staffs of "professional revolutionaries." Now for the first time the skeleton was adding live flesh, with blood abundantly circulating in its veins and arteries, with a highly developed nervous system and a powerful set of muscles. The parties swelled from the inrush of new recruits so that their leaders looked on with secret horror: what will happen when the old guard is dissolved in the politically inexperienced, credulous mass? Will not the decisions of these masses be accidental? Will not the parties become unstable associations shifting like weathercocks to the moods of the formless street? In a word, revolutionary democracy was faced by an unprecedented task, that of organizing and intrenching its achievements, of training and educating the masses which had poured into its ranks, of disciplining them, creating a harmonious system of party organs. For this any quantity of the most skilled party forces would have been insufficient, and genuine, disciplined and reliable party men were not "any quantity" but a very limited contingent. To take enough big party figures to fill the government, ministries, and chief organs of local self-government would have meant bleeding the party organization and the Soviets. An elemental instinct of party self-preservation forced them to be stingy in handing over to the government their big leaders as prisoners of the government apparatus; it inoculated "party patriots" with instinctive repulsion to the government.

No, it was not theory or doctrine which won out in the ranks of Soviet democracy, but a direct feeling of the "burden of power," when the socialist doctrinaires of "bourgeois revolution" proposed, with "profound theoretical justifications," to shift this burden to the shoulders of censitary democracy. At that very moment the bourgeois parties, which had preferred to receive power from the hands of the Tsar and were terribly afraid of accepting it from the hands of the revolution, ceased to resist. Shulgin was saying: "Better take power ourselves, or it will be taken by some scoundrels who are already being elected at the factories."

The initiator of the Soviet's decision to transfer power to

censitary democracy, Sukhanov, realized that this meant "intrusting power to the class enemy." Still he proposed it, while "assuring democracy complete liberty of struggle against this enemy." He favored intrusting the class enemy with power on conditions which "must assure democracy a complete victory over it in the not distant future," but which must not "deprive the bourgeoisie of hope of winning." This was clever dialectic, but absolutely inapplicable to the course of events. Sukhanov and his friends wanted but one thing: "To guarantee complete political liberty, absolute freedom of organization and agitation." Behind the censitary leaders peered "the shadow of Stolypin's Imperial Duma," so the Soviet had to add the condition of "immediate measures toward summoning a Constituent Assembly."* By his own admission, Sukhanov "quite consciously neglected the other interests and demands of democracy, no matter how indubitable and essential." The question of the war he also left out of consideration. Censitary democracy might refuse to create a government to carry on a peace policy; in that case Soviet democracy would have had to accept power under conditions which would make peace the most urgent point of its program. The attitude of the army was particularly mysterious, and an immediate clash would probably ruin both the front and the revolution.

This ingenious construction had one defect. Intrusting power to a group under any conditions presupposed supervision of their fulfilment exercised by those who had set the conditions. Such control is simple and natural when the people in power are body and blood of those who exercise the control. But when supervisors and supervised belong to different camps, at bottom alien and hostile, this assures but one result: a permanent struggle with no juridical instance of appeal. The more certainly since there was no agreement on

* "We agreed with Steklov," says Sukhanov, "on the following: we proposed not to insist to the Progressive Bloc on the term, 'Constituent Assembly' . . . but to accept any other name for it, while categorically stating its full powers . . . But this was not needed."

the forms of supervision. This exposed the complete political bankruptcy of the original nucleus of the Soviet. Evidently it did not realize that supervisors are always responsible to the people for the supervised. It thought that by transferring power to the bourgeoisie, while keeping it on "short leash" by its "conditions," it could later part with it and begin its "struggles." It relied on the censitary government's being both a party to the struggle and an impartial umpire enforcing the rules of "honest battle" on both sides. But, first, the censitary government, which existed by the grace of Soviet democracy, could be a genuine government only if, in return for absolutely honest observance of the agreement, it enjoyed the full support of Soviet democracy. Secondly, what was meant by an "honest struggle with equal weapons" between the government and those who had agreed to intrust it with the power of state? Under normal conditions, in peacetime, with a national representative body, that would mean an appeal to parliament, a vote of no confidence in the government, its resignation, or a general election. But a provisional revolutionary government is a phenomenon *sui generis*. It always possesses fuller, but briefer, power than an ordinary government, for it exists until the creation of, and for the purpose of creating a previously nonexistent, national, representative body, and until it has fulfilled this mission, it acts without responsibility, dictatorially. A normal, legal dictatorship (not one established by force) presupposes later responsibility for honest and vigorous fulfilment of its mission. It does not presuppose a day-to-day, prohibitive control, under which it ceases to be a dictatorship. The leaders of the Soviet who supported Sukhanov's view displayed much shifty dialectic, with more than a touch of Machiavellianism, but no political maturity. And it was especially important for the government's personnel to be fully suited to its purpose. But the creators of the compromise felt differently. "The last point, the personnel of the government, was decided without difficulty. It was resolved not to interfere, but to let the bourgeoisie form its ministry as it saw fit."[4]

This indifference to the government's personnel was very characteristic of the times. It measured the *intellectual inertia* of prewar socialism, which everywhere in Europe acted as an *irresponsible opposition.* The farther Social Democrats sat to the Left in parliament, the more consistently they defended their passive attitude of irreconcilability. Steklov and Sukhanov believed sincerely that their indifference to the personnel of the new Russian government, their readiness to hand power to the censitary bourgeoisie, was a sign of their *political Leftness.* They forgot that the irresponsible opposition of European prewar socialism corresponded to its weakness as against the united bourgeoisie. The Social Democratic party of Germany could wage violent battle against the bourgeois majority in the Reichstag; militancy united its ranks without affecting the course of public business. Such was not the case in Russia. At every step the censitary government felt its own weakness, while each "irresponsible" gesture of its Soviet "opposition" was taken by the excited masses as a signal to attack the remnant of the Tsarist Duma, still tolerated, for some unknown reason, as a mockery of the people. Such was the feeling of the most energetic elements of those masses which had made the revolution; to compel them to feel differently was not in the power of the Soviet Machiavellis who had made the agreement with the Progressive Bloc.

We have already noted the reaction of the clever monarchist, Krivoshein, on hearing the membership of the Provisional Government. If its composition is compared with the "Ministry of Defense," planned in 1915 to enjoy the public confidence, while still responsible to the Tsar, the chief difference consisted in replacing Rodzianko as President by Prince Lvov,* and in including Kerensky who had succeeded in com-

* This was done at the insistence of Miliukov, who, according to V. D. Nabokov, was later inclined to consider this a mistake.

bining membership in the Provisional Committee of the Duma with that in the Presidium of the Soviet, and who was half Laborite and half Social Revolutionary. This was the sole tribute to the universal recognition that the country's feeling had long since, even before the revolution, become more Left than the Progressive Bloc. Kerensky's inclusion was proposed by the extreme Right wing of the Bloc, by the Nationalist, Shulgin.

> We must get headway . . . You know, when a yacht is on its left tack, before tacking to the right, you must bear further to the left, to gain momentum . . . If power is thrust on us, we must seek support by enlarging the Progressive Bloc to the Left. I would invite Kerensky, as Minister of Justice, let us say . . . Right now this post has no importance but we must snatch its leaders from the revolution. Among them Kerensky is really the only one . . . It is much better to have him with us than against us.[5]

This maneuver was executed by the censitary leaders, and not unskilfully. As for Soviet democracy, it would seem as if it too gained by this: it secured within the Provisional Government its own "eye," without which no *preventive* control would be feasible. However, this amendment scarcely remedied the general abnormality of the situation, while it made inconsistent the position of Soviet democracy, which claimed it was not participating in the Provisional Government and hence was not responsible for it. Guided by this idea, the Executive Committee of the Soviet, by a majority of two thirds, decreed not to delegate any representative to the Lvov-Miliukov ministry. But Kerensky had already made up his mind to join the Provisional Government at any price. To achieve this he chose a very ambiguous means. He evaded participation in deciding this question in the Executive Committee of the Soviet, of which he was a vice president. Suddenly he appeared at a session of almost two thousand members of the plenary Soviet, and announced that he had been offered the position of Minister of Justice; not having had time to ask the sanction of the Soviet, he had had to decide on his own; as Minister of Justice he held in his hands the representatives of the old régime and was unwilling to let them go; as minister he had already issued instructions to release all political prisoners and to let the Social Democratic deputies (the Bolsheviks who had been exiled for agitating against the war) return with special honor from exile; he asked for confidence, was ready to die for the revolution, and, if he was not trusted, was willing to resign as vice president of the Soviet. At the proper passages Kerensky received his meed of applause and promptly retired, again refusing to take part in deciding the general question of the participation or nonparticipation of representatives of the Soviet in the government. After his withdrawal, the question was again raised and settled, without specific discussion of Kerensky's position, in favor of *nonparticipation*, almost unanimously, against a minority of fifteen votes. However, Kerensky did not give up his vice presidency of the Soviet, nor did the Executive Committee of the Soviet dare to erase his name automatically from the list of the Presidium.

This ambiguous situation ruined the entire combination. Kerensky, it is true, could claim an exceptional position within the Provisional Government: in it he alone represented the Soviet world, the world of revolutionary democracy. However, he began a hidden conflict with that world, and the Soviet could no longer regard him as an organ of control over the Provisional Government. On the contrary, the censitary government tried to use him as its battering-ram against the Soviet. Kerensky's own personality and political sense determined whether his presence would introduce a fresh current into the work of the censitary government. Kerensky, in summing up his activity later, and, of course, exaggerating somewhat in order to capture the hearts of Right-wing *émigré* society, described his rôle among the censitary leaders:

> The only organic element of power was the Soviet of Workers', Soldiers' and Peasants' Deputies, of the first session; it played a

positive rôle, for it created the flesh and body of the governmental principles. And this was said, not by me, Kerensky, but by other members of the Provisional Government; even the commander of the Petrograd district in March and April, 1917, General Kornilov, said that he never began anything without the Soviets. *I was the most conservative minister*, for then I did not recognize people like Steklov who have now gone over to Bolshevism.[6]

Thus the situation was hopelessly confused. The very man who was supposed to correct from the Left the work of a Right-wing government, unsuited to the country's feeling, proved, by his own admission, "the most conservative minister." The very man through whom the government, sensing its own weakness, sought a connecting link with Soviet democracy, secretly boasted of his permanent though hidden conflict with the latter. If Kerensky, as Miliukov said, "used and even abused his position within the cabinet," by "stressing his rôle as the 'hostage' of democracy,"[7] yet he himself had no illusions. He always emphasized his usual "above-party" position, as a man "apart."

I always speak in my own name, for myself, and I bind no one. It was so in 1912 when I entered the Imperial Duma, despite the decree of my party boycotting the election. It was so throughout my work in the Duma, and during the war as well. It was so in 1917 when I entered the Provisional Government *against the decree of the Petrograd Soviet*, the organ of revolutionary democracy, led by both the Russian Socialist Parties.[8]

Relations between Soviet democracy and censitary democracy were twisted into a Gordian knot by that very minister who represented the Soviets to the censitary leaders and the censitaries to the Soviets, who was a member of the central organs of both bodies and always regarded himself as entitled to act against the will of both.

CHAPTER SEVEN

THE REVOLUTION AND THE WORKERS

THE Russian Revolution burst forth with sudden and primitive force. Many generations of fighters had longed for it passionately, believed in it and sacrificed everything for it. Ever broader masses came to place in it their deepest hopes and yearnings. Each class in its own way dreamed of it as the beginning of a new life.

Of all classes it was the urban proletariat that associated the most definite prospects with it. Its more enlightened section, taught in the rather arid and matter-of-fact school of Marxism, was proud of its emancipation from all Utopias. True, it was out-and-out socialist. But socialism to it was the culmination of a long historic road, in which the natural phases of organic evolution could not be skipped arbitrarily. It pictured the first phase as the democratization of the factory within the democratic state. On this basis it foresaw its own rebirth as a social class intellectually mature, a political vanguard organized along many different lines, possessed of full rights, a class destined during the natural decline of capitalism to fulfil a great historic mission, at once revolutionary and constructive.

This feeling dominated at least the skilled strata of the Russian working class. But the chaotic and tumultuous course of the Russian Revolution proved this evolutionary prospect a mirage. No wonder that the workers began to reflect: perhaps what had been labeled a mirage was the longed for reality.

This process of readjusting began with the first days of the revolution.

The weeks of revolution created an absurdly contradictory situation in the factory districts. "He who was nothing became everything"; but "everything" in fact alone, while remaining "nothing" in law.

Needless to say, Tsarist Russia was utterly ignorant of the "new factory," in which the owner was not an Asiatic despot, but a "constitutional monarch" bound to his factory "subjects," the workers, by a system of "fundamental laws," comprising a collective agreement. In prerevolutionary Russia the right of the entrepreneur in his factory was identified with that of "the master in his own house"; it was regarded as a social, rather than a legal phenomenon. The Russian bourgeoisie insisted that relations between capital and labor in Russia were "patriarchal," and did not require regulation or interference from outside the factory.

The absolutism of the Tsar in the state and of the entrepreneur in the factory harmonized perfectly, supplemented each other. The appearance on factory territory of anything like a "labor union" or even of "concerted action" was regarded as "rebellion," just as in the civil arena the citizens, with respect to the sovereign authority, were subjects who had personally sworn fidelity to it, and in whom even the collective submission of a petition was regarded as a crime against the state.

From the early nineteenth century documents have been preserved concerning the arraignment before a military court of delegates chosen by the workers to present complaints against their employer to the Tsar. For "wilful departure from their command" and for "annoying" the sacred persons of the imperial family with "invented complaints" they were condemned "to beating with the knout, excision of the nostrils and life exile to the galleys," or else to "be hanged until dead." Even in the early 1870's there were genuinely servile factories in which the "workers' rules of the manufactory," confirmed by His Majesty, imposed upon the workers the "duty of unquestioning obedience to the decrees of the manufactory" in the shops and also in the "living quarters," the workers' barracks. There an elaborate system of fines was enforced by the "home administration, elders, watchmen, and sentinels."

On the eve of the twentieth century Russia knew no liberty of strike or coalition. The government's secret circulars declared punishable "even the striving to enjoy their legal rights if by violent or illegal means" (circular of December 5, 1895). The employers were often forbidden by administrative interference to make concessions to the workers under "illegal" pressure of the strike. The political police, in Russia a "state within the state," attacked Witte's very moderate projects tending to legalize to some degree labor organizations and strikes. On the other hand, according to the program of Zubatov, the famous head of the Moscow political police, a certain quasi organization of the workers was to be created outside the law, through workers' committees in various factories; general oversight of the committees was to be concentrated in the secret police, which for this purpose would appoint special agents from among reliable workers, to fight the revolution with the support of the somnolent and conservative elements of the working class.

It was only at the beginning of the twentieth century, in 1903, that Russian legislation created the first legal channel through which the workers could submit their needs to the employer: the "factory elders." But it did this in so pitiful a form that the workers often boycotted the elections and contemptuously called this "law on factory elders" the "law on factory doorkeepers." The Revolution of 1905, during the government's helplessness and the owners' confusion, laid the first foundations of a factory constitution, with elective factory committees and an embryonic system of collective agreements. But counterrevolution came. The workers' organization declined. Militant associations of capital grew up (by 1907 there were 120) forbidding their members to shorten the working day, to allow the workers' deputies to interfere in regulating the hiring, discharge, and payment of the workers, or above all to agree in direct or camouflaged form to pay for time lost on strike. As security these associations required deposits of their members, which were forfeited if they weakened or dropped out. The conquests of the revolutionary period were gradually eliminated. This was furthered through systematic destruction of labor organizations by the police.

Organized lockouts began to be applied more frequently against strikes. The Lodz manufacturers announced, in a special memorandum: "The history of lockouts shows that only the second and third lockouts make the workers obedient." In the revolutionary year, 1905, the workers lost 30% of their strikes, in 1906 34%, in 1907 58%, in 1908 68%. Discharges and arrests of workers' deputies by the police were a constant occurrence. The working day reverted to the prerevolutionary norm of 10–10½ hours. "A ray of the new dawn seemed to break for our workers, but not for long. The more enlightened workers have been discharged. Everything is as before," reads a typical report from a working-class district.

Just before the World War there was a new advance in the labor movement. In 1911 the workers lost 51% of their strikes, in 1912 41%, in 1913 only 31%. The number of strikes, which varied in 1909–11 between 300 and 400, with total participation as low as 46,000 in 1910, again exceeded 2,000, with 725,000 to 860,000 participants annually. This advance and its achievements had not succeeded in modernizing the structure of the Russian factory when they were cut short by the World War. The further evolution of the factory was simple. At first the government cherished a grandiose bureaucratic Utopia: organizing all war industry as a state monopoly, serving all the needs of defense without the aid of private or civic initiative. The methods of this organization were at times more than peculiar. Rodzianko tells how he once encountered a crowd of people on their way to the county seat, under armed convoy as if prisoners. He learned that this was a peculiar method of "mobilizing" trained shoemakers to stitch boots for the army! Only in May, 1915, when the front was without clothing, shoes, or ammunition, did the bankruptcy of bureaucratic procedure force the government to have recourse to the organized effort of private industry. Its voluntary mobilization was tardily begun through the War Industries Committees, which aimed to adapt Russian industry to the needs of national defense, to abolish competition and to secure the most sensible allotment of military orders. The government's failure to cope with this task and its appeal to private capital tremendously raised the confidence of the Russian bourgeoisie. "The commercial and industrial class of the twentieth century," declared Professor V. Storozhev in *News of the Moscow War Industries Committee*, "is no longer a purse from which the state may take as much as it likes, repaying with occasional titles, orders, or the granting of hereditary nobility." "In the great European War the commercial and industrial class acts as a real force, for which both the bureaucratic privileges of the old and the democratic tasks of the new period must make way."[1]

However, the entrepreneurs had no serious quarrel with the "bureaucratic privileges of the old"; these were only family tiffs. It was the "democratic tasks of the new period" that suffered from their alliance. First, workers subject to military conscription were attached to plants working for national defense. In case of strike they were menaced by dispatch to the front. Secondly, through Article 87; i.e., by emergency decree, the labor laws were repealed, and the employment of women and children immediately expanded, together with overtime. Thirdly, the servile labor of prisoners of war was offered to manufacturers in great quantity. Finally, enrolment of "yellow" labor, Chinese and Korean, was widely practiced. Not content with this, the Right press strenuously prepared public opinion for the universal militarization of the industrial workers. The factory was to become a barracks under absolute military discipline; the factory administration was to obtain the full powers of army officers over the workers. Special wartime laws already in force threatened the workers with forced labor for ceasing work. The militarization of war industry implied a still greater threat: flogging had already been introduced at the front!

Underneath, the workers were stirring. A certain safety valve was provided by the factory elections of delegates to the Workers' Group connected with the War Industries Committee. At the second congress of the War Industries Committees the group appealed to the employers, pointing out the measures adopted in all warring countries to attach the workers to the cause of national defense. The functions of coöperative and trade-union organizations had been enlarged, the former to regulate national consumption, the latter to mobilize and distribute labor. The Workers' Group appealed to the Russian manufacturers to break with the traditions of factory feudalism. The group attempted to secure something tangible for the Russian workers: recognition of the right of coalition, creation of arbitration boards to settle conflicts between capital and labor, and resistance to "militarization" of the factories. It suffered a complete defeat. The government and the entrepreneurs merely attempted to revive the dead-letter law on factory elders, the owners trying to make them tools of the factory administration. Meanwhile, the government shut down the unions of printers and metal workers, sole survivals of an embryonic and camouflaged trade-union movement. The bill for arbitration boards, drafted by the Workers' Group, was rejected by the Minister of Commerce, Prince Shakhovskoy, pending decision of the general question of legalizing unions. Attempts of the Workers' Group to mediate in conflicts at the Lessner plant and the "Naval" plant in Nikolayev were rejected by the factory administrations. It was also completely unable to prevent dispatch of strikers to the front after conflicts at the Nobel machine plant and the Admiralty shipyard. This explains the adoption by the Workers' Group of more radical tactics, the appeal for a mass demonstration at the opening of the Duma, a change which led to its arrest. That arrest saved it from complete discredit among the working masses.

Such was the situation in the factories before the revolutionary days of February and March, 1917.

The strike movement, which had broken out intermittently here and there in the second week of February and spread gradually between February 23 and 25, suddenly turned into a general strike. Since it was due less to factory troubles than to the food and political questions, it alarmed the police and government, while the factory administrations were not everywhere involved in the struggle. In some places, as in Kolpino, the factories were closed temporarily "for overhauling." Less often, as at Putilov's, the strike was met with a lockout, and the factory "closed indefinitely." Usually, the factory administration withdrew as the struggle grew hotter and even disappeared completely when the police invaded the factories or were beaten off by a shower of stones. During the weeks of revolution the factory districts were the military base of the uprising. Some factories became workers' fortresses. The factory management kept "out of harm's way," and the workers felt themselves the sole masters. This situation was of the greatest significance for the mentality of the factory proletariat. The contrast between this actual state of things and the preceding régime of "war-industry feudalism" was incredibly sharp. Here was the first problem of the revolution, clamoring for solution. The censitary government was far from understanding either its urgency or its complexity. Yet it was plain that the prerevolutionary factory was an anachronism, ill-suited to the new era, and that the workers who had made the revolution would never again submit to its autocratic labor laws. Hence, a new system, even though temporary and transitional, the "constitutional factory," must be guaranteed them at once. Else it must be recognized that the workers could not soon be lured back to work. Chaos, interregnum, permanent conflict between workers and management, would become the rule, everywhere provoking guerrilla warfare in industry.

The Soviet of Workers' Deputies had the courage, as early as March 5, to urge immediate renewal of work in the factories. It would be an irremediable blow to the revolution if the soldiers, who had formerly had to face a hail of lead empty-handed through fault of Sukhomlinov & Co., were again left in that state by fault of the revolution. But the Soviet also realized that the return to the factories could not mean acceptance of the prerevolutionary factory system. The president of the Soviet, Chkheidze, dotted the *i*'s:

"On what conditions can we work? It would be ridiculous for us to go back to work on the old conditions. Let the bourgeoisie know that . . . In setting to work, we shall at once begin elaboration of conditions on which we will work."

The Petrograd Association of Manufacturers, having discovered arbitrary attempts by the workers to fix the length of the working day and to usurp the right to remove factory managers, took an important and reasonable decision: to consult the Soviet and settle disputes by agreement. It was not easy to part with the owner's absolute sovereignty "in his own house," in his factory. But the prestige of the revolution was too strong. On March 2 the central organ of the Russian commercial and industrial bourgeoisie, the Council of Congresses of Representatives of Commerce and Industry, warned the entire commercial and industrial class of Russia and all its organizations of "the necessity for concessions," while urging it "to forget party and social discord and rally around the Provisional Government."

By agreement between the Soviet and the Association of Manufacturers arbitration boards were finally created with parity between employers and workers. The Factory Committees were recognized as legal representatives of the entire personnel of operatives in dealing with factory management and public authorities. The main achievement was the immediate and painless introduction of the eight-hour working day.

This important conquest of the Soviet was welcomed with tremendous enthusiasm. It gave the Soviet unprecedented popularity among the workers and strengthened its authority for a long time to come, besides making it easier to carry out the previous decision for the general return to work, which the extreme Left, especially the Bolsheviks, were already trying to hinder. Their fronde was led by the Organization Committee of the Moscow ward (in Petrograd); it delayed the end of the strike for several days in protest against failure to refer this question back to the wards and factories. The "Dynamo" factory declared out and out that it "would not submit to the Soviet, or coöperate with it," for a general strike could not be called off until the old government had been completely destroyed and something done to end the war; as long as this was not done, calling off the strike; i.e., the return to preparing ammunition for the world-wide massacre, was not acceptable to the workers. The objectors were quite unsuccessful. One thousand one hundred and seventy delegates against thirty voted on the first ballot for immediate return to work; on the second ballot there were only fifteen votes against the return to work.

Events soon showed how rational this decision was. The tremendous victory of Soviet democracy in securing the eight-hour working day was certain to provoke a counter-attack. Plenty of people were dissatisfied with the conciliatory policy of the Petrograd Association of Manufacturers. They now began an energetic undercover campaign, joined by all those who were dissatisfied with the overturn and afraid to attack it openly but greedily awaiting the first signs of dissension within the victors' camp.

A contemporary writes of this anti-Soviet campaign:

> The agitation was carried on at every street corner. During the last ten days [of March] on streets, in tramcars, in public

places one could see workers and soldiers, in the last stages of irritation, linked in a fierce battle of words. There were also physical encounters. Matters were becoming most alarming.

Of course, the workers were accused of excessive demands, of absolute unwillingness to work and of ignoring the interests of the front. The starting point of the agitation was, by the way, the eight-hour working day. Fishers in troubled waters were speculating on the inability of the muzhik in the soldier's gray cloak to understand this proletarian demand. There is no such standard of work at the front or in the village. Yet here were factory loafers, unwilling to work longer hours, enjoying a free and easy life by other people's sacrifices in the trenches!

The soldiers demanded restraint of the workers and control over the factories. They even threatened reprisals and punishment. "Well, just wait," one could hear everywhere, "we'll show you what's what in your own workshops. We'll set a soldier of ours with his rifle beside every one of you loafers. And in case . . ."

Indeed, the factories began to be visited by armed soldiers, carrying out inspections and using force. Groups of soldiers from near-by garrisons and even from the field army began to arrive for this purpose. The "goading of one part of the population against the other" seemed close to its goal. Serious excesses were expected any hour.[2]

How this feeling was stirred up at the front is shown by a report from the committee of the First Army Corps. The corps commander, General Bulatov, had sent this telegram to all regimental commanders:

There is no linen; it will not be delivered before mid-April, then only in half quantity, there is no surplus clothing; it is not sent from the rear; no tobacco is being brought up. *Announce all this to the soldiers, explaining that in the rear the workers are working very little.* The discipline of the regiment depends entirely on your activity.

The committee branded this attack as an attempt to provoke the soldiers against the workers, the more suspect since on this the "discipline of the regiment" was to be built—one asks, for what purpose?

Rumors were set afloat and proved to be lies; two important Moscow papers, *Russkoye Slovo* and *Russkiia Vedomosti,* reported that the Tsarskoye Selo garrison, consisting of 75,000 bayonets, had protested against the eight-hour day.

Hence the full significance of the Soviet's insistence on immediate return to work, despite Bolshevist demagogy; hence the Soviet allowed the employers, with consent of the Factory Committees, to prolong work beyond the eight hours, at special overtime rates. Representatives of the Soviet met all the soldiers' delegations, accompanied them to the factories, invited them to see for themselves that the workers were at their lathes and were not idling under pretext of continuing the revolution; occasional stoppages were due to lack of raw material or fuel; the eight-hour day did not mean refusal to work after eight hours' labor in preparing cartridges and ammunition for the front, but extra pay for overtime. Soviet democracy carried on a vigorous counteragitation, through public declarations by soldiers' delegations which had visited the factories, through joint soldiers' and workers' meetings, explanatory resolutions and appeals of the workers to the soldiers, through sending special speakers to the barracks, etc. The resolution of the Minsk Front Line Congress, exposing the "bourgeois slander against the workers," was particularly remarkable. As a result, the first attack against Soviet democracy was beaten off victoriously, even brilliantly; the fortnight's crisis between workers and soldiers left in the army a clear understanding of the hostile maneuver as an attempt to light the flame of fratricidal enmity within the very citadel of revolution, and thus to undermine it.

In the eight-hour working day the Soviet had won a triple victory. It exacted a great concession from the employers. It strengthened its authority against ultra-Left, demagogic attempts to advance by chaotic leaps without the central leadership of the "Workers' Parliament." And it strengthened the bond between workers and soldiers which its secret enemies had tried to sever.

But there were still two faltering points in these first victorious steps of Soviet democracy.

First, the eight-hour-day agreement was a purely local, Petrograd achievement; it had to be carried out on a national scale by governmental decree; this, however, would have required a different composition of the Provisional Government. In Moscow no such agreement was made: the manufacturers declared that they rejected it not from personal (class) interest, but as "citizens" who realized the country's "tremendous lack of commodities" despite the growing "requirements of the army and the people." The Moscow Soviet had no choice but to resort to a method proposed by the Bolsheviks but rejected by the Petrograd Soviet: "to decree" that after eight hours' labor the workers should stop work; i.e., should put through the eight-hour day by direct action. The movement now divided into two channels. In Saratov, Simferopol, Yaroslavl, Omsk, Odessa, etc., the "Petrograd" method triumphed; other cities reported stubborn resistance by the manufacturers and resort by the workers to the "Moscow method." "As soon as Kharkov heard the rumor of the introduction of the eight-hour day in Petrograd, the same question was raised. Although the Kharkov Soviet in principle opposed introduction of the eight-hour day by force, it had to sanction what had already been carried out." The eight-hour day was conquered everywhere; but the workers were not completely satisfied; it was an extra-legal fact and legally remained in question. Return to work was greatly delayed. Both employers and workers were nervous. The workers began to blame the Soviet for failing to make return to work dependent on the legal introduction of the eight-hour day. This was grist to the Bolshevist mill.

The second weakness is clearly presented in a report to the

Workers' Section of the Petrograd Soviet, March 18, by a representative of Narva ward, the workingman, Pavlenkov:

> The return to work in the factories without a preliminary improvement in conditions of labor has compelled the workers to carry on a chaotic, unorganized economic struggle. In various places there has been talk of the need for higher wages . . . Although we have been successful in restraining the natural discontent of the masses, the Labor Section must speedily work out the question of a minimum wage.

Pavlenkov noted that "the productivity of labor, on which depends the success in supplying ammunition to the revolutionary troops, has been inadequate, and the Narva Soviet of Workers' and Soldiers' Deputies has had to appeal to the workers to work conscientiously." He wishes no less attention for another problem: supplying the factories with raw material and fuel, "to adopt all measures to prevent a secret lockout under pretext of lack of fuel."

This describes the general position of the first Soviets. They considered most seriously the extraordinary conditions of wartime, they were inspired by a sense of responsibility; they sought to stabilize the situation in the factories by bringing the defense of the class interests of the proletariat within the framework of an organized and centralized struggle, and through negotiation and temporary agreement between the central organs of labor and capital to prepare for extending these agreements to all Russia and supplementing them by legislation.

What was the position of the other party, the employers? The spirit of concession, displayed by the Petrograd Association of Manufacturers, was viewed by many as a sign of "genuine statesmanship" in handling the problems of economic life, of ability to place the historic interests of Russian industry above the immediate interests of the manufacturers. A conference of manufacturers, meeting as late as June 1, still proclaimed loudly that it would discuss all questions, not from a "class viewpoint," not from the "viewpoint of merchants and manufacturers," but from that of the "salvation of industry and commerce themselves," necessary for the growth of "healthy statehood." But the conference destroyed the effect of that proclamation by stating that "the financial situation of many enterprises makes impossible the further conduct of their business" and that "their closing is inevitable in the immediate future." A plainer proof of the impotence of this statesmanship could scarcely be imagined. It was distinctly felt that the whole affair was a cleverly disguised project for a general lockout.

A prominent representative of the industrial class, a member of many firms, boards, and associations, Auerbach, gives a truthful and sober description of his own class, which he had studied well: "The participation of the commercial and industrial class in the Russian Revolution, of course, may be spoken of only in a very relative sense: by the time of the revolution this class had only begun to crystallize, merchants and businessmen were scarcely becoming aware of themselves as kernels of a social group with its own distinctive nature and its great historic mission." Therefore, "at that time the commercial and industrial class as such did not act in the political arena." "In general, this class was so amorphous and politically inert that it did not even have its direct representatives in the Duma, or its own political program." Important figures of the class were scattered among the various Duma parties, or else were politically indifferent. "The presence in its midst of a rather large number of landowners, often nobles, sometimes bound the commercial and industrial class to the caste of the nobility, which had outlived its own political career"; this "injured the political independence of the commercial and industrial class."

Classes doomed to disappear from the arena of history usually have but one tactic: bitter irreconcilability. They lack the flexibility and elasticity natural in classes which represent not a "vestige" but a "living element" of the period. Its alliance with the nobility infected the commercial and industrial class with the same psychology. It showed the over-zealousness of neophytes who had been taken unaware by the revolution, and who understood only that from now on they could no longer enjoy passively all the blessings of life under the government's protecting wing, but would have to rely on themselves alone to defend their interests. Auerbach describes vividly the feverish haste with which the employers began building up their militant associations; "everything was new, hasty, painfully urgent." "Complete union of whole branches of production was achieved without special difficulty"; the "wild" or unorganized factories practically disappeared. The "associations were built at great expense, but means were always found." Leaders were developed; they hastened to acquire the necessary training and make up for their backwardness in comparison with their opponents. They tried to organize a press to defend the interests of their class, subsidizing (through a misunderstanding, as Auerbach explains in some embarrassment) even "ultra-monarchist and reactionary publications" like the famous *Zhizn Rossii* in Kharkov.

The sudden hothouse forcing of this new class feeling, added to a political immaturity inherited from the past, quickly infected the class of employers with the psychology of a peculiar "industrial-feudal Maximalism."

CHAPTER EIGHT

THE PEASANTS AND THE REVOLUTION

FROM earliest times the Russian revolutionary movement was linked to slogans of agrarian revolution. Even before the emancipation of the serfs, the "masters of the thoughts" of the progressive and critical vanguard of Russian society, the great scholar and economist, Chernyshevsky, and the brilliant philosopher-publicist, Herzen, appeared as socialist theorists of the toiling peasantry. They denied any shadow of legal right to the landowning of the gentry; they regarded the institution of private property in land as alien to Russian life and Russian history. For them the emancipation of the peasants *eo ipso* must mean their recovery of the right to dispose of the land they cultivated. "Land and Liberty" were inseparable.

The view of Herzen, Chernyshevsky, and their revolutionary followers was in full accord with the peasants' fundamental attitude. The Russian village never inwardly accepted the landlord's right to the land. For centuries it waited for a merciful and just Tsar to remove the gentry and put them on "the Tsar's pay." Such a view could persist only in a country in which the former caste of noble serfowners went on living "as of old," clung to its land monopoly, and could not become a class of modern agriculturalists, basing its right to the land on its improvement of agriculture. The peasants clung to the thought that they had been deceived in the emancipation of 1861, that their "liberty" was a false one. The peasants had of old expressed their relation to the gentry and the land in the naïve phrase, "We are yours, but the land is ours."

The accord between the revolutionary intelligentsia and the mass of the people was slow to find expression in real life. The peasants long cherished the hope of a just Tsar, while the revolutionaries tried to convince them that the peasant, not having gotten all the land, had not gained his full liberty, that liberty and Tsar were incompatible, that the autocracy, which had stolen liberty from the people, had helped to steal its land, that the Tsars truly styled themselves "the first nobles" and the "first landowners" of the Russian state. In obedience to a true instinct and despite all temporary failures, the Russian revolutionary movement always "faced the village." The first Russian Marxists had tried to ignore it, but even they were later forced to join in the slogan of "Land and Liberty." Only indescribable oppression, inherited from serfdom, lack of culture, illiteracy, and the darkness of the village, carefully fostered by the servants of the old régime, long kept this slogan from the people. With the greatest patience and self-sacrifice the revolutionary intelligentsia by the beginning of this century had broken the ice. After the Poltava and Kharkov peasant disturbances of 1902, communication between intelligentsia and people grew ever more rapidly. The search for an organization to "fuse" city and village was also successful. The formation of the first peasant "Brotherhood for the Protection of the People's Rights," with the participation of V. M. Chernov, in 1898–99, in Borisogleb district, Tambov province, was constantly imitated; in less than five years many districts were covered by a great network of revolutionary "Brotherhoods," which in 1902 united to form the "Peasants' Union of the Party of Social Revolutionaries." In 1905 an attempt was made to form an even broader Peasants' Union, to include other parties and the nonparty mass; with insignificant modifications it adopted the program and tactics of its predecessor, the Social Revolutionary Union.

The 1905 Revolution was broken up. The peasant movement which had begun everywhere, but, as ever, later than in the cities, was brutally crushed. The peasants in silence nursed their bitterness and thirst for revenge. Every observer of the agrarian movement then realized that the next outburst would not display the earlier good-natured, often naïve forms, but would show the scarlet hue of revenge. Obviously political revolution in the city would immediately be followed by an agrarian revolution. Therefore the zemstvo opposition to autocracy was irresolute and constantly yielded for fear of giving an unintentional fillip to a genuine, popular revolution. But when the revolution came, the village, to the general astonishment, remained mysteriously calm. At least, in the beginning.

This might be due, first, to the great delay with which all urban events reached the Russian village. The dispersion of the villages and hamlets across the enormous Eastern European plain where communication was impossible, reliance on distant rumors, half believed and half disbelieved, and finally the dread felt by the local authorities of announcing the revolution to the peasantry, all helped to make the village a passive onlooker. Even in so militant a province as Tver, located between the two capitals, "the news of the revolution received wide publicity only in the middle of March"; the peasants were often told that "this may still change and go back to the old way." In Smolensk province news of the revolution "was passed on quietly, in a whisper," "everyone glanced fearfully around," "feared his neighbor, his relatives, even himself." In Chekuevsky county, Arkhangelsk province, the priest long continued praying for the "most pious, most autocratic" Tsar, while the police officer donned new epaulets and thus reënforced faith in the stability of the old order. In Ufa province people long heard only vague rumors that "the Tsar had run away, had abandoned the throne, and the soldiers and some workers had gone against him."[1]

Some villages, however, caught up the slogans of the revolution at once. The tocsin was rung and people said: "Now freedom is declared to all, and no one shall oppress us." With shouts of "Hurrah!" the crowds moved down the streets of villages and hamlets, arresting elders, foremen, "commune eaters," "kulaks," police, land captains. A deputation was

A RARE PHOTOGRAPH OF THE "GRANDMOTHER OF THE REVOLUTION," BRESHKO-BRESHKOVSKAYA

From Soviet Russia in Its Early Years. *A collection of photographs presented to the New York Public Library*

chosen to go to the county seat, and a provisional committee to administer the local district. In some cases the provisional committees, on their own initiative, began a house-to-house census of all supplies of wheat, fodder, and stock.[2]

Cases where the peasants' thoughts turned to squaring old accounts were very rare. That demanded especially bitter memories. In Tambov province, in the village of Berezovka, the peasants dug up the body of a landlord, Luzhenovsky, burned it, and scattered his ashes to the wind.* But the general feeling was quite different: forgetfulness of the old, every thought and feeling straining toward the bright future. Even Bolshevik peasants, describing by official assignment the bankruptcy of the February Revolution and the superiority of the October Revolution, cannot but give a vivid account of the first months of freedom.

Many went to the city to secure accurate information of what had occurred. Each brings back several newspapers, they are read ceaselessly, and people rejoice without end . . . The village seemed reborn, it became gay . . . From the first days of the revolution the peasants rejoiced and felt that now life would become better.[3]

The people congratulated each other with the Easter kiss and said: "Now, at last the bright holiday has come." Everyone was dressed in his best, as for a great feast day. Thus three days were spent solemnly in our village to celebrate the fall of the autocracy and the establishment of freedom.[4]

The village overwhelmed the revolutionary city with most touching expressions of gratitude, confidence, readiness to follow its leadership. In naïve expressions it thanked the Provisional Government and the Soviets "for the labors they have borne," it thanked the workers and the garrison which

* The provincial councilor Luzhenovsky, who had commanded a punitive expedition, was killed in 1906 by a member of a militant group of the party of Social Revolutionaries, Maria Spiridonova; she was then tortured by the Cossack officer Abramov, inspector Zhdanov and Governor General von Launitz, all of whom were later executed by sentence of the same organization.

supported the revolution. Without abandoning their century-old dream of the land, the peasants were hopeful that "everything would be arranged" somehow "in a friendly way," that the land would be transferred without "offense" to the nobles, for the latter's abilities could be utilized somehow for the general good. If the noble had not oppressed his peasants particularly and had tried to maintain neighborly relations with them, the peasants were benevolently disposed toward him and sought to facilitate his transition to the new and equal life of toil by some transitional compromise.

In the peasants' instructions it is not uncommon to find a concern for the nobles after their land had been taken for "common use." They would not hear of redemption; but especially in regard to the minor gentry, who had applied much labor and care to the land, the peasants almost everywhere were willing to leave them the mansion house and to assign them adjacent land in accord with the highest norm for the toiler, without haggling as to what absent members of the family were to be assigned a share. Let them at first have something extra, that would serve as a rough partition; later "everything would be evened out." Incidentally, the current hope was not so much that the noble would turn peasant, as that each peasant could begin to live in liberty and comfort, "to be a noble himself." In addition, in most of the peasants' instructions there are special points about the payment of temporary "rations" to the former gentry who might leave the land: they would need to "rest a bit and look around," to arrange their lives anew. The peasants used to say, "The land to the muzhiks, and out with the nobles, let them go on the Tsar's payroll." Now their decisions were not so oversimplified. Able agriculturalists, skilled in seed raising and stock breeding, the muzhiks were not unwilling to put on the zemstvo or coöperative payroll, recognizing the difficulty of replacing them. In general, there was at first a strong desire to "arrange things without offense." Some farsighted gentlemen farmers—their number, true, was small—from the first months of revolution, especially from May on, begin to petition the Ministry of Agriculture to have their estates taken over by the Land Committees and managed under their protection and supervision. They saw that this was the only way to save these cultural centers from destruction.

Whence this almost idyllic calm in the village?

Its first cause lay in the sphere of social psychology. The peasant, whether Great Russian, White Russian, or Ukrainian, was instinctively suspicious of the organically alien city. On the other hand, he had an almost childishly naïve thirst to believe without limit in something or someone, to intrust his fate entirely to someone's hands. He had long concentrated all his suspicion on officialdom, and all his faith in the half-mythical figure of the Tsar, who like God on earth "sees all truth, but will not tell it soon." When life finally exploded that faith, and revolution destroyed the Tsar's power, the peasant sought instinctively to transfer this comforting faith, the earthly variant of religious faith in the justice of a Supreme Being, who rewards people for sufferings endured in this vale of tears. The semimystical Tsar was replaced by the semimystical revolution. Its coming was like the fulfilment of the prophecy of the millennium. The peasants were ready to expect "a new heaven and a new earth, in which truth lives." This faith was above all a faith of sacrifice. At peasant gatherings, after speeches on nationalization of the land, the peasants were urged, before voting for it, to realize fully what it meant. When they were reminded that they themselves would no longer be full and unlimited owners of hereditary allotments (and in some cases of additional land which they had bought), indescribable scenes occurred. Suddenly the entire mass of browned, wind-burned, bearded faces blazed up with a kind of religious ecstasy in the presence of some Higher Truth, and leaping to their feet, the meeting burst into shouts: "We give it! We give our land! We give everything!" In this dream of the millennium the lion lay down with the lamb, and it was not surprising if in his thoughts the peasant parted with the noble "in a kindly way."

The second and more prosaic reason for the original "calm" was that there was at first almost no one in the village to carry out an agrarian revolution. The village youth, the adults, and the bearded elders with graying hair were at the front, in the trenches, or in the overcrowded rear garrisons. Farming was thrust on the old men, adolescents, and women. The emancipation of women by the revolution was prepared by their heroic rôle in wartime, when to their tremendous household work they manfully added all the heavy toil of the menfolk taken for the army. The peasant woman became the corner stone of labor and center of responsibility for the entire household. Till then the peasant woman had never taken any part in "politics." The youth of the village was not admitted to anything serious or responsible. The elders in general were disinclined to innovation and wished only to live out their lives by grandfather's rules. The depopulation of the village had deprived it of its usual political activeness. This factor was counteracted but gradually. The "men of forty" returned to the village from the front by a special decree of the government. "Men on leave" by petition of the village communes appeared. The deserters grew in numbers. Workers from factories closed by the owners sought a place in the village. Finally, the women became more active. The peasant woman was far slower than her husband in joining the revolution, but she brought to it a purely feminine passion and fanaticism.

The ebb of labor from the village had naturally slackened the peasants' land hunger. The peasantry had scarcely enough labor to cope with their own land. History granted the nobles a respite, but this was what ruined them. Feeling that the village was now only an onlooker in the urban revolution, and that there was no irresistible agrarian pressure against their property as at the beginning of the century, the gentry were filled with a hope of holding their positions if the new government aided them, and with a will to fight for them desperately.

But the village had no thought of foregoing its agrarian claims. Indeed, it was not so passive a witness of events as might seem. Through the soldiers who joined the revolution en masse and sent deputies to the Soviets the men of the village were taking active part in events. A huge majority among the "gray coats," the peasantry were no longer defenseless. The soldiers' "instructions" displayed the full demands of the agrarian revolution, usually more insistently, always more thoroughly, than those of the village. But if the peasants decided to postpone for a time the general question of a just land order, they still had their petty, daily questions which, however, shaped their life and work.

Since the lack of land had been overshadowed by lack of labor, great importance attached to a problem absolutely new in Russia's agrarian movement: the allotment of the prisoners of war. It touched to the quick the peasant woman, compelled to bear her own and her husband's burdens. The village was struck by this contrast: female, immature, adolescent, and aged organisms were bent, overstrained, and even crippled by work exhausting for the muzhik in the flower of his strength, while the gentry's farms were served by a bountiful supply of prisoners of war, often familiar with far superior farming methods. By paying these new "slaves" the miserly sum of three rubles a month, the gentry could regularly have thirty or fifty of them at work, getting their labor practically free and providing the most primitive maintenance. They frequently carried out various capital improvements on their estates not directly necessary. They dug ponds and built barns and houses. The war brought the village endless suffering; it gave the nobles fresh possibilities for economic improvement on a big scale. That was not all. The noble, provided with the unpaid servile labor of prisoners of war, became absolutely independent of the village. He could now do without the labor of the neighboring peasants, while they, as before, needed his woodlands, meadows, cattle runs, etc. The noble was formerly obliged willy-nilly to get along with the peasants, to wheedle them. Now he could squeeze them without fear.

From the villages there rose a single cry: it is wrong for the soldier's wife to overstrain herself, it is wrong for his lonely father to be rewarded for his labor by "a broken back or a rupture," while the noble, "the spoiled child" of old Russia, keeps all his great privileges in new Russia. Where is the justice of the new order, where is its popular character? The nobles possess their land unjustly, for not they but the peasants harvest it with their horny hands and water it with the sweat of their toil. Then let them hire harvesters at a real wage—they can afford it, but not the soldier's widow, the family burdened with "mouths" and poor in workers. At their meetings the peasants decided to set things right, to correct the oversight of the new government; how could it supervise everything from distant Petersburg? They appeared in crowds at the gentry's estates, "removed" the prisoners of war and assigned them to the households with the fewest hands, if the prisoners, the unwitting apple of discord, had not fled in fright. Incidentally, the more tumultuously the agrarian movement developed, the oftener the prisoners discovered and preferred a third way out: they joined the peasants in overwhelming the gentry who had been most expert in applying this "sweating system."

A new question appeared. The government demanded that the peasant should not leave unsown and unharvested a single square inch of soil. The cities and army were already pinched for grain and fodder. But the peasants' animal and mechanical equipment, always scanty, had fallen into complete decay during the war. Agricultural machinery, always an article of import, became unobtainable. The old equipment was worn out. How could the peasant but look with envy at the nobles' far superior equipment? In part to spare that equipment, in part because he was not especially attracted by fixed prices for wheat, the noble frequently left a portion of his fields unsown. Obviously, both animal and mechanical equipment of the gentry were far from completely utilized; many agricultural machines lay unused for long periods and the gentry's live stock could stand a considerable amount of extra work.

Why should that be? The government declares sowing the fields a national duty, an obligation to the state. Then it ought to furnish means to fulfil it. It is wrong to permit incomplete sowing on the neighboring estates of the gentry and failure to utilize to the full valuable modern farm equipment and first-class live stock. Exhausted by lack of adult labor, the peasants cried out ever louder, ever more confidently. The noble must not be allowed to leave his machinery unused; it must be inventoried by the local organs of government, and given to the peasants to use, for fair compensation. The same is true of the land which the owner cannot or will not cultivate. Under fixed prices for wheat, agriculture is at bottom a state obligation poorly rewarded by the government; hence the noble cannot be allowed to exact tribute, and far too high tribute, from the peasant for the opportunity to fulfil that duty on land rented from him. Rents must be lowered, for undoubtedly they have been artificially inflated by overcrowding on the land, by the constant growth of the population despite the inevitably backward technique of peasant farming.

All this had its iron logic for the peasants. Now they began to act, to establish, through their local organs of popular government, a new, just system of distributing the prisoners, to demand of each owner exact indication of the acreage he would sow, and to take the rest of his land for the temporary use of the commune, fixing a just price for it. They began to forestall abuses by the noble through fixing fines for nonfulfilment of his declared sowing and reaping program; to figure how to secure full use of the gentry's stock and equipment outside his farms, again for "a just payment." In cases of bad management they began to remove owners or managers and to appoint more suitable ones in the name of the local government body, and, in general, to lower rents and standardize wages of farmhands. When the gentry contested their right to standardize payment for use of their property, the peasants decreed that this disputable question should be left to the Constituent Assembly, and meanwhile the money should not be paid to the noble but deposited with the State Treasury. Since under the old régime the nobles had enjoyed the services of the peasants' organs of self-government (the county boards in registering contracts with peasants, the county courts in suing peasants for failure to fulfil obligations, etc.) without contributing to their maintenance, the peasants set about "restoring justice" by taxing the former privileged groups heavily to support the new organs of popular government.

In some places the nobles, reluctantly perhaps, realized the necessity for meeting the new demands halfway; otherwise they foresaw sharp conflicts and disturbances, without any means for resisting this tremendous, popular pressure. In such cases the two sides arrived at a more or less reasonable compromise.

But in an overwhelming majority of cases the gentry judged matters quite differently. They owned their estates, their live stock, and equipment. They lived under the protection of a code of laws which recognized their unlimited rights of ownership. They realized that the land code could be changed. But by whom? Of course, only by the Constituent Assembly. Even the Provisional Government, with its doubtful legal title, was not entitled to make such changes. That would represent the arbitrary power of a casual revolutionary oligarchy. But even if one might at a pinch recognize in some matters the competence of the Provisional Government, it was absolutely unreasonable to submit to arbitrary interference by some local organ of "popular government," crudely organized no one knew by whom or how. If the Provisional Government had not issued a new law on any question, a legislative "interregnum" was nonsense. The old, unrepealed law remained in force. All the committees and Soviets were bound to act within the limits of the old legislation, to observe it strictly, and to compel the entire local population to respect it. Otherwise, they themselves would be acting illegally and would be liable to prosecution.

The gentry had an iron logic of their own, based on formal law. It was the incarnate philosophy of Volume Ten of the Code of Laws, penetrated with the spirit of Roman Law, with its dogma of the sacred and intangible "Quiritean property," with its *jus utendi et abutendi.* To the peasant mind it was as alien as was to the gentry the peasant axiom: since the people have become master in the state, they have become the full and sole proprietor of *all the land.* The land, according to the muzhik, belonged to God or the Tsar: with the fall of the Tsar the people had become their own Tsar, and naturally entered into immediate control of all the land.

The birth of a new, revolutionary Russia had exposed this antagonism. It had to be solved. It could no longer be hid.

CHAPTER NINE

THE TRAGEDY OF THE RUSSIAN ARMY

THE crisis in the worlds of industry and agriculture was accompanied by another momentous crisis—that of the army.

When the revolution had taken place, and the so-called intensification of the revolution unleashed passions and brought to the surface all evil instincts, the result was the disintegration of the army, tragic in its grave consequences for the state; the army refused to fight, and influenced by criminal agitation, abandoned the front, exposing it to the foe, no longer impeded in his invasion of the country.

This version, formulated by Rodzianko, is widespread in certain quarters, and even claims to be the absolute and indisputable truth. When tested by fact, it must meet with the fate of Ludendorff's famous *Dolchstosslegende* in Germany: Germany was allegedly close to victory when the German socialists and pacifists began their revolutionary propaganda in the rear, "plunged a dagger into the back" of the victorious army, and brought Germany down in ruin.

Not one stone is left standing of either legend after investigation of the facts.

Even the point of departure for the Russian edition of this legend does not stand the test of fact. According to the official version, stated by General Lukomsky, at the beginning of the war "one felt that the entire population had been fused into a single whole, and in a universal outburst of enthusiasm wished to hurl itself on the enemy." However, General Lukomsky is obliged to add, in an aside: "It is true, in certain districts, at certain places in Siberia and on the Volga things went wrong with the mobilization, there were disorders (in Barnaul, in Siberia, even serious disorders)."[1] Obviously these "outbursts" were of a quite different character. What was it?

This question is answered by Maximov, in his *War Years.* Maximov was called to the colors from a village of Smolensk province. In addition, he had spent some time at the beginning of the war as farm-agent in Arkhangel, Vologda, and Volhynia districts. The cities, the middle and educated classes displayed a superficial, artificially inflated "chauvinist enthusiasm"; "the common people everywhere merely accepted the war, and not without murmuring." Everywhere Maximov heard the same reproachful, naïve, "primitively Tolstoyan" conversations:

"What devil has brought this war upon us? We are butting into other people's business."

"We have talked it over among ourselves: if the Germans want payment, it would be better to pay ten rubles a head—and in Russia there are so many millions of heads—than to kill people."

"Is it not all the same what Tsar we live under? It cannot be worse under the German one."

"Let them go and fight themselves. Wait a while, we will settle accounts with you."

"How about letting loose the red cock [peasant arson of landlords' mansions], as we did in 1905!"

Each year Maximov found "ever greater hatred and bitterness against the war." "Recruiting went on in a stern and gloomy atmosphere." At times the peasant women outdid everyone in antiwar feeling; those who were leading away their husbands, brothers, sons they pursued with wild shouts: "Curses on you all, all of you!"[2]

The author may, of course, be suspect as an antimilitarist in principle. Let us examine the recollections of Stankevich, who during the war absolutely rejected all pacifism and, as he put it, "preached participation in the war, not only with the body, but with all the forces of the mind." He makes the regretful confession: "In almost everybody one felt the war was something external, alien; the mass of Russian society never felt the war to be its own cause."[3]

Most convincing of all is the testimony of a man who has been thrown by the revolution into the monarchist camp, Nazhivin. He writes, in his *Notes on the Revolution:*

> In the villages everything was quiet, and we watched a new, extremely curious and edifying process, a kind of rebirth of the village. A new mobilization is declared; throughout the district the wailing of women and children rises; the reservists with their little bags and packages leave for the chief city of the province, and everything quiets down. *There was absolutely no patriotic surge:* the war was accepted because it had been ordered. But anyone would be a fool not to evade it if he could . . .
>
> One mobilization followed another, each more absurd, more senseless than the other . . . Then there burst on us a memorable mobilization in early September. The first and second class reservists had gone, men over forty, many gray-bearded. A groan went up from the villages. Excitement rose ominously. Everywhere new, audacious words were heard. "What does this mean, do they want to bury us all, to have more room for *them?*" Even in church the prayer for the "Most Pious, Most Autocratic Tsar" was interrupted by conscripts' bitter shouts. That, in reactionary, Old-Believer Vladimir province. It was clear: we were ready.

Of course, in other countries too the war was first felt acutely, especially by the villages, simply as a *misfortune,* and then later as an endless burden, as a senseless catastrophe. But in France, England, or Germany military and patriotic propaganda had been perfected, to mold the raw recruits from the provinces. In addition, the peaceful peasant, with no interest in politics, was not an overwhelming majority as in the Russian army. In Tsarist Russia no one bothered to create a great apparatus of propaganda; broadsides and pamphlets would be used by the illiterate soldier to roll cigarettes, and it was enough to shout at him with bravado, "Wheel to the right, attack, march!" In general, "in

Russia, from the first military action nothing was accomplished toward creating the psychology of a great war."[4]

As time went on, the army was more and more a sea "not of soldiers, but simply of muzhiks in gray army coats." These muzhiks had such an innate, naïve, good-natured love of peace, and displayed such primitivism of thought that the intelligentsia, which had "accepted the war," with horror called the Russian people politically the most backward in the world. "Here patriotism seems the monopoly of the cultivated classes of society," said one French diplomat in despair. At times it was like Tolstoy's famous story of the ideal "kingdom of fools," which met the enemy's invasion with offerings of bread and salt: "Why, dear friends, is it because land is scarce among you and you have nothing left to eat that you have set out so far loaded down with all kinds of weapons? So be it, we will divide with you, whatever we have we are glad to share. Why put upon our souls the sin of fighting and killing one another!"

No army, even the most brilliant, was absolutely guaranteed against disintegration, at times astonishingly swift. The methods of modern warfare taxed the "human material" to an extreme. Certain limits could not be passed with impunity. The question was, which people would reach these limits and how soon.

General Denikin perhaps more than anyone grew indignant over the decomposition of the Russian army and generously showered accusations in all directions. Even he recalls, however, how "in the autumn of 1918 the German corps, occupying the Don and Little Russia, disintegrated in a single week"; "they deposed their officers, and in some detachments sold military property, horses and weapons." He appropriately mentions that "fermentation in the army occurred among the victors as well: in the French troops occupying Rumania and the Odessa districts early in 1919, in the French fleet in the Black Sea, in the English troops sent to Constantinople and Transcaucasia, and even in the powerful

English fleet . . . Troops were beginning to disobey, and only *rapid demobilization* and recruitment of fresh, partly voluntary forces saved the situation." The sixth volume of Poincaré's memoirs presents many similar facts, such as the firing upon General Dubail's automobile by his own men.

The Russian army was subjected to these processes of disintegration earlier than the others and hence "swift demobilization" could not save it. This is the heart of the matter, not alleged experimenting with the army by the revolution and particularly by the Provisional Government in defiance of all needs of military science.

Military writers from among the old, prerevolutionary officers, like General Denikin, are anxious to prove that the army was disintegrated by the revolution. They are forced to close their eyes to the crying facts of the army's decomposition prior to the revolution. "Even before the revolution there were one or two cases in which individual units refused to obey; they were sternly suppressed." That is General Denikin's only tribute to an unpleasant truth.

The correspondence of the Minister of War, Sukhomlinov, with the first chief of staff of the commander in chief, General Yanushkevich, paints a far more serious picture. By November, 1914, the third month of the war, Yanushkevich reports with alarm that on the northwestern front "Ruzsky and his assistants have suddenly lost faith in their troops," and a "bad spirit" has grown up, the conviction that "nothing can be done." In December he raises a great alarm:

> Wherever the officers have been killed off, surrenders en masse have begun, sometimes at the initiative of the sublieutenants. "Why should we die of hunger and cold, without boots. Our artillery is silent, while the Germans are potting us like partridges. It is better among the Germans. Let's go!" Cossacks, who by their attack recovered five hundred prisoners, were roundly cursed: "Who the devil asked you to do that? We don't want to starve and freeze again." It is true that these are unfortunate cases, but they are significant. That is why I am so hysterical.

Thus began the tragic era of the Russian army. The artillery suddenly had no shells. In the rear the soldiers drilled with sticks in place of guns. Even front-line battalions had to wait for the weapons of the dead to be gathered from the battlefield. "My hair stands on end," wrote Yanushkevich, "at the thought that for lack of cartridges and rifles we shall have to submit to Wilhelm."

We also have General Kuropatkin's wartime diaries. As early as December, 1914, he notes that "they are all hungry for peace" and "are not fighting so very well." "There were disgusting cases: whole battalions, instead of counterattacking, came up to the German trenches and raised their weapons in token of surrender. They were weary of the hardships of war." Next year he wrote: "About the army, the most discouraging news. They do not blame the lower ranks, but point to the ease with which they surrender." "The lack of cartridges, of munitions, the enemy's obvious superiority predispose the cowardly to surrender, sometimes in entire units."

The commander of the Special Corps of Gendarmes, General Dzhunkovsky, on February 13, 1915, reported to headquarters how two squadrons of German cavalry had caused "an indescribable panic" in the Fifty-sixth Infantry Division during its withdrawal to Verzhbolovo: "The first to run were the officers, the soldiers fled after them; some scattered over the near-by fields, others surrendered without resisting and were driven by a handful of dismounted Germans (forty men, chiefly boys) into the third-class waiting room and locked up there till morning."

Does this signify that the human material of the Russian army was low in quality? Nothing of the kind. Prussian military opinions of the Russian soldiers at the beginning of the war, as collected by General Golovin,[5] leave no possible doubt. The Russians were "naturally good soldiers," "brave, stubborn, adaptable to terrain"; they were excellent marksmen and artillery men; wherever they were well supplied, their stubborn resistance wore down the best German corps like Mackensen's famous Seventeenth; his soldiers, "who throughout the rest of the war showed extraordinary valor," now "reached the limit of their moral strength after being engaged for only a few hours." The same was true of the commanders of the Seventy-first Brigade, of the Fifth Grenadiers, of the One Hundred Twenty-eighth Regiment, and others. "Hell seemed to open out before them"; "a hurricane of fire burst forth"; there was raised up "an invisible wall of fire"; "the regiment very soon reports that its forces are exhausted." The impressions of the battle are "overwhelming," miracles of valor are fruitless, "until panic overcomes the strongest discipline, the discipline of the East Prussian regiments." Even when victory inclines to the Germans, in that first period of the war, the fault is not with the Russian soldier. "The battlefield, littered with Russian dead, shows how great were the Russian losses, and how bravely they fought."[6] To reduce an army of such soldiers to a state of complete demoralization requires a succession of defeats, creating a sense of hopelessness.

What was the cause of the defeats? Strategy. The Russian high command began with a fatal and irreparable mistake. It undertook an offensive "when only one third of its military force was ready," like a man who, "instead of dealing a blow with his fist, snaps each finger in turn." These strategically ignorant, adventurous enterprises sacrificed the finest flower of the prewar army, the cadres for the other two thirds of the army, for the reservists, who, left to themselves, lost a considerable part of their potential fighting value. "A philosophy of strategy, amounting to the simple formula, 'push ahead,'" obsolete methods of calculating strength which reckoned the relation of our forces to the German as 76:70, when, in fact, it was 15:24, and a whole series of similar "strategic crimes" made "the account of the 1914 campaign the history of the reckoning for the strategic errors of the war plan."[7]

Nothing need be said of the 1915 campaign. During the literal extermination of the Russian army, practically disarmed by exhaustion of its munition supply, Paléologue blasphemously refers to the "very valuable coöperation" of the Russian front in the Allied cause, for, at the price of self-extermination, the Russian army was diverting fifty-two enemy corps. Why? In order that all might be "quiet on the western front," aside from the capture and recapture of that "ferryman's house," which became famous throughout the world.

"The struggle," writes Paléologue, "is carried on with an energy worthy of the highest praise. Each battle is for the Russian troops a monstrous massacre . . . The Russian people is enduring these fearful sacrifices without murmuring."

But endurance may have an end. Then it becomes an explosion of blind, senseless rage.

Nineteen sixteen marks a fresh effort, the next to the last, of the Russian front to be the hammer, not the anvil. The army's technical resources have been increased by the country's universal effort. But the final result is the same. After that, is there ground for surprise if Rodzianko was forced to admit: "However strange that may seem, the fermentation in the army in 1916 began with the victorious battles, since the conviction had taken shape that all the fighters' superhuman efforts and sacrifices were at bottom fruitless because of unfortunate and clumsy orders."

There is one sure test of an army's state: desertion.

The Minister of War, General Sukhomlinov, continually drew headquarters' attention to the threatening growth of desertion. "Reports of units of privates wandering in the army's rear arrive continually. Major General Bolotov has personally observed cases of marauding; such a mass of men has broken away from their units that in the army's immediate rear whole units could be formed."

During the last months of the Tsarist régime special units

of military police had to be established at railroad junctions. For capturing deserters there was a special reward "per head": for a private 7 kopecks, for a corporal 9 kopecks, for a junior noncommissioned officer 11 kopecks, for a senior 14, for a sublieutenant 25 kopecks. The ridiculously low rewards were fully compensated for by the abundance of prey. By the beginning of 1917 it was reckoned that there were one and a half million deserters in Russia.

On visiting the front early in 1915, Guchkov brought back the discouraging news that the soldiers were going hungry, there was a complete crisis in artillery, "the loss in infantry, especially of officers, was tremendous." Toward the end of 1915 he made a brief summary of the initial period of the war: Russia had begun the war with five million soldiers, had already lost about four million; of 6,000 field guns the army had lost 2,000, together with 2,000 fortress guns. The field officers had displayed much heroism, but "on top things were bad." The privates "had begun the war with enthusiasm, now they were weary and had lost faith in victory because of incessant retreat."

At a cabinet meeting on July 16, 1915, the portentous words were first uttered by the Minister of War, General Polivanov: "I consider it my civil and official duty to declare to the Council of Ministers that the fatherland is in danger." "Our retreat is proceeding with growing rapidity, in many cases it is almost a panicky flight." "Through their enormous superiority in artillery and munitions, the Germans are compelling us to retreat by artillery fire alone. Because of this . . . the enemy suffers scarcely any losses, while our men perish by thousands." "The troops are undoubtedly wearied by the incessant defeats and retreat. *Faith in ultimate victory and in their leaders has been undermined:* more and more ominous signs of approaching *demoralization* are noticeable. Cases of desertion and of voluntary surrender are becoming more frequent. Yes, and it would be difficult to expect enthusiasm and self-sacrifice from people thrown into the line of battle without weapons and ordered to pick up the rifles of their dead comrades." "Growing perplexity is to be observed at the headquarters of the commander in chief. No system, no plan is to be seen in its actions, in its orders. Not a single bold and thought-out maneuver, not a single attempt to utilize the errors of an emboldened enemy. Back, back, back, that is all we hear from there . . . No initiative is allowed. Not one senior commander knows where and why he is moved . . . 'Be silent' and 'do not discuss' are headquarters' favorite barking commands."

At the following session, on July 24, this picture was supplemented by the Minister of War. "In some places disorders have broken out among recruits and in local garrisons . . . The generals are beginning to concern themselves more with internal politics, trying to divert attention and transfer responsibility to other shoulders." The Council of Ministers referred with bitter irony to the "evacuation and refugee period of military action." On August 4, the Minister of the Interior declared: "I must point out that each time the recruiting gets worse. The police are unable to cope with the mass of slackers. People hide in woods and unreaped wheat." Because of this, the minister was willing to drop the early dissolution of his hated Imperial Duma: "If people learn that the summons of the second category of reservists is being executed without the Duma's sanction, I fear that, in the present state of feeling, *we shall not get a single man.*" On August 16, in connection with headquarters' plans to evacuate by force an area of one hundred versts behind the front, the Minister of War reported: "The army staffs have lost the capacity to judge and understand their actions. They are living in a kind of madness." When asked whence salvation was to be expected, the Minister of War could make only the truly classical reply: "I place my trust in the impassable distances, the impenetrable mud, and the grace of our intercessor, St. Nicholas of Mirlikia, protector of Holy Russia." No franker admission of bankruptcy could have been made.

Had this occurred after the February Revolution, what a shout would have been raised by all the military and semi-military patriots of the old school! But under the autocracy the unvarnished truth did not go beyond the four walls of the cabinet. Hence the entire monarchic press and the nationalist-liberal press can even now revel in the countless virtues of the Tsarist army and the pitiful downfall of the revolutionary army. Facts, however, prove beyond cavil that the revolution inherited from the autocracy an army lacking trained cadres, unstrung, demoralized, and long since hopeless of ultimate victory, with no faith in its commanders or even in itself.

What were the causes of the army's lamentable state?

The first cause lay in the complete bankruptcy of the *military theory* of the leaders of the Tsarist army.

The man who was perhaps most fateful for the Russian army and the outcome of the war, General Sukhomlinov, a man of astounding frivolity and intellectual laziness, had the audacity to say at a professors' meeting of the Military Academy that he "could not even listen calmly to the words, '*modern warfare.*' As warfare has been, so it has remained. All these things are pernicious innovations. Take me, for instance; for twenty-five years I have not read a single military book." The people around him were of the same stamp. The words "firing tactics" they still regarded as heresy. They were all the deafer to the prophecy of military science that the next war would become, above all, "a struggle of cannon and machine fire." In the twentieth century they still repeated Suvorov's eighteenth-century aphorism that "the bullet is a fool, the bayonet a brave fellow."[8]

The best Russian military writer abroad, General Golovin, after careful analysis, concludes that the Russian general staff had no military doctrine of its own, but merely tried to copy the Germans or French. These attempts, not adapted to the peculiarities of its own forces and environment, inevitably remained lifeless scholasticism. Russian actions in East Prussia betray "our general staff's lack of preparation to carry on large-scale strategic operations," "the strategic phantasticality" which did "everything to make our troops suffer defeat."[9]

A fatal consequence of strategic illiteracy was countless error in preparation. Russia began the war with 850 charges per gun, while in Germany the standard of 3,000 was surpassed. Despite all warnings Russian fortresses were to the very end built on the old system, and doomed by modern gun fire "to be transformed rapidly into a heap of ruins." As the commander in chief, Grand Duke Nicholas, put it, our armies were forced "to beat off attack practically with their bare hands." The general staff failed to foresee either the probable duration of the war or its fundamental character. "Only a very few of the military authorities admitted the possibility of its lasting more than a year"; the majority of them thought it would be over "within six to nine months."[10] The eloquent experience of the Russo-Japanese War, one of sieges and position, was ignored; that was a colonial war, the forms and methods of which had no significance for serious warfare. "The possibility of a war of position on the western front was denied absolutely"; it was expected to offer "purely field warfare with separate sectors of position." A continuous fortified front from the Baltic to the Black Sea "was not admitted by anyone as possible, and could not even be imagined."

The second cause of the army's decline was the frightful state of its armament and equipment.

The World War brought many "new words" in military technique. First place here belongs to poison gas and tanks. There was also a colossal development of military aviation and the most extensive use of heavy artillery, not only to besiege and defend fortresses, but to destroy trenches and barbed-wire fortifications; that is, to prepare for the attack. And, finally, the complicated system of trench construction, with its communications, with the preparation of concentration points for the attack; that is, the tremendous development of field fortifications.

In all these innovations the old Russian army was taken unawares. It had no coal-gas collectors. Gas production had to be organized from the ground up. Eventually a well-known military chemist, General Ipatiev, accomplished this brilliantly, but Russia's inevitable backwardness had been very harmful to the front. Tanks "could not be produced in our own factories: in all, twelve were turned out, pitiful semblances of tanks, unfit for battle."[11] On the average the Germans had 12 heavy guns per army corps, the Russians 1 unit of heavy artillery to 3 or 4 corps. The Germans also had the upper hand in other types of artillery: 112 light guns and 26 howitzers per corps as against 96 and 12 for the Russians. In general, the Russians had 3½ guns to a battalion, the Germans 7. But these figures give a very incomplete idea of the enemy's technical superiority. As early as December 15, 1914, headquarters warned the front to economize on shells, for the first battles had used up all the supply considered sufficient for the entire war.[12] One must realize what this meant in practice. General Denikin describes the struggle near Przemysl in the middle of May, 1915.

> Eleven days of frightful thundering by the German heavy artillery literally blew up whole rows of trenches with their defenders. We scarcely returned the fire: there was *nothing* to reply with. The regiments, utterly fagged out, beat off one attack after another with their bayonets or rifles, blood poured, ranks thinned, mountains of graves grew . . . Two regiments were practically annihilated . . . by gunfire alone . . . Messieurs the French and the English! You, who have attained unprecedented levels of technique will be interested in this absurd fact drawn from Russian reality: when after a three days' silence, our only six-inch battery received fifty shells, this news was immediately telephoned to all regiments, all companies, and all our soldiers breathed a deep sigh of joy and relief.[13]

General Golovin reports the engagement of the Revel

Regiment near Turau, with a loss of more than 75%. General Verkhovsky saw people go mad on the battlefield, so "shattering was the impression" of "the enemy's obvious superiority," so profoundly "was the soul oppressed by the feeling of utter defenselessness." His diary is dotted with such entries: "We scarcely see the enemy's infantry, it has nothing to do, for the fiery waterspout of the artillery solves all the German's problems quickly and simply. With gnashing of teeth, with silent suffering in its heart, our army draws back, harboring in its soul its indignation toward those who brought on us such humiliation and helplessness."[14] The Russian airplanes were inadequate even for ordinary reconnaissance, while the Germans used them as a regular means to correct their murderous fire. To this must be added "the miserable equipment for communication, the almost complete lack of field radios, the pitiful supply of telegraph equipment." General Lechitsky summed it up: "We are wild, stupid people. We have just come out of the woods. When will we learn to fight?"

The third cause of the army's discouragement was the low level of its commanders. Here there is and can be no room for disagreement.

No revolutionary could have written a more appalling description of the army's condition than that drawn from the correspondence of the Minister of War, Sukhomlinov, with the chief of staff of the commander in chief, Yanushkevich. Names flash by. There is General Lukomsky, who "is trampling under his untidy feet" a most important branch—military supply. There is General Kaulbars, who "without fail ruins whatever he touches." There is Prince Oldenburg, nicknamed "muddlehead pasha." Others the rulers of the army call "irresponsible people," with "sclerotic heads," who commit the "most frightful stupidities." For others "the gallows are too good," but they continue to occupy very important posts. About others Yanushkevich philosophizes: "In times like these people with sick minds should not be given such responsible work—why, by spring a catastrophe may strike the entire country because of this." At a secret session of the committee of ministers Sazonov said of General Yanushkevich himself: "His presence at headquarters is more dangerous than the German armies." Yanushkevich and Sukhomlinov realized that in many cases "the heads of the guilty must be pounded," excepting themselves of course from among the culprits. "A house cleaning must be carried out from above," they resolved in alarm, as if sensing that in time the soldiers themselves might begin the house cleaning from below, wholesale and without fine distinction, punishing the just with the guilty.

With dread they expected a "catastrophe throughout the country" by the spring of 1915. And the surprising thing was not that it finally came, but that it did not occur until two years later.

In 1916, at the April and December conferences at headquarters, the front commanders summarized the general situation. They reported "complete disorganization in Petrograd," the "universal opinion that we had everything, but could secure nothing" (General Ruzsky); "insufficient transport, hence insufficient provisioning, which depresses the spirits" (General Evert); disorganization of transport (General Gurko); "impossibility of coping with a colossus of twelve million people, to be fed by the state" (General Shuvayev); growing frequency of riots among the troops, both spontaneous ones due both to economic causes (Evert) and to war-weariness or propaganda (General Ruzsky, General Brusilov). It was asked what measures should be taken against each of these defects; General Shuvayev replied pessimistically that it was not a matter of "taking measures" as in ordinary disorders, but that it was high time "to take account of reality."

The higher generals lacked the moral courage for that. Even officers like Rodzianko's son, recommended by his father as "calm and well balanced" (no question of his devotion to the monarchy), fell into profound despair, and, in spite of improvement in the supply of guns and munitions, appealed to his father:

> You must inform the Emperor that it is a crime to kill off people so uselessly . . . Everyone in the army feels that without cause matters have taken a turn for the worse; the men are magnificent, we have munitions and guns to spare, but the generals lack brains. It is also too bad we have no airplanes. No one trusts headquarters or his immediate commanders. All this may end in embitterment and breakdown. We are ready to die for the fatherland, but not for the generals' caprice. During battle they usually stay in safe places, seldom appear on the firing line, while we die. Both privates and officers think that unless this system is changed, we cannot win. This must be realized.[15]

Finally, the future hero of the first counterrevolutionary (Kornilov) movement, General Krymov, during a special trip to Petrograd with a large group of officers, declared:

> Things cannot go on any longer like this. Because of the complete lack of continuity in orders and of a carefully elaborated plan, because of careless appointments to the highest posts in the army, our brilliant successes have been nullified; among the soldiers distrust of the officers as a whole and of their immediate commanders in particular is growing; *the army is gradually disintegrating*, and discipline is threatened by complete decline. It may easily happen under such conditions that the soldiers will refuse to advance, and, what is most horrible, under the influence of a criminal agitation, which no one is combatting or can stop, this winter the army may simply abandon the trenches and the battlefield. Such is the ominous and continually growing feeling among the troops.

In truth, could there be any other feeling? "Why, only by the blood of this cannon fodder," wrote General Verkhovsky, "have we endured three years of war. How could confidence have been created?" "Only heroic measures to renew the greater part of the commanding body could help." "From certain units," he noted on December 8, 1916, three months before the revolution, "we have heard a definite and alarming murmur: we will defend ourselves, but will not attack."[16]

To complete this picture of the army's decay under the Tsarist régime, we must refer to one other source of disintegration, the disciplinary methods used by the officers toward the soldiers, methods unthinkable in the army of a civilized country, methods proper to the worst Asiatic despotisms, degrading the soldier and trampling his self-respect in the dirt. "Crudeness and cursing were frequent, sometimes stupid and wilful abuse," admits Denikin in an aside. That was not all. In 1915 flogging was officially introduced. An effort was made to combat "finger wounds" by the *death penalty*. Denikin tries to justify crude physical discipline by the low level of the privates and the death penalty by the inefficacy of other methods of combating desertion: the danger of losing one's life at the front was surpassed only by the danger of the firing squad. One thing is clear: when the mass of soldiers has lost all faith in its commanders, to empower the latter to inspire that faith by flogging and the firing squad is only pouring oil on the fire. It feeds the flames of vengeful bitterness and mutual hatred, and leads directly to merciless extermination of the officers by the soldiers. It is ridiculous to point to "subversive propaganda of elements alien to the army," when the most powerful agitator among the soldiers is the action of their commanders. He who soweth the wind reapeth the whirlwind.

CHAPTER TEN

THE PROVISIONAL GOVERNMENT

WE left the Provisional Government at the moment when Prince Lvov, its president, appointed by the Tsar himself, was announcing the make-up of his ministry, and the able Tsarist minister, Krivoshein, in rueful perplexity, pronounced it too far to the Right, and hence dangerous not only for the revolution, so alien to him, but even for his cherished fatherland.

Indeed, the cabinet was obviously an anachronism. As early as August 13, 1915, the newspaper of the leader of the progressive industrialists, Ryabushinsky, had published a list of the proposed "cabinet of defense," with the familiar figures of the future Provisional Government: Miliukov, Guchkov, Shingarev, Nekrasov, Konovalov, V. N. Lvov, Yefremov, and its future Ambassador in Paris, Maklakov. Their cabinet was to contain Tsarist bureaucrats acceptable to public opinion: Krivoshein as Minister of Agriculture, General Polivanov for War, Count Ignatiev for Education. Since such a ministry needed a head who would link the "civic leaders" with the officials, Rodzianko was proposed as prime minister instead of Prince Lvov. As we see, there was not much difference between the two. Instead of having to provide for three bureaucrats, the main group had to make room for a "hostage" of revolutionary democracy. Maklakov yielded the Ministry of Justice to Kerensky; Shingarev exchanged Finance for Agriculture, giving Finance to Tereshchenko who had suddenly come into prominence. In the Ministry of Education the main group was strengthened by a Cadet, Professor Manuilov, while Guchkov, instead of Internal Affairs, took the War and Navy. Internal Affairs went to Prince Lvov, who also became premier. The living bond with the court and officialdom, Rodzianko, was now unnecessary. That was all.

In this list three men stood out: Miliukov, Kerensky, and Lvov.

P. N. Miliukov was the real inspiration of the Progressive Bloc in the Imperial Duma and creator of the strategy of the Cadet party.

A man of many-sided education, a superior scholar in his special field, with a fine and flexible mind, well balanced and calm, more the lecturer than the apostle of a political creed, Miliukov also had a decided taste for political life, the will to power and the discipline of a well-trained professional fighter. He had another quality of special value for a political leader: he was not discouraged by failure, he accepted defeat philosophically, and like a true sportsman he bore from each defeat unshaken faith in the possibility of *revanche*, and zest in preparing for it. He had many qualities which go to make a really great political leader, almost all the qualities—except one or two. His chief weakness was a complete lack of feeling for popular, mass psychology. He was too much a man of the study, hence, a doctrinaire. The studious side of his nature had been moderated by the long schooling of parliamentary life and struggle, which had taught him to swim with ease in the whirlpool of parliamentary combinations, to manage the backstage manipulation of the changing feelings and tendencies of the Duma semicircle, that peculiar little world, which, in Russia more than elsewhere, was isolated, protected against the pressure of the street. He never spoke the language of the people, the worker, the peasant, the soldier. For him it was a tremendous and alien force, the "faceless object of the activity" of the real leaders, who, for him, were statesmen and legislators. A typical parliamentarian, he was a splendid mediator between disputing parties, a creator of compromises, of elastic formulæ which rubbed out contradiction, smoothed away sharp corners, made verbal concessions that did not prevent him from putting through his own program. He possessed a high degree of caution, of nicety in choosing his moment to act, of ability to wait patiently for a favorable situation, economizing his strength and not overexerting it in struggling against the current. While remaining at heart a doctrinaire, he elevated into a dogma in itself the art of tacking, of discovering flank attacks and the line of least resistance. For this very reason he was meant for quiet, normal times, when life follows deep, well-trodden paths, not breaking virgin soil recklessly, not for times when irrational popular passions rage, when the entire situation changes constantly, when mighty subterranean shocks overthrow the most magnificent constructions like a house of cards.

Miliukov's chief antagonist within the Provisional Government, A. F. Kerensky, was an absolutely different type. His nature had an organic force of its own, a certain impetuosity, impressionability, unquiet searching. Both men were ambitious, as behooves politicians. But in contrast to the coldly calculating Miliukov, who knew what he wanted and plotted his path beforehand, Kerensky lived by the imagination, and his imagination was capricious. Miliukov lived by reason, Kerensky trusted intuition. He filled his sails with the breath of his own restless fantasy, letting it bear him where it would. His speech was extravagant, hyperbolic, and turgid, sometimes to the point of paroxysm. Unlike Miliukov's retarded political pulse, Kerensky's pulse beat feverishly. He was neurasthenic, and at times he came very close to a genuine hysteria. Leaders of the crowd must be flesh of its flesh, they must be infected and infect others with the resistless force of passion. Such leaders are often born actors, consciously or unconsciously seeking the way to the hearts of people around them by theatrical words and gestures. There was a good deal of this acting in Kerensky; he poured out his secret and profound spiritual being in visibly artificial forms.

In Miliukov everything was stable, settled, systematized. In Kerensky everything was illogical, contradictory, changing, often capricious, imagined, or feigned. Miliukov looked down on most people with whom he had to deal; this self-appraisal was so profound that it never appeared on the surface, never offended the sight or ear. Kerensky was tormented by the need to believe in himself, and was always winning or losing that faith. To maintain it, he required the obeisance of those who surrounded him and a sharp, insolent demonstration of his superiority to anyone who dared contest, doubt, or remain indifferent to it. Miliukov could refer to himself in the third person. Kerensky always abused the personal pronoun. Miliukov was inspired by the complicated combination of his own political trajectory with those of important political luminaries whom he encountered or who followed in his path. Kerensky demanded obedient "fellow travelers," revolving about him, whom he could manipulate as he wished and abuse roundly in moments of ill feeling. It was hard for him to endure the presence of great and independent characters, he felt freer with nonentities around him. But he possessed a remarkable power of suggestion, an indomitable energy and capacity for spiritual soaring. In his best moments he could communicate to the crowd tremendous shocks of moral electricity; he could make it laugh and cry, kneel and soar, swear and repent, love and hate to the point of self-oblivion, for he himself surrendered to the emotion of the moment with complete self-forgetfulness. Miliukov was infinitely superior to Kerensky in mind, equally inferior in elemental impetuosity. As moral and psychological types, they were antipodes. Miliukov the politician and publicist fenced with Kerensky playfully, condescendingly, like a master with a fiery novice, but he was on his guard, as if suspecting that this untaught boy might suddenly throw aside the clumsy rapier and snatch a bomb from his pocket. Kerensky sometimes tried to treat Miliukov haughtily, as a liberal phrase-maker, not a man of action; secretly he bowed before a certain strength in him, which, despite its strangeness, im-

KERENSKY (CENTER) AS MINISTER OF JUSTICE IN THE PROVISIONAL GOVERNMENT

From Soviet Russia in Its Early Years. *A collection of photographs presented to the New York Public Library*

posed respect and forced him intellectually to "draw in his horns."

Having practiced his diplomatic talents in the Duma corridors and in party conflicts, Miliukov felt himself called to transfer them from the microcosm of parliamentary politics to the macrocosm of international policy. He could not picture any completion of his life path except as Minister of Foreign Affairs, creator of the foreign policy of new Russia. He worked zealously, preparing himself for that task. Kerensky felt he was destined to become the "soul" of the revolution, "the uncrowned king" of the minds and hearts of a Russia aroused by the upsurge of renewal, the man who, without compulsion, voluntarily, would be raised aloft and told: Lead us! show us the path! As for his concrete rôle in building the new life, being a dilettante by nature, he evidently left the choice of that to inspiration and postponed it till the last minute.

The third prominent member of the Provisional Government was Prince George Lvov. He was third, but should have been first, as head of the government. He was thrust to the fore by Miliukov, to counteract another candidate, Rodzianko, for Miliukov naturally assumed that under Lvov he would find it easier to be the real leader. In contrast to the not very clever, but stubborn and flighty Rodzianko, Lvov was gentle, tactful, and courteous. He was clever, but not conceited He had behind him a long life of public activity. He had earned universal respect by fidelity to his work and his people. As against Miliukov, he was less involved in party quarrels; indeed, he would have been an ideal figurehead for a moderately progressive cabinet in normal bourgeois times with a clever pilot like Miliukov. Prince Lvov, at bottom, was an enlightened conservative. He and Miliukov might perfectly well have been the Right and Left views of a single political visage. But Lvov had to lead the government at a time when the life of the country had been rudely turned upside down. And he continually felt the strong psychological pressure of Kerensky, who, in his eyes, was something of an oracle, through whose lips he seemed to hear the unknown but invincible external element, revolution.

Prince Lvov whimsically combined the new stirrings of revolution with the Slavophil ferment of moderate Russian liberalism, penetrated by nationalist ideology with its peculiar Great Russian Messianism. In his speech of April 27 he said: "The great Russian Revolution is truly miraculous in its majestic, calm advance. . . . The freedom of the Russian Revolution is world wide, universal in character. The soul of the Russian people is a world-wide democratic soul by its very nature. It is ready not only to fuse with the democracy of the entire world, but to go before and lead it along the path of human development under the great principles of liberty, equality, and fraternity." This somewhat diffuse and vague idealism of the first revolutionary premier reversed normal relations between him and Miliukov: the strictly realistic, even drily positivist mind of the latter, in its prosaicness yielding no whit to the economic materialists of the socialist camp, could only be shocked by this amalgam of nationalist Messianism and revolutionary internationalism. Prince Lvov, at bottom more conservative than Miliukov, was now farther to the Left. Soon after the Provisional Government had split into two camps, Lvov with Kerensky and two young ministers, Tereshchenko and Nekrasov, who had pinned their faith on him, was in the group which removed Miliukov from the Ministry of Foreign Affairs although it was to him more than to anyone else that Lvov owed his premiership. Later, Miliukov did not conceal his regret at having preferred Lvov to Rodzianko.

Rodzianko, a big landowner, officer of the Cavalier Guards, president of the nobility and courtier, page, then Kammerherr, a massive figure with the voice of stentor, was colorful, imposing, portly, authoritative, and self-assured, like all people of remarkable height and imposing voice. He had a strong dose of stubbornness and majestic patriarchal narrowness. Witte jokingly remarked that Rodzianko's chief and undoubted merit as a statesman was his excellent bass. The fact that the government preferred to do without him was to him an added excuse for imagining that he had been placed *above* the government. After Grand Duke Michael had mentioned in his manifesto—or rather in the manifesto prepared for him—that the power of the Provisional Government was derived from the Provisional Committee of members of the Imperial Duma, Rodzianko became confirmed in his pose and psychology of "progenitor." He assumed that the Provisional Committee had not exhausted its rôle in creating the Provisional Government, by consent of the Soviet of Workers' and Soldiers' Deputies. This government was merely a ministry which might resign; then power would revert to its original source, to the Provisional Committee, and to its president, Rodzianko. According to this idea, the members of the Provisional Committee were actually a kind of "sovereign rulers." Unfortunately for Rodzianko, Prince Lvov, Kerensky, and the others immediately turned their backs on the institution which had created their government, or rather they tossed it aside like a ladder, once useful, but now in the way. Unfortunately for him, the country also turned its back. Rodzianko began to cherish the idea of convoking the Imperial Duma to serve provisionally as a parliament for the new Russia. But the Provisional Government had no intention of convoking it, while the Duma, which had submitted to dissolution by the Tsar, plainly could not meet against its will. Then Rodzianko thought of convoking all four successive Dumas, an absolutely absurd enterprise from the legal viewpoint, for each Duma canceled the powers of its predecessors. Miliukov personified the reason of censitary Russia, Rodzianko its prejudices, Lvov its harmless dreaming.

The first Provisional Government lasted but two months and failed to justify any of the expectations placed in it.

Of course, many extenuating circumstances could be of
fered on its behalf. Its problems were unusually complex
Wartime conditions confused their solution still more. Th
prevalent conceptions of Russian censitary society, by thei
narrowness and class limitations, were a hindrance in under
standing some of them. But even in questions in which th
leaders of the Duma Progressive Bloc possessed indisputabl
competence, the government displayed a truly mysteriou
capacity for endless delay.

There was, first of all, the problem of local self-govern
ment. The zemstvo had always been the palladium of Russia
liberalism, the elementary school, the foundation for Rus
sia's democratic order. No one could allege lack of prepara
tion here. In addition, after the First Imperial Duma th
Cadet party had adopted a method which many people ha
then ridiculed, but the fruits of which might come in hand
now; it had prepared various drafts of laws, including on
on local government. On a question like county governmen
on a casteless basis, many thoroughgoing drafts had bee
provided still earlier by progressive sections of educated sc
ciety. From some source or other the Provisional Govern
ment could have taken a ready-made draft, and thus ac
quired those new organs of local authority, without which i
was doomed to helplessness, constantly making decisions bu
without the means to enforce them. The revolution ha
created an interregnum in the provinces. The old bureau
cratic apparatus had been swept away or paralyzed by uni
versal boycott. Anarchy could be avoided in one of two way
As in the French Revolution, monarchical centralizatio
might be replaced at once by even more vigorous and merci
less revolutionary centralization, by covering the countr
with a network of revolutionary commissars endowed wit
dictatorial powers. Or the new structure of a democrati
order could be begun from below, by creating ready-mad
forms of a new organic and harmonious order, based on elec
tion and broad local autonomy. Neither way was chosen.

For the first way, the government of censitary democracy lacked determination and confidence. Since by its very idea it was a provisional, multiple dictator, it lacked that intensity of will and audacity which produce genuine dictators. It was even less capable of intrusting dictatorial power to commissars dispatched to the provinces. The Minister of Internal Affairs, Prince Lvov, did order all governors and land captains deposed and replaced by provincial and district presidents of zemstvo administrations. But these favorites of the old zemstvos were almost always local gentry, members of the class least able to find its bearings in the new situation. They were a variegated mixture of all the prerevolutionary zemstvo tendencies, even including typical "die-hards." Selected for economic and administrative activity, even the best were seldom able with firm hand to lead the local population into the new conditions, to guide them in elaborating the forms of a new revolutionary system of law. In many regions these presidents of zemstvo administrations were so repugnant to the people that no one took their appointments seriously. Others, astounded by the new mission suddenly set them, went to Petrograd, to the Ministry of Internal Affairs, expecting to receive uniform instructions. They were told that this was a sign of the "old psychology," that questions must "be solved not by the central government, but by the people," and that "the commissars of the Provisional Government, sent to the provinces, were not to stand above the local organs, but merely to connect them with the central government and to facilitate the process of organizing them." Thus the country was covered, not with a network of hierarchically subordinate agents of the central government, but with a network of advisors, instructors, and informing agents.

As for creating some new local authority from below, the Provisional Government, with typical complaisance and trust, left that to life. In some places zemstvo and city dumas and administrations were hastily supplemented by representatives of the broader and more democratic public: sometimes by representatives of the "Soviets," sometimes by elected delegates from trade-unions, coöperative organizations, from the most diverse groups and in most varied and arbitrary proportions. Elsewhere, the old zemstvos, dumas and administrations were merely empowered, like other centers of public activity, to contribute representatives to special "committees of popular government." Again, they were declared "annulled." The result was an extremely variegated and disorderly picture. One was struck by the lack of any rational or logical juridical principles. In some localities two centers of government were created simultaneously by different methods; they then disputed each other's powers and even arrested each other. Such conditions occasionally favored the personal dictatorship of an ambitious adventurer. "Committees of popular government," "public committees," "executive committees," and others with no less resounding titles appeared arbitrarily, organized no one knew how, with varying radii of action, and no harmonious system of subordination or delimitation of power. The pressure of some and the conciliatoriness of others alone determined their relations. Chaotic multiplicity of governments became "dialectically" its opposite, the absence of government. Prince Lvov responded to this situation with the comfortable and reassuring argument: there was no need for a program for creating local government, that program would be worked out by life itself, the embryos of local self-government already existed, they were preparing the population for future reforms, the present situation was transitional, the defects of the "self-born" organs were unimportant, for even they were transitional and temporary. So, in the capital, various commissions in leisurely fashion were preparing perfect legislation for local self-government. They forgot that nature abhors a vacuum. Life cannot wait for laws which mature too slowly, and the longer administration and even legislation by usurpation persists, the harder it is to compel these substitutes for government to make way for the genuine article.

If the Provisional Government had *immediately* published any of the numerous bills drawn up by the progressive fractions of the Imperial Duma to reform self-government as a whole, and county and zemstvo government in particular, whatever its imperfections—and they could easily have been corrected later—that new system would have been a salvation, compared with the "interregnum" which continued throughout the administration of the censitary government. Uncertainty fostered among the people the pernicious habit of seeing public affairs after the revolution handled by very undemocratic organizations, with dubious powers and unstable and arbitrary rules. The ease with which the Bolsheviks, at the end of 1917, destroyed the democratic zemstvos and dumas, which had not had time to strike deep root, is explained in part by the tardiness with which they were created and by the long period during which organizations like the Soviets and the revolutionary committees had exercised without hindrance the functions of government as an everyday phenomenon of the revolution.

What can explain this delay on the part of the Provisional Government, a delay which left it without an apparatus which might have become its local channel and executive? Not party egoism. In the backward provinces, especially at first, the ideas of the revolution scarcely found adequate expression. Zemstvo and city duma leaders often constituted practically the entire cultivated stratum of society. The immediate introduction of real local self-government, in close contact with the electorate, would have given them the incontestable authority of popular election and increased their political importance. The censitary government, overwhelmed by events in the capital, had no time to think through the situation in the provinces. National enthusiasm at the fall of the old régime was so great that its successors were literally inundated by a cloud-burst of congratulatory telegrams, expressing confidence, support, unbounded hope. As a whole the government perhaps had no special appetite for power as such. But under the warm shower of national greetings and ovations it put aside its first worry as to whether to take power or not. The terrifying revolutionary crowd was not so frightful after all. It was very confiding, naïve, and generous with ovations. Its leaders, it is true, were not so confiding, but unwillingness to shoulder the responsibility for government made them conciliatory. The universal rejoicings seemed to have reënforced the government's position. Why should not the transitional situation be prolonged?

Good-natured Lvov was not alone in his passively idyllic mood. The restless Kerensky, who had tasted power, drew the emotional content of his first speeches from the contrast between the old government, surrounded by many concentric circles of troops, public police, gendarmerie, and secret police, and the new government which by the moral weight of its word accomplished more than the old government by an avalanche of repression. The honeymoon of the new government was a period of peculiar "governmental Tolstoyanism."

Paying tribute to its past, just before its internal crisis and reorganization, the Provisional Government, in an appeal to the country, declared that "as the basis of government administration it assumed, not force and compulsion, but voluntary obedience of free citizens to the government which they had themselves created. It sought support not in physical, but moral force. Not one drop of the people's blood had been shed through its fault, forcible restraints had not been created for any current of public thought." This was true, for the honeymoon of the revolution, a time of general exultation and holiday-making, was not over. But without "compulsion" no government, certainly no revolutionary government, could exist. The theory thus proclaimed was the most harmful of Utopias, absolutely obscuring to the public mind one of the most important problems, the problem of power during revolution. How could the politicians of censitary Russia, proud of their "political realism," have signed such a document!

Finally, there were many urgent and absolutely uncontroversial measures which had to be adopted, and which evoked fresh outbursts of whole-hearted enthusiasm. The abolition of the death penalty, which at other times might have provoked the resistance of the Right wing of society, was now greeted with universal enthusiasm. The Left welcomed it on principle, for motives of pure humanity, as a demonstration of the magnanimity of the victorious revolution. It reassured the Right for the fate of the last overzealous defenders of the now fallen government. The Provisional Government abolished religious and national limitations which had denied civil rights to tens of millions of people. By a political amnesty it opened the doors of countless common and galley prisons, restored to relatives and friends tens, hundreds of thousands of people, condemned by mere administrative order to the ice-bound North, the furnace-like deserts of Central Asia, and the tundras of vast Siberia. It repealed the most barbarous measures applied to the population of enemy territories occupied by Russian troops (liberation of civilian "hostages," etc.).

The weakness of the first Provisional Government lay in its complete failure to understand its own rôle in the struggle of social interests. The censitary Provisional Government was astonished to learn that working-class districts considered it a "bourgeois" government. Its most experienced politician, Miliukov, even in 1921, could assert that "the most exacting imagination could not regard the Provisional Government as an organization which would defend the interests of the 'bourgeoisie' and oppose democratic reforms."[1] He had an oversimplified conception of the bourgeois class position. When the Bolsheviks paraded placards, with an equally oversimplified slogan, "Down with the ten capitalist ministers!" the members of the Provisional Government exchanged glances: there was a professor, a writer, a zemstvo doctor, a lawyer, an engineer, a farmer, and only one capitalist, Tereshchenko, included purposely to offset the "unbourgeois" character of the government, as the single exception which proves the rule. What sort of capitalists were they, and what sort of bourgeois "class politicians"! Quite the contrary. They were simply the "brain of the people." The aims and duties of the government, reasoned Miliukov, "were above party, and common to all parties."

But what makes a government bourgeois, if not its anxiety to perpetuate the given régime, which is at bottom bourgeois, and its rejection of all efforts to change it radically? "It could not be otherwise," reasoned Miliukov, "since all its current measures were merely formal and preparatory. It was simply preparing conditions for the free expression of the people's will in the Constituent Assembly, without predetermining how the latter would react to all the current problems of building the state, to political, social, national, and economic questions." This reasoning is typical of Miliukov. His arguments would have been comprehensible if the convocation of the Constituent Assembly had been expected within some two or three months. But even at that time he felt that elections in the region of the front could not begin until late autumn. Miliukov assumed that in a country that had seen almost a century of constantly increasing social fermentation active impulses would relax and be content with bare forms of democracy, not of democracy in operation, but of the mere promise of democracy, void of any social content.

For the working-class districts there were two prime questions; refusal to predetermine them could signify only descent below the level of human existence. First, the working day of the proletarian must have its standard eight hours, after which the worker should have the recognized right to higher compensation. Secondly, his real wages must not be subject to daily, automatic, and merciless reduction by inflation.

The first Provisional Government preferred to remain a passive onlooker while the eight-hour working day was gained for the Petersburg proletariat by direct negotiation between the employers' association and the Soviet. True to its "refusal to decide things in advance," it turned over to the Soviet the defense of labor's most lawful and elementary interests. Compelled to speed up the pace of currency inflation, it did nothing to offset its effect on real wages. And it wanted the trust of labor democracy!

It tried to maintain this same viewpoint of "no advance decision" in the agrarian question. The new Minister of Agriculture, Shingarev, a Cadet of fluctuating tone, made his début by pronouncing "absolutely baseless" the "rumors circulating among the population about an early large-scale land reform, including confiscation of private lands." That these rumors should not result in "reducing the area sown," he "guaranteed to the producers the enjoyment of their next harvest."[2] On March 9, after reports of agrarian conflicts in Kazan province, the government resolved to take repressive measures and to hold participants in them responsible. Its Tolstoyanism was cracking at the seams.

At that time even the Council of the Moscow Society of Agriculture realized that it was dangerous to postpone agrarian reform any longer. A half century before, the news of the government's taking up the question of abolishing serfdom had at once put a stop to disorders among the peasants; in order to quiet the village, it should be informed that "the government would immediately take up the solution of the land question in favor of the toiling peasantry, as the economic form best suited to the country's economic life." But the Provisional Government could not make up its mind to anything. On March 17 it appealed to the people to refrain from seizing land; it referred to the extreme complexity of the land question, requiring long preparation, and promised to complete this work before the Constituent Assembly met. But it was unwilling to "decide in advance" the content of the projected "land law."

On March 28 a special conference was organized to deal with the problem of establishing conciliation boards to avert misunderstandings over land questions.

Peshekhonov, a great Russian statistician, economist, and publicist on the extreme Right of the socialist camp, had just written:

> Conferences are not needed. We need swiftness and energy of decision and execution. Broadening and replacing old norms and relationships cannot be postponed till the Constituent Assembly, and even less till the creation of new legislative institutions. The Constituent Assembly and the new legislative institutions will merely have to give form and sanction to what will have been accomplished in the process of revolutionary reconstruction: it is impossible to postpone this. The entire question is whether it will take place anarchically or in organized form.

He recalled the universal demand of the progressive parties in 1905 for the creation of a network of democratically organized Land Committees to prepare for reform, and pointed out a whole series of vital and immediate questions, such as the area sown, use of pasture, regulation of rentals, and lumbering. "If these questions are not settled immediately, the result will be anarchy and a different order from that for which all democratic parties are striving. But even that order will have to be sanctioned. The Constituent Assembly cannot overpower the revolution."[3] The Provisional Government, he asserted, had long been powerless to combat anarchy. Should it dispatch punitive expeditions against the the peasants?

An indirect reply to this was contained in the telegraphic command, dispatched by Prince Lvov on April 8 to the provincial commissars, under their personal responsibility, to suppress agrarian disorders by all legal means, including the use of military detachments. The government's "Tolstoyanism" and verbal renunciation of the use of "force and compulsion" evaporated without leaving a trace as soon as the gentry's landed privileges were involved.

But still the authoritative Peshekhonov, well known as a cautious "possibilist" who twelve years earlier had left the party of Social Revolutionaries and since then had frequently attacked its social radicalism, was heard. On April 21, about a month after his article, an important law, drafted with his help, was published, establishing Land Committees, both central and local, with two functions: preparation of the land reform for the Constituent Assembly and elaboration of urgent partial measures pending the settlement of the land question as a whole.

The Chief Land Committee was composed of twenty-five members appointed by the Provisional Government, of elected representatives from the provincial Land Committees, of representatives of all shades of public opinion from the Soviet to the Provisional Committee of the Duma, of representatives of scientific and economic societies and of coöperative organizations, and finally, of representatives of all political parties from Bolsheviks to the "independent Rights" or monarchists. The Provisional Government used its right of appointment to send to the Central Land Committee 22 Cadets, 2 Social Revolutionaries, and 1 Laborite.

The provincial Land Committees were organized in far from democratic fashion: in addition to the representatives of the district Land Committees and elected representatives from the zemstvos and city dumas, they included chiefly local judges and officials. The district Land Committees were organized on the same principles. This network could not come close to the people. The county Land Committees, elected directly by the peasants, were optional, and their competence was strictly subordinate to the district committees.

The Provisional Government evidently assumed that the committees would be primarily institutions for collecting local agricultural statistics as a basis for local plans and proposals regarding the future land settlement. Their main business, imposed on them by the delay in convoking the Constituent Assembly and by the urgency of many controversial questions—"the issuing of obligatory decrees on questions of agriculture and land relationships"—was restricted by the sacramental formula: "within the limits of the legislation in force and of the decrees of the Provisional Government." And since no such decrees were planned, in order to avoid predetermining the people's will as expressed in the Constituent Assembly, this meant that the Land Committees were chained like galley slaves to the iron ball of the existing legislation; that is, to the Tsarist land code.

But the Provisional Government showed itself much pleased with its brain child. In an explanatory proclamation it expressed its certainty that the agricultural population could now wait in complete calm for the Constituent Assembly to meet.

Its resolve to preserve existing land relationships till the Constituent Assembly met was not shaken in the least. It proclaimed: "And let our valiant warriors, the defenders of their native soil, be at ease. Let them be certain that in their absence and without their participation no one will undertake to decide the land question." The men at the front were concerned about something entirely different. The press, including the official *People's Newspaper of the Provisional Government*, more than once reported facts, such as the declaration made at the Peasants' Congress by a representative of the Eleventh Army, that the "offensive would be assured and the army's enthusiasm increased 50% if the government immediately published a decree transferring all land to the peasants without compensation."[4]

At the various peasant congresses the same feeling was expressed with even greater vigor. For instance, the second provincial congress in Samara at the end of May offers a striking picture. The most eloquent speeches of the Populist

Socialist, Igoyev, concerning the government's refusal to settle the land question prior to the Constituent Assembly produce the opposite effect. The peasants' faces become severe. Brows are tensed. The murmurs grow. Exclamations: "Again wait and wait!" "Why confuse us, muddlehead!" The soldier, Lukyanov, expresses the general feeling: "We peasant soldiers have been patient enough at Lodz and Stokhod, you can understand our impatience for the land. The workers took their eight-hour day at once, the peasants need not wait." "In parting with our peasants as they went to war," says a peasant, Yegorov, "we told them: First, defend our land; second, conquer it for the peasants. They did just that, the entire revolution is that. The soldiers, disappointed four times over about the land, are beginning to be afraid they will lose it." A representative of the Union of Military Deputies declares: "We will not drop our weapons even after the war, we will not drop them until the banner 'Land and Liberty' is the banner of the state. During the Constituent Assembly we will keep our guns ready, but remember that the next command is 'set.' "[5]

The soldier was not worried at having the land question decided in his absence by the state in favor of the peasantry. He realized perfectly that in dividing the soil those organs would not forget him, if they were truly popular in character. On the contrary, delay in settling the land question from above created the danger of attempts to decide it from below by an outburst of plundering and unorganized seizure of the gentry's land and property. Then it would be "first come, first served." This might result in a dangerous stampede home from the front in order not to be too late for the "black partition." It could be forestalled only by calming the peasantry at home and at the front through government action, proving that this time the provision of land for the peasant had been undertaken in all seriousness. Too long delay caused confusion, and awakened age-old mistrust. "The workers got the eight-hour day without any Constituent Assembly because they knew how to put pressure on the employers: let's put pressure on the gentry." The pressure was turned on full. It was stimulated by the government's inactivity.

Finally there was a third vital question: the nationalities.

As far as the Poles were concerned, the urgency of the question was grasped by the government. In a special manifesto it proclaimed the idea of the complete independence of ethnographic Poland, uniting its three parts, Russian, Austrian, German. However, it forced this splendid idea into the doubtful framework of Pan-Slavism. Poland was to enter an alliance with Russia and join in the general "plan of struggle against militant Germanism." "Joined to Russia by a free military alliance, the Polish state would be a firm bulwark against the pressure of the Central Powers upon the Slavs." Poland's political structure was to be worked out by "a Constituent Assembly convoked in Poland's capital." Simultaneously, the Russian Constituent Assembly was to consent to modifications of Russia's western boundaries necessary to form an independent Polish state.

That seemed a great step forward for Russian liberalism. Previously only one Russian party, the Social Revolutionaries, had abandoned the principle of the *united* All-Russian Constituent Assembly, and referred to "Constituent Assemblies" in the plural. From this principle it derived its demand for a Constituent Diet for Finland, and settlement of the new relationship by free agreement between the Constituent Assembly of Russia and that of Finland.

This path, however, was not taken by the Provisional Government. It haggled long and stubbornly with the Finns. It repealed all Tsarist acts in violation of the Finnish Constitution; it promised, "for the development of the constitution, to work out and carry through the Diet enlargement of its budget rights, including the right to impose tariff duties." It was even more stingy toward the Lithuanians, who demanded administrative autonomy, and the Ukrainians, who insisted chiefly upon Ukrainization of the schools, courts, and administrative personnel, and on the appointment of a special commissar for Ukrainian affairs in the Provisional Government.

Miliukov, upon whose initiative it was decided to promise Poland complete independence, explained that the claims of the Finns and Poles were more incontrovertible than those of other nationalities; in the second place, and above all, their military situation was entirely different. In case of a German landing operation Finland offered a direct approach to Petrograd. Poland was completely occupied by German troops; the manifesto of the Provisional Government

> reënforced the hopes of the Poles and strengthened their resistance to German and Austrian attempts to form a Polish army of a half-million men and to bind Poland by bonds of a new statehood granted by the Central Empires. Extension of the same rights to other nationalities of Russia was not demanded by such urgent reasons, would predetermine the future arrangement of Russia, and hence must be postponed till the Constituent Assembly.[6]

Miliukov refused to budge from this stand. It was an empty, unprincipled, opportunist, and in its consequences, a dangerous position. It shook belief in his sincerity in recognizing Poland's independence; made it appear a result of military and political rivalry with the Central Powers. It contained no new principles on which the revolution might solve the nationalities problem in its totality, principles which could mean only *federalism,* transformation of Russia into a United States of the East European, Siberian, and Turkestan plain. Instead of giving fresh hope to Russia's oppressed nationalities, instead of beginning gradually but in fact to "unburden the central government" of the "internal affairs" of all special national and cultural areas, the Provisional Government again hid behind the Constituent Assembly, behind the principle of "no predetermination." It forgot that failure to meet half way in time the wishes of the nationalities now awakened to historic life meant driving them to *separatism*. The threat of joining the enemy begins to appear the best weapon in the fight for national rights.

In a word, in the labor, peasant, and nationalities questions the censitary government exposed its complete creative nullity. It solved none of them, but tangled still further the Gordian knots bequeathed by the old régime. It made its final slip in a quite different and no less urgent question: foreign and military policy.

CHAPTER ELEVEN

THE PROVISIONAL GOVERNMENT AND ITS FOREIGN POLICY

IN his *Days* Shulgin tells how Kerensky, during the street disturbances of February, 1917, burst into the room of the Provisional Committee of the Imperial Duma, handed them a folio of papers saying, "Hide them! They are the secret treaties with our Allies!" and hastened off. In all the turmoil there was no place to hide the state secret contained in that folio; it had to be concealed beneath the table with its long hanging cloth, in the same room.

What unconscious symbolism!

The confused heritage of old Tsarist diplomacy, burdened with overdrawn notes, and now bequeathed to the new Russia, was hastily hidden under the table. These secret treaties had been concluded by the Allies in various combinations and without each other's knowledge. Identical territorial acquisitions had been promised simultaneously to different Allies. At Versailles the victorious Allies later found it a long and difficult task to untangle this confusion.

The new Russia did not know what to do with this diplomatic inheritance. Its weight would cut its shoulders and burden its democratic conscience.

Bolshevism advanced the abrupt revolutionary demand: publish these documents immediately, and thus deal a moral blow to the World War. The Cadets, led by Miliukov, were at the opposite political pole: an heir, in accepting the legator's property, also accepts his financial obligations, and all his rights of suit, so new Russia was bound unconditionally by the secret treaties, and must not depart from them. United Soviet democracy, led by the bloc of Social Revolutionaries and Social Democrats, could follow neither Lenin nor Miliukov.

The one-sided publication of the secret documents of the Entente prior to the end of the war or the German Revolution, which would simultaneously expose the secrets of Wilhelm's diplomacy, it regarded as a blow, not at the war as such, but only at one warring side. It meant disrupting the Entente from within, and consciously or unconsciously abetting Hohenzollern Germany.

But Soviet democracy considered it absolutely necessary to break through the web in which the Allies had entangled themselves by the initiative of Tsarist diplomacy. From this viewpoint new Russia was morally entitled to postpone till after the war the exposure of all the filth, the unceremonious greed, the saturnalia of predatory appetites, expressed in the secret treaties, but only on condition of immediate annulment of their binding force. Of all the inter-Allied treaties it left only one in effect: the obligation to end the war by a general peace, not by an egoistic, separate withdrawal from the World War. From now on the new Russian diplomacy must strive to elaborate a positive, concrete program of universal democratic peace, a peace without victors or vanquished, a peace which would not leave behind either chauvinist triumph or insatiable thirst for revenge.

Miliukov could not carry out this policy. From the outbreak of the war he had staked everything on the country's patriotic enthusiasm. He had cleverly turned it against the yearning for a separate peace, which, luckily for him, had been associated with the program of Rasputin's reactionary clique. He had regarded the alliance with England and France as a promise of Russia's future imitation of them in domestic reconstruction. Earlier, during the Balkan War, he had given new life to the motifs of Neo-Slavism which were to undermine the Hapsburg Empire. He had formulated an extensive program of Russia's territorial acquisitions, including Constantinople, and the Bosphorus and Dardanelles, unification of Poland under the Russian scepter, including Posen, Cracow, Lwow, and Danzig, East Prussia as an additional Baltic province, Sub-Carpathian Russia and Bukovina, as Ukrainian lands, and the territories of Hither Asia which had once been Greater Armenia.

Military failures did not lead Miliukov to abandon these plans for conquest. Whatever Ally tipped the scales in favor of the Entente, the victory would be common, and then would be the time to present the old treaties. The new pacifist ideas did not move him from his accustomed track. "In all his speeches he emphasized vigorously the pacifist aims of the war for liberation, but always linked them closely with Russia's national duties and interests."[1] An enduring peace required the destruction of the military power of the Central Empires, their forcible disarmament, and the "organization of Europe" by the victors. *Mutatis mutandis,* the German imperialists were as eager to be the "pacifiers" and "organizers of Europe," in accord with their "national duties and interests." Miliukov shrugged his shoulders at the idea that the socialist parties of the various countries could, during the war, agree on some general plan of democratic peace and then, by peaceful pressure or threat of revolution, break down the resistance of the warring governments. He was firmly convinced that only the Russians took this seriously. "The overwhelming majority of socialists of both warring groups has adopted the national viewpoint," and neither Zimmerwalds and Kienthals nor even Stockholm conferences could move them. Still less could be said for their governments. Although with reluctance, he had to continue the policy of Tsarism: he carried on that policy because no other policy was possible, except a separate peace with Germany; i.e., a camouflaged alliance with victorious Germany. Later, when his card placed on the Entente was topped by the Bolsheviks, Miliukov went quite calmly to the zone of German occupation, to seek salvation in friendship with the enemy of yesterday: that same Miliukov who had not shrunk from casting on his socialist opponents the suspicion of Germanophilism, for which the crowd was then ready to stone to death.

Miliukov stood with both feet on the well-trodden path of the old Realpolitik. Its point of departure was the *sacro egoismo nazionale*, while its façade and signboard boasted of the "last" war, the war "of liberation," the war "to end war." Soviet democracy sought new paths in foreign policy. It tried to end the war, not by military fortune, but on a foundation of right. It broke with secret diplomacy. It tried to appeal to the peoples against the governments to strive for a juridical organization of all humanity, for the subjection of the jealous sovereignties of separate states to a supranational supersovereignty. It wanted what was then termed a mad Utopia, and has since made the career of able statesmen like Briand.

A collision was inevitable. Soviet democracy published its famous "appeal to the peoples of the world." It urged all peoples to make an honest and heroic effort to rally from the war hypnosis, to seek a peace without victors and vanquished, without one-sided dictation and helpless submission. It appealed particularly to the German people, whose armies were menacing revolutionary Russia, to overthrow the empire of the Hohenzollerns, as the Russian people had the Romanovs, and then to take joint measures to stop the World War. Meanwhile, it declared its firm intention of defending by force of arms the boundaries of the Russian Revolution against the armies of German imperialism.

The Provisional Government took a step forward in publishing an appeal to its citizens. "The aim of free Russia is not to dominate other peoples, not to rob them of their national property, not to seize by force other peoples' territories, but to establish a firm peace, based on the self-determination of peoples. The Russian people does not strive to increase its power abroad at the expense of other peoples, nor does it aim to enslave or degrade." But the close of the appeal again mentioned the "full honoring of our obligations toward our Allies"; the specter of the secret treaties was again evoked, and the fine words of the appeal as a whole were called in question. Tsarist diplomacy, while placing its seal on the scandalous contents of the treaties with one hand, with the other had traced the words of the Tsar's first manifesto on the declaration of war: "God is our witness that, not for vain and worldly glory, not for violence and oppression have we taken up arms, but only to defend the Russian state."

Miliukov himself proves that the ambiguity of the appeal was no accident. Only "after yielding to the majority had he consented to publish the appeal on war aims." He purposely chose the least binding form, "not a diplomatic note, but an appeal to the citizens." He selected "expressions which would not preclude his former understanding of our foreign policy, and would not require him to make any changes in that policy."[2] In other words, Miliukov merely consented to *pretend* to choose a new path. When Nekrasov tried to persuade the representatives of Soviet democracy "to interpret the evasive terms of the appeal as a concession by the government," Miliukov "reserved his right, in case the compromise should be interpreted in one-sided fashion, to explain it in his own sense, and to elucidate its vague terms in accord with his earlier policy."[3]

The subtle, refined craft proper in dealing with a practiced diplomat is seldom helpful in dealing with a democracy of toilers. Russian *émigré* revolutionaries were now returning to Russia via England and Scandinavia, and in the Executive Committee Chernov soon made a report explaining that all the communiqués, interviews, etc., of the Russian Ministry of Foreign Affairs meant but one thing: the revolution had made absolutely no change in the foreign policy and war aims of Tsarist Russia; the agreements concluded by Tsarist diplomacy were still considered inviolable for revolutionary Russia; no one abroad had even heard of the proclamation on war aims, intended solely for home consumption. This was confirmed by the "representatives of Allied socialism" who came to Russia at that time. Some of them also represented their governments. Miliukov later accused them of "yielding more to the Soviet than was reconcilable with the common interests of the Allies and their own national interests."

As a matter of fact even Albert Thomas felt that the question of peace had been greatly complicated by Russia's claim to Constantinople and the Dardanelles. This had unleashed the appetites of other Allied countries, and nationalist currents seeking equivalent "compensation" had taken the upper hand. Thomas assumed that Russian renunciation of excessive demands would aid in securing a revision of war aims in other countries; for example, the plans of French chauvinists to seize the entire Rhineland and break up Germany. As a realistic politician, he felt that Germany would fight to the last man against such schemes, and that even if peace were made on such conditions, it would be but a brief interlude before a new war.

Having discussed the situation, the leaders of the Soviet resolved to try to get the Provisional Government to communicate officially to the Allies the contents of its proclamation on war aims in the form of a diplomatic document. They learned that Miliukov refused categorically, and in general declined to make any *démarche* to the Allies toward revising war aims and drawing up a publishable peace program; in other words, he refused to abandon secret diplomacy with its burden of secret treaties and to adopt open diplomacy under public control.

This refusal marked the beginning of a crisis in the government. A bitter political duel now began between Miliukov and Kerensky. The latter seemed to adopt the "Zimmerwald" position.

"Russian democracy is now master of the Russian land," he declared in conversation with the Frenchmen, Moutet,

Cachin, Lafont, and the Englishmen, O'Grady, Sanders, and Thorne.

> We have resolved once and for all to put a stop in our country to all attempts at imperialism and conquest. . . . The enthusiasm which fills Russian democracy does not flow from any partial ideas, not even from the idea of the fatherland, as old Europe has understood it, but from ideas which compel us to think that the dream of the brotherhood of the entire world will soon become a reality. . . . We expect you, in your countries, to exert on other classes the same decisive pressure that we here in Russia have exerted on our bourgeois classes, which have now proclaimed their renunciation of imperialist ambitions.

Kerensky did not fail to point out that he alone within the government represented revolutionary democracy. That was true, and untrue. He was the only minister who also held a responsible position (vice president) in the Soviet; but he did not formally "represent" any one in the government. On the other hand, he was not entirely "alone." Even in the question of the "fatherland vs. humanity," he had two faithful allies, Nekrasov and Tereshchenko. These two were a peculiar type of "internationalist," associated not with socialism but with Russian Masonry. The Slavophil Internationalist, Prince Lvov, and the Masonic Internationalists, Nekrasov and Tereshchenko, supported the "all but Zimmerwaldian" Kerensky, and Miliukov had to capitulate, at least in form. The declaration on war aims was dispatched to the Allies as an official document. But even here the diplomat's resourceful mind found a way out: Miliukov added a preface identifying the declaration on war aims with the "lofty ideas" "constantly expressed by many outstanding leaders in the Allied countries." He declared that in Russia there was a "national striving" to carry the war "to a decisive conclusion," to obtain "sanctions and guarantees" (annexations and indemnities?) which would make new wars impossible. Finally, he once more promised to "fulfil Russia's obligations to the Allies."

The terms of the original proclamation, which Miliukov himself called "evasive," through this commentary were made more than ambiguous.

Miliukov's constant reference to Russia's obligations had already helped the Bolsheviks pass resolutions at the biggest factories in Petrograd (Triangle, Parviainen, etc.), demanding publication of the secret treaties, in order to examine Russia's obligations toward her Allies, and to discover whether their fulfilment was compatible with the democratic conscience of a revolutionary country. They were presented with another trump in their game.

The majority in the Soviet was literally astounded by Miliukov's note. It inclined to regard it as a deliberate stab in the back, a gesture of provocation, a challenge. In any case, it felt it had been deceived. Instead of the promised communication to the Allies renouncing a policy of conquest, here was an attempt to dissolve the previous and not entirely satisfactory assurances in a sea of conventional diplomatic commonplaces.

Even the date of Miliukov's note seemed a mockery. It was dated April 18, Old Style, and this was May 1, New Style—the day on which the international holiday of labor and peace was traditionally celebrated in Russia. On this day the streets of Petrograd had witnessed big demonstrations, and the working class of Russia felt its might as never before.

The startled Executive Committee of the Soviet assembled on the night of April 19–20, and had not yet had time to discuss what had happened, when news came that the Finnish, Kuxholm and One Hundred and Eightieth Infantry and the Second Baltic Fleet were marching spontaneously from their barracks to the Marinsky Palace, to arrest the Provisional Government. In all working-class suburbs crowds were gathering to demonstrate in the center of the city. "Treason! Provocation!" No other words could describe the government's action.

Measures were immediately taken. Soviet delegations were

sent to urge the soldiers and workers to refrain from action, since the Soviet undertook to liquidate the conflict with the government. Fortunately, the Marinsky Palace was empty. The military detachments which had collected, after tranquilizing speeches by the Soviet's orators, returned obediently to their barracks.

That evening the Provisional Government met with the Executive Committee of the Soviet. The members of the government read a series of reports on the country's grave, almost critical position, as if trying to create an impression that quarrels about the texts of the declarations were a mere bagatelle, in comparison with the imperative necessity for making every effort to avert imminent catastrophe, in which all conquests of the revolution would perish. With tremulous voice Guchkov described the tragedy of men of his type; compelled to choose between dynasty and fatherland, they had renounced their oath and joined the revolution, but now saw that this last, heroic remedy brought no salvation. Prince Lvov said that the government was not clinging to power; it was willing then and there to yield it to the leaders of the Soviet, if they thought they could cope better with the situation. The representatives of the Soviet became thoughtful: at bottom they felt an even greater repulsion for power and its responsibilities than before. Yet outwardly they held firm; the seriousness of the general situation increased the need for a logical and active foreign policy. Sukhanov spoke of the extreme danger to the new revolutionary Russia with each day that the war was prolonged beyond absolute necessity. Chernov criticized severely the entire activity of the Ministry of Foreign Affairs. While acknowledging the abilities of his political opponent, Miliukov, he concluded that the latter might be very useful, for example, as Minister of Education; as Minister of Foreign Affairs he would remain a source of weakness and discord in the government and the country, for by his public recognition of the Tsarist war aims, he had become absolutely unacceptable to the democracy of toilers.

Tseretelli sought a formula to which the Provisional Government could agree without inward difficulty, in order to satisfy fully the aroused political conscience of the masses.

Finally, by the evening of April 21 it was agreed that the government would give an official explanation of two points in its note. On April 22 it explained that the reference to the national desire for "a decisive victory over the enemy" meant desire for the triumph of the idea of renunciation of conquest, while "sanctions and guarantees" meant, not one-sided punishment of the defeated (as originally understood in Soviet circles), but a system of international tribunals, limitation of armaments, and similar universal measures. The soviet majority considered it unnecessary to insist further or haggle over words. It was willing to facilitate the government's retreat. More important than any texts was Miliukov's defeat and the growing possibility of his retirement.

But late on the evening of April 20, when the Soviet "Centrists" had succeeded in calming working-class and military Petrograd, bourgeois Petrograd went down to the street, to give moral support to its minister, menaced by working-class democracy. Miliukov spoke to the demonstrators from his balcony. When he said that behind the shouts, "Down with Miliukov!" he seemed to hear "Down with Russia!" the bourgeois crowd burst into prolonged and noisy applause. It longed for the well-tried formula, "I am the State," the never-failing attribute of a "strong government." The bourgeoisie was soon to feel that from a civilian this formula was far less imposing than from a man on whose shoulders there quivered a general's epaulets.

The rumor of the bourgeois demonstration on the previous evening sufficed to rearouse working-class Petrograd on April 21. The movement was begun by Vyborg district, where the Bolsheviks were especially strong. This time the Vyborg district acted in defiance even of the Central Committee of its own party. Its slogan was "Down with the Provisional Government!" It proposed to repeat the February days, and perhaps carry out a new overturn. Lenin and his staff considered this premature and rash, but they were helpless. The demonstrators could not be dissuaded even by a delegation from the Soviet, headed by its president, Chkheidze.

Meanwhile new and alarming reports had come. Military detachments with artillery had again appeared on the Palace Square. This time they were led by the commander of the Petrograd district, General Kornilov. Other military detachments refused to obey him, and in great excitement were holding meetings, asking the Soviet what they should do. Civil war seemed about to break out again on the streets and squares of Petrograd. That evening clashes began between groups demonstrating for and against Miliukov and the Provisional Government. Shots rang out. The Red Guards of Vyborg district resolved to prove that the streets of Petrograd belonged to them, and not to the bourgeois "well-dressed public."

As always, each side blamed the other for the clash. Both suspected provocation by some third "sinister force." The Cadets talked of Germans backing the Bolsheviks, the Bolsheviks of monarchists backing the Cadets.

At this point the Soviet realized that the time had come, not for words, but for decisive action. Under its pressure General Kornilov had to rescind his orders. The artillery disappeared from the Palace Square. To avoid all attempts by the Right or Left to use armed force, all the barracks were informed that without a command of the Executive Committee, sealed with its seal and signed by specially named and empowered persons, no military detachment was to stir. The Executive Committee also forbade all street demonstrations for three days. The Soviet's automobiles dashed through the streets scattering these categorical commands; as if at the wave of a magic wand, everything became quiet.

Thus the Soviet acted as dictator, but only for a few hours, and only to forestall any further provocation to civil war. We know now that Kornilov, like Krymov, was indignant at the government's helplessness, and thirsted for the "ruthless mopping up of Petrograd." The Soviet robbed him of that chance. The strong-willed, ambitious general could not endure this affront. He handed in his resignation. The Provisional Government was entirely on his side, and was sincerely horrified to think that the Soviet had dared to encroach on his prerogatives. Once more it declared with indignation that the "power of the commander of the troops of the Petrograd military district remains in full force, and control of the troops may be exercised only by him." The Soviet did not argue. It did not want a dictatorship, and had merely exercised it at a critical moment since no one else could have done what had to be done. It then returned to its domestic affairs. It did not even pause to reflect that it had, in effect, usurped the rights of the district commander. Such had not been its intention; it was only the result of its effort to prevent a civil war. The government itself realized this; it mentioned in its proclamation that the order of the Soviet "was evidently intended to forestall attempts of individual persons or groups to call out the troops." That was true, although even the district commander became just such an "individual" in the eyes of the Soviet when he aroused its suspicion because of his rash impulses, which might have touched off a civil war. But the Provisional Government as a whole also feared and did not want a civil war. It could be dissatisfied because someone else, and not it, had done what had been done. That was its real tragedy.

That which it could have suspected earlier now became clear to the government. Relations between it and the Soviet could easily be defined. On the one hand, formal power without real force, on the other actual strength without formal power. Powerless government, and governmentless force.

This divorce between governmental power and actual strength had to be ended as soon as possible. Such was the general conclusion. In particular, Miliukov, as Minister of

Foreign Affairs, had become a great danger to the entire government.

Under other conditions all the authority lost by Miliukov would have been gained by Kerensky. But Kerensky had made a terrible blunder: the odious addition to the note was no surprise to him, as it was to the Soviet leaders. Kerensky "later tried to deny" that he had assented to this note; an official communiqué immediately explained that the "note of the Minister of Foreign Affairs had been carefully considered by the Provisional Government, and its text adopted *unanimously*." Kerensky's popularity, which had grown rapidly since the first days of revolution, tottered for the first time, and seemed on the verge of collapse. It was long before Kerensky could forgive Miliukov for that moment of weakness which he had to justify even to his most devoted friends. Sharp scenes occurred within the government. Kerensky presented his resignation. General Kornilov insisted on resigning. Guchkov's resignation seemed imminent. Least of all was said of the natural step; namely, Miliukov's resignation. A group was growing which demanded a resignation of the cabinet and a coalition with representatives of Soviet democracy. They caught up Chernov's idea of transferring Miliukov to the Ministry of Education.

Meanwhile Kerensky published a letter written for him by Chernov, explaining why revolutionary democracy had been ignored in forming the government and why he had entered the cabinet on his own risk. Noting the beginning of a new era—its responsible participation in governing the country—he concluded that revolutionary democracy, whether through the Soviet or the socialist parties, would delegate to the government its formal representatives who would report their activity to it; he promised that such would henceforth be his own rôle.

Soviet circles still hesitated as to whether or not to adopt such a novel line of conduct. At one session of the Executive

Committee, participation in the government was rejected 23 to 22, with 8 abstentions. At the next meeting it was adopted 41 to 18, with 3 abstentions. When this decision had been adopted, it turned out that the censitary part of the government originally had in mind, not forming a genuine coalition government, but rather bringing into the cabinet, preferably for the newly established post of Minister of Labor, one more socialist, some labor leader, like Plekhanov, who by the historical popularity of his big name would reënforce the government's badly shaken authority and be a living shield against attacks from the Left. Negotiations dragged on and more than once seemed on the verge of complete fiasco, although efforts to arrange a coalition were made not only by Kerensky, Nekrasov, and Tereshchenko, but also by such a skilful diplomat as Albert Thomas. In Soviet circles a movement grew in favor of taking direct responsibility for the government's policy only on condition of real, numerical preponderance within the cabinet. The All-Russian Congress of Soviets of Peasants' Deputies, then in session, expressed this as a demand for a Soviet majority within the cabinet. In addition, the unsuccessful experiment in the provinces with Prince Lvov's commissars and instructions led them to demand with insistence that Internal Affairs be transferred to socialist hands. That would have been difficult without the retirement of Prince Lvov, a chief defender of the idea of reorganizing the government along coalition lines. There was much disagreement about Chernov; the crisis had broken out and the question of the coalition been decided in his absence. The Left wing of the Social Revolutionary party demanded that the Ministry of Foreign Affairs be transferred to him; the majority of the party considered that, as author of the program for "socialization of the land," he should take over the Ministry of Agriculture, in order to prepare the land reform. The Cadet party, unable to forgive his victorious campaign against Miliukov and his participation in the international conference at Zimmerwald, objected to his participation in the government. Finally, Chernov, summoned from Moscow by telegraph, protested against exchanging a Soviet for a government post; he conditioned his assent, first, on participation of the Social Democratic leader, Tseretelli, in the government, and, second, on the transfer of the Ministry of Supply, so closely connected with agriculture, to some socialist; but the Cadet Shingarev clung to this post. Kerensky, who but recently "had dreamed of raising justice in Russia to an unprecedented height,"[4] had turned cold, and thirsted to replace Guchkov. He was now dreaming of placing the revolutionary army "on an unprecedented height," and crowning it with laurels of victory. To reconcile all these difficulties was like "squaring the circle."

At one moment Nekrasov, convinced that a coalition government could not be formed, proposed establishing a dictatorship and intrusting power to some military leader, popular in society and politically unambitious. As a candidate he suggested General Manikovsky. This proposal merely seemed extravagant. It indicated how far the members of the government had lost confidence. Obviously, censitary government was neither good nor bad, it was simply not government.

The country needed a government which could maintain intimate contact with the forces which grew with the revolution, which could direct them to the wheels that moved the new mechanism for the reconstruction of Russian life. But the revolution could be led only by a government that went ahead, breaking open a path and lighting it, not one that dragged after, constantly retarding it.

The first Provisional Government tried in vain to treat a great revolution as a petty palace revolution. It could try to accept the revolution, but without drawing revolutionary conclusions. This was the secret of its uncreativeness.

The coalition government at last saw the light of day. The great leader of Social Democracy in the Soviet, Tseretelli, became nominally Minister of Posts and Telegraph, actually minister without portfolio for general policy. A close associate, Skobelev, became Minister of Labor. The leader of the Party of Social Revolutionaries, Chernov, became Minister of Agriculture. Kerensky took War, transferring Justice to an assistant, Pereverzev. The Populist Socialist, Peshekhonov, took the Ministry of Supply. These six men (as a matter of fact, fewer than six) were considered the socialist minority in the government. Miliukov was replaced by Tereshchenko, while Shingarev went to the Ministry of Finance. The rest were unchanged.

At the next congress of the Cadet party Miliukov, now in retirement, declared bitterly: "I did not leave, I was put out." He cast a poor horoscope for the new government. Its program he considered too "indefinite; it hid the embryo of future conflicts." He was convinced "that a clear and definite statement of its program was an impossibility; the coalition was a compromise which paralyzed the government from within, as it had been paralyzed till then by pressure from without."[5]

At bottom Miliukov was right. In accepting the coalition idea, people were looking backward, not ahead. They were trying to correct a mistake of the past, instead of solving the problem of the present and future.

The first period of the revolution had presented tasks common to liberal and labor democracy alike. But liberal democracy had shouldered alone the unbearable burden of revolutionary government. Now the toilers' democracy came to its assistance; its representatives hastened to correct its work, and were hitched in the same harness. Meanwhile new tasks had come to the fore, and inner unity in solving them had already become impossible.

"Better late than never" does not always hold true. The misfortune of the coalition was that the combination of conditions and problems which had made it so difficult to get along without a coalition was gone. During the first months of revolution the men of the Duma opposition and the men of the revolution had coöperated throughout the country in uprooting the vestiges of the autocratic and bureaucratic régime, and in creating the skeleton of a new, popular, democratic government. First of all, the country needed the *forms* of a free state, founded on public law. A place for them had to be cleared, they had to be forged in coöperation. Then the question arose as to the *social content* to fill those forms. Here the two groups were bound to part company. The era of joint action and that of separation followed in natural sequence. But in organizing the government this sequence was turned topsy-turvy. In the period of united action, liberal democracy and the toilers' democracy were divided; when they joined forces, the hour of their natural separation was already striking.

The diarchy which had paralyzed the government's activity and marked the irreconcilability of censitary and Soviet democracy, did not disappear on being transferred within the government. This dualism was merely modified: it now paralyzed the plans and intentions of the separate and heterogeneous halves of the cabinet. From now on neither was strong enough to carry out its own policy, while each was strong enough to prevent its partner from fulfiling its own program. The result was a deadlock which only exhausted and irritated the participants. The government, helpless for good or ill, furnished fewer *concrete* causes for acute indignation, it took fewer incautious steps. But more and more dissatisfaction was concentrated on its scanty achievements, or rather on its lack of achievements. Its divergent parts canceled each other out. The natural result was a policy of marking time.

CHAPTER TWELVE

INDUSTRIAL CONFLICT

PEOPLE assumed that the new Provisional Government would strike out on fresh paths, especially in the labor and agrarian questions.

Labor legislation, according to the declaration of the coalition cabinet, was to be based on "the struggle against economic breakdown through establishing control over production, transportation, exchange and distribution of production, and the organization of output when necessary." It could not be otherwise. Miliukov rightly says that "industry was more and more *obliged to subsist at the expense of the state* and was already menaced by the approaching crisis"—a crisis in transportation, supply of raw materials and fuel and replacement of equipment. It was absurd to finance industry without supervising it. The approach of the crisis did not allow of a policy of *laissez faire, laissez passer*. Protecting the interests of labor assumed that the government would restore to health economic life as a whole.

To discuss and prepare drafts of laws for regulating labor conditions prior to their examination by the government, a special "Labor Committee" had been organized under the first Provisional Government. It included eight members from workers' organizations and eight from the industrialists'. The ninth member, who presided, was the Minister of Labor. It invited witnesses and specialists with a consultative voice.

Valuable light is thrown on its activity by the memoirs of Auerbach, a representative of the employers and a director in many industrial corporations.

> The Ministry of Labor was definitely Menshevist in its directing personnel, and drew strictly Marxist scholars into its work. . . . With their wide erudition the latter with remarkable

ase reënforced their arguments by reference to laws and cus-
oms of all countries, to resolutions of congresses, etc. The re-
orts which preceded examination of draft bills were carefully
nd sensibly prepared. It was obvious that everything had been
hought out and arranged. Our avowed enemies, the members of
he workers' fraction of the committee, were armed to the teeth.
When, at the first session, we were showered with formulæ, quo-
ations, persons, and cities, and all this with unusual ease and
ven grace, we seemed absolutely routed before the battle
egan.[1]

What had the representatives of the Russian bourgeoisie
o oppose to the defenders of labor? Very little, as Auerbach
dmits. "Carefully concealing our despondence, but realizing
ur lack of preparation, we tried to make up for it by elo-
uence and ingenuity." Evading a discussion of the essence
f the drafts, they chiefly emphasized their "inopportunity"
during wartime. "In this way the moment of decisive struggle might be delayed, but it could not be averted or escaped
without defeat." The Russian bourgeoisie took to heart the
slogan, "Back to the study!" The Council of Congresses of
Industry and Commerce organized a special Labor Section.
It began feverishly to collect materials, draw up reports,
memoranda, and notes, frame amendments to drafts, write
counterdrafts, etc. "We felt ourselves sufficiently armed,"
admits Auerbach. "Nevertheless, we, of course, could not
hope to overtake our opponents who had spent years in
preparation. We had to educate ourselves so that the explo-
sions of shrapnel, crammed with formulæ, citations, names,
should not start a panic in our own ranks."

Gradually the employers' representatives felt out their
opponents' weak spot. "All drafts introduced into the Labor
Committee involved considerable expenditure for the treasury and oftener for the national economy" (i.e., for the employers). So the capitalists began to figure out "how much
each 'conquest of the revolution' would cost the country";
by these calculations they "provoked panic among their ad-

versaries." Even in uncontroversial questions, such as security in illness, disability and old age, which "in principle had our sympathies," says Auerbach, "we only shrugged our shoulders at the problem of how to carry them out at once and on a universal scale, without causing complete derangement."

Of all the draft laws examined by the Labor Committee (freedom of strike, eight-hour day, limitation of child labor, security against old age and disability, labor exchanges, etc.) only two became law. The "absolutely harmless" law on labor exchanges and that on insurance against illness (based on the Ghent system; i.e., imposing half the expense on the workers and half on the employers) aroused no dispute. For a revolutionary period such a result was nil. "The other bills, thanks to ruthless criticism, went back to the bureaus of the Labor Ministry, never to return." The employers' state of mind is illustrated by their calling the unrestricted right to strike "antisocial." Prohibition of child labor in factories ran "counter to stern reality." The proposed restriction of adolescent labor in agriculture was "a curiosity." When Auerbach notes with satisfaction all these entirely negative victories won by the employers' group, he knows perfectly well whom the Russian bourgeoisie, by its stubborn resistance, enabled to profit by this pitiful product of the coalition's work. These bills, pigeonholed in various bureaus, "after the Bolshevist Revolution were issued by the Soviet government either in their original form or in the form proposed by the Workers' Group in the Labor Committee." Need one be surprised at the growing sympathy for the Bolsheviks among the workers? The Bolsheviks' best ally was the obstinacy of the Russian bourgeoisie, which, through parity representation in the committee, nullified its work.

The second side of the industrial question was that of organizing the supervision of production. On its earliest approach to that problem the coalition showed its first split. The Minister of Commerce and Industry, A. I. Konovalov, one of the most progressive representatives of his class, was unable to stand the pressure. By May 11, like Skobelev and Tereshchenko, he had concluded that the country must tax excess war profits severely, appoint special government commissars to manage plants with acute conflicts between capital and labor, establish government supervision, and in a few places nationalize plants directly. A week later Konovalov caused a great sensation by his resignation. His pretext was that government control was to be effected through a network of special committees, modeled on those existing in the leather industry and others, on condition of their being democratized. "The imposition of democratic organs, under present conditions of Russian reality," declared Konovalov, "will place people without economic experience in most industrial plants and will bring disorganization instead of improvement." Were such worn-out arguments decisive, no government would ever have passed from a bureaucratic and autocratic régime to modern, parliamentary democracy. Naturally experience comes with practice, and the new social elements, now in power, were less experienced than the old bureaucratic caste. This usual but quickly remedied defect was counteracted by greater freedom from routine and greater initiative. The transition from the employers' factory autocracy to public and state control, to economic democracy, was bound up with the same difficulties as the transition from the imperial government to a parliamentary régime.

Konovalov's resignation happened to coincide with the arrival in Russia of the English Labor Minister, Arthur Henderson. As a progressive European, he was greatly astounded by these purely Asiatic prejudices displayed by the most progressive representative of the Russian bourgeoisie. At a meeting of the Moscow Board of Trade Henderson said: "You should know that all industry, all work for supplying the army, has been brought under strict supervision by the English government, and there are almost no conflicts with the workers. . . . The interests of the state must come first. . . . Do not think that this is socialism," he hedged. "This is merely a temporary necessity, for the state is fighting for its very existence, for its integrity." Finally, Henderson emphasized the reverse of the medallion: "When the war began, we asked the workers temporarily to renounce the struggle for their rights, and they did so in the interest of the state. At times the workers have worked seven days a week with no holiday or rest."

Henderson's declarations evoked a response from many firms with predominantly English capital.* They complained no less than their Russian colleagues of the serious plight of industry and the conduct of the workers. But instead of appealing to old Asiatic methods, they turned to European ones. They petitioned the government to "take over supervision of their plants on the basis of the government supervision exercised in England." In press, public, and government circles this declaration made a strong impression. The Left-wing press (Social Revolutionary *Delo Naroda*) regarded it as "a lesson to the Russian industrialists." The bourgeois press emphasized the fact that the "government supervision exercised in England" abolished the workers' right to strike, and it asked insistently whether the Russian labor organizations and socialist parties would consent to that. Of course, the answer could only be "No." The English workers could speak with a certain satisfaction of their "wartime conquests," added to a high prewar standard of living. Nothing of the sort held true of the Russian workers. If the Provisional Government had made up its mind to introduce a democratic supervision of production, its most essential element for labor would have been regulation of real wages. Then strikes, the only other means for saving the workers' standard of living from automatic reduction by inflation, would also have disappeared.

* Neva Yarn Factory, Neva Stearine, Neva Cotton Textile, Voronin Factory, Liutsh and Gesher Factories, Spasskaya Cotton Spinning, Kalinkinsky Factory, Russian Oil, William Hartley Corporation.

The Russian industrialists, disturbed by the mere fact that socialists had entered the government, on May 10 sent to it a large delegation, led by the president of the Council of Congresses of Commerce and Industry, a former Tsarist minister, Kutler. This delegation tried to prove that demands for higher wages threatened to swallow up the entire fixed capital of industry. They minimized the fact that the value of their fixed capital was reckoned in the prewar par currency, the wage increases in inflated currency. They then tried to scare the Provisional Government by predicting the universal unprofitableness of plants, their abandonment, the necessity for the state to take them over, and thus to nationalize nothing but deficits. Leaving no doubt as to his hidden threat of a lockout, Kutler laid down his cards and spoke of an "object lesson" to the workers, which would halt them on the path of ruin, in their striving to secure "privileges at the expense of society and national economy as a whole."

The socialist ministers, Skobelev and Tseretelli, easily showed how the dominance of selfish, private interests in industry had created huge war profits and lowered the workers' standard of living. Chernov exposed the fictitious character of their calculations, and warned against "shameful experiments" with lockouts, which, in a period of revolution, might prove a suicidal playing with fire. In these negotiations even Konovalov supported the united front of both wings of the Provisional Government, and protested against the employers' camouflaged threats. Accused of treason to his class, he soon gave way, however.

Konovalov's resignation showed that the Russian bourgeoisie could not coöperate with the moderate socialist wing as urged by Henderson. No big industrial leader or expert would take his place. The moderate socialists were now faced by a dilemma. Should they give up the coalition with the political representatives of commerce and industry, or, for the sake of the coalition, renounce the extensive program of reconstruction which they had laid down? They flinched and gave way, a fatal retreat! They dropped the idea of publishing a special government declaration, drafted in two variants, socialist and bourgeois, Skobelev's and Stepanov's. Both drafts referred to the need "to interfere forcefully in the country's economic life and to subject it to state control and regulation." Both proposed to syndicalize private enterprises in the chief industries under state supervision. Instead, the government issued a proclamation by the Minister of Labor to the workers, appealing to their self-discipline and self-restraint and many other fine feelings. In bewilderment the workers asked what the Provisional Government was doing in industry besides addressing moth-eaten sermons to the workers. This was the main weakness of the Provisional Government: instead of acting through legislation and administration, it used their substitutes—appeals and exhortation.

The employers were not content with checkmating all attempts at new labor legislation.

Through their most militant leaders, Von Ditmar and Tikston, the manufacturers demanded that the government "confirm to the entire population the fact that all laws not repealed by decrees of the Provisional Government continue in full force and violation of them entails corresponding punishment." This was an attempt to profit by the physical impossibility of revising at once all the legislation of autocracy, the fruit of centuries. The employers also cast doubt on the legislative competence of the Provisional Government in the most acute questions between masters and workmen. To counterbalance the Petrograd agreement for the eight-hour day and attempts to introduce it on a national scale by decree of the Provisional Government, the Moscow Board of Trade declared:

> The question of the eight-hour day cannot be regarded as a matter of mutual agreement between employers and workers, since it has general governmental significance. The entire popu-

lation is interested in its solution, and hence it cannot be the object even of provisional legislation, but must be decided by the will of the entire people through properly organized legislative institutions. . . . Representatives of industry do not regard it as possible of solution at present, however benevolent their attitude toward the interests of the workers.[2]

If the fundamental problems of labor legislation are beyond the competence of the Provisional Government, while all old legislation not repealed or replaced remains in force, the result is obvious. Under the Provisional Government the workers must live by the old Tsarist laws, submitting to the methods of the autocratic factory, with the masters' assurances of their "benevolent attitude" toward the workers.

Even toward the feeble beginnings of the new factory legislation, such as the law concerning the Workers' Committees in the factories, the manufacturers behaved disloyally. This law declared (#9a) that the committees had full power to represent to the administration the interests of the workers "in questions concerning the mutual relations between employers and workers; such as wages, hours of labor, rules for factory discipline, *etc.*" The employers did not wish to recognize the "etc." Contrary to the obvious sense of this enumeration, they maintained that questions of hiring and firing were exempted. Many owners refused to allow a committee member to be present at the hiring of workers. Although the law plainly stated (#16) that *all* disputes regarding its application were to be referred to conciliation boards, the employers by an ultimatum demanded that disputes over hiring be excluded. The associated manufacturers of the Southern district asserted that "industry can continue to exist only if the hiring and firing of employees and workers is the *exclusive* right of the employers." The All-Russian Conference of Employers' Organizations demanded "the removal of interference by Factory Committees in the sphere of competence of the factory administrations." The Urals manufacturers announced that "no factory administration would recognize any committees or boards, that it was master of the factory, and would do as it wished. As for governmental and public control, the manufacturers had not recognized such control and would not do so."[3]

Mediation by the Soviet of Workers' Deputies, which had solved painlessly the question of the eight-hour day, now met with open hostility. At the Kurzon Factory in Rostokino, the owner refused to deal with the "conciliator" from the Soviet of Workers' Deputies, invited by the Workers' Committee; he declared he "did not recognize him," and, revolver in hand, drove him from the factory, as an "intruder." Just previously the association of the steel and iron industry had notified its members that the "new commissions, formed by the Soviets of Workers' and Soldiers' Deputies, being arbitrary and usurping the power and rights of legal organs, cannot be admitted to the factories." A campaign was now begun against the workers' elected representatives, who were compelled by their duties to be away frequently from work. The Council of Associated Industry decreed that "in case of a worker's systematic absence from the factory, he ceases to be a worker, and hence, by Art. 104 of the Rules of Industry, not yet repealed, he should be regarded as having withdrawn from the workers' personnel." The administration of the Bogoslovsky mining district announced that "employees engaged in elective duties to the injury of their regular work will be replaced with other persons." A special explanation had to be issued by the Ministry of Labor, stating that factory-owners had no right to discharge members of Factory Committees except with the sanction of the conciliation board or court of arbitration. Yet the government's own administration in the Putilov Factories rejected this explanation, and insisted on its right to discharge members of the committee of employees *before* a decision was rendered by the conciliation board; it even threatened to discharge all its employees. This brought but one result. It created an atmosphere of excitement, conducive to strikes, which resulted in mass participation by the Putilov workers in the October Revolution.

In the Petrograd agreement between the Association of Manufacturers and the Soviet of Workers' and Soldiers' Deputies, the most telling defect was the absence of any agreement regarding the bases for a standard wage. This was a most pressing question for all Russia. For the provinces it was even more important than for Petrograd; in wage level Petrograd was an oasis in a Sahara of primitive exploitation.

The historian must answer two questions: (1) were the workers' demands for higher wages justified, or had their pay been increased before the revolution as much as was possible; and (2) were the employers justified in their claim that the volume of their profits was insufficient to satisfy the workers' demands?

The first question has been answered by persons and institutions beyond all possible suspicion of prejudice in favor of the factory proletariat.

One of them is an army commander of the Tsarist régime, General Ruzsky, hailed by the Octobrists and Nationalists as a "national hero," and trusted by Right spheres. At a secret meeting of the Council of Ministers on August 10, 1915,

> General Ruzsky referred to the condition of the workers in the Petrograd factories; they were enduring extremely intense labor and the entire burden of the high cost of living; the factories had failed to raise wages and the workers had to resort to exhausting overtime work to avoid hunger; most serious attention must be given to this question and swift measures taken, since strikes and disorders are possible; the war would then be absolutely hopeless.[4]

Perhaps the situation of the workers had improved after 1915? Let us examine a later document from a source even more hostile to socialism and labor. The summary of the chief of the Petrograd Gendarme Department for October, 1916, contains this admission:

"The economic situation of the masses, despite the enormous rise in wages, *is worse than awful.* While wages have risen 50% for the mass, and only for certain categories (machinists, founders, electricians) 100–200%, articles of prime necessity have gone up 100–500%."

The experienced gendarmes realized how fruitless it was to catch individual "agitators" when the most eloquent agitator was life itself.

The manufacturers continually retorted that regardless of the pressure exerted by the workers they had always raised wages parallel to the rising cost of living. The workers riposted that the opposite was true:

> The overwhelming majority of the demands made on the factories have been left unsatisfied. Isolated strikes have usually failed; where the workers have obtained an increase in wages, the manufacturers have passed on the wage increase (even adding to it), thus causing prices to outstrip wages. This has been aggravated by the decline of the ruble. We are falling into a vicious circle, from which there is no escape except through vigorous measures by the government.

Which of the disputants was right? Objective material is furnished by the decisions of the arbitration courts. Whether they were constituted on a basis of parity, or by a special commission of the Provisional Government, or by the Ministry of Labor, or by the less "proletarophile" Ministry of Commerce and Industry, the result was always the same. Rates of wages prepared by the workers, or sometimes slightly higher, were always accepted. This is no cause for surprise. The data of the Moscow Labor Exchange showed that from February to July, 1917, wages increased by 53%, while prices of prime necessities rose by 112%, on the average, rye bread 150%, potatoes 175%, clothing and shoes 170%. Confronted by an impartial authority, the employers had to surrender. This drew on them the protests of their own central class organizations. The Petrograd Association of Manufacturers, which at the beginning of the revolution had yielded to the spirit of the time on the eight-hour day, now turned sharply to the Right and forbade its printers' section to sign the new rate scale with the Printers' Union; this caused a rupture between the association and its master-printers' section. A compromise achieved in the engineering trades in Petrograd was protested by the Main Committee of United Industry. It declared that submission to arbitration by its engineering section was "not voluntary, but due to the threat of all factories of that category to strike," while governmental arbitration was a crying violation of the "necessary freedom of contractual relationships."

Since the inflation was a cause of the soaring cost of living, decisions of arbitration courts in the workers' favor were of small assistance. The new wage scales were obsolete when introduced. There was no way out except through government regulation of wages, based on a subsistence minimum reckoned by official and periodical price indices. Nominal wages would then increase automatically without the pressure of trade-unions and strikes. But so vigorous a measure, if proposed within the government, would have blown it to pieces. Its bourgeois section would never have been reconciled to it, especially since it involved the general establishment of state control over industry.

The necessity for such control arose logically. The longer the war lasted, the more industry worked for the front, for defense. The government was its customer. The government also granted the entrepreneurs enormous loans to enlarge their plants and improve production, and supplied them extensively with non-interest bearing advances on orders. When a plant began to decline, the government took it under its direct management. A paradoxical situation had arisen. As long as a plant flourished, the government assisted in maintaining its prosperity, the fruits of which went into private pockets; if production became unprofitable, it was thrust upon the government's shoulders, but only after all possibilities of fresh loans and advances had been exhausted. The entrepreneur was the government's agent. He worked more and more with government money, and was able gradually to withdraw his own capital from the enterprise.

When confronted with the workers' demands, the entrepreneur constantly asserted that "a very large percentage of the plants are undoubtedly working at a loss." The workers met all such assurances with ironical scepticism. Generally speaking, the average profits in Tsarist Russia, compared with Western Europe, were enormous (a lure to attract foreign capital into Russian industry). During the war, as everywhere, they grew considerably. Annual profits before and after outbreak of war were: for the Cable Factory 1.4 million rubles and 3.34 million; for Sormovo Factory 2.17 million and 3.79 million; for Kolchugin 2.17 million and 4.72 million; for the Corporation of Tula Factories 1.86 million and 8.39 million rubles.

During the heat of the argument as to whether Russian industry could bear the burden of higher wages, the newspapers were publishing official reports which sharply contradicted the employers' complaint. The Sormovo Corporation declared a dividend of 17½%. The size of the dividend offers but a feeble idea of the firm's real profit; almost half its net profit, a sum of over 4.8 million rubles, was written off as depreciation.

The Kolomna Machine Factory, with fixed capital of 15 million rubles, and liquid capital of less than ½ million, ended the year with a profit of almost 7.5 million rubles.

Of course, such a state of things could not last forever. Conditions in industry were bound to grow worse as general economic conditions deteriorated. The wartime "flowering" of industry, abundantly watered by inflation, was a contradiction: it was based on the forced *creation* of means of *destruction.* It mercilessly wore out the living strength of the worker and the country's equipment; it overstrained the endurance of the consumer. It was soon felt in the disturbance of transport, the breakdown in supplying raw materials and fuel, the decline of productivity. Plainly, the best time for skimming the cream from the "wartime prosperity" of Russian economy was over. The auspices were gloomy. "Economic ruin" must inevitably affect the provisioning of the army, its supply of weapons, hence, its fighting power. But military defeat meant burdens of direct or concealed tribute imposed on the vanquished, hence, relentless taxation of the poverty-stricken country. This created a great temptation for capital to desert in time. It handed out dividends lavishly and concealed profits by all sorts of "deductions" and "writing off." It wore out or cashed in the property of the plant and thrust the pitiful remnants upon the government's shoulders. It transferred funds to neutral countries, where a broad field of international commercial activity had been opened up, through semicontraband middleman activity between the warring powers—in other words, it became a Russian branch of international speculation. Such was the line of least resistance now opened to capitalist acquisitiveness. The Provisional Government imposed restrictions on the transfer of money and the export of foreign exchange, but the exodus of capital continued by roundabout and undetected paths. To justify its desertion capital needed a pretext: the workers' demands were a splendid excuse. Such conditions opened a tremendous sphere of activity for "sharp dealers" among the capitalist class. Some appeared as deliberate provocateurs of class warfare and economic chaos, others as unconscious tools of history. The former took care to transfer their activity to countries safe from revolution; they were a minority of the big business men. The majority, usually small capitalists, became scapegoats for the sins of their entire class.

The main struggle between entrepreneurs and workers was soon concentrated in mutual recrimination. The employers accused the workers of absolute negligence of discipline, of allowing productivity to decline, of blind, selfish greed, destructive of the very existence of industry. The workers, on the other hand, accused the employers of planning a camouflaged lockout with the intention of abandoning production entirely.

The workers' countercharge was not an invention. According to Auerbach,

> in the Council of Congresses of Industry and Commerce people were discussing the proposal to use the lockout as a reply to the onslaught of the tumultuous and unrestrained masses of workers; but that seemed, in a national sense, just as odious as the workers' strikes—it would seem like a blow at the army's rear. The moral position of the manufacturers would be impaired, and the consequences of such a step, without the government's support, appeared very gloomy to most. Finally they concluded that life itself would furnish an object lesson, without any organized "action," through the inevitable and gradual closing of the factories, which in fact was soon observed.[5]

The general, simultaneous, and demonstrative lockout was rejected. The fears of the industrialists were justified: the leaders of the lockout would have been torn to shreds, and the army would have been first to demand their ruthless punishment. If the government had tried to protect them from the people's wrath, it would have been swept away even more swiftly and completely than the autocracy. Individual lockout, "not wholesale, but retail," was dictated by the instinct of self-preservation.

However, murder will out. On May 10 the leader of the industrialists' delegation, Kutler, declared that unless the government protected the interests of the manufacturers, an object lesson to the workers would be inevitable through stoppage of production. The Minister of Agriculture, Chernov, immediately called a spade a spade, and uttered this warning: "Take care, you are beginning to play with fire, the consequence may be a conflagration which no one can localize." Some time later a leader of Russian industry, P. Ryabushinsky, publicly pronounced even more menacing words: "Perhaps, to escape from the present situation, we need the bony hand of hunger, the poverty of the people, which would seize by the throat all those false friends of the people, all those democratic Soviets and committees." These fatal, unforgettable words echoed and reëchoed across the country. Everywhere they sowed wrath, hatred, thirst for revenge. The misery, hunger, unemployment, hardships, accumulated in every corner of Russia, all this world of human suffering and hopelessness responded violently to this irresponsible threat with a helpless gritting of the teeth and a convulsive clenching of fists, ominous portent of the future avalanche of that maddened "Bolshevism of the street."

Words did not remain mere words. The Leather-Working Corporation presented the Factory Committee with a seven-point ultimatum; if it was not accepted, it threatened to "pay off all the workers, foremen, and clerks, and close the factory." The administration of the Bogoslovsky mining district sent a courier from Petrograd with nine conditions; only in case of their acceptance was it "willing to attempt to carry on business in the district any longer." At this time, in the Preparatory Commission of the Labor Division attached to the Ministry of Commerce and Industry, during the discussion of the right to strike, the representatives of the manufacturers "insisted very energetically on including in the bill impunity of lockout." The bourgeois *Commercial and Industrial Gazette* states that "among owners of plants we remark a considerable slackening of interest in their business, in securing materials, fuel, and everything necessary for the plant. All this prepares the way for further closing of plants" (September 3).

Naturally the owners' neglect in keeping plants supplied for continuous production could only be understood by labor as deliberate sabotage. The workers began apparently paradoxical attempts to interfere in the management of production and reduce the stoppage or prevent the closing of factories. The trade-union of textile workers, together with the Factory Committee, started up the Ferman Factory, the closing of which the workers explained as "deliberate sabotage." The well-equipped factory, under a new manager elected by the workers, began to operate normally. The union, recognizing that "it cannot yet become the owner of the factory," proposed that the government confiscate it and appoint a commissar to whom the union would transfer the factory operating at full capacity. After the announcement by the administration of the biggest shipyard in the South, Naval, of a reduction of production to one half without guaranteeing regular wages for the future, the committee of workers and employees decreed that delegates be sent to the places where the products needed by the factory were prepared or extracted, to deal with the committees of those plants and to continue operation under the workers' control. The G. Bronner Factory was more than once stopped by its owner. The workers took over its management; new orders and even fresh credit were secured to start up the plant. The owner sued the workers, took over the factory, and again forced it to shut down. Finally it was requisitioned by the government. The most notorious case was the so-called "Likinsky sabotage." Its villain was the owner of a textile factory, Smirnov, member of the employers' organization in the cotton spinning trade, president of the Moscow War Industries Committee, and one time State Comptroller in the Provisional Government. His factory proved to be well supplied with cotton, but peat had not been collected, while the workers' offer to gather it was rejected. After Smirnov had closed the factory, the workers discovered a three months' supply of fuel. The owner brought suit to arraign the Factory Committee for arbitrary interference. Demonstrations of hungry unemployed began, the near-by factory center of Orekhovo-Zuevo was aroused. The Moscow Soviet tried to move the Ministry of Labor, the Ministry of Commerce and Industry, the Textile Commission. All this was fruitless, and the conflict continued till the October Revolution.

On June 8, at the Moscow Exchange a special conference

was openly assembled to consider the "question of stopping work in the factories of the Moscow district." Some one suggested timidly that the shutdown be postponed till winter, in order to do something to "satisfy the commodity hunger." But the majority revolted against this, allegedly in the interests of the workers who would find it easier to get work in the autumn wheat harvest or coal mining. As a matter of fact the Russian textile industry had enormous supplies of goods on hand (the Bolshevist government later subsisted on them for a long time), and they could be sold more profitably after stopping production.

The class of entrepreneurs, which had fought so hard against interference by the workers' organizations, now decided to give them a decisive part—in planning the funeral ceremony. On June 20 delegates of the employers' organizations met delegates of the Moscow district Bureau of Soviets of Workers' and Soldiers' Deputies and representatives of the government Supply Section. The Soviet dictated the rules of "coming to a stop with brakes on": (1) no factory to be closed if raw material and fuel were available; (2) where closing was recognized as inevitable, to wait for it to be sanctioned by a special commission and not to discharge workers pending its final decision; (3) in such cases to summon a general factory conference, whose resolution should be sent for final confirmation to the representatives of the Soviet and of the Supply Section; (4) in cases of partial reduction in the number of working days per week, not to cut wages proportionately; (5) while the factory was closed, to list the workers as on the permanent force, though without pay; and (6) to reopen the factories not later than one month before the beginning of elections to the Constituent Assembly. The employers agreed. Some agreed because they had inwardly lost all interest, and were preparing to shake the dust from their feet. Others, because under conditions of commodity famine they could find better use for their capital in commerce and speculation than in industry. Others naïvely imagined that in the interests of the country's industry they were taking a step, cruel perhaps, but extremely clever and salutary.

If they had known that a cruel caprice of history would make this a step toward their economic suicide, probably they would not have decided so lightheartedly to follow their leaders—"the blind leading the blind." The Russian employing class, an involuntary and unconscious suicide, received from Bolshevism merely a coup de grace, and, perhaps one should add, the professional services of the grave digger.

It would be ridiculous to deny the importance of discord with the workers during the revolution. It was due not to the workers' unendurable condition before the revolution, and the employers' indifference alone. Nothing compels one to believe that the management is always to blame and labor never. No revolution in history has escaped deterioration of labor discipline, afterwards revived with difficulty and against the resistance of the masses. That was true of the February Revolution. But even among the workers there was a valuable and well-organized kernel, with a highly developed consciousness of its working-class dignity, a dignity which did not permit it to soldier on the job or to try to live without working. It also had a deep love for its work, professional pride, even a peculiar "poetry of the machine," like the peasant's love for his field. Workers of this type more than once showed that they could swim against the current, resist the chaotic spirit of rebellion, slackness, and irresponsibility of the motley mob which had invaded the factory during the war, in part to escape being sent to the front. And, in the question as to which of these two elements would dominate the labor movement, much depended on the employers' conduct. But industrial-feudal Maximalism, the absolutism of the employers, created its antipode: the Maximalism of expropriation, the absolutism of the proletarians, who pictured socialism in simplified form as a simultaneous confiscation of all factories and the immediate expulsion of owners and managers, to be replaced by sovereign Factory Committees.

Back on March 13 the representatives of the Factory Committees of the biggest artillery plants, assembled in Petrograd, had realized their peculiar situation. By the almost universal flight of the Tsarist administration, these factories had been left in the workers' hands. In their resolution the representatives declared that they "do not undertake responsibility for the technical, administrative, and business organization of production"; their hour had not yet struck, that was to be postponed "until the complete socialization of all production." By the end of May, however, at the first general conference of Factory Committees, members stated from the floor: "The Factory Committees, willy-nilly, are compelled to interfere in the economic life of their factories, otherwise they would have closed down long since." "That is inevitable if we wish to live and to save production for the future." There are only two possibilities: "to submit to shortening of production and to discharge, or to interfere actively, to take over control of production and regulation of work in the plant." The further matters went, the oftener the strikers presented their ultimatum: if by such and such a date the conflict is not settled, "we will demand confiscation of the factories and mills which have not concluded collective agreements" and "we will begin practical measures to prepare for confiscation by inventorying goods, machines, etc." At this stage there appears the full Bolshevist plan: to put through "direct" workers' control by self-sufficing Factory Committees, and to transform that control into complete domination of the factories and introduction of an elected administration.

Among the workers there were influential groups of Social Revolutionaries and Social Democratic Mensheviks, who understood how helpless scattered local Factory Committees would be in organizing production. They were inspired by the constructive idea of organizing a complicated system of public and state control, with participation by the organized consumers (coöperatives) and producers (trade-unions and Soviets), based on obligatory syndicalizing of the plants and standardizing of both profits and real wages, avoiding industrial conflicts by strictly legal methods of settlement. The employers' stubborn, blind resistance and the helplessness of the Provisional Government frustrated these plans. Two irreconcilable camps then stood face to face without a buffer.

One camp said: no limitation whatsoever of the owners' rights, no interference by government in "freedom of contract" between employers and individual employees, and above all *no soviets or committees.*

The other view was summed up in the words of a working-class delegate from the Putilov Factory, who advanced rifle in hand to the tribune of the Petrograd Soviet and shouted: "Must we workers tolerate this government longer? You have gathered here to discuss, you compromise with the bourgeoisie. Then know that the worker will not stand it any longer. There are thirty thousand of us Putilov workers. We will have our way. *Let there be no bourgeoisie!*"

Two Bolshevisms stood face to face. Each fed its opposite. Caught between them were elements which tried to forestall their life-and-death struggle.

The stubbornness of the employing class predetermined the outcome of these attempts. This is a characteristic fact: in the Soviets, so hated by the bourgeoisie, the Bolsheviks were still a minority without influence. The Social Revolutionaries and Mensheviks predominated. But the Factory Committees, the organs which clashed most directly with that bourgeois "inverse Bolshevism," were won almost without resistance by the Bolsheviks. The first Petrograd Conference of Factory Committees gave the Bolsheviks an overwhelming majority over the united forces of the Social Revolutionary and Menshevik Bloc. That was an evil omen. But it was not understood. From this original citadel, the Union of Factory Committees, Bolshevism gradually spread to the Soviets, the trade-unions, etc. If Bolshevism was forged by Lenin, Trotsky, Zinoviev, and their ilk, its path was cleared by industrial leaders like Von Ditmar, Tikston, and Ryabushinsky.

The latter believed that even the temporary accession of the Bolsheviks to power would not make any change; democracy would be bankrupted the sooner in the person of the Bolsheviks, and the "bony hand of hunger" would quell the workers and force them to return with bowed head. How mistaken they were! In the workers there ripened an intense, gloomy determination to accept any hardship or hunger, if only they could discard those owners, the mere sight of whom enraged them. At other times they would probably have shrunk from a leap in the dark. But war created a false illusion of the extreme ease with which the factories could be nationalized. Their work was based on government orders and government payment; under such conditions there remained but one short step to nationalization. Secondly, the owners' "inverse Maximalism," the conceited stubbornness of men convinced of their indispensability, enraged the workers. For them it became a question of honor, no matter what the cost, to prove to these gentlemen that they were wrong. A dangerous exaltation was growing in the workers: a strong desire, having forever left the shores of the bourgeois world, to disappear in some unknown ocean rather than turn back. It was a peculiar heroism of despair. Although despair is a bad counselor, it is irresistible because it creates fanatics.

This section of the workers began to act as if it wished even at this late date to justify the employers' complaints that it was impossible to continue work. They exasperated every conflict. They harried the engineers from the factory. They beat up hated members of the factory administration. They fired on them. Finally they began to attack the owners.

On September 20 a telegram was sent from Kharkov to the Provisional Government:

A part of the workers of the factory of the General Electric Company on September 18 arrested all persons connected with the higher administration, demanding consent to an increase in rates for unskilled workers. The administration, having refused, was held under arrest about thirty-six hours, while no help was rendered either by the state's attorney's office or by the government administration. . . . As a result, the conduct of the workers of the General Electric Company was imitated in the factory of Gerlach & Pulst, where the administration was likewise subjected to arrest for twenty hours. Today, September 20, in like manner the administration of the Kharkov Locomotive Plant has been arrested. . . . The united revolutionary organizations, led by the Bolsheviks, at their last session, September 19, adopted a resolution which reads: "If within three days we do not satisfy the demands of the unskilled laborers through the arbitration commission, then the United Revolutionary Committee undertakes to solve the conflict without flinching at the most strenuous measures, including arrest of the entire Association of Manufacturers, if necessary."

Such telegrams began to arrive more and more frequently. The most alarming ones were from the Donets Basin, where, the coal operators complained, "General madness is about to grip the masses."

Those were the first flashes of that bloody dawn of the Red October and of the civil war which it brought.

CHAPTER THIRTEEN

THE GOVERNMENT AND THE AGRARIAN CONFLICT

THE coalition government proved incapable of digging a channel for the labor movement. It was even more helpless in formulating an agrarian policy.

In this question the rôle of the Labor Committee in working-class policy fell to the Chief Land Committee. The first Provisional Government had appointed 25 members to it: 2 Social Revolutionaries, 1 Populist Socialist, 1 Laborite, and 21 Cadets or Cadet sympathizers. The elected members included representatives of the provincial Land Committees, one from each province; representatives of various organizations, so arranged that the delegates from the Workers' Soviets were offset by representatives of the Provisional Committee of Members of the Imperial Duma, representatives of the Peasants' Soviets by delegates of the rival Peasants' Union; representatives of the Union of Coöperatives and of the largest agricultural societies; 11 representatives of various political parties, 5 from the socialists, and 6 from the bourgeois parties. *Ex officio* it included the Minister of Agriculture and the vice minister, and a president especially appointed by the Provisional Committee—the aged nonpartisan Populist, Professor Postnikov. The Chief Land Committee was given a wide measure of autonomy. This institution, with its very moderate majority, seemed likely to restrain effectively the activity of the socialist Minister of Agriculture, Chernov.

All these measures failed. The representatives of the provincial Land Committees met only for special sessions; despite their undemocratic composition, these committees reflected local feeling, which was rapidly turning to the Left. Of the other fifty or so members, only about half met regularly. The turning point in the work of the Chief Land Committee came during the first session, which began on May 19. On May 20 a special commission proposed to the general assembly this decree: "The land reform should be based on the idea that all agricultural land must be transferred to the use of the toiling agrarian population." The nonsocialists joined forces to pass an amendment eliminating "all" from the formula. At first it was eliminated by the slight majority of four. But after the Minister of Agriculture, Chernov, interfered, demanding a roll call, to the dissatisfaction of the authors of the amendment, the question was revoted. The roll call showed 14 votes in favor of keeping the word "all," only 4 for its elimination, with 9 abstentions. This showed the instability and lack of political courage among the Cadet opposition. The majority, consolidated by this first step, grew in numbers and in strength, while the opposition could not recover from the blow. The Right elements had no unity, and were indifferent to an institution whose work they disliked. Their absenteeism came to border on passive boycott.

The Chief Land Committee was very cumbersome and at times seemed incapable of real work. But at its first session it elected a fairly homogeneous board, which established close contact with the Executive Committee of the Soviet of Peasants' Deputies. Thus there developed a "triangle" of agrarian policy, with the Board of the Chief Land Committee as its center, and the Social Revolutionary Ministry of Agriculture and Soviet of Peasants' Deputies influencing it from both sides. But the more closely the three sides of this triangle fused, the harder it became to get its policy adopted by the coalition government.

In one field of work it was absolutely independent of the Provisional Government, and was preparing for the Constituent Assembly—in the elaboration of the legal bases of the new land order to be created by radical agrarian reform. In order to build it on firm foundations, the Ministry of

Agriculture organized a special land and agricultural census, based on the rich material of Russian zemstvo statistics, supplemented by the methods of the best foreign agricultural statistics, those of the United States. Agrarian reform was to be based on the most exact census possible of the country's agricultural resources. Its chief aim was not bare, equalitarian justice, with its leveling down to the lowest standard. The entire reform was aimed to raise productive forces on the new, purely peasant basis. The motive power back of that improvement was to be the individual interest of each toiling peasant, harmoniously coordinated with the interest of society and the state. The reform was not to make the former owner a helpless client of an omnipotent, paternal state. It proclaimed the equal right of all toilers to the soil; both he who wished to settle on the land and he who had already settled on it were to be given a strictly defined totality of rights, and could set going a system of law to invoke them.

A no less complicated task was to define concretely how the equal right of the toiler to the land was to be expressed under varying conditions. The country's entire income from agriculture, divided by the number of people engaged in it, expressed abstractly that "equality of right to the land." For each homogeneous agricultural district, and for each main branch of agriculture, this income quota would be expressed as an area of definite size, corresponding to its income, and calculated according to average local conditions. The unoccupied land of a given locality was to be divided into such lots. As for existing peasant units, slight divergences above or below this average would be balanced, not by crude partition, but by heavier taxation of the "extra-allotment surpluses" (based on their average net return), to go to a special fund for settling the unallotted lands. A return from an allotment, raised above the average by more diligent cultivation, by greater intensity of method, by the introduction of improvements, etc., was to be left untouched by taxation. Personal interest, the irreplaceable motive power of agricultural progress under modern conditions, was thus left in full force. Economic changes were to be detected by a well-organized statistical system, and all "norms" were to be revised periodically. The final result should have been a flexible system of peasant economic balance, with extensive freedom of personal enterprise. The enlargement of the peasants' land supply by wiping out large-scale landowning was not the heart of the reform. It was merely the original fillip to promote the reconstruction of that economy, to advance agricultural civilization and technique in an organized and planned way, based on the free union of toil and land.

Twenty-four commissions and subcommissions, under the Ministry of Agriculture, toiled ceaselessly, preparing for the Constituent Assembly a detailed plan of land reform and land organization. The work of these commissions, rudely interrupted by the October Revolution and completely abandoned, was later consulted frequently by the legislators and agrarian organizers of the Bolshevist Revolution. But they neglected its underlying purpose, the logical connection of its separate parts as elements of a single plan, calculated for at least a decade.

The Chief Land Committee and the Ministry of Agriculture were everywhere in close contact with the local population. They could not confine themselves to the academic work of planning the new agrarian order. Day-to-day existence brought its own burning problems, requirements, and conflicts. The village's most urgent needs had to be satisfied while leaving freedom of action to the future Constituent Assembly.

On the eve of the first session of the Chief Land Committee, on May 17, the Social Revolutionary Minister of Justice, Pereverzev, with Chernov telegraphed an administrative order to all notarial bureaus, stopping all dealings in land. But rumors spread persistently that on May 25 he had canceled that order under pressure by the majority in the

Provisional Government. On June 1 the question of "measures to preserve the land supply intact till the general solution of the land question by the Constituent Assembly" was referred to a conference of representatives of four ministries, the Land Banks, the mutual credit associations, and coöperatives. There it was pigeonholed. On June 7 a new telegram of the Minister of Justice removed all prohibition from tax contracts, purchases of nonagricultural land, and several other classes of contracts; on June 23 he ordered "the circular instructions concerning land contracts repealed." This was a course of "zigzags." On June 29 Chernov succeeded in putting through a law to wipe out the Stolypin land reform. Immediately afterwards he suffered two serious defeats. The Provisional Government rejected a bill approved by the Chief Land Committee, on the use of meadow lands. This bill was to protect the interests of the peasantry which, at the emancipation of 1861, had been deprived of its due share of meadow lands; it transferred excess meadow land to the state. The cabinet rejected another bill to regulate fisheries through mediation by the Land Committees; private monopolies and fisheries contractors had encroached on the interests of fishermen and consumers.

Obviously, the same fate menaced all other bills, particularly that regulating rental relationships and utilization of forests. Diametrical opposition developed between the viewpoints of the Ministry of Internal Affairs and the Ministry of Agriculture. On June 11 Prince Lvov made a special report to the government on the mass of "revolutionary" decrees issued by local organs of popular government, in violation of the lawful rights of the landowners. He proposed that such decrees be declared invalid, and especially urged the necessity of a public declaration to this effect, signed jointly by himself and Chernov. The latter refused categorically, for the lack of new agrarian laws from above made "separate legislation" from below inevitable. Despite the imperfections of local legislation it was a lesser evil than efforts to compel the people to abide by the old Tsarist land laws, efforts which could end only in agrarian disorder and anarchy.

The idea of sabotage, of refusing to sow their fields, had become popular among a part of the landowners at the beginning of the revolution. In many places relations between peasants and landlords had now become so tense that the gentry could only abandon farming and passively watch it die. The Land Committees could no longer remain mere onlookers. In Ranenburg district, Ryazan province, a center of the more obstinate landlords, resolutions of village and county assemblies favoring abolition of rent contracts and the "black partition"* compelled the Land Committee "to undertake to regulate this question." At a meeting of specially invited landowners, "influenced by the frightful impression caused by loss of almost two million poods† of wheat on their estates, by the empty fields, by scraggly cattle lying in courtyards and dying on many estates," the committee made a radical decision. Part of the estates it resolved to take under its direct control, part to divide up for provisional use by the peasants. This decree and the following compromise decree were canceled by higher authority. Everything went back to the original state, with one result: "plowing was broken off."

The second plenary session of the Chief Land Committee met from July 1 to 6. The Mohilev delegate reported that "throughout the province proclamations were pasted up, signed by two princes, Lvov and Drutsky-Sokolinsky, who threatened severe punishment to all violators of the old land order." This made the peasants ask if the revolution had really happened, if it was not a dream. The representative of Kursk province reported that the provincial Land Committees were forced to work under terrible conditions. They were to bring order into land relationships, eliminate disorder and anarchy, but were not given money for travel expense. A

* *Chernyĭ peredel:* direct partition of the gentry's lands by the peasantry.
† 1 pood = 0.32 cwt.

simple resolution was ripening in the peasants' minds: "We will not give the landlord a single kopeck of rent in the district, but will turn all this money into the fund of the Land Committee." The Ministry of the Interior refused to countenance far less serious steps. When the Bogoroditsky district Executive Committee taxed the gentry's land equally with the peasants', the Ministry of the Interior denounced it as "arbitrary action"; it suggested that, in case of a deficiency in funds for the land agencies, the peasants might take up a collection. Encouraged by this support, the landlords in some places refused to pay local levies; then, as in Lifland, the county committees inventoried and auctioned their property. Everywhere attempts of the Land Committees to regulate rental relationships and rates met with threats of court action. The provinces vociferously demanded the new laws promised by the Provisional Government; the Minister of Agriculture could only reply that "the bills presented to the Provisional Government did not meet with unanimous approval."[1]

This second session examined and approved in its fundamentals the draft for a new decree on Land Committees, to replace the original and now obsolete law. On July 16 that draft, which democratized their personnel and enlarged their competence, was accepted in final form by the Board of the Chief Land Committee, but "was not confirmed by the Provisional Government." Instead, a decree of the Provisional Government, dated August 25, added to the Land Committees' representatives of the Treasury, the Nobles' and Peasants' Land Banks, and where they had no branches, the managers of the Treasury branches. Instead of democratization, bureaucratization.

The second session gave unqualified support to the Ministry of Agriculture. It declared that the work of the Land Committees "was being delayed by certain instructions of the Ministry of the Interior"; "the central government was extremely backward in not having supplied the committees with a single general measure, nor issued a single general law"; only "by reversing this situation could the country be guided to the Constituent Assembly and saved from an arbitrary solution of the question."[2]

Even the local agents of the Ministry of the Interior saw plainly the unreality of their minister's policy. The district commissar of Samara province decreed as follows: "I direct the county committees to carry into effect the decrees of the Samara provincial congress immediately and without hindrance, as obligatory for all citizens. The telegram of the Vice Minister of the Interior, Leontiev, of July 27, is not to be executed." That was only a beginning. Later there was a great epidemic of resignations by district and provincial commissars of the Provisional Government, because of the impossibility of carrying out instructions sent from the capital. Even less respect was shown by the Soviets to telegrams from the central government. That of Kazan replied: "Circulars from the Ministry cannot choke the voice of the peasants. . . . Threats of prison and other punishment will not deter the Soviet from carrying out the will of the people."

Prince Lvov could not endure this breakdown of his entire policy. After he had received a delegation from the Union of Landowners, which demanded a precise answer to all its questions and was extremely pleased with the result of its interview, Lvov presented his alternatives: his resignation or Chernov's.

The Union of Landowners had first appeared in 1906–07 a product of the fright aroused by the first symptoms o agrarian revolution. After the triumph of Stolypin's re action, the nobles calmed down, and the Union broke up. In November, 1916, it reappeared, founded by a group o thirty-three persons, headed by the Court Master of Cere mony, Count Orlov-Denisov, and the Court Master of th Stalls, N. N. Shebeko, with 4 kammerherrs, 6 kammerjun kers, 1 Jägermaster of the Court, 2 state secretaries, 3 princes

5 state and actual councilors. The president of the board of directors was one of the wealthiest men in Russia, proprietor of several hundred thousand dessiatines in seven provinces, P. N. Balashov.

Under Tsarism the Union had pursued chiefly material aims. It had a contract with the Ministry of Agriculture to furnish from 2,385,000 to 4,170,000 poods of vegetables and dried fruit for the army, at very profitable prices, and with advance payment of 50% of the total order. The revolutionary government had revised the overgenerous terms, and finally canceled the contract. Then the Union became primarily political. In a memorandum to "His Excellency, the Minister President of the Provisional Government" from the Union of Simbirsk Landowners, it protested against statements of the Minister of Agriculture on the necessity "for solving local economic conflicts in the interests of the toiling peasantry." It demanded either full restoration of all property rights of the landowners, or their exemption from all taxes and levies and a moratorium on mortgages. Various local sections of the Union demanded "parity" in land committees for landowners. In the supply committees they demanded a majority for the "producers, not for the consumers" (Kuban Union of Wheat Growers). Sometimes (e.g., Union of Landowners of Rostov district) they decreed "to deprive of bread the cities from which people come to agitate for the eight-hour day or for the removal of war prisoners from field work." Orators at congresses of the Union demanded for the landowners liberty to fix the price of wheat: "*They* want fixed prices, but we want a firm government." The Samara "Union of Sowers" demanded "an immediate decree declaring null and void all decrees of the Peasants' Soviets, institutions which have not received from the government power to establish any norms whatever, likewise the decrees of land and other committees" which exceed their powers. Sometimes they issued an ultimatum, "that no laws on the land question be issued until the Constituent Assembly," for "the Provisional Government has no right" issue them. At the congress of the Union in Odessa distri Sidorenko declared that "they will have to march over o dead bodies before they take our land." The congress te graphed Kerensky demanding Chernov's removal. It d clared that the Provisional Government "had resulted nothing but anarchy, bacchanalia and disorder." Its A Russian Congress protested against sending a telegram greetings to the Provisional Government: "We do not wish thank them for robbing us."

The delegation of the Union now returned to its congre greatly pleased with Prince Lvov. In demanding that t Provisional Government choose between them, Prince Lv formulated his accusations against Chernov quite in t spirit of the Union. "He issues decrees which undermi popular respect for law; he does not combat the striving seize the land, does not standardize and guide land relatio ships into the proper channel, but he even seems to justi the fatal, arbitrary seizures occurring throughout Russi and confirms what has already taken place."

In his own way Prince Lvov was, of course, absolute right. Chernov's bills did not attempt to force land relatio ships back into the *old* channel. On the contrary, they open favored the peasants' irresistible striving for the land, t right to which belonged solely to labor, in the popular co ception of right. Chernov felt that the only way in which t agrarian legislator could escape "confirming an accomplish fact," whatever form it might take, was through legislati which would not always lag behind reality, as it had so fa but would hastily dig a new channel for its irresistible cu rent.

Lvov's withdrawal from the ministry merely made a pla at the head of the government for Kerensky, and in this co flict he was for the first and last time on Chernov's sid Utilizing the simultaneous resignation of the Cadet ministe over the Ukrainian question, and pressing home his adva

THE ARRIVAL OF PRIME MINISTER KERENSKY (LOWER CENTER, IN KHAKI UNIFORM)
IN MOSCOW FOR THE STATE CONFERENCE

Courtesy of the Muzei Revolutsii, U.S.S.R.

tage, Chernov finally put through his legislation forbidding dealings in land until the meeting of the Constituent Assembly. The only concession which he had to make was to substitute for the prohibitive form of the law an outwardly mild and permissive one: land contracts required in each case special permission of the local provincial Land Committee and confirmation by the Minister of Agriculture.[8] In the Soviet of Peasants' Deputies and the All-Russian Central Executive Committee of Soviets, Chernov received noisy ovations. The policy of inaction, of helpless attempts to hem the peasantry within the framework of the prerevolutionary land code, seemed ended once and forever.

This hopeful feeling was jarred by a sharp dissonance. The commander of the Southwest front, General Kornilov, had isued an order for the entire frontal area on July 8; under pain of criminal prosecution and loss of property rights and arrest, he forbade all "arbitrary interference" in land relationships by local agencies. The order particularly prohibited compelling the gentry to raise the wages of war prisoners or removing these prisoners from the large estates to work for the soldiers' wives. The order provoked a ferment in both village and army. The general was not joking. The Poltava provincial land commissar was indicted for violating these decrees. The military authorities ordered such cases examined without delay; if necessary, military force was to be used. Emboldened by this example, civilian justice, represented by the state's attorney's offices, became active outside the frontal area. They began to arrest members of the Land Committees. The latter lost all authority among the population, and their further activity became impossible.

Chernov took a new step: on July 16 he issued "instructions to the Land Committees." He confirmed the right of the Land Committees to take over land which the landowners were unable to cultivate, and to distribute it among the peasants. He confirmed the power of the local Land Committees as mediators in revising rental contracts between owners and lessors.

Peasants in a privileged situation, after deducting norma feed requirements for their own cattle, were to surrender th rest for war needs at fixed prices. The instruction permitte compulsory utilization of the gentry's animal and mechani cal equipment, but required consent by Land and Suppl Committees and direct supervision by them. The Land Com mittees were to supervise protection of forests against preda tory lumbering and to secure for the peasants the privileg of taking wood for the actual needs of their households an for public institutions. Protection of model farms, bloode cattle and valuable crops was provided for. In conclusion the instruction recommended that the Land Committees g half way to satisfy the just and well-founded demands of th toiling peasantry, that they regard themselves as the author ized organs of the state and count on the full support of th Ministry of Agriculture; the latter, in turn, would do every thing it could to issue new laws, in order to "end the presen precarious and indefinite situation in land relationships, th cause of similar precariousness and indefiniteness in th popular conception of right and law."

The Ministry of Agriculture was at once attacked by th Ministry of Justice: "The application of Sect. 4, Art. 7 o the decree on Land Committees, because of the right grante to Land Committees of issuing obligatory decrees affectin agricultural and land relationships, would mean limiting th right to dispose of private property."

It is hard to believe that such a view could be proclaimec not in the revolution, but even during the World War, whic had long since made private property a social functior hemmed in by a multitude of limitations and instructions beneath the Damocles' sword of requisition.

Simultaneous circulars were issued by the Ministries o Supply and the Interior. Chernov's circular had been a ra of hope for the local authorities; the other two discourage them profoundly, especially that of the Interior, drafte under Prince Lvov, though signed by a temporary substi tute, Tseretelli. This circular ignored the irresistible transition of the village from one land order to another. It was drawn up in the phrases of the old administrative Utopia: "resolute measures" against "violators of the law," no "overstepping their power" by the Land Committees, threat of reprisals "under the full severity of the law." Here is one reply from the provinces:

The circular telegram of the Ministry of the Interior of July 18 has been dispatched to the provincial commissars. Copies are already in the hands of all gentry, and within a few days will be known to the entire people of toilers and will arouse alarm for the future of agrarian reform. . . . Comrades! You are misled by people who are sowing whirlwind and anarchy. You are remote from the feelings of the village.[4]

Chernov's instruction was an attempt to build a bridge between the action of the government and the feeling of the village. How could such cautious instructions have raised this tempest?

By now the alarm and anxiety of the gentry had reached their high point, their bitterness demanded a scapegoat. The victim was the Land Committees toward which the Cadet party and censitary Russia felt like the hen that hatched duck's eggs. General Kornilov's dictatorial gesture, plainly calculated to win the landlords' hearts, had given them fresh hope. But by his instruction Chernov had sanctioned the activity of the Land Committees, made them executors of a higher will, and invited the people to deal directly with them. This blocked the government's path in its surrender to the vigorous pressure from the Right.

The government discussed whether the Ministry of Justice could formally indict the Ministry of Agriculture for overstepping its powers. But another loophole was discovered. The Bolsheviks had suffered a first big defeat in their attempt to bring the masses on to the street, to compel the Soviet to take over all power. Kerensky had brought troops from the front to Petrograd. Arrests of Bolsheviks began; all the Right raised its head, demanding dispersal of the Soviets as well as the Bolsheviks. Chernov was the chief target of the anti-Soviet campaign. To avenge his defeat of the previous May, Miliukov led the attack. His newspaper, *Rech*, accused Chernov of "defeatism," because he had participated in the Zimmerwald conference of socialist parties, which had urged the slogan of the struggle for the earliest possible democratic peace. In his literary activity during the World War, Chernov had always carried on a determined polemic against defeatism.[5] He was also accused of helping to publish literature "with German money" for Russian prisoners of war in Germany. The sole pretext was his participation in the "Society for Spiritual Comfort to Russian Prisoners of War," which published a periodical, *Na Chuzhbine.* The Society included Left-wing Internationalists, like M. A. Nathanson, and Right-wing Defensists, thoroughly patriotic leaders, like Colonel Oberuchev. In some German concentration camps the military authorities had even taken steps to prevent the circulation of this periodical. The bitter political struggle in Russia had now reached its apogee. It did not stick at its choice of weapons. The slogan of censitary Russia was, "No Zimmerwaldian on the government benches." Later this slogan was repeated publicly at the Moscow State Conference by the Cossack general, Kaledin, and the Right-wing Cadet, Maklakov. The words "Zimmerwald," "defeatism," and "German money" were identified in the Philistine mind. To combat the Great Land Reform openly was harder than to take the roundabout path of personal slander. The wave of filth was rising higher. Finally, rumors spread that Burtsev and Shchegolev, investigators of espionage, held documents convicting Chernov of "serving the Germans."

Chernov now demanded that the government investigate all his actions; he declared that he would give up his ministry for a time, to facilitate the presentation of accusations. In the Soviet, especially among the peasant deputies, this news caused an outburst. The peasants declared that in the villages this would be like tossing a spark into a powder magazine. The intransigent gentry would raise their heads; the peasants, now losing all hope of a legislative solution to these urgent questions, would have to rely on their own forces and embark on the most desperate acts: an All-Russian pogrom of the gentry would result. Only with great difficulty could Chernov calm them by the assurance that the slanderers would quickly be discredited. The alarm spread among the provincial peasant congresses then in session. The Tambov Congress declared that "Chernov's withdrawal and delay in passing his provisional laws will inevitably cause disorders and anarchy in the village." The Voronezh Congress telegraphed: "Chernov must remain as Minister of Agriculture, the peasants' minister. He has our support, the peasantry believe in him, hope with him at their head to carry out the socialization of the land." The crisis in the Ministry of Agriculture evoked response in the army; a flood of the strongest telegrams demanded Miliukov's arrest and threatened that the army would punish the sowers of slander and demoralization.

After Burtsev and Shchegolev had refuted all reference to incriminating documents alleged to be in their possession, in accord with the report of the Ministry of Justice the government recognized that the accusation had no factual basis. In the new coalition cabinet Chernov was again Minister of Agriculture. To give partial satisfaction to the Cadets, Kerensky sacrificed Tseretelli, evidently not without secret pleasure; more moderate than Chernov, Tseretelli was a dangerous rival to Kerensky because of his influence within the government.

On July 30 Chernov convoked a conference of representatives of the Ministry of Agriculture attached to the provincial Land Committees. As one, they insisted that the duties intrusted to the Land Committees required the grant of corresponding powers. Without such powers and new laws to guide them, the Land Committees could only run afoul of the courts or else disband. A special delegation was sent to Kerensky to make energetic representations. "The head of the government replied that all questions could not be answered at once, and asked them to inform the local population that new laws would be issued within the next few days."[6]

Nevertheless, Chernov's attempt to turn this promise to advantage by passing a law regulating the use of forest commons ended with the usual failure. This was one of the most sensitive spots for the village, for the price of lumber had been boosted by speculators beyond the peasants' purse. After several sessions of the Provisional Government, filled with sharp clashes, the study of the bill was interrupted, and later transferred to a special juridical commission. It was returned to the Provisional Government only on October 10.

The Chief Land Committee made one more effort to influence the government. A fresh warning, signed by its president, the moderate nonpartisan Professor Postnikov, was sent to Kerensky. The letter complained of the "irresoluteness of the Provisional Government in carrying out measures to bring order into the new land relationships." Under such conditions "the Land Committees, left to themselves, without definite standards and limits, were trying to satisfy, each in its own way, the urgent demands of reality"; this resulted in a chaotic variety of local decisions. "The situation is rendered more acute by attempts of the organs of government to execute existing laws, to apply risky measures, including arrests of local Land Committees." Life was moving swiftly; the government's slowness could only sharpen the present serious situation. The president of the Chief Land Committee predicted that persistence in this policy would lead to complete anarchy and sabotage the entire agrarian reform.

"On August 9 the Provisional Government at last devoted

a special session to the agrarian question. After listening to a two-hour report by V. M. Chernov, the government took no decision."[7]

At this session the Right wing of the government attacked Chernov. It accused him of publishing his numerous (in all, fourteen) drafts before they were adopted by the Provisional Government, while in the provinces all the Soviets, Land Committees and local branches of his party of Social Revolutionaries seized upon them as if they were already law, and began to carry them out. Chernov replied that he would continue to publish his drafts—as was, incidentally, the practice of all the Ministries—because he considered it obligatory for the Provisional Government to work with public knowledge. The idea of passively resisting the agrarian revolution, now advancing with irresistible tread, was both objectionable and futile. They could either formulate this enormous change in the country's agrarian order through legislation, or, by obstinate but helpless resistance, they could provoke an explosion, chaos, a Pugachev agrarian revolt. In Yelshinsky district, Smolensk province, 14 county Land Committees had been arrested; in another district, 70 men, described by the district Land Committee as "the best, most experienced people, trusted by the population." If things went thus, declared Chernov, three fourths of Russia would have to be hailed into court. Whoever thinks that this is possible in a country shaken by revolution is blind.

But Chernov and the majority of the Provisional Government were, in Lassalle's expression, "barbarians to one another"; they spoke different languages.

Chernov's continuance in the Provisional Government had become absolutely purposeless. He had so stated several times to the Central Committee of the party of Social Revolutionaries; each time the reply was that his resignation would bring catastrophe. But in the leading circles of the party the opinion began to take shape that perhaps Chernov's policy could be saved by sacrificing his person. This was due, as in Tseretelli's case, to Kerensky's difficulty in putting up with independent personalities in his government.

Kerensky's open conflict with the commander in chief, General Kornilov, now exposed their very confused and ambiguous relations, and gave Chernov a pretext for breaking with Kerensky in decisive fashion and returning to the Soviet.

The first result of his withdrawal was a fresh blow at the Land Committees. On September 8, the Provisional Government subjected the Land and the Supply Committees to the control of special administrative courts.

After that, however, there seemed to be some improvement. S. L. Maslov, personally "neutral," was willingly accepted by Kerensky as Minister of Agriculture. The first gain was the promise of the Minister of Justice, Malyantovich, to free the arrested members of Land Committees. However, fulfilment of this peculiar and informal amnesty was postponed. Some of the arrested members were released from prison only by the October Revolution.

Chernov now began defending his policy energetically through the press. He tried every means, including an appeal to the elementary common-sense of the gentry.

> The preventive rôle of the Land Committees has not been understood, nor their services appreciated, and those who have been most ungrateful are those whom they have in fact saved from something worse, the landowners. . . . They have not stopped to consider what would have happened but for the Land Committees. The Land Committees have sifted out the peasants' requests. The landlords do not realize that they are sawing off the branch on which they lean.

At the Peasants' Congress of Tambov province, a relatively quiet region, the delegates noted with intense alarm the sudden, ominous flare-up of a pogrom movement against the nobles. Its secretary concluded that, because of delay in carrying out the ministry's declaration, "such disorders are inevitable: beginning in one county, they will blaze up like a conflagration and spread throughout the country. If the declaration is not carried into effect, the village will soon drive out the Soviets of Peasants' Deputies and the Land Committees: so far we have given it nothing but words."

The farther events unfolded, the more insistent Chernov's campaign became. Finally he cried, with the voice of one crying in the wilderness: "We cannot delay. The government's responsibility at such a moment is too great. Stop the conflagration, decree at once transfer of the land to the control of the Land Committees!"

But to the end the government kept to its snail's pace. It was only in the middle of October that Maslov introduced a bill "for the regulation of land and agricultural relationships by the Land Committees." To get it through the "eye of the needle" of the Provisional Government, Maslov consented to a number of changes in Chernov's policy. Lenin, in exultation, rang the tocsin: "The Social Revolutionaries . . . have betrayed the peasants, they have betrayed the Peasants' Soviets, they have gone over to the side of the landowners!"[8] Even that did not help. The government met to discuss this draft on October 24; the discussion was suspended to cope with the emergency question of defending the capital. The Bolshevik coup d'état was beginning its triumphant march through the streets.

Meanwhile, left without the guidance of a clear, firm government policy, the agrarian problem had moved irresistibly toward a collision between two Maximalisms, that of the peasants, and that of the gentry. "We do not admit the possibility of alienating the land without compensation," Count Olsufiev stated at the Saratov provincial congress of landowners, "because that would be not an act of authority but out-and-out robbery." Thus, the gentry's "landed sovereignty," in this view of property, was superior even to the sovereignty of the state.

The peasant could sooner agree that the noble should pay for his age-old and unjust use of the "common," "God's," or the "Tsar's" land, than accept the idea of paying him for the land, "watered with the muzhik's bloody sweat." The peasant with his semimystical idea of Mother Earth rejected compensation. But he had other motives, profoundly practical.

At the very beginning of the revolution Professor Katzenellenbaum figured out the cost of land redemption. "The total compensation would equal five billion rubles."[9] The state was on the verge of bankruptcy. Russia had to renounce the land reform or else effect it without compensation.

There was another side to the question. Professor Katzenellenbaum figured that "after effecting the compensation the Treasury would have to pay three hundred million rubles in annual interest on old and new debts." The peasants paid the nobles about three hundred million rubles annually in rent. After reform the same three hundred million rubles would still rest on them, but under another name.

"Was it for this that we fought for decades? For this that we made the revolution?" This cry burst from the lips of the peasants when the partisans of compensation tried to explain how the financial side of the land reform could be organized.

"Such orators did not please our muzhik. Why, down with all orators who want us to pay the gentry—what the devil is such liberty worth?"[10]

For the landlords, without a positive solution of the question of compensation, a provisional, "conciliatory" policy had no sense. Were they asked to accept a compromise? Perhaps it was worth accepting if it stabilized their position for the future. But the compromise was provisional, until the land question as a whole was settled by the Constituent Assembly. What would happen then? Obviously, the complete elimination of private agriculture. Then, what would the gentry gain by a compromise, and what would they lose by rejecting all compromise? They would gain nothing, and had nothing to lose, for in the Constituent Assembly their cause was plainly lost beyond hope.

Of course, under a policy of compromise all the progressive estates and more elaborate technics of the gentry would be preserved and pass into the new agrarian order. Only the signboards would change. The private estates would become model farms run by the state, the zemstvo, or the district co-operative societies. The state, progressive peasants, and the socialist Minister of Agriculture, Chernov, wished to achieve that through the plan for a national land reform. But the injured gentry? Was it not more tempting to say: If all this is not to be mine, then let no one have it! The worse, the better! Let them break into the mansion, tear it down brick by brick, and divide it by "equalization," let them plunder the forest, let them ruin, burn!

At the All-Russian State Conference the official representative of the Union of Landowners ended with the famous phrase: "You say our landed property is done for? So be it! We see that the partition of the land is not to be averted. Let there be a partition, let there be a 'black partition,' but not a Chernov partition!"

A social class in danger of complete disintegration inevitably develops a nervous instability which to it seems a "heroism of despair." Among the numerous appeals circulated among the landowners special interest attaches to one document. "Future proletarians, Russian landowners, unite!" Thus began the appeal of the "Union of Unfortunate Landowners." Its practical conclusion read:

> Since the socialists did not recognize autocracy, even when it enjoyed universal recognition, we cannot recognize the criminal, plundering republic. We cannot escape ruin, nor our children hunger, because we shall never submit to the commands of a criminal government which wishes to legalize seizure, downright robbery, and theft. We shall find no place in our reckless fatherland, just as the socialists found none. But the socialists had recourse to revenge and terrorism when they had no other path.

Hundreds of thousands of impoverished landowners can certainly secrete one tenth of their number, and these unfortunates one dark night will go with boxes of matches and bottles of kerosene to tens of thousands of predatory villages and hamlets, where sessions will shortly be held in touching unanimity by Soviets of Workers', Soldiers', and Peasants' Deputies, who have fled there after the bankruptcy of the factories and mills, and they will carry out an All-Russian conflagration, sparing neither houses, forests, nor crops. In this terrible, inevitable revenge we shall gain our only consolation.[11]

This and similar documents were regarded as mere curiosities, like the anonymous threats daily showered upon the socialist Minister of Agriculture, Chernov. There were the usual angry outpourings, death sentences from real or fictitious organizations, ultimatums, ordinary letters, and missives written in blood for greater effect.

The threat of guerrilla warfare in the village might become a reality if the gentry could coöperate with prosperous elements in the village itself, and not merely with the kulaks, a class of money-lending parasites, hated by the village, a class economically important, but scattered and weak in numbers. They would have had to coöperate with a group comprising almost one fourth of peasant Russia, the "separated peasants," favored by Stolypin's land policy, which aimed to create in Russia the economically strong farmer of the Western European type. The gentry did, indeed, plan to join with these elements in a national "Union of Landowners," which entered the political arena with a great deal of noise and fireworks. But with a few exceptions the results of its activity fell far short of the effort expended. The "separated peasants," forced to choose between the doomed gentry and the many millions of peasants, usually did not hesitate long. Indeed, they could not hesitate.

The newspapers of that time abounded in reports like the following:

In the village of Svishchevka, Spazhkovsky county, Saratov

province, the small farmers and "separated peasants" joined together and decided to support the party of Social Revolutionaries. In order to avoid disputes over the land until the Constituent Assembly meets, they decided to leave each the land he had, but anyone unable to work his land with the aid of his own family should surrender it to the commune through the Land Committee.

Decision. July 14, 1917, we, the undersigned citizens of the village of Anastasino, Shiroko-Ustupsky county, Atkarsky district, all owners of "separate plots," have learned that the big landowners and gentry have formed a union to defend their private property, and to draw us, the "separated peasants" into it, to increase their numbers. Profoundly indignant at such impudence on the part of the landowners, we declare in advance that we "separated peasants" will never betray our unfortunate, landless brother peasants, nor enter into any such union with our eternal enemies. We await the Constituent Assembly, our free lands we give to fellow members of the commune who have no "separated" holdings. We have, and have had, no objection to turning our "separated" holdings into the commune.[12]

In some spheres the Union of Landowners did find a favorable response. At the congress of its Ryazan section a local leader of the landowners' movement, Kazakov, cheered the delegates with the news: "The Council of the All-Russian Union of Landowners has established close contact with the Council of Congresses of the Representatives of Industry and Commerce, and has the sympathy of the banks, especially the land banks." In Tambov and Penza provinces the unions of landowners and manufacturers joined hands. A telegram to the Ministry of Internal Affairs from Tula, describing the anarchy in the province and demanding the dispatch of a regiment of cavalry, was signed by the Union of Landowners, the Union of Industrialists, and the "Union of the Clergy of the Tula Diocese."

In the village itself the Russian landowners gained certain successes. For instance, their Novgorod-Seversky section had over 3,000 members by July, that of Poltava 2,500, those of Sergievo, Odessa, Ekaterinoslav, and several others about 500 members each. Of course, on the tremendous, gray-coated peasant sea these were scarcely ripples. Probably the chief activity of the Unions was in organizing the torrent of complaints which showered upon the Provisional Government, attacking the peasants' initiative, and demanding redress of injured property rights. The Ministry of Internal Affairs replied with a similar flood of telegrams to its commissars in the provinces, and their replies indicated again and again the falseness of the complaints. From a very uneasy district (Ranenburg, Ryazan province) the district commissar reported:

> Of the enormous quantity of complaints not one has been confirmed by careful investigation. Personnel and funds were wasted, all to follow up false denunciations. These were undoubtedly attempts to undermine the strength of the Land Committee and to sow discord among the population, a thing which was easy in the first two months of the revolution.[13]

At the second session of the Chief Land Committee the representative of Nizhni-Novgorod province reported that there was only one topic among the peasants: We are tired of waiting, we have waited three hundred years, and now that we have conquered power, we do not want to wait any more."

What were they waiting for? They were told: For the Constituent Assembly. Unfortunately, this assembly was postponed with depressing regularity. No better means for sickening the peasant of the Constituent Assembly could have been invented.

And so the idea that there was no need to wait for the Constituent Assembly and that the land must be seized at once found ready soil. At the second session of the Chief Land Committee a Smolensk representative reported the talk of the peasants in Sychevsky district: "They say of the Constituent Assembly: Well, Nicholas was overthrown without the Constituent Assembly; why can't the gentry be driven from the face of the earth without it?" The Bolsheviks, who were on the job, nudged them: They can be. You have only to set up a workers' and peasants' dictatorship and settle all problems "in two shakes of a lamb's tail," with a mere flourish of the pen at the foot of revolutionary decrees.

The gentry were not at all scared by this. Dictatorship, Bolshevism, what difference to them if the Constituent Assembly would not leave them their land, or pay them for it? The "worse, the better"—let everything be done in the most abrupt and despotic way. On this *reductio ad absurdum* the revolution would break its own neck.

Later even a progressive and cautious landlord and Octobrist, Shidlovsky, wrote:

> I think that the Bolsheviks, without suspecting it, did Russia a colossal service, an unforgettable service, in dispersing the Constituent Assembly, presided over by Chernov. Nothing good could come from it, while it would have done no less harm than the Bolsheviks, though without dictatorship or terrorism; I feel that if the country was doomed to experience a severe crisis, it is better to have all the scorpions at once than gradually.[14]

If people could say this after having experienced the scourges of dictatorship and terrorism, it was all the easier for them to uphold this "negative Maximalism" when the "dictatorship of the proletariat" was merely a vague, abstract idea, which had not yet revealed its contents of blood and terror.

For a moment the gentry saw a ray of hope, not in creating a powerful organization which would dam up the peasant movement, but in the schism and disorganization within the movement.

The peasantry had joined Soviet democracy. They had added to the existing Soviets of Workers' and Soldiers' Deputies the Soviets of Peasants' Deputies, dominated by the party of Social Revolutionaries. Earlier, in 1905, there had been a nonpartisan "All-Russian Peasants' Union." After friction with the "Peasants' Union of the Party of Social Revolutionaries," its leaders now undertook to maintain a parallel competing organization, the All-Russian Peasants' Union.

On March 12 there was a first appeal, "To all the peasantry," from a self-appointed Chief Committee of the Peasants' Union. Without reservation it backed the "sacred union of all classes." It urged the people not "to inconvenience private business, not to interfere in its concerns. . . . Let even the gentry sow their fields." Incidentally, the appeal favored "restoration of free exchange, destroyed by the Tsarist government," in other words, abolition of the policy of fixed prices for agricultural products. It was in the country's interest to protect industrial capitalism for, where industry and commerce are "free of state interference," they enrich the country and the treasury. Where they "do not find proper conditions," capital "may easily be transferred to other states" and even make its way "to the banks of our enemies."

The Peasants' Union did not dare attack the Peasants' Soviets directly. It even took part in organizing the All-Russian Congress of Peasants' Soviets. The Soviets, in its view, were temporary organizations, to last only till the Constituent Assembly, to supervise the Provisional Government and support the socialist ministers. The Peasants' Union, on the other hand, was to be the permanent political organization of the village. The Chief Committee of the Peasants' Union let it be clearly understood that, unlike the Soviets, which supported the socialist ministers, the Peasants' Union would give unconditional support to the Provisional Government as a whole.

The logic of the situation compelled the Peasants' Union to convoke an All-Russian Congress of its own directly after the All-Russian Congress of Peasants' Soviets. This separatist tendency of the Union was arousing alarm among the leaders of the Peasants' Soviets. The peasant movement was being deliberately split. The leaders of the Union had to choose between it and the Soviets. Many of the Union's most promising leaders now urged the liquidation of the Union. The socialist ministers, Peshekhonov and Chernov, also declined to participate in the congress of the Union. The remaining members of its Chief Committee stubbornly defended their enterprise and succeeded in assembling their congress on July 31 in Moscow. After the presiding committee of the congress refused the floor to those who protested in favor of a single organization and of absorbing the Union into the Soviets, the minority withdrew demonstratively. Part of the delegates dispersed. The rest, amounting to under one hundred and fifty, later less than one hundred, insisted on electing an Organization Committee. Defections at once began in this. Beside the All-Russian Congress of Soviets of Peasants' Deputies, with its 1,353 delegates, the Moscow congress of the Union was a negligible quantity. After the congress a struggle started in the provinces between the Soviets of Peasants' Deputies and the branches of the Peasants' Union; the former were victorious and the latter lost all importance, except on the Don and in the Ukraine.

Characteristically, the congress of the Peasants' Union, under strong pressure from the Left, displayed its "Rightness" only in the field of abstract policy. In the social sphere it cruelly deceived the hopes of censitary democracy. Instead of "freedom of exchange" it demanded control and fixed prices for industrial goods, "transfer of all land to the use of the toiling people without compensation," and destruction of "private property in land."

The gentry could now only try to postpone as long as possible the convocation of the Constituent Assembly, and meanwhile squeeze all they could from their estates. The estates could be mortgaged and remortgaged, thus gaining for their owners far more than by government compensation. The "cream could be skimmed" by cutting down the valuable forests and selling off the best animal and mechanical equipment. Parceling, real or fictitious, could be resorted to in order to conceal a surplus of land over and above the norm guaranteed against confiscation. Land could be sold to foreigners whose property rights would be defended by their governments. Unbridled land speculation was rife.

The peasantry at once sensed the new menace. "Beware the masters do not twist us around their finger again," "Be careful not to let the land slip," was heard everywhere. The first and universal demand of the village was now the prohibition of all contracts of sale, mortgage, donation, etc., until the meeting of the Constituent Assembly; secondly, to avoid this partial decline, the estates, with all their stock, equipment, meadows, etc., must be taken under the control of the local Land Committees. This added a new dispute to the quarrels about rentals, prisoners of war, wages on the estates, use of hay fields, forests. It implied constant invasion of the nobles' farmyard by the peasant. Had the owner sent the blooded cattle away? Were the rumors true about his mortgaging the land or selling the forest? Regarding the noble's estate as the lawful heritage of the emancipated people, the village set up its own guardianship over it. Where the nobles consented, peaceful and even neighborly relations were restored. Where the gentry resisted—and where did they not resist?—their Maximalism provoked the gloomy counter-Maximalism of the peasants.

The soil was prepared for Bolshevism. It began to penetrate, taking on a primitive aspect in a primitive environment.

A Bolshevist peasant describes the birth of village Bolshevism in Tambov province:

At the meeting the peasants split into two groups. One proposed to take the estates from the nobles in an orderly way and divide up all the property proportionately among the population, but to preserve the gentry's buildings for cultural purposes. The other group proposed to burn down all the estates immediately, not leaving one stone on another; "by orderliness," they said, "we shall never drive the nobles from the estates."

The poor peasants favored the second group, the proletarians, and they were the majority. At exactly ten in the evening the crowd, feeling its gigantic power, approached Romanov's estate. They broke into the house, dragged the owner out to the street in only his nightgown, and the vengeance began. . . . They set fire to the wheat and the estate, and began to plunder the house.

The fiery signal was caught up by other villages: the peasants of Yaroslavka went to plunder and burn the Davydov estate, the peasants of Tidvorka and Yekaterinino burned the Ushakovs' estate, and Komarov's, the village of Bashovo burned Volosatova-Zaeva, and during the night of September 7–8 a sea of conflagrations swept over the estates of our country. On the morning of September 8 along the road to the village crowds of people were straggling with stolen property: some with wheat, others with a bed, cattle, or a broken armchair.[15]

In Chernigov province, on the estate of the former president of the nobility, Sudienko, "the stock, equipment, furniture, etc., were divided by the peasants, each taking whatever he could. The land was divided among the peasants, and all the buildings burned down. In the mansion house there were many historical treasures, and an enormous library, which the peasants tore up to roll cigarettes. Paintings by famous artists were torn off before the house was burned and used to make trousers. . . ."[16]

The nobles did not want "Chernov's partition" at any cost. They preferred the "black partition" and they had their "black partition."

Oh, yes, they thought it would turn out differently. They thought that the peasantry's rushing headlong into wild excesses would help serve to rouse the Provisional Government from its irresolution and lead it to send military detachments to subdue the peasants.

That was stark madness. There was no better means of demoralizing the army than to send it, with its 90% of peasants, to crush the movement of millions of its brethren.

In Samara province the soldiers' wives raised a rebellion:

Let us go and mow the grass of the gentry; why are our husbands suffering for the third year? The gentry brought a detachment of soldiers from Hvalynsk. But when the soldiers, who were peasants themselves, saw the muzhiks mowing the rich grass, they tried their hand at mowing; they were tired of their rifles. The peasants fed the soldiers, talked to them, and then set to work all the harder.

In Tambov province a military detachment came at the summons of Prince Vyazemsky. It was greeted by a roar from the crowd: "What are you doing, coming to defend the prince, coming to beat your own fathers? Throw the devils into the river!" The commander took it into his head to fire into the air. He was struck by a stone and ordered the troops to disperse the mob, but the soldiers did not stir. The officer spurred his horse and escaped from the enraged peasants by fording the river. His detachment scattered and let the crowd surround the prince, whom they arrested and sent to the front as a "slacker." At a near-by station he was lynched by a detachment of Siberian shock troops on their way to the front.

In Slavuta, Izyaslavsky district, Volhynia province, a detachment of fifty Cossacks was sent to the Sangushko estate to pacify the peasants. A detachment of infantry from the front was also quartered nearby. The Cossacks went out to reconnoiter in the woods. The soldiers then "set out with the peasants. First, they burst into the prince's palace. The prince tried to flee. The soldiers quickly scattered to search for him. They overtook him near a steep bridge and tossed him on their bayonets; three times they lifted Sangushko on their bayonets, at the fourth thrust the bayonet went straight to his heart. The soldiers and peasants, without wasting time, carried three iron chests from the mansion, with several million rubles in gold, silver, and paper money, distributed the money to the poor, and then burned the chambers of the prince. The peasants went boldly out to divide the land, afraid of no one."[17]

Gray-uniformed peasants, aroused by the revolution in the city, were sent against the village, which would not and could not go on indefinitely under the Tsarist agrarian laws, once Tsarism had fallen. A more suicidal policy could not have been invented.

CHAPTER FOURTEEN

IMPASSE IN THE NATIONALITIES PROBLEM

THE famous geographer, Élisée Reclus, said, in 1905:

> The Moscow Revolution, like the French Revolution, will occupy a definite place among outstanding periods in the life of mankind. . . . To the working class will belong the initiative of emancipation. The peasants will also be drawn into the process of the great revolution. But another question besides class division is arising, a question which undoubtedly agitates profoundly the peoples of Russia, with their different languages and different levels of national development. What is called Russia is a limitless expanse of earth, conquered by the Tsars and inhabited by various oppressed peoples; finally, there is the huge country of the Ukraine, robbed of the right to its native language and its free literary development. The Finns, the tribes of Turanian origin, Bashkirs, Tatars, Kalmucks. . . . Six million Jews, shut off in their pale. . . . The Georgians to whom the Tsars solemnly promised full respect for their independence; the Armenians. . . . The chain of oppressed peoples stretches far into the depths of Asia. . . . They all await freedom, which revolution will bring them!

The venerable geographer seemed to foresee that great "Congress of the Peoples of Russia" (Poles, Ukrainians, White Russians, Lithuanians, Letts, Esthonians, Georgians, Moslems, Moldavians, and Cossacks) of September, 1917, which proclaimed the federal form of government alone worthy of the new Russia. This congress was greeted by a special representative of the Provisional Government, who expressed complete sympathy for its fundamental idea. At that very time the Provisional Government was engaged in bitter conflict with the largest of the "subject" nationalities, the Ukrainians.

Of all the Great Russian parties only the party of Social Revolutionaries had adopted the federal form of state in its program. It was strongly opposed by all bourgeois parties, including the most progressive of them, the Cadet party. The Cadet leaders and jurists played a significant rôle in turning against the Provisional Government all or almost all the smaller nationalities. The federal idea also penetrated with great difficulty among Russian Social Democrats, whether Bolsheviks or Mensheviks.

There were doctrinaires of united Statehood (with a big S), idolaters of centralized government; it alone could determine the scope of local and regional self-government by its own "grace." There were also doctrinaires of economic unity and centralization, of the concentration of the "fatherlandless" proletariat through the growing concentration of "fatherlandless" capital.

Both overlooked the fact that if the French Revolution had given to the world the Declaration of the Rights of Man, the Great Russian Revolution must proclaim the rights of nationalities—those living, collective individualities and agents in mankind's cultural history, which no doctrinaire in the world could dissuade from their fundamental idea: man is not for the Sabbath, but the Sabbath for man; in other words, national economy and the state are for the people, not the people for the state and national economy.

Kiev was the center of the Ukrainian movement. The revolution there had been entirely bloodless. Local public leaders, from Board of Trade and War Industries Committees, zemstvo and municipal institutions to editorial boards of newspapers and student organizations, coöperative societies and trade-unions, organized a Council of United Civic Organizations. This council elected an Executive Committee, responsible to its electors, and at the same time regarded as local representative of the Provisional Government. The cities in the Ukraine were considerably Russified. This affected the national composition of the Executive Committee, which, in its overwhelming majority, was alien to the Ukrainian movement. The Executive Committee of Civic Organizations was, at bottom, a rallying point for the Russian minority in the Ukraine.

A day or two later another organization arose, at first of very modest appearance. It included delegates from the Ukrainian Scientific Society, the Ukrainian Pedagogical Society, the National Ukrainian Union, and from coöperative and student organizations. It took the name of "Central Ukrainian Rada" (i.e., Soviet or Council). It sent greetings to Prince Lvov and Kerensky and expressed its hope that "in free Russia all the lawful rights of the Ukrainian people would be given satisfaction." Simultaneously it appealed to all provincial organizations to send delegations to the Provisional Government to state the urgent needs of the Ukrainian people, to create cultural and educational organizations, and to collect money for a national cultural fund.

At first this organization attracted little attention. The limelight was fixed on the Civic Committee and on the Soviet of Workers' and the Soviet of Soldiers' Deputies. The older censitary city duma was reorganized by admitting representatives of democracy. A struggle flared up in the Soviets between Bolsheviks and Mensheviks. Trade-unions were growing impetuously. Aside from these purely urban movements there was growing, almost unnoticed, a Ukrainian national movement. It was in close touch with the peasantry, that underlying mass of the Ukrainian people which had preserved unchanged its own national life, transmitted from the historic past. Late in March the Kiev provincial zemstvo announced its ambition to become "the national Ukrainian zemstvo." A Central Ukrainian Coöperative Council was formed. On the holiday of the revolution national Ukrainian banners and placards with "Long live Free Ukraine!" made their appearance. An assembly of Ukrainian officers declared itself the "Officers' Military Rada." An independent Ukrainian military club was opened. Recruiting for a Bogdan Hmelnitsky regiment of volunteers began.

By April the Ukrainian movement occupied the front of

the stage. The first purely Ukrainian demonstration was organized, with tens of thousands of participants. The demonstration was politically variegated. Placards with "Hurrah for the federal republic!" and "A free Ukraine in a free Russia!" vied with "Independent Ukraine with its own hetman!" Before the portrait of Taras Shevchenko, the Ukrainian national poet, the crowd swore not to rest until it had built a free, autonomous Ukraine. A resolution was adopted, pledging support to the central government and voicing the expectation that it would recognize Ukrainian autonomy and take measures to Ukrainize local institutions. That brilliant demonstration greatly stimulated the sentiment of the Ukrainian nationalists.

In mid-April the Central Rada was greatly strengthened; it was joined by the Ukrainian Social Democratic party. In the first week of May the Rada sent out a call for a Ukrainian congress; it invited representatives of all cultural, political, trade-union, and similar organizations which favored Ukrainian autonomy. This news caused a sensation. The alarm was first raised by the Kiev committee of Bolsheviks; it had learned from the Jewish socialist organizations that the Rada was said to be planning to proclaim this congress a Ukrainian Constituent Assembly. The Bolsheviks in principle expressed their opposition to dividing the proletariat by governmental compartments. They resolved to carry on a bitter struggle against Ukrainian separatism and to press the Ukrainian Social Democratic party to oppose "centrifugal forces."[1] This question was discussed at a conference of all the socialist parties and at a joint conference of Soviet and nonpartisan political associations. The president of the Rada, the historian Hrushevsky, gave reassuring explanations. The Ukrainian National Congress was preceded by party congresses of the Ukrainian Social Democratic party and of the newly formed Ukrainian party of Social Revolutionaries; the latter included in their demands for Ukrainian autonomy the organization of a separate Ukrainian land fund. Both parties, with variations, favored autonomy for the Ukraine and the federal reconstruction of Russia. This viewpoint was also accepted by the Ukrainian National Congress, dominated by moderate Ukrainian nationalists, the so-called "*postupovtsy*," "radical democrats," and "autonomist-federalists." The congress was greeted by the Kiev commissar of the Provisional Government, while the president of the congress, Hrushevsky, in his reply promised "full support" to the Petrograd Provisional Government.

Despite this exchange of official greetings, the fact remained that the movement of urban revolutionary democracy, a movement of a national minority (in the Ukraine), and the Ukrainian movement proper with its interest fixed on the village, seemed to be proceeding on two different planes, eying each other with distrust and without comprehension.

This distrust only needed an occasion to break out. It soon appeared. At the transfer point about three thousand soldiers had been collected, to be formed into detachments and sent to the front. The idea was proposed, and at once backed by the Rada, of forming an integral Ukrainian unit, a Bogdan Hmelnitsky regiment. The Rada pointed out to the authorities that national union greatly enhances combat value; the yearning for union among Ukrainians, scattered throughout the army, was very strong; it was better to guide it than to leave it unsatisfied and thus furnish food for agitation. The Rada drafted several measures for creating Ukrainian regiments among units at the rear. It advocated this for the front too, but only insofar as it could be done without a sharp break which might affect current operations unfavorably.

On the day after the Rada's resolution the idea of forming a special Ukrainian regiment was rejected unanimously by a joint session of the Executive Committees of the Soviets, the Civic Committee, the Committee of Deputies of the Troops of the Kiev military district, and the Coalition

Council of Students. That was a real vote of "no confidence." The reply came quickly. Two days later, on May 1, there was a Ukrainian military holiday. It was celebrated by the soldiers who had declared themselves the first Ukrainian regiment and had accepted the slogan of "War to a victorious finish under the banner of the Ukraine." The regiment voted its confidence in the Provisional Government, the Soviet of Workers' Deputies, and even the Imperial Duma. When the president of the "nonnational" Soviet of Military Deputies, the Social Democrat, Task, attempted to persuade them to renounce "Ukrainization," he barely escaped arrest. The commander of the army district, General Hodorovich, asked the soldiers to disperse and reassemble that evening to discuss the question. At a conference lasting until a late hour their representatives refused to cease regarding themselves as a Ukrainian regiment.

The minority (Russian) elements of revolutionary democracy were too insensitive to what was going on under their eyes: like the army leaders they fanned the fire of nationalist passion by their unrestrained attacks. The cause of the Ukrainian fermentation was obvious: the formation of national Polish units from Polish soldiers. The Ukrainians had suffered greatly from the Poles and had aided Russia's historic triumph over Poland; they were greatly disturbed by this injustice; even in free Russia they were not allowed what was granted to the Poles. A Ukrainian Social Democrat, Neronovich, was more than right when he declared that the work of organizing Ukrainian regiments should be undertaken by Russian and Ukrainian democracy together, for otherwise "the cause would be captured by the Ukrainian 'die-hards' and used for their chauvinist purposes." Another member of that party, Vinichenko, warned it that any other solution of the question "might provoke disorders in the rear and at the front." But even General Brusilov, a "possibilist" among the army leaders, shared the most obstinate prejudices of the "dominant nationality." He declared: "The Kiev garrison is strong enough for the chief commander of the district to put down disorder." It is easy to see how provocative this sounded to the Ukrainians, and how they were bound to react to the order "to dispatch three thousand Ukrainians to the front in the usual formations."

This was characteristic of that period. People who considered themselves, unlike "party fanatics," representatives of a "realistic policy" in the revolution, continually made categorical decisions in the name of "statehood," without stopping to reflect whether they could carry them out or would have to abandon them. That was what happened now. On May 5, the Ukrainian Rada "accepted with pleasure the declaration of the chief command concerning the formation of the first Ukrainian regiment." Had that consent been given a week earlier, it would have aroused in Ukrainian circles an explosion of enthusiasm for the common cause. Granted after stubborn but short-lived resistance, it was merely a sign of weakness, it undermined the government's authority, raised doubts of its sincerity, and made people think that concessions could be wangled from it only by facing it with accomplished facts.

The Ukrainian "separatists"—at that time all Ukrainian parties disclaimed any ties with the uninfluential but aggressive group under that name—now raised their heads. Having learned of the coming regional congress of Soviets, they urged small credit organizations and others to send as many delegates as possible. About two hundred appeared at the congress, which of course they dominated. The organizers of the congress lost their heads. They declared that the county assemblies were not Soviet organizations, and consented to admit only two representatives from each district and four from each province. The peasants became excited, and demanded that they all be admitted. After long and wearisome negotiations, they were all admitted to the first ceremonial session. The congress, instead of uniting the peasantry and the city folk, the Ukrainians and non-Ukrainians, effectually divided them into two camps. The peasant section of the congress passed a resolution demanding a federal republic, national and territorial autonomy for the Ukraine, a central Ukrainian land fund, and gradual Ukrainization of military units. After the organizers of the congress had declared that only two delegates per district would be admitted to the following sessions, the peasant section resolved to consider that as mockery of the peasants, to boycott the regional congress and go home. A formal rupture was now a fact.

The minority national groups, Great Russian in sympathy, dominant in the cities, tried to evade the eloquent reminder of the Ukrainian village that they were not the real masters of the country, and were just as much immigrants as were the Ukrainians in Great Russia. But the village was not alone. The conference of Ukrainian students, held at about that time, declared that all Ukrainian parties without exception had a common minimum platform: "A Russian federation of free democratic republics, among which one free republic will be the Ukraine." That was an indirect vote of "no confidence" against the Russian democratic parties.

Before the close of the regional congress it was learned that a Ukrainian General Army Committee had been formed and had appealed to the Minister of War to obtain from all military detachments lists of generals, officers, and noncommissioned officers who regarded themselves as Ukrainian soldiers and officers. It asked him to form a Ukrainian division with all branches. The Ukrainian General Army Committee was to be allowed to complete the partially formed Bogdan Hmelnitsky regiment, and so forth. Then came the congress of the "Village Coöperative Union." It determined to take part in the All-Russian Congress of Soviets of Peasants' Deputies, in order to press for "immediate and solemn" recognition by the Provisional Government of the Ukraine's right to autonomy. An All-Ukrainian Union of Cadets was formed. Finally, on May 18, the Ukrainian Army Congress assembled about seven hundred representatives of Ukrainian groups and organizations in the army and navy.

Debates at this congress showed that it would have been advantageous for Kerensky to lean on the Ukrainian movement. Many orators favored continuing the war to a victorious close, to unite Galicia and Sub-Carpathian Russia to the Ukraine. Shapoval, Masiuk, Belokon, Lutsenko described the redoubled energy with which the Ukrainians, united in national regiments, would fight, if behind them they had an autonomous Ukraine, and before them the still unconquered natural borders to the west.

New voices were also heard, irritated and aggressive. "Poland's independence has been proclaimed, and Finland's autonomy. Poland was conquered, while we joined Russia as equal to equal. Why have we not more, but fewer rights than Poland?" In this propitious atmosphere chauvinistic voices sounded. "All Great Russians, peasants, workers, and intelligentsia are hostile to the Ukrainians." "The Ukrainian people have taken an active part in the revolution, but not in order to await the pleasure of the Constituent Assembly which, without a Ukrainian majority, may refuse us autonomy, as various Soviets of Workers' and Soldiers' Deputies are now doing." "They tell us that now is no time, that the fatherland is in danger. But what fatherland? Our fatherland is the Ukraine, not Russia. The hour has passed to wait for or beg a favor. We are a power, we too have bayonets."

Ukrainian Social Democracy sounded a sobering note.

The revolution was made by the workers and soldiers, and thanks to them we can now assemble and organize. We must not abandon our ally, Russian democracy, though we disagree with it on some points. The best people of Russia, including the Soviets of Workers' and Soldiers' Deputies, are alarmed by foreign and domestic events. Let us watch for the right moment, we are bound to the Russian state by economic and political bonds.

Vinichenko appealed to the common sense of the most militant delegates.

> Yes, we have power now, and it is growing continually. But we must not forget that the Ukrainian soldiers are scattered throughout the state. Will our force be sufficient for an armed struggle? We must organize. . . . We are not going to attack Russian democracy with the bayonet, and we shall not allow it to attack us.

The congress was restrained from adopting overaggressive decisions. To the request that the Provisional Government publicly recognize in principle the autonomy of the Ukraine, it added the wish for a special minister on Ukrainian matters and a representative from the Ukraine at the future peace conference. This last demand aroused special opposition among Russian circles in the Ukraine. Their attitude has only to be compared with the conduct of the British bourgeois and nationalist government which willingly admitted representatives of all the dominions to the peace conferences.

The Army Congress held a joint session with the Coöperative Congress. A telegram was read from the Petrograd Executive Committee of Soviets. The question of national troops was being discussed by a special commission, assisted by the general staff and the nationalities organizations. It was to be placed on the agenda of the First All-Russian Congress of Soviets. The Executive Committee requested the congress to appeal to all Ukrainian soldiers to refrain "from arbitrary, unauthorized action" pending the decision of the All-Russian Congress. Again tumultuous scenes occurred. The final session of the Army Congress determined to send a special delegation to Petrograd to discuss the manner of organizing Ukrainian army units. At the same time it appealed to the soldiers, "for the salvation of the Ukraine and of Russia, to refrain from arbitrary withdrawal from their units."

Kerensky visited Kiev early in June. The leaders of the

Central Rada, Hrushevsky and Shulgin, spoke frankly: although the Ukraine had once had its own statehood, "we do not strive for independence," we only want "autonomy within a federal Russian republic." In this form "the Ukrainian movement is not a menace to Russia, but a strong support; the Provisional Government must lean on it if it wishes to save Russia." Generally speaking, "only decentralization can save Russia, otherwise it will perish." Kerensky promised to do what he could "in accord with duty and conscience." He pointed out that in this question he had to "combat the same impatience as in the ranks of Russian democracy." "You speak of the sanctioning of an accomplished fact by the Constituent Assembly, while we should like the assembly to prepare the way for that fact." The negotiations ended with Hrushevsky's declaration that the satisfaction of the intense desires of an entire people could not always be postponed with impunity. If that occurred, the Central Rada "could not answer for the consequences." Kerensky responded that in any case he remained a "friend" of the Ukrainians.

On June 10 the All-Ukrainian Peasant Congress met, and on June 17 the Second Army Congress. The conflict with the government was now coming into the open. The new commander of the Kiev army district, General Oberuchev, a Right-wing Social Revolutionary of the "Kerensky trend," had referred in a special order to numerous arbitrary actions in organizing Ukrainian detachments and electing Ukrainian officers, which had raised the "specter of civil war." The Ukrainian delegation had met with no success in Petrograd. "Unfortunately," said Vinichenko, "the Ukrainian delegation was received, not by the socialist ministers, but by Lazarevsky and Kotlyarevsky, who in fact created the government's attitude toward us."*

* Lazarevsky and Kotlyarevsky were prominent members of the juridical commission of the Provisional Government; it was entirely Cadet in composition; it took over questions requiring a first-class funeral, with all the ceremonies of juridical formalism. The socialist ministers were not visited by the Ukrainian delegation and some of them heard of its mission only after its departure.

On June 11 a telegram came from Kerensky declaring the Ukrainian Army Congress "inopportune." Since no obstacles were placed in the way of the Polish, Cossack, Aviation, and All-Russian Army Congresses arranged for at about the same time, this prohibition could be understood only as a blow at the Ukrainian movement. At the Peasant Congress it evoked a tempest of passions. Soldiers appealed to the congress "to follow the example of their glorious ancestors, who knew how to fight for freedom and right with sword in hand." Speakers who pointed out that they must "march with those Russian socialists who recognize the rights of all peoples and of the Ukrainian people, not in words, but in deeds," were heard coldly. An orator who declared that the Ukraine "would secure freedom and land only when Russia had them" was shouted down. Not long before, the least influential group, the "Separatists," had advocated recalling the Ukrainian deputies from the All-Russian Peasant Congress, proclaiming the Central Rada the Provisional Ukrainian Government, convoking a Ukrainian Constituent Assembly and summoning all Ukrainian soldiers to join a national Ukrainian army. Now the congress all but passed these proposals. The situation was saved by the Ukrainian Social Democrats and Social Revolutionaries. The autonomy of the Ukraine cannot be introduced without harmonizing it with the other peoples inhabiting its territory, argued the Social Democrat, Martos. Beware of the slogans of the "Separatists," urged the Ukrainian Social Revolutionary, Zalivchy. "Our democracy will be lost, and we will not get the land if we establish only the independence of our republic. . . . We must press the Russian bourgeoisie, but we must combat the Ukrainian bourgeoisie. Do not imagine that because the landlords talk our speech, they are on our side." The appeal to the social antagonism of the peasants against the Ukrainian landlords and bourgeoisie had its effect, and the congress refused to follow Stepanenko's Separatist group. On a vote as to whether the Ukrainians were to strive for autonomy or independence, only nineteen supported Stepanenko's type of independence, but only fourteen opposed it. The Ukrainian movement was approaching a crossroad.

On June 17 a meeting of three thousand people protested against Kerensky's prohibition of the Army Congress and almost accepted the proposal of the "Union of Ukrainian Sovereignty" to proclaim the political independence of the Ukraine at once. After the meeting the crowd, reënforced by the First Ukrainian Regiment, went to St. Sofia Square and raised the Ukrainian yellow-and-blue banner over the city duma and at the monument to Bogdan Hmelnitsky; to the sound of the cathedral bells they swore "not to return to their detachments without settling the autonomy of the Ukraine."

Urban democracy, faithful to its Great Russian orientation, underestimated the significance of what was happening. At a joint session of the Executive Committees of the Soviet the two parties exchanged sharp words. People learned that the Provisional Government had rejected the Ukrainians' requests with its sacred formula of "wait till the Constituent Assembly." The Cadets, Mensheviks, and Right-wing Social Revolutionaries defended the Provisional Government. The Ukrainian Rada was accused of double-dealing in justifying its action by the elemental force of national feeling, while in fact inflaming that feeling. A Menshevik, Dorotov, asked what guarantee there was that Ukrainian bayonets would not drive the non-Ukrainians from the Soviet tomorrow.

The representatives of the immigrant nationalities, predominant in the cities, found it difficult, with their Russian orientation, to cease considering themselves masters of the situation, and to accept the position of national minorities content with the usual guarantees of minority rights. They alarmed themselves with phantoms; by their hopeless struggle they increased the real danger.

Kerensky refused to withdraw his prohibition, disregarding the question of how to compel submission. His refusal merely exposed the bankruptcy of the Provisional Government, this time, of the coalition.

The Second Ukrainian Army Congress now decreed: "Since the right of assembling and holding congresses belongs to the Ukrainians, as well as other free peoples, prohibition of the Congress by the Minister of War cannot be considered lawful, and the Congress will certainly execute its decrees." The awkward action of the district commander, Oberuchev, added oil to the flames. Acting on unchecked and false rumors "that the Ukrainian Congress at 2 A.M. had decreed the immediate seizure of the local branch of the State Bank and Treasury," he brought troops, in full field equipment, and occupied those buildings. He hastily issued a communiqué, expressing the hope that he could avoid decisive measures, inevitable "in case of attempts to summon the people to civil war by a somewhat overexcited section of the Ukrainians." He invited the citizens "to observe calm," which he had just lost, and "not to believe rumors," which he had so incautiously believed. At the Army Congress the action of Oberuchev and of the chief of police, Leparsky, was branded as provocation. They were denounced as "heads of the counterrevolutionary, anti-Ukrainian hydra." Unusual excitement was aroused among the Ukrainian population. Countless street meetings were held from early morning to late at night. Nevertheless, at the congress Vinichenko successfully defended the thesis that the Ukraine was not ready to declare itself an independent state. But the Ukrainians could not wait for the Constituent Assembly, for, as he said pessimistically, "it is still open to question whether the Constituent Assembly will ever meet." The congress upheld the aim of Ukrainian autonomy, and resolved to attain it "by direct action"; it promised the Central Rada the assistance of all Ukrainians under arms in the rear or at the front.

To fulfil this platform, at the suggestion of the Ukrainian Social Revolutionaries, a solemn manifesto was published with great pomp. A parade of the First Ukrainian Regiment was held. The bells resounded from St. Sofia Cathedral and St. Michael's Monastery. The clergy celebrated a service and proclaimed "Long life!" to the Ukrainian people, Ukrainian government, troops, and elders. The crowd hurrahed for the Ukrainian people and the Central Rada, and on bended knee repeated Shevchenko's "creed."

In the Soviet each side heaped accusations on the other. The Russian Social Revolutionaries and Mensheviks accused the Ukrainian socialists of abandoning socialism for nationalism and joining the chauvinist bourgeoisie. The Ukrainian socialists hurled back the same accusation: the coalition with the Russian bourgeoisie in the Provisional Government had infected the Russian socialists with the spirit of bourgeois centralization and Great Russian nationalism. After the balloting, the Ukrainians and Bolsheviks, left in the minority on different questions, withdrew in demonstrative protest.

Distrust of the Central Rada was growing rapidly in Russian bourgeois circles. It fed particularly on the fact that even before the war a small and variegated group of Ukrainian *émigrés* (Basok-Melenevsky, Skoropis-Yoltukhovsky, etc.) had determined to copy the tactics of the Poles, who, in expectation of a World War and Russia's defeat, had decided to take the Austro-German side and with their assistance to strive for the resurrection of an independent Poland. The Ukrainian group had organized a "Union for the Liberation of the Ukraine," and entered into relations with the Austro-German general staff, undertaken to form volunteer detachments, first of Galician Ukrainians, later of Russian-Ukrainian war prisoners. After the Russian Revolution the "Union for the Liberation of the Ukraine" broke up; individual members petitioned to be allowed to return to their fatherland. Those who were successful met with obvious mistrust among democratic circles in the Ukraine. Their representatives were not admitted to the Central Rada. Even in May the Rada had rejected all relations with the "Union for the Liberation of the Ukraine." When Skoropis-Yoltukhovsky sent from Stockholm to the Ukrainian national fund money collected among the prisoners in Germany and Austria, the Central Rada rejected it. This did not deter the Cadet leaders and writers from again and again accusing the Ukrainian movement of an "Austrian orientation," in other words, of treason to the state; that is, to the revolution.

It was now discovered unexpectedly that the Bolsheviks were trying to shift their stand. Instead of a "bitter struggle" against separatism, they decided to "support the direct action proclaimed by the Ukrainians in the revolution." They were fiercer even than the Ukrainians in attacking the ban on the Army Congress, and the "imperialist policy of the central government." They urged the Ukrainians to break with their national bourgeoisie and to join the Bolsheviks in fighting for power. The social Maximalism of the Bolsheviks had proclaimed its willingness to join hands with the nationalist Maximalism of the Ukraine, to storm the government together. Matters were taking a dangerous turn. In the Soviets and the Civic Committee voices were raised blaming this abnormal alliance on the mistaken policy of the Russian organizations, reluctant to take a single step to meet Ukrainian demands, which would in any case have to be satisfied.

Within the Provisional Government the socialist ministers, without in every case approving the Rada's policy, in principle always considered as absolutely just the striving of the Ukrainian people for autonomy. Both Tseretelli and Chernov recognized the right of every nationality, including the Ukrainian, to self-determination. The fact that it "determined" on autonomy, not on breaking off every bond with the All-Russian state, was proof of political maturity and farsightedness. The Great Russian, Chernov, long since a convinced federalist, was firmer in this conviction than the non-Russian, Tseretelli. But they were a minority, as were the Cadet ministers who defended the opposite view, that of relentless centralization. The government's decision depended on the intermediate group, on the triumvirate of

Kerensky, Tereshchenko, and Nekrasov, and their supporters. This triumvirate was inclined to accept the proposal of the socialist ministers. Two ministers were sent to the Ukraine: Tseretelli, for the socialist wing, and Tereshchenko for the bourgeois. At the last minute they were joined by Kerensky and Nekrasov, on their own initiative. As a result, the negotiations were conducted by the Kerensky triumvirate, together with Tseretelli.

The chief work in achieving a political agreement fell to Tseretelli, and the negotiations were completed with relative ease. The Rada, previously the organ of a single nationality, was transformed into a kind of regional preliminary parliament by the addition of a fair representation (based on proportional numbers) for other nationalities in the Ukraine. The Rada had its own executive organ, the Secretariat. The Secretariat was also the local agent of the Provisional Government, and received formal confirmation from it. Thus, the autonomy of the Ukraine was combined with the unity of the revolutionary front of nation-wide democracy. This provisional situation was to last until the Constituent Assembly, and by that time the Central Rada was to have ready a draft of the definitive statute of autonomous Ukraine, and the bill for a Ukrainian land fund.

The negotiations on the army question, conducted primarily by Kerensky, took a different turn. The military section of the bill was "sharply opposed by the Ukrainian Social Democratic party and the Ukrainian General Army Committee." Kerensky rejected the system of territorial formation of troops, which would have meant modifying the general plan of mobilization. He accepted only "a closer national union" of the Ukrainians in separate detachments, insofar as the Minister of War might find it "technically feasible and not injurious to the army's fighting power." Direct activity in this sphere by any national Ukrainian organizations was rejected, but special Ukrainian delegates, appointed by agreement with the Central Rada, were to be attached to the cabinet of the Minister of War, the General Staff, and the commander in chief.

During these difficult negotiations the district commander, Oberuchev, forbade the troops to participate in a ceremony in the Rada's honor, while the General Army Secretariat summoned them to participate. Despite the official ban, the Ukrainian detachments turned out to demonstrate in favor of creating a Ukrainian army. Again and again the government's authority was shaken by issuing decrees which it could not enforce.

Finally the agreement was approved by the Rada, by a majority of only 100 to 70, with many abstentions. It had still to be accepted by the central government. Although "the ministers had reported to the government in Petrograd by direct wire . . . confirmation of the agreement, expected by that evening, had not arrived."

In the absence of the four ministers, there were in Petrograd four socialists, partisans of the agreement, four Cadets, hostile to it, and three waverers. Everything depended on chance. The early return of the absent ministers was essential. Once in Petrograd, they presented the text of the "decree" as concerted with the Ukrainians. It was only with the greatest difficulty, they added, that they had obtained its acceptance by the Central Rada, and any modification to the Ukrainians' disadvantage would mean breaking off the agreement.

The Cadet ministers regarded this as a "violation of the fundamental bases of the coalition," and "obvious proof of the impossibility of its continued existence."* The pointed resignation of the four Cadet ministers aroused the greatest excitement in the capital; turbulent demonstrations were held in favor of transferring power to the Soviets. There was no less excitement in the Ukraine. Anti-Cadet feeling there led the Ukrainian Committee of the Cadet party to repudiate its leaders in Petrograd and declare that "the creation of a

* Miliukov.

single organ or regional authority in the Ukraine is opportune and expedient," while the Cadets' "withdrawal from the government is incomprehensible and dangerous to the welfare of the state."

Miliukov's party thus encountered one defeat after another. Even its inner unity was endangered. The socialist members of the Provisional Government had to face Nekrasov and Tereshchenko with the alternative: either an end to the coalition, or else an attempt to organize from Left-wing Cadet and allied elements a new party to coöperate with the toilers' democracy in a creative alliance. After long hesitation they announced they had not secured the backing of any substantial groups.

The proposal was made in the wrong quarter. A Left-wing but nonsocialist party could best have been founded by Kerensky, with Nekrasov, Tereshchenko and others as his zealous assistants. For some unknown reason Kerensky imagined himself a Social Revolutionary, and that party shared his delusion. As a result, the farther events progressed, the more ambiguous the situation became: Kerensky and the party engaged in continual undercover conflict, while to many people Kerensky was the personification of Social Revolutionary policy, and the party had to take responsibility for all his "words and deeds."

The crisis of the coalition, caused by the Cadets' withdrawal over the Ukrainian question, the withdrawal of the industrialist representative, Konovalov, over labor policy, and Prince Lvov's ultimatum on the agrarian problem, was complete. The Central Committee of the Cadet party stated the alternative: either greater homogeneity in the government, or else abandonment of majority voting as against the Cadet minority within the ministry. The second alternative in practice meant giving the Cadet minority the right of veto in every question.

After a long government crisis Kerensky decided that a broad coalition government to include Cadet, commercial, and industrial circles could not be organized on a narrow platform of revolutionary democracy. He also refused out-and-out to form a more homogeneous government of the Laborite type. Yet the moderate Soviet parties dared not organize a government of their own. They would have to face a violent attack by all bourgeois parties, while their rear was undefended and at a crucial moment they might be dealt a blow in the back by demagogically reckless Bolshevism.

Thus, when a new delegation from the Ukrainian Rada, including the personnel of the General Secretariat of the Ukraine, arrived in Petrograd to formulate the agreement concretely, it learned that everything had to be begun all over.

The author of the agreement, Tseretelli, was no longer in the government. He had been dropped for the sake of coalition with the Cadet party (instead of Chernov, whom the Social Revolutionary party refused to sacrifice). The Cadet "juridical commission," that grave digger of all innovations, again appeared on the scene. In it a deciding voice was asserted by old school political scientists, Kokoshkin and Baron Nolde. As Miliukov said, Kokoshkin "aimed to correct, as far as possible, the injury done to Russia by the July 2 agreement." The General Secretariat, the regional organ of the Provisional Government, was greatly reduced in scope. It was to administer five incomplete provinces instead of nine. Supply, Posts and Telegraph, Justice, Railroads, and War were removed from its jurisdiction. A third of the remaining portfolios were allotted to non-Ukrainians. In emergencies the Provisional Government might deal directly with local authorities, ignoring the General Secretariat. There were many other reservations and restrictions, sometimes petty but no less irritating. Several times the negotiations were on the verge of collapse. For a while the commission of the Provisional Government closed its sessions to the Ukrainian delegates. "It was obvious," Vinichenko reported to the Rada, "that certain ministers wanted us to provoke a break." The leading parties of the Rada, however, had sufficient political intuition not to push matters to a rupture between the Ukraine and the rest of Russia at that uneasy time, when Russia was caught between two fires, between the Kornilov rebellion, now about to break out, and the Bolshevist putsch, in process of preparation.

The Rada accepted the instructions for the General Secretariat after sharp criticism even from those who favored their acceptance. The Ukrainian Social Revolutionaries called it "that shameful document." The plenum of the provincial Soviet of Peasants' Deputies described it as "an insult to democracy." The motivation of the Rada's acceptance was worse than any rejection. It asserted that the original agreement had been violated by the new instructions; they displayed the tendencies of Great Russian imperialism; by giving the non-Ukrainian nationalities a disproportionate representation in the organ of regional authority, they broke up the unity of Ukrainian and non-Ukrainian democracy.

Tseretelli's great effort at pacification was undermined. Worst of all was this public evidence of the unreliability of the government's pledged word. Its method was always the same—one step forward, two half-steps back.

Next to the Ukraine the biggest nationality problem was Finland. Here again each wing of the Provisional Government spoke another language.

From the beginning the censitary government had entered into a juridical dispute with the Finns: with the overthrow of the autocracy, who inherited the rights of the Russian crown in Finland?

According to the Right-wing Cadet, Maklakov,

the Finns presented proposals which implied the transfer to the Finnish representative body of the rights of the Russian Emperor; i.e., the Grand Duke of Finland, after the latter's abdication. . . . This was logical; but this theory led directly to independence, both *de facto* and *de jure*. The Cadets did not want that, and tried to prove that the Provisional Government, recognized by the Russian people, had inherited all the rights of the autocrat, including his rights in Finland.

How could that be proved? By Nicholas' abdication in favor of Michael, and Michael's abdication in favor of the Constituent Assembly? By the ukaze of Nicholas II appointing Prince Lvov Premier of the Provisional Government? These documents could not be considered the basis of the authority of the Provisional Government, which, moreover, changed its personnel several times. If the Tsar of Russia was also Grand Duke of Finland, and if all joint Finno-Russian questions had been decided by parallel Finnish and Russian legislation, then the death of Russian autocracy severed Russo-Finnish dualism. The prerogatives of the Russian Tsar might pass to the Duma, to the Constituent Assembly, to the Provisional Government, to anyone, on the Russian line. The prerogatives of the Grand Duke of Finland must likewise pass in the Finnish line. In this juridical sense, as Maklakov admits, "right was on the side of the Finns' claims; our attempts to prove that the rights of the Grand Duke of Finland had passed to the Provisional Government had no basis."

To the socialist ministers this dispute was scholastic. The Russian Emperor, like all persons crowned by "the grace of God," bore an extremely long and wordy title. By some ancient, almost prehistoric claim, he also declared himself "heir to Norway." Would the Provisional Government be *eo ipso* a collective pretender to the "Norwegian heritage"? For the Russian socialists Finland was an independent state organization which, like Russia, gained by the revolution an opportunity to settle its fate independently. The Constituent Assembly of Russia and the Finnish Diet, also possessed of constituent powers, should come to an agreement, as equal with equal, regarding their future relations: whether Finland should be a member of the Russian federation, an ally, or merely a neighbor.

The socialist ministers could easily have made such an agreement with the Finns. But they were a minority in the Provisional Government, heirs to the long legal dispute between the most learned political scientists of the Cadet party and the equally learned jurists of Finland. Maklakov said of the Provisional Government:

> It defended Russia's interests as Stolypin had once defended them. But the Cadet jurists had now to attack that theory which they had formerly defended against Stolypin. When the Finns began to insist on the omnipotence of their Diet, the Provisional Government, like Stolypin or Bobrikov, used violence, placed a lock on the entrance to its building, as Stolypin had once done to the Tauride Palace. The Provisional Government resorted to measures which tranquilized no one, but led to a rupture between the two countries.[2]

The socialist ministers, prisoners of the coalition, reluctantly confined themselves to insisting that dissolution of the Diet meant merely a fresh consultation of the people by immediate election of a new Diet. When the Finnish Social Democratic party, on principle, came to the Diet building, tore the seal from the door, and held a session by way of demonstration, the socialist ministers had to be satisfied that no bourgeois minister urged reprisals. The Russian troops in Finland would not have allowed them in any case.

The socialist ministers and the Soviet leaders tried frequently, but usually without success, to serve as mediators between Finnish democracy and the Provisional Government. Chernov also attempted this; he was visited by a delegation of the Finnish parties, which pledged its solemn word that, if the Provisional Government accepted without change a draft law prepared by them enlarging the rights of the Diet, they would not present any new demand or cause fresh difficulty before the meeting of the Constituent Assembly or the end of the World War. By a majority vote of the ministry the draft was referred to that same "juridical commission."

Petty haggling with each nationality now awakening to

historic life, constant dread of getting the worst of a bargain, obstinate striving to postpone and evade payment on the notes presented by history, such was the policy bequeathed by the Provisional Government of the censitary parties. The coalition government lacked sufficient strength to renounce this heritage.

The powerful inspiration of revolution forced it to pronounce great words. But its petty and shortsighted deeds were in complete disharmony.

The nationalities policy of the Provisional Government lacked any broad sweep. The Duma, "involuntary revolutionaries" at bottom, hoped that if Tsarist Russia, like Hapsburg Austria, was a "prison house of peoples," the mere destruction of this prison régime, leaving the state centralized as before, would evoke universal enthusiasm and satisfaction. They did not realize that the more heavily the oppression of the autocratic régime had borne down the stubborn spring of the peoples' national feelings, the stronger the force of release. It did not occur to them to proclaim the new Russia a free union of all peoples, a union to which nothing would bind them except the "mutual guarantee," advantageous for all, of a purposeful association for the sake of the community and of profound cultural and social bonds.

The Provisional Government was obliged, albeit reluctantly, to consent to the reorganization of the army according to the principle of national territories. But this Ukrainization, Esthonization, etc., of regiments and divisions might recreate the army on new principles or disintegrate it still further, depending on whether a general formula was found to solve the nationality question for all the peoples of Russia. The Provisional Government could have helped settle this question by establishing a special "Council of Nationalities." In the first period of revolution those elements which led in the awakening of the subordinate nationalities were, on the whole, far removed from the extremes of separatism to which they were later driven. There was full opportunity to enter the new path arm in arm. But instead of a guide in their national resurrection they found the Provisional Government too often a stingy, cold-hearted and evasive protector of the historical privileges of the "dominant" Great Russian nationality. From it concessions could be forced by blackmail, by facing it with irrevocable accomplished facts. This caused disorganization in the rear, and even more at the front. The national units listened attentively to what was going on in their homes and repeated all the disputes and solutions there. Instead of a great power for constructive work, the pressure of the nationalities was turned into a destructive force.

CHAPTER FIFTEEN

IMPASSE IN FOREIGN POLICY

BESIDES the impasse in domestic problems there was another in foreign policy.

Revolutionary democracy expected Tereshchenko to carry on an active policy, to revise the diplomatic heritage of autocracy, the infamous secret treaties, and for this purpose to convoke an Allied conference. In addition, Soviet democracy was ready to carry on an active foreign policy of its own. It was to prepare and convoke an international conference of labor organizations and socialist parties, to organize a simultaneous peace movement in all countries to reject aggressive aims and work for a genuinely democratic peace. Such a peace would mean, not the arbitrary expansion of some powers at the expense of others, but the organization of Europe on a basis of law, elimination of the future possibility of war and striving for economic coöperation among all states.

The policies of the government and of Soviet democracy were to supplement and aid each other.

The first replies of the English and French governments to the coalition were disheartening: Miliukov rightly remarked that "for the new government their publication would be a severe blow." They exposed the rupture of political unity in the Allied front, and political unity was the core of strategic unity. France and England stood on the treaties. Revolutionary Russia had but one logical course. If it was unwilling to conclude an immediate and separate peace with Germany, it could only declare its war against the Central Empires a *separate war;* i.e., a war with a purpose absolutely different from that of its former Allies. This idea had already appeared in certain socialist circles. There was much both *pro* and *con.* The political separation of the Eastern from the Western front, from a strategic point of view, would give Russia a much-needed freedom of action. Throughout the war she had been condemned to serve as an auxiliary to her Allies. She had always begun offensives not when and where required by a general war plan of her own, but as required by military difficulties of some Ally. This hampered Russian strategy, and savored too much of pulling the chestnuts out of the fire for others. On the other hand, separation might hit Russia in her vulnerable point, military supply, for which she depended on English deliveries *via* Murmansk. Of course, Russia's separate war against the Central Empires would be better for England than a separate peace; a skilful diplomacy could have played on this. The transformation of Russia's war against the Central Powers into a separate war assumed two possibilities: either fresh negotiations with the Allies, to make the separate war again an Allied war by working out a positive peace platform, the publication of which would clear the stifling atmosphere which had Europe gasping; or else the separate but simultaneous conclusion of peace. After all, the United States, after refusing to ratify the Treaty of Versailles, officially liquidated the war with Germany by a separate act, as if it had been a separate war. When people in Russia spoke of a separate peace, they usually meant something quite different, the hasty withdrawal from the war at its critical moment, which for the Russian public meant a camouflaged betrayal of Europe to Hohenzollern Germany. They almost never thought of a separate peace of the American type.

The position of France and England was not so immovable as it seemed. The delegation of French socialists, led by Marcel Cachin and Marius Moutet, left Russia with a great change in feeling. With the help of Albert Thomas, they arranged a secret discussion of war aims by the Chamber of Deputies. The last secret treaty with Tsarist diplomacy was then made known for the first time. It had been concluded less than a month before the autocracy's overthrow. It provided, neither more nor less, for partitioning Germany and creating a special Rhineland buffer state. The treaty caused a great sensation in the chamber. It found few supporters. Attacks on it were so severe that the head of the government, Ribot, announced that since Russia had renounced her claims to Constantinople and the Straits, France could abandon the February treaty, which had been merely intended as "compensation."

This path was also taken by English diplomacy. Through the London correspondent of the Petrograd *Stock Exchange News*, a clever semiofficial communiqué was forwarded. "Neither the partition of Turkey nor the partition of Austria-Hungary were corner stones of English war policy," but had been "merely a concession to Russia's military program." All other questions of reshaping internal European boundaries (Alsace-Lorraine and Trentino, autonomy of Poland and Bohemia) "affected England from the viewpoint of the interests of her Allies." References to the original imperialist sin of Tsarist diplomacy as the source of their own imperialist fall from grace were, of course, only a maneuver, but revolutionary Russia did not care how English diplomacy justified its own past. The conclusion of the note stated plainly that "if the Russian government wishes, the British government is quite willing to reopen, and, if necessary, to revise, prior agreements with its Allies."

In principle, the path of revision was open. This was still far from the goal. The Gordian knot of the secret treaties was greatly tangled. Russia's military weight had declined. The problem was whether Russia could find real allies in her struggle for a democratic peace. With the entrance of the United States into the war, new horizons opened.

The central organ of the biggest political party in Russia, the party of the Social Revolutionaries, the *Delo Naroda*, published an article by Chernov, urging an immediate and radical change in new Russia's foreign policy, the closest possible rapprochement with the United States, based on similarity of aims. This idea brought response even from the old professional diplomats. The former Ambassador to Washington, Baron Rosen, came in person to the Social Revolutionary headquarters to express his accord.

Russian official diplomacy, under Tereshchenko, failed to display the requisite flexibility and activeness. According to the Russian "vice ambassador" in London, Nabokov,

> the Provisional Government showed lamentable shortsightedness in not using this moment to establish close contact, not only with the government of the United States, but with the country at large. Enormous possibilities lay open. At that moment we could have won the sympathies of the American people forever. The Provisional Government merely replaced one Bakhmetiev by another, as ambassador.[1]

The fault was not entirely Russia's. If not Tereshchenko and the official diplomacy, at least the moderate parties of Soviet democracy were quite ready to stretch out a hand to Woodrow Wilson. But he found no common tongue with them. Not without malignant joy Miliukov noted that "for Tereshchenko most unpleasant of all was the text of the American note, which Francis refused to modify by a single word," and which "was certain to cut the ground from under the new course in Russian foreign policy; in that Wilson was merciless."[2] Wilson had no such conscious purpose, this was a colossal misunderstanding. Having just abandoned neutrality for armed intervention in the World War, poorly informed of the position of the Soviet, he did not understand its efforts to break through the network of secret treaties, its firm intention to prevent a peace poisoned by lasting inequality between vanquished and victors. Wilson replied to the Russian note by a dissertation on an entirely different subject, why war must be waged and peace not made with Hohenzollern Germany. But the Soviet needed no demonstration of that. Russia had long been in the war, and the Soviet had long since devoted its effort to enhancing the fighting power of the Russian army. Instead of answering the profound and tormenting queries of new Russia, Wilson replied with a victorious polemic by the Wilson who had resolved to take part in the war against the Wilson of neutrality, while imagining that he was thus converting the Russians to the true path. The sermon was misdirected. It missed the mark and perpetuated a state of mutual miscomprehension. German circles in the United States, attacking Wilson's decision to abandon neutrality, snatched for the popular slogans of pacificism; Wilson set about identifying pacificism and pro-Germanism, which, in Russia, was water to the mill of the worst Right-wing chauvinist enemies and slanderers of democracy. Wilson did not suspect this, but that did not improve matters. He was given a sharp retort. Both Cadets and Bolsheviks rejoiced malignantly at this misunderstanding. The Cadets saw it as proof that Miliukov's policy was alone feasible. The Bolsheviks mocked the hopes placed in Wilson; he was as much an imperialist as the rest, only he camouflaged his nature with hypocritically repulsive sermons, and the moderate majority in the Soviet had been stupid to nourish such illusions.

But the Soviet never had any illusions on this question. Its leaders well remembered Wilson's message to Congress, in December, 1914, urging the United States to develop its domestic life and resources and to busy itself in supplying its own and other peoples of the world. America realized all the advantages of neutrality for a wealthy capitalist country. It had captured the markets of the world. Its own production increased the more it was needed by countries which had to adapt their own industry to unproductive, purely military consumption.

The Soviet leaders understood perfectly the further logic of development. An overseas power had to work for that warring party which controlled the ocean, hence for the Entente. The longer the war lasted, the greater the rôle of credit. Indebtedness of the Entente to America grew enormously. America had invested so much capital in the cause of the Entente that it could not afford to let it be ruined, as it would inevitably have been had it finally lost the World War, or had the war been prolonged to the point of exhaustion.

Independently of Germany's staking "all or nothing" on her absurdly provocative proclamation of ruthless submarine warfare against neutral merchant shipping, the moment was bound to come when the creditor would have to step from behind his debtor's back and place his "Brennus' sword" on the scales of history. The Soviet leaders had no intention of demanding of the Americans a romantic altruism. On the contrary, the profound material interest of the United States in a certain policy would be the best pledge of its constancy. It was not enough for the creditor to save his debtor from ruin. The peace must not contain the embryo of a new war or lead the debtor to undermine his strength by unproductive expenditures for competitive armaments.

No matter how prosaic the source of the desire of influential business circles of America for the earliest possible restoration of order in Europe, the fact of this interest was a positive factor. Without it President Wilson might have dreamed of a League of Nations, of the right of self-determination, of the "rule of law" in international relations, as many had dreamed of it before. But he could not have set in motion the great power of the United States, to implant at least part of those principles in the Versailles peace treaty, otherwise so alien to them.

In his plans for pacifying Europe President Wilson could have only one absolutely sincere and reliable ally: new Russia, the Russia of the toilers' democracy, the Russia of the proclamation "To the Peoples of the World."

Wilson did not realize this. The price was his tragedy, his isolation during the Versailles negotiations, his final failure, despite a slight success in form, and the swift eclipse of his popularity.

Albert Thomas left Russia with a note by Tereshchenko.

"The Russian Revolution is not merely a revolution in the domestic structure of Russia, but a mighty movement of ideals, showing the will of the Russian people to strive for equality, liberty, and justice both in the domestic life of the state and in the sphere of international relations." Hence its obstinate yearning "to achieve a general peace on conditions forbidding any violence, no matter what its origin, and any imperialist purposes, no matter what their form." "Russia's unity with her Allies" was to "assure a general agreement on all questions, based on the principles of the Russian Revolution." Finally, welcoming the assent of the Allies in principle to revision of war aims, the note proposed convocation of a special inter-Allied conference "in the immediate future, when favorable conditions arise."

Confident of Tereshchenko's honest support, Soviet democracy hastened to create these "favorable conditions" by calling an international socialist congress at Stockholm. The socialists of the Allied countries had come to Russia to preach activization of the war against the Central Powers and to oppose meeting the socialists of the enemy camp before conclusion of peace. They left Russia, strongly impressed with the moral atmosphere of the Great Russian Revolution and ready to meet it halfway. Albert Thomas and Henderson returned with the firm intention of helping to make the Stockholm congress a success. A special Soviet delegation was to work abroad. Even Ambassador Buchanan advised his government to grant passports to Stockholm for the sake of peace between the Provisional Government and the Soviet.[3]

But the attempt to organize the Stockholm congress failed. It met an unexpected obstacle. The Provisional Government, by Tereshchenko's pen, had eloquently explained the will of the Russian people to overcome all desire for conquest. It had just declared publicly that "from this will the members of the Russian Provisional Government derive their strength; in service to it they see their duty." Could anyone suspect that the mine was being laid in this very quarter?

On August 3, the Russian chargé d'affaires in London, Nabokov, sent Tereshchenko a long telegram, informing him of currents hostile to the Stockholm congress and, in particular, of certain statements of the Conservative leader, Bonar Law. He concluded:

> To safeguard our relations as an ally of England, in which the overwhelming majority in public opinion and government is opposed to the conference, I consider it extremely desirable for me to be enabled to state clearly to Mr. Balfour that the Russian Government, like the British cabinet, considers this a party question, not a matter of state, and the decisions of the conference, if it takes place, as by no means binding on the further course of Russia's policy toward her Allies.

This wish of Nabokov, a diplomat of the Tsarist school, to assist the anti-Stockholm agitation within England and strengthen the position of the Conservatives against Henderson within the government was comprehensible. But who could imagine that, instead of a sharp reprimand, he would receive a sympathetic reply from Tereshchenko? On August 8, Nabokov, who had been awaiting the reply "with intense impatience," received the following telegram from Tereshchenko:

> I fully approve the declaration to the English Government, as proposed by you. You may tell the Minister of Foreign Affairs that the Russian Government, finding it impossible to forbid participation of Russian delegates in the Stockholm socialist conference, considers, however, this conference exclusively a party matter and its decisions as in no measure limiting the government's freedom of action.

In diplomatic language it meant that for the Russian Ministry of Foreign Affairs the Stockholm conference was at best an unavoidable evil. But that was not enough for Nabokov. He added his own commentaries to Tereshchenko's reply, as an indirect attack upon Henderson's and MacDonald's efforts. The latter had just made a special trip to Paris to help put through the Stockholm congress. Nabokov added a direct attack on the radical press, which asserted that Russia was anxious for the Stockholm "universal socialist peace conference."

The next day Nabokov was invited to call on Lloyd George, who already had on his desk a telegram from Albert Thomas which showed that Nabokov was not alone. It was short and clear: "*Kerensky ne veut pas de conférence.*" The "sharp little Welshman" declared Nabokov's note to Balfour "a document of the greatest importance," for it gave him "full liberty to ban the conference." Lloyd George informed him that he had already demanded that Henderson, as a member of the government, exert the necessary pressure on the Labor party conference. Henderson confined himself to reporting to it that "a slight change had evidently occurred in the attitude of the Russian Government to the conference"; he had not changed his own attitude, and still defended the conference. Then Lloyd George, realizing the impossibility of referring to Thomas' telegram, urged Nabokov to allow the publication of his note to Balfour. He depended on that to prove that Henderson's conduct at the Labor party conference had been a "violation of his duty to the country and the government, and hence he must resign from the government." Knowing that Kerensky was at heart with him, Nabokov consented to publication of a part of his note. Lloyd George now referred triumphantly to an "official communication indicating that the attitude of the Russian Government to the Stockholm conference differed very essentially from that which had been assumed." Balfour welcomed it as "fresh proof of the identity of views between the Russian and British Governments in the question of the Stockholm conference." Under this pretext the English Labor party delegates were denied passports for Stockholm.

Thus Nabokov sapped Henderson's position. But the button was pressed from another quarter, as shown by Thomas' telegram. Whence this report? Nabokov informs us: "Later

Tereshchenko told me that in personal conversation Kerensky had spoken against the conference, and that he, Tereshchenko, had confidentially reported that to M. Petit, a member of the French embassy in Petrograd, who was in direct communication with Thomas." Tereshchenko knew perfectly to what use such "confidential" communications were generally put.

Thus, through Nabokov and Petit, Kerensky and Tereshchenko blocked the organizers of the Stockholm conference, who were confident of their support, and underhandedly overthrew Henderson, who was doing everything in his power to strengthen their government. This was a brilliant illustration of the value of their promise "to draw their strength from the will of the Russian people to bring justice into international relations."

Again and again we are reminded of Kerensky's later statement that at bottom he was the "most conservative of ministers." That was his right. The misfortune was that he preserved most carefully the appearance of being the most revolutionary of ministers. This disharmony between appearance and essence pervaded Tereshchenko's activity as well. "Under his administration," says Miliukov, "the Allied diplomats knew that the 'democratic' terminology of his dispatches was an involuntary concession to the demands of the moment, and accepted it with condescension so long as they were sure of gaining in essentials by making concessions in form. . . . Tereshchenko's policy, at bottom, merely continued Miliukov's."[4]

In other words, in foreign policy the coalition government turned the revolution back to the situation which had provoked the first crisis. At that time two external forces had neutralized each other; the censitary government and the Soviet. Now this was effected by the two factions within the government. In neutralizing each other, they condemned the coalition to a policy of marking time in foreign policy too.

The foreign policy of Soviet democracy was caught in a

blind-alley. But the democracy did not perceive the true cause. It did not suspect the real authors of the failure of the Stockholm idea. The Allied governments seemed unreliable, while in their countries the popular movement for a democratic peace was still too weak to exert pressure on them. Soviet circles began to feel that the influence of the Russian Revolution had been weak so far because Russia herself had less and less weight in the scales of international politics. Its enemies and its allies seemed to think that the peace spirit of the Russian Revolution was only the unconscious expression of its military weakness. Hence a dangerous idea: to help the Minister of War prove by an active offensive that the revolution had increased Russia's military strength, and that her voice in international affairs must be rated much higher than before.

At all events, the convocation of an inter-Allied conference to revise war aims had been decided upon. The Provisional Government was planning to send a delegation, including elected representatives of the Soviets. In order to avoid a complete fiasco at this conference, Soviet democracy was now unwilling to make haste. First its own weight must be increased. That could best be achieved through victories by the revolutionary armies at the front.

This shift of revolutionary thought was hailed in nonrevolutionary circles with the liveliest satisfaction. It suited the spirit of the times. Many other influences had long worked to urge revolutionary democracy on this path. There were the delegations of Allied socialists, closely bound to their governments, with the secret mission of arousing Russia to renewed activity. An especially strong impression was made by the Belgian delegation, headed by Vandervelde and De Man. It touched many hearts by the tragic fate of its people and by its plea to be saved through an offensive. All censitary Russia urged this path. For it the only justification of revolution was that it might save the country from the military ruin and national humiliation to which Tsarism had led it. In particular, the propertied classes regarded a military victory and its concomitant chauvinism as the only way to avoid aggravation of the social revolution. Finally, there were intermediary elements, for whom Kerensky was a pillar of fire, who staked the honor of the revolution to prove on the battlefield free Russia's superiority over Tsarist Russia.

The militant blasts of the press grew louder. It preached, hymned, trumpeted offensive, offensive, offensive. A single sobering word against its unanimous chorus gave one the reputation of being a Bolshevik, a traitor, even a German agent.

Yet the logic of the situation was clear. Either the army authorities were actually preparing an offensive at the front, in which case the noise of the press was a criminal warning for the enemy's benefit; or else the leaders considered an offensive premature, and this irresponsible newspaper outcry was a criminal attempt by petty politicians to blackmail the army into action unjustified from the military viewpoint.

At the congress of the Social Revolutionaries late in May, its leader, Chernov, had raised this question in an acute form. We have no revolutionary army, he said, but a

> rather disorganized mass of people out of whom an army can be created; this work of creation is not complete. Is it possible that at this very moment, when this work of creation has begun and is progressing, people at the rear should begin shouting for an immediate offensive, urging an act the consequences of which are difficult to weigh beforehand, particularly for civilians? What does this mean? It may mean driving the army into military adventure, ending in its complete destruction.

Then those "vociferators of the bourgeois press" would be the first to express their malignant joy and blame the revolution for the army's collapse. Perhaps they already hoped "to warm their hands by that fire which would consume the

Russian army if it allowed itself to be urged prematurely into a military adventure."[5]

This warning merely embittered relations within the government, between Chernov, who had risked making it, and the majority of the government, with Kerensky at its head.

Later it appeared that this warning coincided with the opinion of many military specialists, including several Allied military attachés. Their fears were reported to responsible leaders, including Miliukov. Miliukov was also visited by a special delegation from headquarters, headed by Novosiltsev, to warn against an immediate offensive. In Brusilov's speech at the conference of army commanders at headquarters we read: "At the beginning of the operation I indicated to you that success was not particularly to be counted upon." All these warnings died away within four walls.

The army continued to suffer from the underlying antagonism between the commanding officers and the mass of soldiers, while the field officers were caught between hammer and anvil. There were only two ways to end this state of affairs. Either that of the French Revolution: to give the revolutionized army revolutionary leaders, if necessary from among the field officers, whose intimacy with the soldiers and revolutionary enthusiasm would compensate for their inexperience; or the opposite method: to turn the clock back and grant the old generals unlimited power to purge the army unmercifully and reduce it to unquestioning obedience. The coalition government could not adopt the first method: agreement with the old corps of generals was an absolute condition of the compromise on which the coalition was founded. The second method meant political suicide: having secured complete control of the army, the old generals could easily turn it against the revolution. A halfway régime was set up. The soldiers had their "committees." "Coalition" relations still had to be arranged between them and the commanders. This rôle was assigned to commissars of the Provisional Government, miniature Kerenskys, as it were, balancing between two hostile parties. As if an army could be united and strong under conditions which made civil government divided and weak.

The chief commissar of the front, Stankevich, set the tone for all the commissars and officers with influence over the committees. A faithful follower, Vilenkin, president of the Fifth Army Committee, stated his attitude to the committees as follows: "The task of our committee was to bring the army to such a state that at the order of the army commander any detachment would unhesitatingly arrest the committee. Then we leaders of the committee could say: Our duty to the country is done." Kerensky, Stankevich, Vilenkin, and their ilk failed to achieve this, and it was only thanks to this failure that they were not arrested in a body by General Kornilov during his revolt. Events reversed everything: "There was no regiment that would not have arrested its commanders but for the resistance of the committees."[6] To lead such an army to an offensive was to tempt certain failure.

The result of the Kerensky offensive varied. In some sectors "the offensive was absolutely hopeless" from the beginning. In the Dvinsk region, "General Danilov tried to convince headquarters that the offensive had no chance of success. In conversation with me," writes Stankevich, "commanders of corps and divisions said openly that they saw no chance for success in this offensive, provoked, in their opinion, entirely by 'political motives.' " The soldiers, led by persons who saw no purpose in what they were doing, lacked all enthusiasm for the offensive. Somehow, all, or almost all, not without the aid of punitive detachments, were gotten under way. Then general confusion developed. "They occupied some points—moved ahead in some places—brought prisoners from somewhere—met sharp fire from the enemy. There was almost no conception of the general progress of the attack. Companies were confused and lost their officers. No one led the offensive, everything went by inertia, but the force of inertia was soon exhausted." As a result they returned to the point of departure.

On some sectors the troops were not lacking in offensive spirit. "The original moment of onslaught was magnificent: the attacking troops advanced willingly, rushing forward at command with red flags." Before the Second Army, "the Austrians as usual surrendered in entire regiments." But on the front of the Seventh Army things went worse, the offensive enthusiasm was exhausted quickly. In places the soldiers faced barbed-wire entanglements, not destroyed by artillery, and were helpless: "They were not trained or equipped to overcome these obstacles." The chief commissar of the army was "tremendously impressed by the striking technical deficiencies." "With our technical equipment in this state, the attack had no chance for success in the face of the enemy's severe artillery fire, even had the morale of the troops been of the highest."

The offensive was begun haphazardly by people who drove themselves to believe in it. Even Kerensky, "after inspecting the front and returning to headquarters, said to Brusilov: 'I do not believe in any possible success of the offensive.' "[7] Under such conditions his duty was to cancel the offensive. But Kerensky lacked the moral courage. After the breakdown of the offensive, the Austro-German counteroffensive and the catastrophic rupture of the southwest front, he grasped at General Kornilov's telegram as an anchor of salvation: "I declare that the fatherland is perishing, and hence, unasked by anyone, I demand the immediate cessation of the offensive on all fronts to preserve the army and reorganize it on the basis of strict discipline, in order not to sacrifice the lives of a few heroes who deserve to see better days."

Although Kerensky hated anyone who had warned him in time against the offensive as a dangerous adventure, he rewarded this belated condemnation with the highest military title: he made Kornilov supreme commander in chief. Kerensky was never noted for consistency. To the committee which investigated the Kornilov affair, he said: "I recall that General Kornilov's comment in his July 11 telegram on the necessity for immediate cessation of the offensive on all fronts had great weight in his appointment as supreme commander in chief."[8]

This was an act of weakness. Too feeble to stop in season or condemn his own act, Kerensky eagerly thrust on Kornilov responsibility for liquidating the offensive.

"The military accepted events more calmly," while "Kerensky took it almost as the failure of the revolution. I do not know whether this was realization of the true significance of the failure, or regret for the possibilities which would have been opened up by a successful offensive, both in foreign and domestic policy. . . . Loss of spirit was very abrupt."[9] Denikin is even more definite: "There is no doubt, but that Kerensky did this in despair." Despair was poor counsel. General Kornilov's promotion to the supreme command opens a fresh chapter in the history of the revolution.

The failure of the "Kerensky offensive" merely summed up the results of the policy of the coalition government. In the labor question, in the agrarian and nationalities questions, in foreign policy, and finally, in the military question, the coalition government marked time.

Meanwhile, life moved on. Events were approaching, catastrophes maturing.

The revolutionary country had tried the censitary government, and rejected it. It had tried the coalition government: it came too late, and was as helpless to cope with the new problems as the Duma leaders had been.

What was left?

The answer was plain: a more homogeneous government, composed of those new elements which were a minority in the coalition ministry. In other words, only a Tseretelli-Chernov government could still be tried, in order to carry through that policy for the sake of which they and their followers had entered the government of Lvov and Kerensky. Unlike the broad coalition government, that would have been a government of "narrow coalition," a united front of the democratic parties. It might have included the Social Revolutionaries, the Social Democrats, the Laborites, the Populist Socialists, the Coöperative leaders, and individual dissenters from the Right, like Nekrasov, and from the Left, like Krassin.

Such a government would have had a majority in the Soviets, in the municipalities and zemstvos, and in the future Constituent Assembly: that is proven by the indisputable statistics of the elections. It could have strengthened its position until the Constituent Assembly by convoking a "preliminary parliament," composed of delegates of zemstvos and municipalities; i.e., a parliament based on universal suffrage, but elected indirectly; it could have declared itself responsible to this body, until the meeting of the assembly. This was the only possible democratic government, a government of the majority and controlled by it.

Otherwise, only minority governments were possible, either of the Right or Left. Either would have to be a dictatorial government, breaking up the majority and subjecting it to a minority: a dictatorship of the Right or Left. A Right dictatorship would be a militant dictatorship, directed against the working class, against the revolutionary peasantry, against enlarging the rights of nationalities, against democratizing the army, and in favor of war to a victory which would flatter the national vanity and promise compensation for the war sacrifices at the expense of the vanquished.

Kerensky was at one time believed by many, with fear, or hope, to be moving toward the rôle of dictator through the natural course of events. Lenin always called him "a tiny Bonaparte." Trotsky remarked that, although Kerensky was no Bonaparte, he was "the mathematical point of application of Bonapartism in Russia." Later, at the Democratic conference, organized by the Soviets, Kerensky himself stated that he had repeatedly been urged to set up a dictatorship. He had not consented. Why not? Because it could not be effected? Or because he could not reconcile himself to dictatorship? Evidently, not because of this. On August 27, during the Kornilov rebellion, he exacted written resignations from the members of his cabinet, and justified this "concentration of power" in his own hands—a short-lived but personal power—as follows: "In a struggle against a conspiracy led by a single will, the state must oppose a power capable of swift and decisive action. Such a power cannot be a collegium, even less a coalition." Kerensky had unusual talent for expressing unquestioned truths inappropriately, and giving them illustrations quite unconnected with the "text." As a matter of fact, the Kornilov rebellion, as we shall see, was liquidated by a "collegium"—a very numerous one at that, the Soviets and the army committees. Kerensky perched on his heap of resignations, on the ruins of his own laboriously constructed "coalition," like Marius on the ruins of Carthage, in the beautiful pose of a "doomed man," in disheartening and impotent isolation. He was not the stuff of which dictators are made. He could only copy the intonation and gesticulation of a dictator, and dream what a benevolent dictator he would be. According to General Lukomsky,

> on his journeys to the front, forgetting the fear which he felt in Petrograd before the Soviet of Workers' and Soldiers' Deputies, Kerensky gathered courage and with his fellow travelers frequently discussed the question of creating a strong government, of forming a directory or intrusting power to a dictator. Since most of these companions and intimates were in fact closer to headquarters than to him, all these conversations were reported to us.[10]

According to the acting Minister of Marine, Lebedev, Kerensky said to him in a tone of intense and dreamy conviction: "Oh, if only *they* [the Soviet and Duma leaders lumped together] entrusted power to me, real complete power!" At this time he was neutralizing the Duma elements in the government by the Soviet ministers, and the Soviet elements by the Duma members. Relying on the intermediary group of his personal followers, he could in fact do whatever he liked, repeatedly shifting his majority from Right to Left, and thus deciding in advance all decrees of the Provisional Government in a little group with Nekrasov and Tereshchenko (this was called the secret directory or triumvirate). Dictatorial power was offered Kerensky only by much narrower groups. He referred to "Cossack circles" and certain "representatives of public opinion." That did not carry sufficient weight. Things would have been different had Kerensky's July offensive succeeded and its author returned with the halo of victory. Then the political situation might have made the impossible possible. From this viewpoint, the "very sharp depression" which Stankevich noted in Kerensky after the breakdown of the offensive, need provoke no surprise. His explanation—"the dreams of those possibilities which would have been offered by a successful offensive both in foreign and domestic policy were not realized"—evidently has a far deeper significance than intended by its author.

Right-wing elements, naturally, could agree to a Kerensky dictatorship only with reluctance and for lack of a more suitable candidate. Kerensky was too closely bound by his past to the revolution and even the Soviets to be very militant against them at once. Their hope rested partly on the logic of the new situation which would compel Kerensky to follow the line of least resistance, partly on Kerensky's being a prisoner of those who would have aided him in securing dictatorial power. For them it was a relief when he dropped out of the running as a possible dictator, and intrusted the supreme command to Kornilov, thus offering them a new, full-fledged candidate, and an unexpected chance to take possession of the army, which meant power.

All partisans of a Right dictatorship naturally began at once to organize around the man who held such a vital position for the possibility of seizing power.

For the partisans of a Left dictatorship, the Bolsheviks, it was most advantageous to wait their turn, *reculer pour mieux sauter*. For their "leap to power" one could hardly imagine a better spring board than the defeat by the people in arms of a counterrevolutionary generals' putsch, particularly a putsch for which the way had been cleared by the Provisional Government, in appointing Kornilov commander in chief. The momentum of armed suppression of counterrevolution was to lead to their own offensive and victory.

Meanwhile, the army, which in time of revolution lives the thoughts and hopes of the entire country, had not been left unaffected. In the army question the policy of compromise, of "marking time," was as fatal for the revolution as in the labor, peasant, and nationalities questions.

CHAPTER SIXTEEN

THE ARMY AND THE REVOLUTION

WITH the outbreak of revolution, that which had been hidden was disclosed. The army, that voiceless giant, suddenly found its tongue and began to hold meetings. Excess of blind subordination, of slavish rigidity, of idiotic "eyes front," created a similar, though opposite excess—denial of all discipline, detecting the old régime in the most elementary and justifiable desire to check outrageous slovenliness and criminal negligence. Because mountains of cannon-fodder had been wasted with criminal extravagance to make good failures of military strategy or defects in technical equipment, the desire was all the stronger now to avenge this history by a regard for personal safety which at times became cowardly slacking, dangerous for adjacent military units. Because the commanders' incapacity had been made so obvious to all, the privates now insisted on discussing military orders, thus destroying the bases of the army's very existence. The more the privates' personality had been degraded by "manhandling" and corporal punishment, the stronger was their desire to degrade and even terrorize the officers. Finally, the structure of every army is inevitably stamped by the country's social structure. When revolution overthrows its entire social and political organization, that must be reflected in the army's structure. In wartime, when the army becomes "the nation in arms," the front must live the same feelings, the same thoughts as the civilian rear, or else it will begin armed combat against it. Attempts of the old commanders to preserve intact the structure of the old army have in all revolutions resulted in "punitive expeditions" by the front against the revolutionary capitals; in genuine revolutions they have invariably ended with the temporary "decapitation" of the army, a crisis, radical reform, and absolutely new leadership.

On the Russian front the revolution had created a very complicated situation. In the beginning the negotiations of the Duma leaders with the high command showed that no irreconcilable contradiction divided the government of the Progressive Bloc and the generals. Both of them abandoned the monarch reluctantly, and only because it seemed as if the dynasty could be saved at that price alone. At the conference of the Progressive Bloc on October 1, 1916, Miliukov was sincere in declaring, "Why, we are all monarchists." But it was not equally easy for all members of it to abandon the monarchy. Moreover, the Progressive Bloc had to lean on its own Left wing, and seek allies from the Left, even at the price of losing support from the Right. The result was a misunderstanding. The chief of staff, General Alexeyev, finally regretted having aided in securing the abdication of Nicholas II. He drew his own conclusions, unfavorable to Rodzianko's person; even this typically old régime politician seemed to him insincere and suspect because of his coöperation with the men of the "Left." Rodzianko too felt it would be no easy matter for him politically to work hand in hand with Alexeyev. But during the absence of the commander in chief his place was automatically taken, according to the military code, by his chief of staff; thus General Alexeyev became the army's head in fact, and shortly in form. The Provisional Government did not accept* the Tsar's appointment of Grand Duke Nicholas as his successor—it could not have accepted it, even had it so wished. The least painful course seemed to be to replace him by General Alexeyev, and the supreme command was intrusted to him. A paradox now occurred: the more conservative "Provisional Committee" of members of the Imperial Duma on March 19 addressed a

* Properly speaking, using the same fiction of unbroken legal succession, it asked the Grand Duke to resign the high command, and thus avoided the necessity for reversing the "Tsar's August Command."

GENERAL ALEXEYEV (LEFT)

From Soviet Russia in Its Early Years. *A collection of photographs presented to the New York Public Library*

serious warning to the more radical Provisional Government. Considering General Alexeyev's previous activity and "failure to understand the present moment," the committee urgently advocated that "General Alexeyev be relieved of the post of commander in chief." The president of the committee, Rodzianko, wrote (March 18) to the president of the government:

This appointment will not lead to success in the war. Realize that General Alexeyev has always felt that the army should command the rear, that the army should command the will of the people, and that the army must head the government and all its measures. Remember General Alexeyev's accusations against the representatives of the people [the Imperial Duma], that a chief culprit of the approaching catastrophe was the Russian people in the persons of its representatives. Remember that General Alexeyev insisted strongly on the immediate establishment of a military dictatorship. . . .

From General Alexeyev's "Diary" of those days, we know now that this first leader of the Russian revolutionary army, when by himself, always called the Soviet of *Soldiers'* Deputies the Soviet of *Dogs'* Deputies! The old psychology which had dictated that odious sign, "No admittance to privates and dogs," penetrated Alexeyev to the marrow.

Alexeyev was considered a weak character. As chief of staff he was given General Denikin, temperamental, abrupt, unyielding, determined to ignore completely the existence of all soldier collectives or organizations. Several of the highest posts were offered to a man of like tendencies, General Krymov, who refused them all and complained to Denikin:

How can we possibly work under such conditions, when the Soviets and the unruly soldier mob do not let the government take a single step? I offered to clean up Petrograd in two days with a single division, of course, not without bloodshed. . . . Not at all! Guchkov dissents, Lvov cries, "Lord-a-mercy, that would provoke such complications, such commotions."

Finally, at the seat of government, command of the Petrograd military district had been intrusted to General Kornilov by the Tsar's command (this was concealed from the public). He "defined the political situation as Krymov did: a government without power, and the necessity for a stern purge of Petrograd."[1]

The "Provisional Committee" of Duma members, which did not yet consider its rôle exhausted, made an interesting attempt to acquaint itself with the true state of the army by sending special delegates to the front. One of them reported:

> We talked with many officers. Many have absolutely no realization of the true situation and ask us: "Could you not have consulted the army before making a revolution?" They are displeased that this was done without asking them, so to speak, hastily, by civilians who did not consult them. Some commanders have been very tactful. After the revolution, abdication, etc., they quietly removed all portraits [of the reigning family]; in some units the portraits are still hanging in provocative manner. When the soldiers demanded that the portraits be removed, the commanders refused, not because they felt the portraits must hang or because their love of the old régime required it, but because, in their opinion, discipline did not permit their removing them: "What, the soldiers demand, and we obey their demand?" This attitude is ominous for the future. Some of the soldiers said frankly, "So-and-so is our commander, we will kill him, we have organized his murder." We said: "Calm down, the Provisional Government will solve this question in one way or another, it will adopt measures so that the commanders will be of the right kind."

The government adopted, not measures, but half-measures. "Measures" were taken *from below.*

> Some of them [the commanders] understand their task, but others are quite unwilling to realize that a change has occurred and that they must change themselves. They are indignant at the new commands, including Guchkov's order to treat the soldiers courteously: they say such things are done by people at the rear who have nothing in common with the army.

A division commander replied briefly and expressively to a Duma member regarding this order for polite treatment of privates: "Even so, I have flogged those rascals and I shall continue to flog them, and if they do anything, I shall hand out fifty strokes of the cat."

It was not the socialists, nor the Soviet, but the Provisional Committee of the Imperial Duma that declared: "This is a counterrevolutionary state of mind."

Could it have been otherwise? No.

The intimate assistant of Grand Duke Nicholas, General Danilov, admits in his *Russia in the World War*, that even before the fall of the autocracy, "besides the opposition, the only real force was the army, educated by its monolithic commanding body in a spirit of profound devotion to the fatherland, which it identified with Russia's ancient governmental system." This "monolithic" body, carefully selected during several centuries, had suffered great losses on the battlefield and been strongly diluted by the democratic body of young lieutenants drawn from all classes. Yet the higher the rank in the military hierarchy, the more monolithic it was. The few exceptions were not always fortunate: individuals from the top ranks of the army supported the new régime more frequently from opportunism, lack of principles, and selfish ambition than from sincere inner reconstruction. General Denikin does not deny that "Russian professional officerdom as a whole cherished monarchist convictions." The situation was especially bad in the imperial guard.

The guard officers, isolated within their caste and its obsolete traditions, were recruited exclusively from the nobility, while part of the cavalry guard came from the plutocracy. . . . Undoubtedly, the guards officers, with few exceptions, were monarchists *par excellence* and bore their ideal inviolate through all revolutions, trials, evolutions, struggles, downfalls, Bolshevism and volunteer armies, sometimes secretly, sometimes publicly. . . . With valor, occasionally with heroism, in military and civil life, it [this body of officers] preserved for the most part the intolerance of a closed caste, an archaic class aloofness and profound conservatism, sometimes with symptoms of statesmanship, more often with a strong inclination to reaction.[2]

These elements could not but react against the spirit of revolution which was penetrating the army. The clash was inevitable. The privates sensed the aloofness, the inner repulsion of their commanders for that new thing which brightened their own lives so radiantly. They felt it when the officers hid it, as well as when they displayed open hostility.

An army can exist only as a monolith. The old régime had created that monolith *from above*, the new régime had to create it *from below*. The old régime had compelled the field officers and privates to identify their sentiments with those of the commanders; the revolution reversed their rôles: the commanders had to identify themselves with the democracy of the army, or make way for a new commanding body produced by that democracy. The farther the revolution advanced, the more acute this necessity became. At first the privates spoke up timidly ("They are still scared by the old régime," said one letter); they presented complaints and requests; soon they gave way to impatience and excitement. The commander of the One Hundred and Eighty-second Infantry Division wrote that "the nerves of the soldiers are strained to the point of exasperation"; he did not know how to cope with "the approaching conflagration." In March the Duma members reported after visiting the front that "the soldiers are expecting something." But soon, without waiting any longer, they set about purging their commanders themselves.

General Dragomirov complains:

Arrests of officers and commanders do not cease. New accusations have been added to the old ones, of adherence to the old régime or injustice to the privates. . . . Arrests of generals and officers by privates have resulted in removing displeasing commanders; impunity of the privates means in practice that they can dismiss anyone merely by threat of violence against his person.

Dragomirov, as a military expert, was absolutely right. Renewal of the commanding body cannot be left to the initiative of the privates. A revolutionary army requires no less severe discipline than an old régime army, but one "not of fear only but of conscience," a discipline reënforced by a *fresh consciousness of civil duty*. That this discipline may triumph without a psychical rupture, there must be no temptation to violate it *at the call of revolutionary conscience*. Revolutionizing the personnel must be effected from above lest it take place from below.

The generals of the old school merely laughed sceptically when told that the army could be recreated with the aid of revolutionary enthusiasm. "As if the ordinary private would face death more willingly if told that he would die for the revolution! As if that magical word would abolish animal fear for one's own skin!" But the militant, revolutionary spirit was offered, not in place of discipline, but as the foundation for a new discipline, to replace the old "our faith, the Tsar, and the fatherland."

Later the Bolsheviks showed that merciless discipline, absolute unity of command and abolition of all commissars and soldiers' committees were feasible in a revolutionary army, not at once, but only after a process of reconstruction. This could be accomplished only by people who were at the opposite pole to the hated old régime and appealed to the army in the language of revolution and in the name of revolution. The Bolsheviks showed that a revolutionary army could be led only by going *ahead of it* in the revolutionary process; excesses of revolutionary zeal injured the army less than attempts to halt the revolutionary process.

In conflicts between privates and commanders the field officers at first sided frequently with the privates. There was a chance to unite the field officers and the mass of privates against the commanders and their satellites among the privileged officers. Through this union alone could the old army have been recreated and resurrected as a revolutionary army. Trust the field officers, who lived the same trench life, in direct comradeship with the privates! Promote capable field officers boldly, choose from them genuine leaders for the revolutionary army! This would have been the program of a truly revolutionary government. With this slogan the leaders of the French Revolution had reorganized the royal army. But a censitary government could not choose this path. It could not follow Danton's slogan: *De l'audace, encore de l'audace, toujours de l'audace!* Its slogan was one of cautious conservatism: *Quieta non movere!* Its program was compromise. This meant perpetuating the dualism in the army, letting the army be devoured by mutual mistrust between lower and upper ranks, assigning to the field officers the most ungrateful rôle by putting them "between hammer and anvil." The new government did not place its stake on the field officers; robbed of all support, the latter served first as a buffer and finally a scapegoat for other people's sins.

The first Minister of War in the Provisional Government, Guchkov, did make an attempt to "freshen up" the corps of commanders. He purged its lists, which, as Denikin admitted, were "clogged," removing about a hundred generals. Against "Guchkov's proscription lists"* a frightful clamor was raised among the army's commanding staff. Discharged generals, officers who had fled or had been driven from their units by the self-assumed power of the privates, swamped headquarters, which was soon described as "a hornets' nest of reaction." Guchkov's measures were child's play compared with what the French Revolution did to its armies. Up to July, 1793, 593 generals had been retired. Yet the French army of that day was tiny beside the Russian army of the World War.

Guchkov could not cope with the task. He made way for

* Denikin.

Kerensky. The latter was expected to display great revolutionary energy and determination. Yet he did not even tackle this task. His enthusiastic supporter and immediate assistant, Stankevich, says plainly that, to relieve the generals of "a feeling of instability after Guchkov's purge," he "displayed *special conservatism* toward the commanding staff, making it plain that every new man, because he was new, was worse than the old"; he displayed this conservatism by Kerensky's instructions.[3]

Kerensky was not phrase-making when he said that he was "the most conservative minister."

The culminating point in the fermentation and disintegration of the old army was certainly Petrograd. There the military forces had not watched the events of the revolution from the side line, as they had at the battle front. At Petrograd they were boiled in the pot of revolution. They emerged the chief figures of action. Discord between soldiers and commanders was expressed in the heat of struggle, where there is no room for evasion, where "whoever is not with us is against us."

In Petrograd adherence to insurrection meant violating discipline by an action for which the military code knows no penalty but death. Officers and privates fought, not with words, but weapons. The revolt of many regiments was begun by firing on their own commanders. How could it be otherwise when, during the first days of insurrection, the commanders had led their soldiers on to the street, lined them up, and ordered "Ready!" "Fire!" The "gray coats" had besieged the revolutionary factories, and sometimes taken them at the bayonet by order of their commanders. Even on February 26, on Nevsky Prospect the shooting was so intense that the pavement was strewn with corpses of unarmed people, including old men, women, and children. The first three regiments to revolt, the Volhynian, Lithuanian, and Izmailovsky, having killed some officers and compelled the rest to flee, were led to the Duma by a civilian, Attorney Sokolov. The very sight of an officer's coat or epaulets aroused an explosion of mob wrath. The belated attempt of one officer, Stankevich, to join the insurgents all but ended tragically, while his proposal to go to the Tauride Palace met with distrust.

This was a blow at the army's structure, a crushing, irremediable blow. Stankevich's rank did not blind him to the essence of the tragedy. The privates who had violated discipline and killed their officers were by universal recognition heroes, emancipators of the country from its centuries-old yoke. Within a few days that had become the official version, obligatory for the commanders as well. The main thing was not that some officers had tried to prevent the soldiers from accomplishing that feat; they had been killed. But what of the officers that remained and now joined in the chorus of eulogy? Why had they not led their soldiers in orderly ranks to achieve that feat? Why had they compelled the soldiers, in a disorderly mob, in an explosion of elemental wrath, to sort out their rifles and rush on to the street?

Now that the victory was a fact, the officers joined in. But was that sincere, and for long? During the first minutes they had lost their heads, hidden, put on disguise. What if all the officers had come back the next day? What if some had joined in within five minutes after the sally of the privates? It was still the privates who had led the officers, not the officers the privates, and these five minutes were an impassable chasm.

A shining example of this chasm is the famous "Order Number One" to the troops of the Petrograd garrison, issued during the revolutionary "interregnum" by the Petrograd Soviet and drawn up by a commission of delegates of the revolutionary military units.

This Order, for military leaders, quickly became something terrible, unspeakable, ruinous for the army: a kind of bomb, intentionally cast by a criminal hand at the foundation of army discipline. Yet most points of that Order contain nothing so terrible for people acquainted with the military discipline of modern armies outside Russia.

Its point of departure was simple: "The strictest military discipline in line and in fulfilment of service duties"; outside the barrack, line, and trench the private is a citizen with full rights.

Its reforms in external discipline—prohibition of the familiar address, "*ty*," to the soldiers, and in general of rude treatment of them, use of the simple "citizen general" instead of the pompous "Your Excellency," and so forth—were frightful only to people who worshiped the petty magnificence of title.

But slightly more serious was the abolition of the obligatory attention and salute when off duty, which had made the private's stroll through streets crowded with officers a genuine torture, with the risk at any minute of overlooking an officer and being confined to the guardroom.

Three points of the Order regulated the private's relation to his elected *political* organizations, the Soviets and committees. Of course, on the principle that the army was outside politics, these points were heresy. But the army which had just made the revolution and was defending it could not be declared "outside politics"—that was simply stupid. Secondly, the commanders who demanded that "their" soldiers be left outside politics did not renounce interfering in politics. On the contrary, they were already dreaming of a "severe purge of Petrograd," and even offered to carry it out; the battering-ram to be used was those units which were indifferent to politics and unquestioningly submissive to their commanders.

Another point required execution of only those orders of the military commission attached to the Provisional Committee of the Duma which did not contradict the orders of the Soviet of Soldiers' Deputies. But that "commission" was just as much a political and self-formed organ as the Soviet; limitation of its rights did not contradict any military rule.

However, the central point, the fifth, would have been impossible in an army. "Every sort of weapon, such as rifles, machine guns, armored automobiles, etc., must be kept at the disposal of company and battalion committees, and in no case handed over to officers, even at their demand." This point signified a vote of no confidence in the officers, set up as a rule for the privates.

Worst of all, this point was more than justified.

Order Number One was signed on March 1. On that day General Ivanov, with dictatorial powers to subdue Petrograd, brought his train, with a special battalion of St. George soldiers to Vyritsa. On the following day, arresting and terrorizing the railwaymen, he attempted to reach the Tarutinsky Regiment, in order to occupy Tsarskoye Selo. On March 1 troop trains were still being dispatched to him from the northern and western fronts. Only on March 3 was Miliukov's proposal finally dropped "to assemble the military force necessary to defend the Grand Duke" (Michael), and place him on the throne. Still aiming to defend Michael's candidacy, Rodzianko and Miliukov talked themselves hoarse trying to persuade one military unit after the other "to disperse to their barracks," "to find their officers and to place themselves under their command"—for they "will not teach the soldiers anything bad and would act in full accord with the Duma." The "Provisional Committee" of the Duma, "the only government, which all must obey," needed "the coöperation of military force acting in an organized way." At this time, in the opinion of officers close to Denikin, "a single steady battalion, commanded by an officer who knew what he wanted, could have reversed the entire situation."

The Duma leaders evidently took fright at their own haste; on that same March 1, Colonel Engelhardt, appointed to the military commission by their Provisional Committee, issued a special order. Against attempts to take weapons from the privates it threatened "the most determined measures," including the firing squad! This was considerably more serious than the mere refusal to hand over their weapons, as in the Soviet's Order Number One!

On March 5 General Ivanov took leave of his St. George Battalion and urged it henceforth to serve the Provisional Government as faithfully as it had the Tsar. On that day the Petrograd Soviet issued Order Number Two, explaining that it had not instituted election of officers. Order Number One did not apply to the front. While subordinate politically to their Soviet, the soldiers were subject in questions of military service to the legal military authorities.

But could these belated recognitions change in the least that tremendous, incorrigible, fatal thing which had passed between upper and lower ranks of the army during the unforgettable days of late February and early March, 1917?

The chasm remained. With each fresh shock it deepened until it finally split army and country and made them clash in civil war.

The upper ranks demanded that everything return to its normal state, that the army forget the events in the rear and go back to its previous purpose: that of fighting to a victorious finish. They had reconciled themselves to the fall of Nicholas II only because of their professional and military interest: the old régime had plainly been leading both army and country to destruction. They would accept even a revolution, but only if it furnished better organization for war, greater chance for victory.

Nicholas II was gone. New people were in the government. Now what? Let them justify themselves.

The out-and-out officer turns "civilian" thinking upside down. For him the entire country is only a "rear" for his army, an appendage to serve it. A Great Revolution? A place can be found even for it, if it earns it, on the running board of a supply wagon, serving the front.

Hence, as soon as the *façade* of the state was changed, "the incident was closed" for the army command.

Was it closed for the country? For its toiling masses? For them it was the reverse: the revolution was not to be justified by serving the war; the war had to find its justification in serving the revolution. But this could be only if the revolution went beyond the façade.

Before the revolution the masses had been appealed to in vain. No patriotic enthusiasm had stirred in them. Poverty and enslavement, beyond certain limits, kill any feeling for the fatherland. There is *nothing to defend* in the fatherland. Even the bogey of hostile conquest has no effect. There is nothing to lose. It can be no worse.

The task of the revolution is then to fill with a new social content the naked *forms* of liberty now proclaimed, within the new structure to create for the people values that they will defend even by their own blood.

CHAPTER SEVENTEEN

THE COUNTERREVOLUTION AND GENERAL KORNILOV

THE Kornilov drama is one of the most gripping pages in the history of the revolution. The passions which raged about this movement have not yet subsided. Some regard it as a mad attempt, which destroyed the inner balance of the country—hence the prelude to Bolshevism. Others viewed it as the only means—had it been successful—to forestall the Bolshevist catastrophe. For some it was the political adventure of a foolhardy, ambitious man; for others, the hopeless, tragic, sacrificial outburst of a "heroism of despair." For some, it was a plot arranged in cold blood with "malice aforethought." Others regarded it as due to "great provocation" by the general's enemies and ill wishers, anxious to rise at his expense and carry out his program without him and by his ruin. Some consider it a symptom of the social counterrevolution which had been silently ripening; others look upon it as an unselfish struggle, devoid of political or social nuance, to establish at the front conditions which would make victory possible or at least ward off the annihilation of Russia, hence of the revolution.

The historian of the Russian Revolution must deal both with the "Kornilov legend" and with the "Kornilov enigma."

Eager for adventure, impatient of discipline, by origin a plebeian, Kornilov seemed to some a man of great diligence, beyond reproach in pecuniary matters, of modest habits and great personal courage. To others he appeared abrupt, unbalanced, painfully sensitive, ambitious, and cocksure. On Left-wing, revolutionary General Verkhovsky, Kornilov "made a strong impression. . . . Kornilov has a lion's heart, you feel the hot blood of a fighter pounding in his veins . . .

but when he begins to talk politics, you sense that it is not his element."[1]

Kornilov began his career as a solitary scout. He ended it in a bitter, brilliant, but unsuccessful guerrilla campaign against the numerous but poorly organized Bolshevist bands of the North Caucasus. Kornilov felt, and was right in feeling, his ability to accomplish something extraordinary. He was merely mistaken in its scale and character.

In 1915, through rash disobedience of orders, Kornilov was captured by the enemy. In the autumn of 1916 he escaped. Rumor and later advertising wove of this flight a great heroic legend. Reality was much more prosaic. As was later proven to the Austrian military court, a Czech, Franz Mrnak, for 20,000 gold kronen, which Kornilov promised to pay in Russia, had disguised him as an Austrian soldier and brought him from the military hospital to the border. Mrnak was detained, Kornilov escaped and proceeded to talk too freely to reporters in Russia. Mrnak was condemned to twenty-five years' military imprisonment. The volubility of the man he had aided cost him dear.

After the February Revolution the president of the Provisional Duma Committee, Rodzianko, begged the Tsar's headquarters, in order "to establish complete order and save the capital from anarchy," to appoint "a militant general"; namely, "the valiant hero, known to all Russia, Lieutenant General Kornilov," as commander of the Petrograd district. General Alexeyev "most humbly reported" to the Tsar by telegraph, and secured "the consent of His Majesty the Emperor" for this measure, "to tranquilize the capital and establish order in the troops" which had just overthrown the existing "order." Nicholas II wrote on this telegram: "Execute."

Once in Petrograd, Kornilov visited the Soviet. That was a curious interview. Of course, the Soviet had not the slightest inkling that it was discussing their joint task with a general appointed by "most august command" to defend "order." Such things were carefully concealed.

As a prisoner in Austria Kornilov had often expressed his wish "to string up all these Miliukovs"; he now had to support these "gallows birds" against still worse ones, the leaders of the Soviet. All Russia was turning Left, and General Kornilov moved Left as far as Miliukov and Guchkov. When, in April, tumultuous demonstrations of workers and soldiers demanded Miliukov's resignation, Kornilov hastily brought out his cannon and led cavalry to the Marinsky Palace. To avert civil war, the Soviet had to act as a revolutionary government and forbid all demonstrations and attempts to bring the troops on to the street. Even Kornilov's troops appealed to the Soviet, asking what Kornilov's orders meant, and whether they should obey them.

Kornilov had then hardly formed a plan for dictatorship. But he was deeply offended that the Soviet by a single gesture had established order, while he was powerless. He had had no luck at all with his Petrograd mission. "Kornilov's unquestionable weakness was his inability to organize the administrative side of his work," writes Stankevich.[2] In addition, as soon as Kornilov lost direct contact with the soldiers, his charm for them vanished. His austerity, his "sometimes rough treatment" of his subordinates, left one impression under fire at the front, quite another in the rear. "If he had often succeeded in mastering a military unit by personal fearlessness or a picturesque word, there were now times when the troops refused to leave their barracks to greet their commander, or whistled at him, or tore the St. George banner from his car." He was in too complicated a situation; he "could neither influence the government, nor exact the respect of the Soviet." Feeling that the Soviet was usurping his power, he decided to resign. There was another reason, Denikin adds: "The commander of the Petrograd district was subordinate, not to headquarters, but to the Minister of

War. . . . Guchkov resigned, and Kornilov did not wish to remain subordinate to Kerensky, a vice president of the Petrograd Soviet." Worst of all, Kornilov departed with the conviction that "a rigorous purge of Petrograd was inevitable."[8]

Before resigning, Guchkov tried to have Kornilov appointed to command the northern front, in place of Ruzsky, who had been relieved by Alexeyev for "weakness and opportunism"; i.e., for yielding to attempts to democratize the army. Alexeyev objected flatly, citing Kornilov's "insufficient experience as commander." Guchkov insisted on the "need for a strong hand" on the northern front and "the desirability of keeping Kornilov in the immediate vicinity of Petrograd in view of future political possibilities." Alexeyev refused to sacrifice strategy to politics. "Guchkov insisted, Alexeyev refused. The commander in chief had never been so unyielding toward the ministry. Alexeyev threatened to resign." The creator of Russian world-war strategy dreaded intrusting an entire front to a man of such impetuous, stubborn, and unbalanced character.

The dispute ended with a compromise: Kornilov was given the Eighth Army (on the southwestern front). "He immediately made friends with Boris Savinkov, commissar of the Provisional Government for that army, and began to intrigue against the commander of the southwestern front, whom he soon displaced," says Brusilov, seizing only the outward form of events. Kornilov did not intrigue. He merely belonged to the "militant" or "irreconcilable" generals, who naturally opposed the "opportunists" and even more the generals who favored democratizing the army. And Savinkov did not "make friends" with Kornilov; he had found in him the powerful battering-ram he had long sought.

Once a brilliant figure among revolutionaries, a leader of the terrorist "Militant Organization" of the Social Revolutionary party, Savinkov was now inwardly empty. He had lost faith in people and looked down on them. He was hostile to his former friends and by them suspected of a bent for adventurism. A man of brilliant talents and even more striking defects, audaciously self-assured, restless, laconic, with flashes of stilted eloquence and tragic exaltation, he exaggerated his strength, and believed that on the horizon of the revolution his star would outshine all others. During the war this potential regicide, a former Social Democrat, later a Social Revolutionary, and then toying with individualistic anarchism, shocked his former friends by declaring that during war any step against Tsarism or capitalism was a blow against the fatherland. His closest partisans turned their backs on him, and he repaid them with like coin; a few continued to be impressed by him, and these he was the first to despise. The militant bent of his soul, developed by years of terrorist guerrilla warfare, had grown unnoticed into a passion for war for its own sake, a strained, unhealthy, "apocalyptic" passion. He had no clear, positive program. He lived by negative slogans. The old friends, toward whom he nourished the fresh hostility of a renegade, had intrenched themselves in the Soviets; the leitmotiv of Savinkov's policy became the emancipation of the government from the influence of the Soviets, and of course of parties, for Savinkov felt himself an outcast in his own party. In the government he found a man who seemed created for his purpose. For Savinkov Kerensky was the long-sought embodiment of the personal principle in the revolution, able to resist all parties, Soviets, and committees—a kind of supra-party political "superman." Savinkov saw through the inner weakness of this "superman," and by putting himself at his disposal counted on mastering his will and using his popularity. Kerensky dreamed of a "dictatorship of the word." Savinkov, his soul scorched, perhaps seared, by the flame of austere terrorism, hinted that, while that was all right for a time, at the critical moment *gegen Demokraten helfen nur Soldaten.* He needed a general not oversubtle in social matters, requiring political guidance, but able without a flicker of the eyelash to issue the order "Ready! Fire!" no matter how many the human targets, nor who they were. Savinkov suddenly discovered Kornilov; he could not have imagined a fitter instrument. Thus Abbé Siéyès had once hoped to control young Napoleon Bonaparte.

In his book on Kornilov, Savinkov refers to his plan for emancipating the government from the influence of Soviet democracy. "The first step was General Kornilov's appointment to command the southwestern front." This step was hindered by the fact that Kornilov was a military failure, or, as Stankevich delicately put it, "fate had not given him a proper opportunity to display his strategic talents." As soon as success smiled, and Kornilov's Eighth Army had broken through the Austrian line and seized Kalush and Galich, Savinkov made it a spring board to leap, with Kornilov, to the highest commands in the army. "The laurels of Galich were contested, not without reason, by General Cheremisov," but that did not worry Savinkov. He later wrote, "Of course, General Kornilov's military success was for me only a pretext."[4]

Strategy could be and had been sacrificed to politics. Not everyone was easily reconciled. Kerensky admits that "he encountered almost the same resistance from Brusilov that Guchkov had met from Alexeyev."[5] Resistance usually served merely to arouse Kerensky. He had come to trust Savinkov, and no warnings from the Social Revolutionary party center could change his intention of making Savinkov his right-hand man in military matters. "Kerensky insisted on appointing Kornilov commander of the southwestern front."[6]

How did Kornilov and his followers regard Savinkov? "I do not believe in Savinkov," Kornilov once let drop. And Denikin described him:

> Strong, cruel, lacking any restraining principles of "relative morality," contemptuous of the Provisional Government and of Kerensky, for expediency's sake, as he interpreted it, he supported the government, but was willing any minute to discard

it. He considered Kornilov merely a tool in his fight for a strong revolutionary government, in which he would possess paramount significance.

Why should not Kornilov try to use Savinkov as his own tool?

Be that as it may, Savinkov and Kornilov had taken each other's measure as potential opponents. One of Kornilov's intimates, Zavoiko, appeals to Savinkov's right-hand man, Filonenko: there are schemes afoot for proclaiming a dictatorship of Grand Duke Nicholas Nikolayevich; this danger must be forestalled; how far are Savinkov and Filonenko ready to go with Kornilov? The alarmed Savinkov consults his assistants. One of them, a Social Revolutionary, Gobechia, offers to cut the knot: as an old revolutionary, he is ready, if necessary, to sacrifice himself, to go and kill General Kornilov. Kornilov is also on his guard: before his decisive interview with Savinkov he hastily calls up the faithful Tekinsky Regiment. Savinkov says to Kornilov: "General, I know that, if necessary, you will not hesitate to have me shot, and you know that I will do the same in cold blood if I come to the conclusion that you are thirsting for power, for dictatorship. Let a strong alliance arise from this mutual appreciation: our aim is the same, but we must achieve it together, and, for the sake of painless success, include Kerensky." Kornilov agrees, the alliance is concluded. Savinkov does not have to send Gobechia with a revolver, Kornilov does not have to use his Tekinsky Regiment.

The allies begin their compaign. Only two days after Kornilov's appointment to the southwestern front, he telegraphs an ultimatum to the Provisional Government. The moment is well chosen. There is a catastrophe on the front. The unfortunate "Kerensky offensive" has been followed by a strong German counterattack. The only successful army, Kornilov's Eighth, now under Cheremisov, is in danger of being outflanked, surrounded, annihilated. Kornilov demands extraordinary powers for the commanders, demands that these powers be incorporated in the army regulations. "If the government does not ratify the measures which I propose, and deprives me of the only means for saving the army . . . I, General Kornilov, will lay down my powers as commander."

Kornilov does not spare the government. He hits directly at Kerensky; he refers disdainfully to people who "think to govern with words on fields where death and the disgrace of treason, cowardice, and egoism reign." He threatens: "Either the revolutionary government shall wipe away this disgrace, or else, if it cannot, other people will be brought to the fore by the inevitable march of history." Who are these "other people"? It is not hard to guess: "I, General Kornilov, all of whose life has been spent in devoted service to the fatherland, though unasked, declare that the fatherland is perishing." His candidacy as savior was announced.

Later, it turned out that this telegram had been revised and toned down by Savinkov. Its original text contained a "hidden threat, if the demand made on the Provisional Government were not executed, to proclaim a military dictatorship on the southwestern front." After gaining Kornilov's consent to cut out this passage, Savinkov declared to Kerensky that he backed "every word" of Kornilov's statement.

The telegram was secret, and Kerensky was reconciled to its contents, including its unpleasant references to himself. But, dated July 11, it appeared on the twelfth in the *Russkoye Slovo.* Everything was spoiled. Kerensky was furious. A headquarters conference of all front commanders was arranged. Kornilov was told that he need not appear.

Savinkov's plan for "marrying" Kornilov and Kerensky and forming a new, purely military triumvirate to decide the fate of the revolution seemed ruined. It was rescued by two misunderstandings during the headquarters conference.

The first misunderstanding, a surprisingly petty one, was between Kerensky and Brusilov. The latter describes it:

We were told that the minister would arrive at 2:30 P.M., but he came an hour earlier, while I was busy with my chief of staff issuing field orders. I could not reach the station in time to welcome him. In view of the urgency of the questions we were deciding, General Lukomsky also advised me not to go. . . . Our work was interrupted by the appearance of Kerensky's adjutant with the minister's demand that I appear at once at the station with my chief of staff. That same day I heard that Kerensky had fumed and raged at the station, had ominously declared that the generals were spoiled, that they should be brought up sharp, that I wished to ignore him, that he required more attentiveness, for the "former ones" had been met by standing at the station in all weathers for hours on end. . . . All this was very petty and ridiculous, especially beside the tragic situation at the front which I had just been discussing with my chief of staff.

This episode is reported identically by other participants in the conference: Denikin, Lukomsky, and Alexeyev. By the next evening Alexeyev had concluded that "Brusilov's days were numbered"; he did "not surmise that Brusilov's hours were numbered."[7]

The second misunderstanding was with General Kornilov. His absence from the conference, due to disfavor, now turned to his advantage. The conference was nervous, the debates sharp and fruitless. Denikin's speech was a formal arraignment of the government, "which has trampled the Russian banners in the dirt," and of Kerensky, who must repent everything he had done "if he has a conscience." Kerensky's reproof to Ruzsky was excited, almost hysterical. Nothing concrete was formulated. Against this background Kornilov's "nine points" were a miracle of practicality. In one point Kornilov, an enemy of commissars and committees on principle, urged, this time in accord with Savinkov, "the establishment of commissars in corps now without them, while empowering them to ratify death sentences." In another he suggested "at once effecting the most thorough and merciless purge of the commanding body." Kerensky, who had just had a sharp conflict with this commanding body and had heard so many bitter attacks on the commissars and committees, on the government and Soviets, imagined that this represented "a broader view." He was cruelly in error: Kornilov was merely transferring to the commissars the odium of passing death sentences, while by a purge of the commanders he meant expulsion of the "opportunists" and their replacement by irreconcilables.

The wheels of history began to turn. On the way from headquarters to Petrograd in his private car, Kerensky and Tereshchenko, with Savinkov and Filonenko, who had been specially invited, discussed various measures "to save the army and the country." They considered removing from the government the Left ministers, Chernov and even Skobelev, and replacing the "weak" Brusilov. Kerensky, Savinkov relates, "asked me point-blank who should replace the latter. I mentioned Kornilov. General Kornilov was appointed commander in chief." Neither were his political protectors ignored: Savinkov was made Minister of War, and Filonenko, his *alter ego*, an unprincipled adventurer, became supreme commissar at headquarters.

Kerensky did not suspect that, as the popular saying has it, he was "exchanging the cuckoo for the hawk." He quickly felt the hawk's talons. In reply to his appointment Kornilov wired: "As a soldier, bound to furnish an example of military discipline, I accept, but, as commander in chief, I report that I accept the appointment under these conditions: (1) responsibility to my conscience and the entire people, (2) absolute noninterference in my field orders, hence, in the appointment of higher commanders." Then: the demand that all punitive measures adopted at the front be applied to the rear, and, in general, fulfilment of the "nine-point" program which Kornilov had presented to the "council of war."

Even a convinced follower of Kornilov like Denikin shrugged his shoulders over that "very original constitutional form of the commander in chief's sovereignty to last till the Constituent Assembly," expressed by Kornilov in the winged words, "responsibility to my conscience and the entire people." But Kornilov was not bothered by "constitutional forms," provided he had dictatorial powers over all military concerns. Kerensky too had defined his prerogatives curiously in a general order issued on taking over the War Ministry: "*Taking in my hands the military power of the state,* I declare the fatherland in danger" . . . "I will allow no requests for resignation, due to desire to escape responsibility." Kornilov was in part carrying on a camouflaged polemic against Kerensky, in part parodying Kerensky's own statements. Savinkov says he again calmed Kerensky, assuring him that this new rebellious document had merely been palmed off on Kornilov by some casual intriguers, and that the general's signature, so incautiously given, was not to be bothered about. "I even liked Kornilov's vehemence then," Kerensky later admitted. "I advanced him steadily, against the opposition of his superiors and the hostility of Left groups." Kerensky was unconcerned that he had appointed Kornilov commander in chief "despite the opinion of the military authorities."[8] To act as a "superauthority," that was Kerensky all over.

This was not the last complication. In appointing Kornilov commander in chief, Kerensky had also appointed General Cheremisov his successor for the southwestern front. But Kornilov was absolutely serious in demanding sole power to appoint the higher commanders. He refused to recognize Cheremisov, and appointed General Baluyev. Two men appointed by different authorities were about to clash. What was to be done? The duumvirate, Savinkov and Filonenko, set to work. As supreme commissar, Filonenko summoned Cheremisov to the telephone: he could straighten out the situation by a "voluntary" declaration that he could accept his appointment only from Kornilov. The astonished general declared that he was not hired for the personal service of Kornilov or anyone else, but served only Russia. Finally, in reply to Cheremisov's comment that orders of the Provisional Government could not be canceled by the backstage intrigue of "sinister forces," Filonenko said with irony: "Kindly include in these sinister forces Savinkov and Filonenko," and broke off the conversation.

Meanwhile, the commissar of the Eighth Army had taken alarm. During the "Kerensky offensive," the action of Cheremisov's Twelfth Corps had been most successful. A new military star seemed to be ascending, one which had completely accepted the revolution. The commissar protested that "the situation can be saved only by outstanding men like General Cheremisov." Filonenko's threat of Kornilov's resignation provoked no panic in the commissar of the army which Kornilov had commanded before Cheremisov; comparing the two men, he preferred Cheremisov.

The conflict between Kerensky and Kornilov had to be settled. A comedy was acted out. On the twenty-fourth Kornilov took over his duties as commander in chief. The next day Cheremisov arrived at the staff headquarters of the southwestern front. Before he had left his train he was handed a telegram from Kerensky, relieving him of the command of the southwestern front, and placing him "at the disposal of the Provisional Government"; that is, depriving him even of the army which he had saved from a crucial situation and the corps with which he had achieved a brilliant victory.

From that moment his opinion of Kerensky was unshakable. During the Bolshevist overturn, as commander of the northern front General Cheremisov did not lift a finger to rescue Kerensky's helpless government.

Kerensky and Kornilov now stood face to face.

Kerensky had not yet seen through Kornilov. He saw in him a "difficult" character, instead of a definite plan and a firm policy. Kornilov's challenging conduct was like a clarion call to supporters and allies. The chief committee of the Officers' Union at headquarters declared publicly that if they failed to accept Kornilov's "nine-point" program, which alone could save the army, the members of the Provisional Government would "answer with their heads." Real forces were mobilizing about the candidate for dictator. For the first time since the revolution those forces seemed to spring from the ground.

During the revolution and its "honeymoon" all defenders of the Tsarist régime had somehow evaporated, vanished without trace. As a matter of fact they were merely lying low. They were waiting for discord and strife to develop among the victors. The first government crisis, the replacement of censitary by coalition government, had been a signal for counterrevolutionary groups to awaken. From early summer all kinds of antigovernment and anti-Soviet societies and unions sprouted like mushrooms after a rain. Because of unfamiliarity with conspiracy, most of them existed publicly, camouflaged under a legal aim; within this legal framework there were various stages of conspirational organization, like the narrowing circles of Dante's *Inferno.* Since the flower of all classes was in the army, most of these organizations drew their strength from the corps of officers, and inclined to act, as Miliukov said, "by those means at the disposal of a military milieu." That meant a military plot, for a purely military overturn. But concrete plans were not clear. They agreed, not on a positive platform—that was beyond most of these elements—but on what had to be stopped, and who had to be destroyed. At bottom, they agreed on the principal thing: to stop the revolution, disperse the Soviets, lay hold of the Provisional Government incidentally, if it interceded for the Soviets, and then—"whatever God gives."

Denikin was close to the truth when he said:

They were preparing for any event: a Bolshevist attack, fall of the government, collapse of the front, support for a dictatorship, or finally, for some members, restoration of the autocracy; at first neither a pretender to the throne nor a dictator was mentioned.

The restless Purishkevich led one secret group, the "Society of the Russian State Map." Later, to the Bolshevist Revolutionary Tribunal, he described his difficult position:

> How could I attempt to restore the monarchic order—which, I profoundly believe, will be restored—if I did not even have a person who should, in my opinion, be the monarch? Tell me who could be that! Nicholas II? A woman, whom I hate more than anyone else? The sickly Tsarevich, Alexis? My tragedy as a monarchist is that I see no one who would lead Russia to quiet waters.

Finding no one in the Imperial family, people began to search outside. They began to dream of a dictator, a Russian Bonaparte, perhaps rather a Cavaignac.

Bonapartism has always been "more democratic" than legitimism. It does not repudiate revolution, but regards itself as its completion, its heir. Hence some of these groups and secret organizations with a leaning to Bonapartism at times dreamed of a "dry putsch," a "legal dictatorship," set up by the Provisional Government or legalized by it *post factum*, or else established with the participation of some part of it, especially its head. One of the best methods for effecting a "dry putsch" seemed to be to involve the Provisional Government in a fight against the Bolsheviks by such ruthless measures, uncompensated even by the shadow of a concession to revolutionary democracy, that non-Bolshevist and anti-Bolshevist Soviet parties would revolt. The logic of events would thus make the fight against the Bolsheviks one against the Soviets, while that in turn would make the Provisional Government the actual prisoner of those forces which would have secured victory for it, and would make it accept, willy-nilly, their demand for a dictatorship. The latter was regarded as a transitional stage, a purgatory leading to the Elysium of monarchy, constitutional perhaps, but anyway monarchy.

Kerensky was to be flattered by the idea of a "dictatorship." V. N. Lvov, a member of one of his cabinets, said later: "He did not want to be a dictator; well, we would make him one." According to Denikin, "the originally vague hopes among both the officers and liberal democracy, especially the Cadet party, attached to General Alexeyev's name." Even before the Tsar's downfall he had almost frightened Rodzianko to death with his idea of a military dictatorship. "Later, or perhaps simultaneously, many organizations made definite proposals to Admiral Kolchak, during his stay in Petrograd." In particular, the "Republican Center," which had a large share in the Kornilov movement, "was then in touch with the Admiral." According to Novosiltsev, the chief conspirator of the Officers' Union at Headquarters, confidential conversations were also carried on with him by the leader of the Cadet party." Then with Savinkov's help Kornilov was moved to the fore. All further search ceased. The "name" was found. What forces rallied around it?

The first to offer its services was "an officers' organization, formed at the initiative of General Krymov, on the southwestern front; it chiefly included parts of the Third Cavalry Corps and the Kiev garrison, guards' cavalry regiment, officers' and technical schools, etc." This organization had been waiting for an elemental catastrophe, such as the collapse of the front. In case the Germans advanced, Krymov planned to withdraw slowly into the interior, continuously organizing the rear on principles of iron discipline. The question of the form of government was unusually difficult for Krymov's organization; there were strong monarchist influences in it, but his antidynastic, conspiratorial past hampered its leader. It had to adopt the policy of "no predetermination" as between monarchy and republic. Krymov was in contact with his partner in the first conspiracy against Nicholas II, Guchkov, and in the Provisional Government, with Tereshchenko, another fellow conspirator.

Second place belonged to the "Chief Committee of the Officers' Union at Headquarters." Under various legal pretexts, it secretly transferred "reliable" officers to Petrograd to form a shock unit. It tried to control the formation of volunteer shock battalions in army divisions and at railway junctions—until Brusilov ratified Colonel Manakin's own project which gave the Soviet organizations direct participation in this. The committee established extensive contact with similar organizations and bourgeois parties. It was headed by Colonel Novosiltsev, behind whom loomed a greater figure, General Alexeyev.

During the Moscow State Conference [Denikin writes] there was a remarkable conversation between the commander in chief and Alexeyev: "General Alexeyev, we shall have to rely on the Officers' Union, your handiwork. Take the leadership of it, if you think that will make things easier." "No, General Kornilov, that will be easier for you, as commander in chief."

Thirdly, note must be taken of a number of Petrograd secret societies and circles, later united as the "military section" attached to the "Republican Center," formed in June. At first the Center proclaimed its support of the Provisional Government against the Bolsheviks, but later began to plan its overthrow. The military section of the Center was run, according to the president of the "Union of Military Duty," F. Vinberg,[9] by a colonel of the general staff, N., and after his departure, by another colonel, Du Cimetière. It numbered two to four thousand active members, that is, supplied with weapons. That seemed a real force. Later it was discovered to contain too many "gilded youths," who played at conspiracy making and squandered the money intended for the "cause." According to General Lukomsky, Kornilov maintained contact with these secret societies through Colonel Lebedev, a founder of the "Military League." At Lebedev's initiative a meeting took place at headquarters between Kornilov and two Petrograd delegates, both engineers. "It was decided," says Vinberg, "to begin active measures in conjunction with and by consent of General Kornilov, who was slated for dictator. It was agreed that power in Petrograd would be taken over by General Krymov as soon as he reached the capital with a special corps." By the time Krymov's troops arrived, "the main forces of the revolution were to have been broken, so that Krymov would only have to establish order."

Lukomsky adds that the representatives of the Republican Center claimed to have 2,000 armed men, but asked to have 100 officers sent to Petrograd toward the end of August. "General Kornilov assented, adding that the officers could be sent from the front, as if on leave. . . . It was agreed that everything was to be ready by August 26."[10]

Many participants in the plot were convinced that the Bolsheviks were planning to seize power toward the end of August. This information contradicts everything we know of the real intentions of the Bolshevist general staff. Undoubtedly, it was spread to justify the attempted overturn. But a part of the conspirators knew perfectly that the rumors of a Bolshevist action were deliberate lies, and even tried to counterfeit such an attack.

This brings us to the fourth group of conspirators: the Council of the Union of Cossack Troops, dominated by an unprincipled, but energetic demagogue, Ataman Dutov; and the Economic Club, the legal camouflage for P. N. Krupensky's illegal monarchist organization. V. N. Lvov, later an unsuccessful volunteer mediator between Kornilov and Kerensky, after the Kornilov uprising heard an important admission from Dutov's own lips: "I was to act as a Bolshevik on August 27, in Petrograd." The pretended Bolshevist demonstration failed, for, as Dutov said, at the decisive moment he "ran to the Economic Club and summoned it to the street, but no one followed me."

Dutov's provocation was ruined by the opposing side. On the eve of it three of the biggest labor organizations, the Executive Committee of the Soviets, the Petrograd Council of Trade-Unions, and the Central Union of Factory Committees, issued a warning:

Comrades and citizens, rumors are spreading through the city that demonstrations are planned. They say that August 27 has been set for a workers' street demonstration. Counterrevolutionary papers write of a massacre planned for August 28. . . . We, the representatives of the workers' and soldiers' organizations, declare: These rumors are being spread by *provocateurs* and enemies of the revolution. They wish to call the masses to the street and drown the revolution in a sea of blood. We declare: No party of the working class and the democracy summons you to a demonstration. The proletariat and garrison of Petrograd will not succumb to provocation.

Still earlier the Bolshevist Central Committee had issued a warning: "Sinister persons are spreading rumors of an approaching demonstration, and carrying on agitation for purposes of provocation, allegedly in our party's name. The Central Committee summons the soldiers and workers not to succumb to this provocation, and to preserve complete discipline and calm."

These maneuvers throw a different light on the activity of the skilful and demagogic paper, the *Living Word* (*Zhivoye Slovo*), which called itself national and socialist. The paper was well financed. It preached dictatorship, and ever dictatorship. It championed a purely Russian Hitlerism ten years before the latter appeared in Germany. Cleverly speculating on the ignorance and irritation of the lower classes of the capital, especially the "infuriated petty bourgeoisie," the paper sold like hot cakes, and stimulated strong discontent with everyone and everything.

Kornilov had only to combine all these various elements in a unified plan. Its military formulation was intrusted to Colonel Lebedev and Captain Rozhenko, while Lieutenant Colonel Golitsyn and Adjutant Zavoiko linked the technical with the political plan. Kornilov did not have to search for assistants. His challenging attitude had given the signal throughout Russia. "Representatives of the Officers' Union, led by Novosiltsev, came and expressed their desire to work for the salvation of the army. Delegates came from the Cossack Council and the Union of St. George Cavaliers. The Republican Center promised the support of influential circles backing it, and placed at Kornilov's disposal the military forces of the Petrograd organizations. General Krymov sent a messenger to the committee of the Officers' Union to inquire, 'Is something going to happen?' and to ask whether he should accept the Eleventh Army, offered to him by Denikin, or remain with the Third Corps, which would 'go anywhere,' as he put it. He was asked to remain with the Third Corps."

The military and conspiratorial aspect of the Kornilov movement has been outlined. Its political and social side has remained in the background.

Much scattered information can be assembled to show what intimate bonds linked it to the landowners and plutocracy. The myth that the Kornilov movement was inspired by the essential need of the state, and was sharply opposed to all selfish private, party, class, or caste interests, collapses utterly.

During the liquidation of the movement the following news item appeared:

> Moscow, September 7. In searching the house of a certain Petrov, 6,500 political pamphlets were found, bearing Kornilov's name. The pamphlets were confiscated. The militia searched the premises of the Administration of the Union of Landowners. Broadsides and four proclamations of General Kornilov, distributed during the days of his rebellion, were found.

This item recalls Kornilov's order forbidding interference with the landowners' rights in the areas adjoining the front. An attempt was made to explain that order as intended solely to aid in supplying the front, which depended primarily on the landowners' estates. Kornilov promised a delegation of Polish landowners to lend them "armed force only to protect crops needed by the army." A very broad interpretation was given to the purpose of this armed force. At a plenary session of the Chief Council of Landowners Count Chapsky asserted that the publication of the order was a direct result of the Union's activity: "We have now secured from the commander of the troops a decree punishing persons who hinder the reaping of crops and hay."[11]

No wonder Kornilov and his followers supported the campaign of the militant Russian landowners, for Kornilov's right-hand man, Zavoiko, was a big landowner and president of the nobility in a district (Gaisinsky) of Podolsk province. Several of the secret societies which had rallied around Kornilov also had a definite agrarian trend. The Council of the Union of Cossack Troops, led by Dutov, had its own agrarian policy, under the slogan, "Not an inch of Cossack land to the peasants." Concretely, this slogan meant that the Cossack elders, by isolating the rank-and-file Cossacks from the rest of the peasantry and arousing hostility between the Cossacks and the "others," would not only preserve the privileged landed property of the higher officers as a whole, but would keep in their hands the profitable function of disposing of the unoccupied army lands, which they rented out.* "The Republican Center assumes that property in land must remain," reads an "Appeal to the Peasants," from the central Kornilov Society in Petrograd. It refers to the "hard labor and sweat of fathers and grandfathers," rejects the possibility of transferring the land to the unpropertied. The "Military League" declared that the solution of questions of everyday life, the agrarian, the labor question, etc., was "a matter for the future, not the present." Denikin admitted that "many participants in the Petrograd organi-

* From the middle of the 1840's the Don Cossack officers had begun receiving sections of army land, first for fifteen years, later for life, instead of money pensions. The superior officers received up to 200 dessiatines, staff officers 400, retired generals 800, active generals 1,600. The "Cossack elders" proposed that this life holding be made hereditary, and the autocracy consented. Instead of "Not one inch of officers' land to the toilers," it was easier to say, "Not one inch of Cossack land to the peasants."

zations belonged to Right circles"; these circles were closely connected with the nobility and big landowning.

There is another important indication of the backstage rôle of the Russian landowners in the Kornilov movement, one so far ignored by historians of the revolution. Much has been written of one "Hollywood" episode in it, the unsuccessful effort at reconciliation made by V. N. Lvov, former Procurator of the Holy Synod in the Provisional Government. Lvov was sincere, but muddleheaded, odd to the point of abnormality. By his well-intentioned but clumsy interference he accidentally touched off the explosives which had accumulated in Petrograd and at headquarters. V. N. Lvov was a brother of the president of the Council of the Union of Landowners, N. N. Lvov, a much abler man. After his first conversation with Kerensky, after gaining his consent to "enlarge the coalition" and to include "parties even more to the Right than the Cadets," relates V. N. Lvov, "I did not see any of the civic leaders, but merely sent my brother, N. N. Lvov, to talk to various civic representatives, telling him that Kerensky had given his consent." Plainly, of the two, N. N. Lvov, not V. N. Lvov did the "sending."

Kornilov was also furnished an "agrarian theorist" of his own, a Professor Yakovlev. He invented his own agrarian project, to undermine the land reform based on Chernov's project. The essence of it was, first, that land would be granted, not to the toilers in general, but to frontline soldiers faithful to their duty, or to their families; secondly, numerous and elastic exemptions from "nationalization" were planned to benefit the landowners. These two peculiarities made the draft a useful tool for dictatorship.

The leaders of Russian plutocracy also attempted to hide backstage. Yet, they could not conceal their participation in the Kornilov movement.

Buchanan, British Ambassador, wrote that he was informed of the plot by a participant, "a big financier." Kerensky complained that in April or perhaps earlier leaders in banking and finance, had set up a special fund to support secret antigovernment and anti-Soviet groups. By his information, these circles had sent Zavoiko to "find a general" who would offer his sword for their purposes. Zavoiko had been in contact with Rasputin's circle before the revolution; it was said that he would have become Minister of Finance but for Rasputin's murder. In Kornilov's cabinet he laid claim to this post.

Kerensky made his charge without having firm proofs; they are now available. In the register of the Moscow branch of the Officers' Union, under No. 19, we find a receipt to the All-Russian Union of Commerce and Industry for a check of 10,000 rubles. After a special mission of the Chief Committee to Moscow and Petrograd, there were "voluntary contributions from nonmilitary people" of 3,500, 4,000, 10,000, and 16,000 rubles. An anonymous "Society for the Economic Resurrection of Russia," through our old acquaintance, Rodzianko, assigns 100,000 rubles to aid a no less mysterious and probably fictitious "Party of Liberty and Order," with the slogan, "Whoever is against order, is against liberty." This "party" proves shortly to be no party at all, but "a military nonpartisan organization" to fight "influences demoralizing the army"—plainly, one of the groups which gravitated to the "Republican Center." Of the latter Denikin says that it had one other advantage over the others—it possessed certain pecuniary means. They were furnished by the moneyed bourgeoisie, which had "raised the alarm after the July days exposed the weakness of the Provisional Government, and offered [the Republican Center] its first pecuniary assistance, in order to save Russia . . . from the even then imminent danger of Bolshevism." The representatives of this banking, commercial, and industrial aristocracy remained outside all organizations, "for fear of being compromised in case of failure."[12]

More concretely, who were these representatives? In the summer of 1917 the representatives of the Officers' Union reported a series of steps among civic leaders. "Russian civic groups, especially the Cadets, promised us their full support. We saw Miliukov and Ryabushinsky. Both groups promised support with the Allies, in the government, in the press, and in cash." "The Moscow group welcomed us, the Petrograd one dodged us. Ryabushinsky's group was more receptive."

During Kornilov's triumphal welcome in Moscow, at the opening of the State Conference, a member of one of the oldest merchant families, the millionaire Mme. Morozov, dropped to her knees before him.

Three representatives, Tretyakov, Sirotkin, and Ryabushinsky, were invited to the secret headquarters conference to discuss the formation of a Kornilov government.

Later, on September 12, when the "Kornilov men" were already in prison, General Alexeyev wrote Miliukov: "I do not know the addresses of Messrs. Vyshnegradsky, Putilov, etc. The families of the imprisoned officers are beginning to go hungry. I strongly request them to help. They will not abandon to hunger those to whom they were bound by community of ideas and preparation." Otherwise, "General Kornilov will be obliged to explain in detail to the court all the preparation, all the negotiations with persons and circles, their participation, to show the Russian people with whom he was marching hand in hand."

Only a few names were mentioned. But Vyshnegradsky, Putilov, Ryabushinsky, Sirotkin, Tretyakov, Morozov—these were the very cream of the Russian business world.

The fusion of the Kornilov movement with the class organizations of big business and landowning required, as a natural complement, alliance with their old political representation, the remnants of the Tsarist Imperial Duma.

Shidlovsky writes:

> About that time a group of young officers from headquarters expressed a desire to negotiate quite confidentially with some of the most prominent members of the Duma. A small conference was arranged in absolute secrecy. The officers asserted that

they were empowered by Kornilov to inform the Duma that at the front and headquarters everything was prepared to overthrow Kerensky, and that only the Duma's consent was needed to have the intended overturn effected in its name, and, so to speak, under its protection. The Duma members looked on this proposal with great caution, and from further questioning concluded that all this had not been arranged seriously.[13]

This account evidently refers to the Moscow visit of a special headquarters emissary, Colonel Rozhenko, in the first third of August. According to Denikin, "at the apartment of a prominent Cadet leader there was a meeting of influential members of the Duma and of political leaders." After Rozhenko's very frivolous report on the conflict which was coming to a head between Kornilov and Kerensky and on the probable need for the cavalry corps, intended to liquidate a possible Bolshevist attack, to liquidate the Soviets and government as well, it became clear "that everyone sympathized with the cause, but no one believed in its success" or "wished to bind himself or the political groups represented." A few days later the discussion was renewed "in a broader group of liberal and conservative civic leaders." For the Cadet party Miliukov declared his "hearty sympathy for headquarters' intention of putting a stop to disruption and dispersing the Soviets," but "the feeling of the masses is such that the party could not furnish any assistance." Rodzianko also declared the Imperial Duma absolutely "impotent"; but in case of success it could be "galvanized" and be brought to participate in "organizing the government."

Kornilov's officers were not entirely satisfied with their reception in these circles. The sympathies expressed seemed overplatonic. One officer, after recounting all these declarations of sympathy, concluded: "Nevertheless, we must draw this conclusion: we are alone." The conclusion was correct. At the critical moment the political circles which favored the overturn would not have led a single person on to the street. That political staff had long lacked even the shadow of an army to answer its summons. The counterdemonstration for Miliukov just before his resignation, "the demonstration of the bowler hats," had been its next to last attempt to review its forces. The last was the effort to organize a triumphal welcome for Kornilov when he arrived for the Moscow State Conference; but it assembled almost exclusively young officers, the very circles which sought in vain for effective support from the civilian population. The Kornilov movement had its façade, rich in the names of yesterday's stars of "high policy," rich in contacts and influence, in prestige with the Allies, in newspapers and money. From it moral support could be demanded for the slogans of the coup d'état, creation of a favorable social and political atmosphere, pressure on the government—that was all. If the plot succeeded, it would sanction it, crown its leaders with laurels, and advance with open vizor—if it failed, it would try to escape unscotched and carry on till better times.

Within these limits the façade began to act. It undertook to mobilize practically the same forces that it had once mobilized against autocracy, merely shifting its front to the Left. All nonsocialist forces were organized in a single antisocialist bloc. As earlier, its soul was Miliukov, Rodzianko its outward leader. Its organization was the so-called "little conference of civic leaders," preparatory to the Moscow State Conference. "Its three-hundred-odd members," writes Miliukov, "represented the most varied political groups and tendencies, from the coöperative leader Chayanov to the landowner, Prince Kropotkin." Its positive platform was defined as "creation of a strong national government to save Russia's unity" (Prince Trubetskoy's formula); its negative, "combating the influence of the Soviets on the government."[14] Kerensky stormed and raged. He told Kokoshkin: "Miliukov is organizing the Progressive Bloc against the Provisional Government as he once organized it against Nicholas II." Denikin agreed with Kerensky: "If many representatives of the new Progressive Bloc—such at bottom was the 'conference of civic leaders'—were not informed of exact dates, they at least sympathized with the idea of dictatorship; some surmised, others knew of the impending events."

The composition of the new Bloc all but coincided with that of the old; its leaders were the same. But it was now a liberal-conservative Bloc. The high light of the conference, for example, was General Alexeyev's speech; as an upholder of military dictatorship even under Tsarism, he would have been impossible for the Progressive Bloc. The same must be said of the leader of the Union of Landowners, Prince Kropotkin, not to be confused with the famous revolutionary thinker. With its front facing the Provisional Government instead of Nicholas II, it was not a Progressive, but a Regressive Bloc.

During the "little conference" a rumor spread that a conflict had broken out between Kerensky and Kornilov, and that Kornilov was in danger of dismissal. All the conspirators' plans would have been upset. The Officers' Union at headquarters was already proclaiming "enemies of the people" any who dared attack Kornilov, and promising him their support "to the last drop of blood." The Council of the Union of Cossack Troops proclaimed Kornilov an "irrevocable commander"; if he were removed, it threatened "to divest itself of all responsibility for the conduct of the Cossack troops at the front and in the rear." The Union of St. George Cavaliers was even more rebellious: "It would give a militant signal to all St. George Cavaliers to coöperate with the Cossacks." The "little conference" hastened to "add its voice to that of the officers, St. George Cavaliers, and Cossacks." Its appeal to Kornilov rang out like a provocation to act: "In the ominous hour of severe trial all Russia looks to you with hope and faith."

When Kornilov entered Moscow, the bard of the Cadet party, Rodichev, ended his greeting with the inflammatory words: "Save Russia, and a grateful people will crown you."

"No wonder," notes Denikin correctly, "people sometimes

felt pricks of conscience. Maklakov told Novosiltsev: 'Tell General Kornilov that we are inciting him to act, especially M. Why, no one will support Kornilov, they will all run and hide.' "[15]

Maklakov spoke the bitter truth. The first to hide was the formal leader of the new Bloc, Rodzianko. No sooner was it clear that Kornilov's enterprise had failed, than Rodzianko immediately denied through the *Russkoye Slovo* all participation in the movement.

Miliukov's position was more difficult. During the panic created by Kornilov's rebellion he all but raised the vizor. The Cadet paper, *Rech*, appeared on August 30 with blank columns instead of its usual editorial. But the proofs of the article, which had been hastily removed when the latest news changed the situation, were brought at once to the Soviet by the typesetters. In it Miliukov welcomed the approaching dictator most warmly. The Cadet press later spoke of the "criminal" methods of the Kornilov movement, softening this by a reference to its noble aims. Its conduct was the reverse of beautiful. Miliukov himself preferred to abandon the political stage for the time being and went to the Crimea.

The Cadet party even followed Kornilov's directions as regarded its members in the Provisional Government.

As early as June, 1917, V. N. Lvov was invited to an apartment with Shulgin, who even in March had yearned for machine guns to turn on the mob, and Colonel Novosiltsev, one of the leaders in the plot. "Shulgin stunned me by declaring that an overturn was being prepared; he wished to warn me of it, so that I could resign immediately after August 15." Lvov at once agreed to comply. Later, on August 21, when he was no longer in the government, a similar warning was delivered through him to the Cadet ministers. The initiative came from General Lukomsky. The Cadets were recommended to resign by August 27, to make the government's position difficult and save their own skins. Lvov's assertions are corroborated by V. D. Nabokov, the former secretary general of the Provisional Government. He carried Lvov's warning to three Cadet ministers, Kokoshkin, Oldenburg, and Kartashev. No such warning was communicated to other members of the government: that was what the Cadets meant by "practicing coalition." All four Cadet ministers resigned on the evening of August 25, thus literally executing headquarters' directions. Of his own initiative Kokoshkin had anticipated this method "of blowing up the government." On August 11, on the eve of the Moscow Conference, he had suddenly told Kerensky that "he would resign at once unless Kornilov's program were adopted today." Kerensky was "stunned" by this. Abandonment of the government by the Cadets "would make further preservation of national balance impossible." Then the Moscow Conference would become an arena of violent conflict, and he would have to dread some adventurous outburst from the Right, such as an attempt to proclaim a "strong government"; that is, a dictatorship.

Kornilov considered the Cadet party completely involved in his movement. When in the Mohilev hospital under guard, after his failure, he issued the following order through Prince Trubetskoy, "Tell them no Cadet must enter the government." Denikin sums up this conversation between Prince Trubetskoy and Kornilov: "The man of politics and public meetings had to spend much time persuading the man of the sword that to present such a demand one must have very concrete promises from the Cadet party." Kornilov had promises only for victory, not for defeat.

The struggle between Kornilov and Kerensky now began. A third element, Savinkov, meddled in it from the start.

Savinkov, and his *alter ego*, Filonenko, claimed that their efforts had "created Kornilov." Kornilov would be the sword to hack away the Gordian knots in restoring the army's fighting power and in settling the question of war and peace. Savinkov, with his tremendous reputation as a revolutionary and terrorist, would be Kornilov's democratic shield, protecting him against blows from the Left. In the second place, by their influence on Kerensky, Savinkov and Filonenko would make possible the painless execution of Kornilov's demands. Without Kerensky and against him success was hypothetical. Kerensky's participation would destroy all obstacles. The fulfilment of the main points of Kornilov's program with the aid of Kerensky and his triumvirate, and with the assured support of the Cadets, as Savinkov reasoned, "would compel the minority, including Chernov, to resign. In addition, by voting for the bill, Kerensky would *ipso facto* take a position openly hostile to the Petrograd Soviet."[16] The government crisis and the reconstruction of the cabinet after war had been declared between the government and the Soviet would concentrate power in a real or formal directory of three or five men, naturally including Kornilov. A quasi-legal coup d'état would achieve the same purpose as individual dictatorship, without its dangers. Evidently Kornilov was given to understand that the "directory" might be a transition to genuine dictatorship. He did not dissent. "I favor a directory, but we must work fast, time will not wait." On August 25 Kornilov was already arranging with Filonenko the membership of the triumviral directory—Kerensky, Kornilov, and Savinkov. The next day, a larger conference with Filonenko, Kornilov, and two of his political ciceroni, Zavoiko and Aladin, elaborated a project for a "Council of National Defense," with Kornilov as president, Kerensky as vice president, and Alexeyev, Savinkov, Kolchak, and Filonenko as members.

From the viewpoint of revolutionary democracy, such plans were a crime against the revolution. Kerensky willingly concurred in this estimate. Yet justice requires us to note that Kerensky himself, by continuing as Prime Minister and Minister of War and Navy and taking over the duties of commander in chief, carried out Kornilov's "governmental scheme," merely putting himself in Kornilov's place. Then with four ministers he formed the so-called "directory," or "Council of Five." Finally, the idea of a "Council of National Defense" was merely borrowed by Kornilov from Kerensky's triumvirate.

Thus the struggle between the "Kornilov men" and the "Kerensky men" became ever more a struggle of persons, not of ideas. That is clear in the quarrel over Kornilov's military program. At the very height of the undercover struggle through Nekrasov the "triumvirate" declared that Kerensky and Kornilov did not have two different programs, but merely two different methods of executing the same program. After the Kornilov defeat Kerensky tried to assert that he had always opposed the introduction of the death penalty in the rear, and militarization of factories and railways. Buchanan's secret dispatches to Balfour prove the opposite.

> Kerensky, so Tereshchenko assured me, agreed with Kornilov, and in principle approved application of the death penalty to several types of crime committed against the state by soldiers and civilians, but the Cadet ministers objected to its application to the latter, for fear it might be used for political purposes against those who abetted the counterrevolution.*

Kerensky inclined more and more to "a Kornilov policy minus Kornilov." After having promoted Savinkov constantly, despite the insistent warnings of the Social Revolutionary party Center, Kerensky now changed abruptly toward him. Savinkov "wanted state policy directed, not by one man, Kerensky, but by three, Kerensky, Kornilov, and myself; Kerensky declared he would never allow that."[17]

Of course, Kerensky preferred the old triumvirate, himself, Nekrasov, and Tereshchenko, to the new one. It was easier to handle. But the old triumvirate was already splitting. Nekrasov was becoming its Left wing, Tereshchenko its Right. This successor of Miliukov, Tereshchenko, was a kind of improvisation, a jest or caprice of history. Of all the qualities necessary for a diplomat, he undoubtedly possessed one, and only one: impeccable dress and elegant manners.

* Telegram No. 1332.

He had a superficial ease of orientation and flexibility of thought, and no backbone; in this he was a typical *Wunderkind*. "As Minister of Foreign Affairs he aimed to pursue Miliukov's policy, but in such a way that the Soviet of Workers' Deputies would not hinder him. He wished to fool everyone, and for a time succeeded. . . . Yet nowhere, in no social circle did he strike deep root, no one rated him high. *Ce n'était pas un caractère.*"[18]

On July 16 Buchanan secretly informed Balfour of Tereshchenko's curious frame of mind: "The blow dealt us on the southwestern front may be regarded as a favor to Russia," he asserted. "Undoubtedly, the enemy have saved Russia. . . . They have helped the government restore the death penalty, subdue the extreme parties, strengthen its positions, and restore the unity of the country." This "defeatism" led Tereshchenko to the Kornilov platform. On July 21 Buchanan telegraphed London:

> Tereshchenko . . . has told Kerensky that he can no longer remain in the government unless the latter acts vigorously. The only thing left is to militarize the entire country, to apply martial law to the railwaymen and compel the peasants to sell their grain. General Kornilov must be admitted to the government, and several members of the government must stay at headquarters, in constant touch with him. To my question whether Kerensky shared his views, he replied affirmatively, but said his hands were tied.[19]

All Savinkov's and Filonenko's calculations were based on this feeling of Kerensky and his friends. But the more they tried to become supreme arbiters between Kornilov and Kerensky, the more distrust they evoked from both. Kornilov "never knew exactly whom Savinkov was going to stab in the back, himself or Kerensky." Kornilov had his own confidants. He was a poor judge of men. Besides, he himself complained that he had no one to choose from. His political milieu was marked by "adventurism and frivolity," even "absurdity." Zavoiko, according to Kerensky, was the emissary of banking and industrial circles to Kornilov. Aladin was a former Duma member, a leader of the "Labor" faction, and a demagogue of the purest water. After the Stolypin reaction he had secretly gone over to the government and worked for Suvorin's *Novoye Vremya.* Aladin had been specially summoned to Russia by a secret telegram from Buchanan to Balfour.[20] There is no doubt but that his journeys and activities were financed by the British Government. Aladin tried to secure an audience with Kerensky, to persuade him to effect changes in the government to secure the "necessary confidence of the business classes, landowners' group, moderate parties, and army command."[21]

Buchanan did not hide the fact that "all his sympathies were with Kornilov." He merely claimed that he had warned against a military coup and urged an agreement between Kornilov and Kerensky. We already know of his negotiations with a "financier who had taken part in the conspiracy." As dean of the diplomatic corps, and in its name, Buchanan even ventured to offer the Provisional Government friendly mediation between it and the general. Buchanan noted in his diary: "There is nothing to be done but to await events and trust that Kornilov will be strong enough to overcome all resistance in the course of a few days."[22] The foreign military representatives at headquarters were even more outspoken: "Many of them called on Kornilov during those days, assuring him of their respect and their wish for his success; that was expressed in especially touching form by the British representative."[23] General Knox was so closely connected with Zavoiko and Aladin as to be practically a participant in the plot. That connection survived the Kornilov revolt. During the Versailles Peace Conference Lord Milner invited the conference to hear a "Russian representative," under the name of "Captain Kurbatov"; the sole person allowed to speak at Versailles in Russia's name was none other than Zavoiko. From Buchanan's dispatches we learn that he was much worried when a Moscow paper referred to the participation of English representatives in the Kornilov movement, and thanked Tereshchenko for promising to shut down that paper.

Kornilov's intimates were already drawing up slates for the future Kornilov cabinet, not overlooking themselves: Zavoiko claimed the Ministry of Finance, Aladin Foreign Affairs; they left places for Savinkov and Kerensky, to make sure of their support. In private there were frank conversations. Kerensky's death alone could assuage the officers' anger. Although Kornilov invited Kerensky to headquarters and guaranteed his full safety in Mohilev, it was always possible that he might be killed by some casual volunteer. On the other hand, during Kornilov's every trip to Petrograd at the government's summons, headquarters wondered if he would return alive. Kornilov went to the Winter Palace accompanied by two cars armed with machine guns. His faithful Tekinsky Regiment carried the guns into the vestibule of the palace and waited there.

At this difficult moment Kerensky, who could not be indifferent to his loss of popularity, tried to restore it. He convoked the so-called State Conference, to represent all organized forces in Russia. The division of seats among organizations, unequal in size and importance, had but one aim: numerical balance between labor and bourgeois elements. The neutral coöperative group, the only one of which Kerensky was sure, would give a slight superiority to one or the other side. This unstable equilibrium of opposing forces left the government in the rôle of superarbiter, exercised by Kerensky and his triumvirate within the Provisional Government between the equally balanced Left, Soviet wing, and the Right, censitary wing.

Prior to the State Conference all relations in and out of the government had become very strained. Toward Kornilov Kerensky had exhausted all his resources of delay. Kornilov had flared up several times and called Kerensky weak or simply insincere and untrustworthy. The Cadets had presented their ultimatum. Savinkov had expended all the resources of his impetuous character. Kerensky finally decided to let him resign. At times Chernov fought alone against all, and, having achieved nothing, was anxious to withdraw ostentatiously from the government and return to the Soviet. In the capitals Bolshevism was growing. The moderate Soviet parties felt more clearly the need for shifting the government's course to the Left. Kerensky needed support to resist that demand, but the "little conference" had just dug an abyss to his Right. The State Conference was irrevocably divided into two opposing camps.

Kerensky planned to frighten these two camps by their irreconcilability and to offer himself as a "superarbiter." ("He has gone to be crowned in Moscow," the journalists joked.) He wished to oppose to the realities of class, national, and party hostilities a sacred object, nay, the mysticism of a Higher Being, "Statehood," with himself as its archpriest. He wished to demand submission to the vast, simple, all-leveling force of national self-preservation for its own sake. The Provisional Government agreed with Kerensky. There were but two ministers who considered this scheme hollow and useless, though grandiose in appearance: the extreme Right, Kokoshkin, and the extreme Left, Chernov. For the first and last time they voted together against the majority.

As the conference approached, Kerensky defined more clearly a second practical aim, to locate exactly the danger which menaced him. His faithful assistant, Nekrasov, on leaving his train in Moscow, in alarm begged a Moscow resident who had come to welcome him to tell him what was being schemed there. Miliukov, the center of all the civic and political support for Kornilov's plot, asserts that "nothing definite was planned . . . no attempt was being prepared to establish a so-called 'strong government,' or any such thing, *at the conference itself*, or by force."[24]

This assertion is contradicted by well-known incidents. During the conference, the corps of one of the participants in the Kornilov plot, Prince Dolgoruky, advanced on Petrograd. It was stopped in time by General Vasilkovsky, commander of the Petrograd district. The Seventh Orenburg Cossack Regiment similarly advanced on Moscow but was checked by the commander of the Moscow district, General Verkhovsky. It is contradicted by the evidence of seven "Junkers" from the officers' guard in the hall of the conference. The commander of the guard, Captain Rudakov, told them that the conference would decide which of three generals (Alexeyev, Brusilov, or Kornilov) would become military dictator, while the Soviets, which "disorganized and corrupted the army and the population," would be destroyed, and the present Provisional Government would be replaced by "honest and able men, truly worthy of the lofty title of rulers of the people." Part of the Junkers appealed to the Moscow Soviet, protesting against this expressed desire to "use them as a blind physical force, to carry through some political intrigue to the detriment of the revolution and of the liberty they had won."[25]

Perhaps neither side really intended to attack the other during the Moscow Conference. But each side expected an attack, and "prepared." Significantly, Kornilov and Kerensky did not meet on arriving in Moscow. While the lieutenants of the Sixth School, the Junkers of the Alexander School, and the never-failing Tekinsky Regiment shouted "Hurrah!" and carried Kornilov on their shoulders, Kerensky reviewed a parade of the Moscow garrison, arranged for him by the revolutionary general, Verkhovsky. The Minister of War and the commander in chief seemed to be holding military demonstrations against each other.

The Moscow Conference merely summed up an obvious situation. The Right accused the workers of making excessive demands, of plundering the national capital, the peasants of seizing land, the subject nationalities of "choosing a moment of deadly menace to the common fatherland, to break their centuries-old bonds," the government of "conniving" at the excessive demands of all three groups. The government, the Right asserted, must "admit it has been leading the country on a false path" and "cease serving Utopias." Miliukov ironically rejected the desire of the Soviet parties "to guide the bourgeois revolution into a socialist channel by the hands of the so-called bourgeoisie." The representative of the Landowners' Union declared that he preferred the "black partition" [*Chernyĭ peredel*] to a "Chernov partition" [*Chernovskiĭ peredel*]. General Kaledin and Maklakov attacked Chernov indirectly, demanding that the government benches leave no room for a Zimmerwaldian. The Left half of the hall replied with a triple ovation for Chernov. General Kaledin protested against the "stealing of governmental power" by arbitrarily created local organs, and demanded "abolition of all Soviets and committees." The entire Left replied by a chorus of "Down with the counterrevolution."

The attacks of the old generals were repulsed by the representative of the front-line organizations, Kuchin. He defended the democratization of the army and showed how helpless the commanders would be in dealing with the army without the committees and commissars. A representative of the front-line Cossacks, Nogayev, denied the right of the ataman's group to speak for the mass of Cossack toilers. He was interrupted by insults, one of which almost ended in a series of duels. In turn the soldiers remained sitting in protest when the hall rose to welcome General Kornilov.

But the interest of the Left did not lie in polemic or tumultuous incidents. Chkheidze read to the conference what the government should have and had not done: an extensive platform of urgent reforms, which rallied the entire front of labor democracy. It was signed by non-Soviet organizations; it was supported by the majority of the representatives of the All-Russian Union of Zemstvos and Cities, the Union of Employees of Government, Civic, and Private Institutions, the Executive Committee of the United Civic Organizations,

GENERAL KORNILOV ARRIVING IN MOSCOW FOR THE STATE CONFERENCE

Courtesy of the Muzei Revolutsii, U.S.S.R.

representatives of the All-Russian Railway Congress, the central and capital committees of the All-Russian Union of Disabled Veterans, representatives of front-line and army organizations, and finally, representatives of the Russian co-operatives. Only the highest ranks of society were left out. Their isolation was depressing.

Tseretelli tried to draw political conclusions. He appealed to the bourgeois section of the conference. Would it respond, was it prepared to march shoulder-to-shoulder with democracy to planned conquest of economic anarchy, to intensive social creation? His speech even evoked applause from the Right; a representative of business, Bublikov, replied that the outstretched hand would not be stretched in vain; but their symbolical handclasp remained merely a personal gesture.

Kerensky's opening and closing addresses dwelt on power, power which binds human beings into state unity, and has its own demands and interests. This abstract form of power majestically ignored the question of social content, which lends significance to the form. Kerensky did not deign to explain the government's attitude toward the program of democracy. In conventional, old-fashioned rhetoric, like that of sermons and Imperial Manifestoes, he demanded submission "to the Will of the Supreme Authority and to myself, its Supreme Head." He waxed indignant at those who "dare pronounce against the Supreme Power and the Russian State words for which they would formerly have had to answer under *lèse-majesté*." He threatened to defend order against its violators from Right and Left by "blood and iron," "to make people remember that there was once an autocracy," and, if necessary, "to kill my soul but save the state." In his concluding address Kerensky tried to exalt this leitmotiv to tragic heights, passing from a pathetic whisper to broken ejaculation. Instead of his policy he discussed his psychology. He wished to govern by persuasive words, by influencing the citizens' conscience. He was driven to measures of severity. If necessary, he would tear from his soul the best, the tenderest flowers of gentleness and trample them underfoot. His heart was turning to stone, he would lock it tight, and forever cast the key into the sea. Outbursts of feminine voices from the loges began to respond to the orator's hysteria. The alarmed members of the government, sitting near Kerensky, expected any moment that his speech would become a nervous attack. Instead of showing strength, he displayed a febrile weakness, compensated by imperious declamation and gesticulation.

According to the government's plan, the conference was not to vote at all, even to express a wish. Scores of orators spoke in succession, without their speeches being summed up. The purpose of the conference remained obscure, its value problematical. Its artificial composition and vague purpose aroused much perplexity. The suspicion arose that it was intended to supplant the indefinitely postponed Constituent Assembly. In the workers' sections of Moscow hostility to the conference was so strong that the Bolsheviks, who had decided to "boycott" it, had no trouble in organizing a general strike of protest.

The position of Soviet democracy, which accepted the conference without enthusiasm, was ungrateful. Reluctantly, bound by its duty to the coalition government, in which the coalition was merely a bare, contentless form, it did what it could at the conference. Kerensky had achieved his purpose. He had scattered his menaces Right and Left, against the military putsch-makers and the Bolsheviks, with but one result: he drove both of them into paroxysms of anger.

CHAPTER EIGHTEEN

THE MUTINY AND ITS AFTERMATH

THE Moscow State Conference left Kornilov in a state of extreme irritation. His personal relations with Kerensky were nearing a complete rupture. Kerensky could not forget how often he had hinted to the commander in chief that his job was to look after the front, not to play politics in Moscow. Only with the greatest displeasure had he allowed him to address the conference, and only on the condition of his speaking about the army and the front as a military expert, and not touching upon general policy. But the boundary was vague in a time of revolution, and Kerensky accused Kornilov of exceeding the agreed limit. Kornilov's ears still rung with Kerensky's veiled threats, so exasperating to the hard-hitting general, unaccustomed to circumlocution. Finally, Savinkov's retirement, decided by Kerensky over Kornilov's objections, was taken by the latter as a final blow to the "Kornilov program."

Only Krymov was pleased. He was long since disgusted with all these negotiations, agreements, conditions, compromises, intermediaries and mediations, with this complicated, chesslike game of politics, in which Kornilov would always be outplayed in the end. Krymov did not believe a single word of Kerensky or Savinkov. His own plan was simple. There was "a strategic reserve of the commander in chief," in which the more reliable units were concentrated. Under some plausible pretext they should be drawn closer to the capital, if possible, to both capitals. Then, by a swift blow everything "Soviet" would be wiped out, the seat of the administration seized, and their will dictated to the country.

The Third Cavalry Corps and the Central Asiatic Cavalry Division were concentrated in the region of Nevel, Lower Sokolniki, and Velikie Luki. They were purged of their doubtful units, and strengthened by more "reliable" ones. The chief of staff, General Lukomsky, at once surmised that this hid some purpose alien to the interests of the front. The region of concentration was excellent if these units were to be thrown against Petrograd or Moscow, but entirely unsuited for strengthening the northern front. Therefore Lukomsky asked to be taken into full confidence or else to be allowed to go to the front. Kornilov laid down his cards. Yes, his purpose was to protect the Provisional Government against Bolshevist and Soviet violence, even against its own will. He would "hang the German placemen and spies with Lenin at their head," and disperse the Soviets. Kornilov wished to intrust this operation to Krymov, for he knew that "he would not hesitate if it were necessary to string up the entire membership of the Soviet of Workers' and Soldiers' Deputies." With the Provisional Government he would probably succeed at the last minute in coming to an agreement, but might have to act without its consent. That was nothing; "afterwards they will be grateful to me."

The purpose of this operation was also clear to the commanders of the several units engaged. According to Prince Ukhtomsky, who wrote a "chronicle of Kornilov's march," although marching orders indicated a tiny place called Usva on the shore of the Baltic as the goal, "the general opinion was that we were going to Petrograd." "We knew that a coup d'état must take place shortly. It was to destroy the power of the Petrograd Soviet and establish either a directory or dictatorship, with Kerensky's consent and participation, which, under the conditions, was a guarantee of the complete success of the overturn." The regiment was "in a splendid state of mind."

After the Moscow Conference the aims of the conspiracy changed. It was now preparing to turn against Kerensky. But two events occurred to turn it back to its old channel.

The Germans crossed the Dvina, pierced the northern front and captured Riga. The front moved closer to Petrograd; headquarters had to include in the frontal belt the entire Petrograd military district, till then directly controlled by the Minister of War. It was impossible to reject this demand. But Kerensky was afraid that the government would be "gobbled up" by Kornilov, as he put it. In this, of course, he was justified. He thought of evacuating the government to Moscow, but realized the bad impression this would create throughout Russia. It would have been interpreted as indecent panic in the face of a still distant enemy. Kerensky came to a different decision. He resolved to take a sharp zigzag to the Right, patch up his peace with Kornilov, make great concessions to him, and guarantee the prompt fulfilment of his program. In return Kerensky wanted Kornilov to banish from headquarters the "Union of Officers" and certain suspicious persons. He decided to hand over the Petrograd military district to Kornilov's control, but to set apart the city of Petrograd with its suburbs, where the Provisional Government was to enjoy military extraterritoriality and govern under martial law. Kerensky insisted on receiving from Kornilov some absolutely reliable military detachment, like the Third Cavalry Corps, but under a commander personally devoted to himself. By capitulating to Kornilov's program Kerensky reckoned on killing two birds with one stone. He hoped to secure himself against another attack from the Left: the most propagandized troops of the Petrograd garrison were to be sent to the front and replaced by fresh, "unspoiled" troops, while the citadel of Bolshevism, Kronstadt, was to be disarmed and evacuated. Savinkov's resignation was now annulled by Kerensky; he was restored to his duties as Minister of War and sent on special mission —to arrange a final agreement with Kornilov at headquarters.

Kerensky expected the next threat to his government from the Right. He was chiefly anxious to establish the military extraterritoriality of Petrograd and secure a reliable military force, and was willing to accept the rest conditionally insofar as it might prove necessary in attaining his central aim. Savinkov, on the other hand, was fascinated by the danger from the Left. For him it was desirable to destroy Kronstadt and the Soviet center of the capital, emancipate the government from the influence of the revolutionary democratic parties, and carry through the Kornilov program in the army. Savinkov told headquarters the government was willing to use measures against Kronstadt and the "revolutionary" Petrograd garrison which would force not only the Bolsheviks but all the Soviet parties into conflict with it. At a secret conference of the principal conspirators—Kornilov, Lukomsky, Krymov, Zavoiko, and Aladin—it was said that "all this looks so fine that it makes me fear we are being double-crossed." The development of the conspirators' plan was henceforth within the bounds of legality. One might say that it was commanded from above. The only point which disrupted their plan was the condition set by Kerensky and Savinkov: the Third Cavalry Corps was not to be under General Krymov. Kornilov had to consent to this condition. But his character contained a streak of Oriental treachery. He had resolved beforehand to break this promise. The advance of the Third Cavalry Corps on Petrograd and the proclamation of martial law in the city were to coincide.

The other event was the "mission" of V. N. Lvov. That well-intentioned busybody decided that he could and must ward off the impending struggle between Kerensky and Kornilov. Kerensky had to be "saved" from the fatal consequences of his own conduct. Kerensky was afraid to break with the Soviets and hence could not rely on those elements which should be his true support. "That," Lvov told Kerensky, "means first, the Cadets; secondly, the merchants and manufacturers; thirdly, the Cossacks; fourthly, the regimental detachments; finally, the Union of Officers and many others." Meanwhile, he asserted, the Soviets were gradually passing into the hands of the Bolsheviks, and were no support for Kerensky; at the same time "indignation at the Soviets is growing . . . is already flowing over and will end in butchery."

According to Lvov, at predictions of the "butchery" menacing the Soviets Kerensky exclaimed, "That's excellent" and jumped up, rubbing his hands. Kerensky also had no objection to enlarging the government to the Right or replacing "Soviet socialists" by what he called "strong-government socialists." Lvov was now convinced that Kerensky had empowered him to negotiate with those Right elements which were to be brought into the government. Later Kerensky stated plainly that "he had not given Lvov any instructions or powers." Lvov hastened to headquarters. He assured Kornilov that Kerensky was not anxious to cling to power, that he had no objection to reorganizing the government through including "all civic elements." In a whirlwind of ideas and plans, Lvov simultaneously recommended enlarging the government and narrowing it, a broader coalition, a limited "directory," a military dictatorship—headed, of course, by Kornilov—and again merely combining the power of commander in chief with that of head of the government. Kornilov said he no longer trusted Kerensky or Savinkov, but was willing to leave them the portfolios of Justice and War. Finally, Lvov and Kornilov agreed on a complete plan: Martial law was to be proclaimed in Petrograd, as arranged with Savinkov; in addition, the government was to resign of its own volition; the administration of current affairs in Petrograd would be left with the collegium of vice ministers, while Kerensky and Savinkov would come to headquarters. There Kornilov would receive from them full civil and military authority and organize a new government including them. After his agreement with Savinkov, Kornilov regarded this as a fresh step by Kerensky toward Kornilov's own program, and did not doubt but that he was treating with a genuine representative of Kerensky. For Kerensky, however, Lvov was merely an unintentional scout to ferret out his opponent's secrets.

Lvov returns to Kerensky. This time he admits that the "real force" from which he brings concrete proposals is the commander in chief. Kerensky is on his guard. Lvov tells all he knows: Kornilov invited Kerensky to headquarters and guaranteed his safety only there, while Kornilov's followers, as Zavoiko had admitted, wished to sacrifice Kerensky to the "popular wrath" of the officers. Kerensky feels that his head is at stake. He is frightened, and at the same time deeply offended that they wanted to leave him the insignificant rôle of Minister of Justice under Kornilov. Kerensky turns Nat Pinkerton and sets a trap for his admirer: he pretends to consent and makes Lvov repeat everything in the presence of a hidden witness. At the height of Lvov's enthusiastic speeches, having secured a "document," a written exposition of Kornilov's proposals, Kerensky gives the signal, and Lvov is arrested. First, Kerensky tries to secure from Kornilov direct evidence of guilt. He calls him on the telephone and pretends to be Lvov. Without repeating Lvov's statements exactly he demands from Kornilov confirmation of all these proposals. Again he plays the comedian, pretending to be willing to go with Kornilov to the last ditch. The spiderlike premier weaves his web, and the big wasp, the commander in chief, flies straight into it.

But the wasp almost broke the spider's web.

During the following days there was great contrast between feeling in Petrograd and at headquarters. Kornilov realized that the first step was the hardest. By going to headquarters Savinkov and Kerensky would burn their bridges. Various difficulties, compromises, and friction within the projected "directory" were possible. But from a directory to a dictatorship the transition was far easier than from a coalition, half-Soviet government to a directory controlled by army headquarters. And after the final decision for a directory, Kornilov told Dobrynsky confidentially: "Still, I have determined to become military dictator, but no one must know of that for the time being."

Things were different in Petrograd. In the Provisional Government Kerensky's report of Kornilov's ultimatum and of the movement of Krymov's Third Cavalry Corps toward Petrograd fell like a bomb. It blew the Provisional Government to bits. Kokoshkin and his friends abandoned it because they could not act against Kornilov. Chernov withdrew because it was difficult for him to act with Kerensky against Kornilov now that events had lifted a corner of the curtain which had till then concealed from the Left wing of the government the long story of suspicious conspiracies, arrangements, and agreements between Kerensky, Kornilov, and Savinkov.

In the greatest haste, without proper collegial decision, without proper form, a telegram was sent discharging Kornilov as commander in chief. It was not sent in the name of the Provisional Government or of the premier. It was sent without countersignature, without number, without the usual address, "Comchief, Headquarters." It resembled a private telegram, signed "Kerensky," and addressed to "General Kornilov, Mohilev."

Kornilov refused to give up his powers, and the chief of staff, General Lukomsky, to whom they passed by military code, declined them. Kerensky ordered the commander of the northern front, General Klembovsky, to stop General Krymov's troop trains. The reply was that his competence did not cover them, since they belonged to the strategic reserve of the commander in chief. Kerensky appointed him commander in chief; Klembovsky refused. All the other commanders telegraphed that Kornilov's retirement would be fatal for the army and Russia; he must remain regardless of political complications.

General Krymov's troop trains were approaching the capital. Detachments of the Petrograd garrison were dispatched in haste. They were puzzled by what was occurring, and regarded the struggle between Kerensky and Kornilov as a family quarrel, indifferent to them and not worth a drop of soldier's blood.

Filonenko, Savinkov's understudy, who passed through this improvised "anti-Kornilov front," on the way from headquarters to Petrograd, later said sarcastically: "The conduct of the Petrograd troops was beneath all criticism." General Verkhovsky's opinion, in retrospect, was no more favorable. "In Petrograd, during the Kornilov days a single cavalry division or a single heavy artillery unit could have dispersed the entire garrison."

After breaking with Kerensky's government, Chernov took a general staff officer, Boyer, and a former volunteer of the French army, Kallistov, and visited the front line. On his return, he reported to the Central Executive Committee. To oppose the troops advancing from the front, infantry detachments were drawn up, with no cavalry reconnaissance in front and no contact between them. The soldiers complained of lack of machine guns and of a ridiculously meager ammunition supply. The troops were drawn up on an irregular terrain, where infantry could easily hold its own against cavalry with the aid of the most elementary field fortifications; for some unknown reason they had neither shovels nor barbed wire nor field engineers. According to their instructions, on the enemy's approach they were to abandon a terrain difficult for cavalry and withdraw to a low plain just before Petrograd, a perfect target for Kornilov's artillery, which could then conveniently cover them with its fire from a hilly and wooded elevation. That would leave to Kornilov's cavalry the very easy task of driving the disordered government troops before it and breaking into the city at their heels. All this was less a plan for defending Petrograd than for the easiest possible surrender to the mutinous general. A special delegation was dispatched by the Soviet to the Ministry of War, where Savinkov with icy politeness answered

Voitinsky, Chernov, and others: "Kindly do not worry, matters will not reach an armed collision, everything will be settled peaceably."

The rump government was in a frightful state. Savinkov relates:

Tereshchenko resigned. Nekrasov proposed transferring all power to the Soviet of Workers' and Soldiers' Deputies. Several ministers avoided spending the night at home. The same panic prevailed at the Soviet [?]. That is my only explanation for Chernov's going to the Tsarskoye Selo front to "inspect" the defense, for Voitinsky demanding that I disarm the military schools, and for Tseretelli and Gots insisting that delegates from the All-Russian Central Executive Committee be present at the district military staff, probably to watch over my instructions.

All this indicates, however, not panic but energetic precautions by the Soviet, mistrustful of the military authorities. Not only Kornilov but the Soviet leaders were wondering whom Savinkov was preparing to knife: Kerensky or Kornilov. Savinkov reports that even his colleague at the Ministry of Marine, Lebedev, denounced to Kerensky a "conversation of criminal character" held during these days by direct wire between Savinkov in Petrograd and Filonenko at headquarters. Nevertheless, Savinkov remained military governor of the capital till August 31; that is, during the most critical days of Krymov's advance. True, in trying to exonerate himself, he was the first to announce publicly that Kornilov "would be handled as a traitor."

On the other hand, the Duma leaders of the "Regressive Bloc" plucked up courage. General Alexeyev was passing through Petrograd. Kerensky offered him the post of commander in chief. Alexeyev refused and in turn proffered his services to effect a reconciliation with Kornilov. The same demand for a reconciliation between Kerensky and Kornilov was made by the chief Cadet leaders. The same advice was given by Ambassador Buchanan. That was what Savinkov and Filonenko were striving for.

Both sides had gone too far to be reconciled. Like Savinkov, Kerensky had publicly proclaimed Kornilov "a traitor to his country." Kornilov did not lag behind; he broadcasted throughout Russia that "the Provisional Government was acting in full accord with the plans of the German general staff"; he "could not betray Russia to the Germans"; therefore he "was opposing the Provisional Government and its irresponsible advisers who are selling their fatherland"; he "preferred to die on the field of honor and battle than to see the disgrace of his native land."

Savinkov and the Right-wing Cadet, Maklakov, attempted to influence Kornilov by direct telephone conversation. The rough and ready general suspected a trap. "I see here the pressure of the Soviet, in which there are people tainted with treason. In this ominous hour of the Fatherland I shall not desert my post."

Kerensky too was inspired with a peculiar courage of despair. He rejected Miliukov's and Alexeyev's offers to go to headquarters as mediators. He also turned down the similar offer of a delegation of the Council of the Union of Cossack Troops, suspecting it of desiring the Cossacks to join the mutinous general.

On August 28 the director of the diplomatic chancery at headquarters, Prince Trubetskoy, communicated to Tereshchenko his observations, typical of the spirit prevailing in bourgeois circles.

A sober appraisal of the situation must recognize that the entire body of commanding officers, the great majority of all other officers, and the best field detachments of the army will follow Kornilov. In the rear he will be supported by all Cossack bodies, most of the military schools, and also the best field detachments. To this physical force must be added the superiority of military organization over the weak civil organs, the sympathy of all nonsocialist strata of the population, a growing dissatisfaction with existing conditions among the lower classes, and in the bulk of the people, dulled to everything, an indifference which submits to the whip. . . . The men now in power must decide whether they will go halfway to coöperate in the inevitable change, thus making it painless, or whether by their resistance they will accept responsibility for new and innumerable calamities.

The Cadet party, led by Miliukov, drew up a plan to secure the voluntary retirement of Kerensky and his companions from the government in favor of General Alexeyev. The latter was to form a new government, to settle the Kornilov "incident" peaceably. To avert civil war, internal conflict in the army, the breakdown of the front, and Russia's ruin, they implored Kerensky and his few remaining followers to make way for the only man still able to save the situation. Finally, his last followers, Tereshchenko and Nekrasov, urged Kerensky to retire and transfer power to General Alexeyev. Around Kerensky there grew a terrifying vacuum. In solitude he wandered through the Winter Palace, recently so noisy, now desolate, and reflected on how short was the path from the Capitol to the Tarpeian cliff.

At a most critical moment in the endless, nerve-wracking negotiations with ministers and candidates to the ministry, when Kerensky held in his briefcase the resignations of all the ministers, and he alone held "the plenitude of power," not knowing what to do with it, and not in the least resembling a lucky dictator, he was visited by an official delegation from the Soviet. It offered its assistance, and set but one condition: relentless suppression of the mutiny. The Soviet did not waste time in words, but acted, acted as it had in the best days of the revolution.

The military detachments drawn up by Savinkov and his assistant, Poradelov, could have been crushed by Krymov's "Wild Division" alone. They were near to simply disbanding, for they identified Kerensky with Kornilov and saw no use in suffering in their quarrel. This would not be the final word in Kornilov's difference with the revolution. All the Petrograd suburbs bristled with barricades ready to encounter the foe. Kronstadt sent so many men that Savinkov tried to send back 2,000, saying they "were not needed." The workers took up arms, organized units of the Red Guard, and prepared to transform each factory and house into a fortress. More than 25,000 men joined the Workers' Militia in the very first days. Scores of agitators were dispatched to Krymov's troops.

The Soviet had no time to legalize its actions. It functioned as a genuine revolutionary authority. Without waiting for the numerous secret Kornilovist societies to choose their moment to act, it began to make arrests. The conspirators' staff at the Hotel Astoria was wiped out. The president of the "Military League," Fedorov, was arrested. Total arrests exceeded 7,000. At many homes searches were made and documents seized with lists of conspirators. Panic gripped the inexperienced plotters. Their organization was crippled by lack of funds, which had been squandered. Colonel Sidorin, sent especially by Kornilov to direct the conspiracy, "from fear of persecution fled to Finland, taking the last remnants of the organization's money, about 150,00 rubles."*

The Railway Bureau organized by the Soviet was feverishly at work, crippling the movement of Krymov's troop trains, just as in March it had disorganized those of General Ivanov. Some detachments were sent in the wrong direction and realized it too late. The station tracks were blocked with coaches. The engines were out of repair. In three places the track was torn up, and loaded freight cars overturned. The railway repair battalion was nowhere to be found. The command to advance on foot was blocked by failure to organize a food supply. The soldiers were literally showered with proclamations from the Provisional Government and Soviets. Kornilov's counterdeclarations did not reach them. Local So-

* Denikin.

viets and garrisons, as in Luga, threatened artillery fire. The telegraph and telephone had to be captured by main force. Individual detachments lost touch with each other and headquarters. The Kornilov soldiers began to refuse to traverse points where they were in danger of clashing with local garrisons. They began electing committees which demanded explanations of the officers and deprived them of freedom of action.

Chernov, then at Gatchina, and a local Soviet military organizer, Vincent Sokolov, were visited at night by a delegation from several front-line detachments, including the Third Don Cossack Artillery unit. On learning that there had been no Bolshevist uprising in Petrograd and that they were not being led to defend the Provisional Government, the artillerymen said they wished to prepare all their comrades to receive a Soviet delegation, and promised that, if any units made an attempt to arrest it, they would fire upon them. The next day, in front of the position of the Petrograd garrison, a cavalry reconnaissance of the "Wild Division" encountered Chernov, examining the positions with a group of officers. Instead of taking them prisoners, they listened to Chernov's account of the general situation and turned back.

The "Wild Division" was to be met by a big Moslem delegation, organized by the Soviet. A great quantity of proclamations from the Moslem organizations and the Soviet was printed in the principal languages of the Caucasus. The automobile of the Minister of Agriculture at once dashed off with them to Tsarskaya Slavianka, where contact between Kornilov reconnaissances and Petrograd garrison units began. There Chernov's place in the car was taken by two representatives of the Cossack military section of the Soviet. They set out boldly for the front-line Kornilov units, where the proclamations were eagerly seized by the horsemen. The officers raged helplessly but did not dare resist.

Petrograd knew nothing of all this. It lived in dread or in hope of military attack. General Alexeyev "thought the government's hours were numbered. It had to be decided what Kornilov should do after his victory."[1]

Those who thought the revolution defeated in advance were sadly mistaken. The Soviets and committees were active. On August 29, on the southeastern front, Denikin and his chief of staff were arrested by the army committee. On the northern front Klembovsky transferred his post to the revolutionary general, Bonch-Bruyevich. Under a false name and with a letter from Kornilov Zavoiko left headquarters "to raise the Don." On the way he was arrested by the Homel Soviet. He boldly dispatched a telegram to Savinkov, such as might be addressed only to a fellow conspirator. "For the general interest and well-being I consider continuation of my journey necessary. I await granting of the opportunity to do so." The commander of a cavalry corps, Prince Dolgoruky, who had left headquarters for Finland as part of a general plan, was arrested en route. In Mohilev things were going wrong. The soldier printers, engaged in running off Kornilov's proclamations under the surveillance of Central Asiatic troops, used the ignorance of their guards to run off Kerensky's proclamation, declaring Kornilov a traitor. A battalion of St. George Cavaliers declared in favor of the Soviet and constantly clashed with the Central Asiatics. In Kornilov's own regiment seven officers had to be arrested for insubordination. On August 28, during a review of the garrison, Kornilov was greeted with tumultuous "Hurrahs" by some units and with stony silence by others. By a threat to strike the railway shopmen and workers secured the liberation of persons arrested for posting Kerensky's telegram at the station. Headquarters ceased receiving weapons, food, or fodder. Revolutionary control of posts and telegraph practically isolated it from the rest of Russia.

The commander of the Caucasus front, General Przhevalsky, had already telegraphed condemning whoever had begun the civil war. The commander of the Rumanian front, General Shcherbachev, Generals Parsky, Danilov, and others, declared for the government.

There could be no further doubt. Kornilov's star was setting. Once again the Soviets had saved Kerensky, who, to Lvov's prediction of the approaching massacre of the Soviets, had replied: "Well, that is excellent—we shall only have to say that we were powerless to forestall it."

If the Soviets reckoned on Kerensky's now siding with them and breaking off his connection with that group which had been ready to hand him over to Kornilov or exchange him for General Alexeyev, they were deeply mistaken. The Soviets, in his eyes, were now too strong. In joining them, he risked becoming their prisoner. The "regressive bloc," on the other hand, was absolutely disorganized by its compromising rôle in the mutiny and its dread of the consequences. All the more reason for offering himself as all-forgiving protector. Had the Soviets been shattered, Kerensky would probably have been willing to make a similar gesture to them. Kornilov's followers would naturally have forbidden it. Would Soviet democracy allow this gesture?

The first test came soon. The ferment among Krymov's troops reached its height. A conference of the soldiers accused their officers of deceiving them, and demanded an investigation of those responsible for this adventure. The latter referred to the Savinkov and Lvov missions, and asserted that they had led the troops against Petrograd with Kerensky's approval. The soldiers decided to investigate for themselves. Their numerous delegation was solemnly received in the Soviet. It was addressed by Chkheidze, Tseretelli, and Chernov. Kerensky also received it. But he quickly interrupted the first man who declared that the soldiers expected the removal and punishment of their traitorous commanders.

On August 29 General Alexeyev told Shapron, captain of cavalry: "Tereshchenko was just here. I am urged to accept the post of chief of staff with Kerensky as commander in chief. If I refuse, Cheremisov will be appointed. You understand what that means. The next day they would execute Kornilov's followers. The rôle that lies before me is profoundly revolting, but what can I do?"

On August 30 Kornilov, still unaware of what was happening to his troops, but sensing that something was wrong, prepared in any event a path of retreat. General Lukomsky acted as go-between. Both sides would stop issuing proclamations against each other; Denikin and others must be set free; General Alexeyev must come to headquarters as mediator. To prove that he sought nothing for himself, Kornilov was willing to transfer the supreme command to Alexeyev, provided "a strong government, independent of irresponsible organizations," was formed. Kornilov still thought he could set conditions.

Alexeyev seized eagerly the chance of a compromise. He was willing to speed his arrival at headquarters, to take over the supreme command painlessly. He "strongly urges Kornilov to keep the administration in his hands" until his own arrival, and by radio sent an instruction from the government "to all, all, all," "to execute the operative directions issued by General Kornilov."

Recovering courage, Kornilov immediately tried to benefit by this halfway legalization of his betrayal of the Provisional Government. He sent Krymov a letter informing him ironically of what had happened, and asking what were "the further chances of exerting strong pressure by the means at his disposal." Finally, he requested Krymov to inform headquarters fully, so that suitable instructions might be given him. "If circumstances permit, act independently in the spirit of the instructions which I gave you."

In other words, the march on Petrograd, the march against the Provisional Government, was to go on. Kornilov did not suspect that there was *no one* to carry on, no one to carry on *with*. The day of August 31 destroyed his last illusions.

That day General Alexeyev again talked with Lukomsky by wire. Krymov had been in Petrograd, on his way to be received by Kerensky. That was one hope less at headquarters. Lukomsky asked if forces were being sent to capture headquarters. Yes, but not through Alexeyev, who must therefore learn in what rôle Kornilov would receive him at headquarters, as mediator or successor. Was Kornilov reconciled to the arrival at headquarters of an extraordinary investigating commission, headed by Shablovsky? Lukomsky replied that Kornilov had no intention of turning headquarters into a fort. He would accept Alexeyev as authorized leader of the army, but he must stop military action against headquarters. The question of the commission was left unanswered: that was too painful.

Military forces were already moving against headquarters. With the consent of Zhdanov, commissar of the western front, Colonel Korotkov, a Social Revolutionary and member of the provisional revolutionary committee of the western front, on August 29 and 30 had organized at Orsha a unit of 3,000 bayonets and 800 swords, with 3 field batteries and 300 machine guns. At Vitebsk a detachment of 1,500 men and 16 guns was being assembled. To them Kornilov could oppose the 2,500 men of the Kornilov Regiment, several hundred of whom, however, had already refused to support headquarters, 5 battalions of Polish troops, and 500 cavalry (chiefly Central Asiatics), the Russian part of which had already declared its loyalty to the Provisional Government. Even these feeble forces were menaced from the rear by the hostile St. George Battalion, not to mention the workers who to a man backed the Social Revolutionary and Menshevist Soviet. The struggle was unequal. In Moscow General Verkhovsky had already loaded fifteen troop trains for Mohilev. "Today," he informed Alexeyev on September 1, "I am leaving for headquarters with a strong armed outfit, to end this mockery of common sense. Kornilov, Lukomsky, Pliushchik-Pliushchevsky and Sakharov must be arrested at once and dismissed. I have summoned you to the telephone, in hope of hearing that these arrests have already been made." Alexeyev interrupted him: "There is no need of your troops. Your movement can be undertaken only at the instruction of the commander in chief." And he threatened to resign unless Kerensky restrained Verkhovsky.

The same happened to Korotkov. "I have seen General Alexeyev, he was dissatisfied, it seems, with my military preparations. He considered every active military step inadmissible, and declared that had he known that force might be applied, he would not have gone to headquarters. From my conversation with him I seemed to be the mutineer. The conversation was most depressing."

Korotkov's unit was stopped, Verkhovsky also had to "demobilize." Unloading the troop trains was more difficult than loading them. Verkhovsky's soldiers like Korotkov's were eager to attack mutinous headquarters. The front buzzed ominously. The commissar of the Second Army reported: "The spirit in the troops has been strongly affected by Kerensky's telegram about the necessity of fulfilling Kornilov's commands until he has taken over those duties. The masses considered this order a forgery."

The command was not a forgery: the only forgery was the reputation which the soldiers had created for Kerensky. That reputation was fading like a mirage.

Alexeyev arrived at headquarters and paid the customary calls on Kornilov and Lukomsky. With the former he had argued in Moscow as to which should head the movement. Now one had to remove the other. After listening to his program of "Kornilovism minus Kornilov," Lukomsky told Alexeyev that all these promises had been made because he alone could liquidate headquarters without bloodshed; afterwards he would be discarded. From Petrograd the Ministry of War was urging him on: "The government is accused of inaction. The Soviets are raging; the atmosphere can be cleared only by showing authority and arresting Kornilov and others." With a heavy heart, poor Alexeyev pretended to show authority: on the evening of September 1 Kornilov, Lukomsky, Romanovsky and Pliushchik-Pliushchevsky were placed under home arrest. Denikin admits that this "was a necessary precaution against the government troops and revolutionary democracy," which were hostile to the mutineers.

Alexeyev addressed the Mohilev garrison. He publicly declared Kornilov innocent of the crimes alleged, and accused the troops loyal to the government of accepting "Jewish money." "He seems to consider us mutineers instead of Kornilov"; "This man will be no better than Kornilov, an apple off the same tree," said the soldiers, clenching their fists.

Alexeyev did not stay long in his post. He complained—with what ground we do not know—that Kerensky opened his correspondence, that Kerensky had pledged his word that Kornilov would be pardoned, but had not raised this question in the government, and so on. Kornilov told him that continuance in his post he would consider moral support of Kerensky's position. Alexeyev retired.

On September 2 the extraordinary investigating commission arrived in Mohilev. Outwardly, it carried on its work in due order. Prodin, Rozhenko, Aladin, Sakharov, vice minister of Communications, Kislyakov, and the entire chief committee of the Officers' Union were arrested. They were first transferred to the Hotel Metropole, and then to a regular prison at Bykhovo station. "After the first examinations by the investigating commission, it became clear that all its members were very favorable toward us, . . . that the investigating commission was trying to spin out its work as far as possible." Kornilov was not examined at all, but was allowed to write out his depositions, which were immediately printed in Burtsev's paper. That paper began to agitate in favor of Kerensky's going to Kornilov and apologizing; it soon collected thousands of signatures in support of this. The inner guard of the prison was intrusted to the Central Asiatic troops, which affectionately called Kornilov "our boyar." "Everyone knew that if General Kornilov wished, he could not only leave whenever he pleased, but *even arrest Kerensky if the latter came to headquarters.*"[2]

In Bykhovo prison,

regular connections with Petrograd, Moscow, and Mohilev were quickly set up; we were informed of everything that happened and corresponded with the people we needed. The staff of the commander in chief likewise kept us informed on all questions which interested us.[3]

General Lukomsky wrote: "Under Kerensky we could have escaped from Bykhovo with complete ease, if we had so wished." Why should they try to escape? Lvov, arrested by Kerensky himself, Colonel Lebedev and many others had been freed by Shablovsky earlier; on October 18 the Cossack captain Rodionov was freed, on the twentieth Zavoiko, on the twenty-second Novosiltsev, on the twenty-fourth five more of the chief committee of the Officers' Union, and only the five chief accused—Kornilov, Lukomsky, Romanovsky, Markov, and Denikin—set themselves free without formality and left with their Central Asiatic guard to escape the Bolshevist unit which moved against Bykhovo after the October Revolution.

It is hard to say what aroused the front more: the Kornilov and Krymov adventure itself, exposure of the close intertwining of Kornilov's "conspiracy" with the "understanding" with Kerensky, or the comedy of the mutineers' arrest and imprisonment.

These were the men who had boasted at the Moscow Conference that for violations of military discipline they gave without hesitation orders *to annihilate entire regiments.* They had preached ruthlessness, reintroduced capital punishment at the front and urged it in the rear. The soldiers demanded that the measures which they had advocated be applied to them. When it was realized that discipline and capital punishment were for soldiers, not for generals, the front swelled with anger and turned black like the sea before a tempest. The Bolsheviks had only to catch the favoring wind and fill their sails.

Thus ended the "Kornilov mutiny." It dealt a fresh, and, it seemed, final blow to confidence between officers and privates. "As a result of the mutiny, distrust of the officers has grown, doubt is cast on all prior orders by Kornilov." In the Forty-fourth Siberian Regiment Captain Zuyev, at a regimental banquet, offered a toast to Kornilov; the soldiers arrested twelve officers. In the neighboring Sixtieth and Sixty-first Siberian Regiments seventeen officers were wounded by a bomb thrown at an assembly of officers, and the commander was removed by the soldiers "for Kornilovism." "Discussion of military orders has become chronic and general," "the army's general state has grown worse, and may be described as approaching complete breakdown." Headquarters' reports abound in cases such as the arrest of fifty officers by the One Hundred and Twenty-sixth Division of the Special Army. The commander of the Twelfth Army describes the situation: "A huge, tired, badly clothed, underfed, angry mass of people, united by yearning for peace and by general disillusionment." Headquarters' military-political sector added that "the same description might without exaggeration be applied to the entire front."[4]

The Kornilov rising was liquidated. What next?

Kerensky again startled the country by a strange appointment. Although a civilian by training and character, he made himself commander in chief. This was in poor taste. He unintentionally reminded people of the old régime; the Tsars, whether or not possessed of military knowledge and capacity, were *nominally* heads of the army. Kerensky's removal to the Winter Palace was another act of bad taste. As his tremendous, unexampled popularity melted away, he lost his self-control, and sought more external attributes to emphasize his extraordinary position. This provoked shrugging of shoulders, sarcasm, or disillusion.

Being at once commander in chief and head of the government, Kerensky had to transfer the Ministry of War to someone else. Everything pointed to General Verkhovsky, who had distinguished himself by energetic measures against conspirators of the Right and anarchy from the Left. Verkhovsky had acquired great popularity among the democratic parties of the Soviets, while at times he established tolerable relations with the moderate wing of the Bolsheviks. His appointment as Minister of War meant a complete rupture with the Kornilov period, with the struggle of the old commanders against the Soviets and government for control of the army. It meant a fresh current in military policy, imparting real homogeneity to the army by bringing it into line with the revolutionary and democratic movement. The sensational appointment as Minister of Marine, in place of the obedient dilettante Lebedev, of Admiral Verderevsky, not long before arrested at Kerensky's command for "abetting" the sailors in their conflict with the government, also smoothed out somewhat the attitude of Soviet democracy to the fragments of Kerensky's cabinet.

Judging by General Verkhovsky's "diary," published as *Russia at Calvary*, of all the generals he best understood mass psychology. He first decided to risk a large-scale purge of the commanders. "I consider," he wrote on September 30, "that the only cause which would induce our masses not to hinder organization of the defense would be Germany's refusal of a just and democratic peace offered by us and our Allies." "Only then will our people believe in the need for the Russian people to continue the war and transform it into a revolutionary war." On October 14 he noted: "Whoever right now shall take into his own hands the question of hastening peace will get control of the government." This feeling made him insist strongly on this question in the Provisional Government. They must "compel the Allies to agree to peace negotiations, otherwise this will cause them inestimable harm." But this by no means signified, as afterwards alleged, that he was leading the government toward a *separate peace*. On the contrary, on September 27 he wrote, "We must do everything, but not surrender; behind us we have huge areas. In case of need we can retreat beyond the Volga, but not withdraw from the war or accept a separate peace." In the Provisional Government he declared that the government must at once reduce the excessively swollen army; it could not be fed, and might from one day to the next disperse because of hunger; the government must give up its offensive tactics; "we must even be prepared for the enemy's pushing us eastward and occupying many important points."

People who made a patriotic virtue of their own wilful blindness raged at the revolutionary general. But even General Alexeyev refused to represent Russia at the inter-Allied Conference at Paris, for he felt "the game was hopelessly and irretrievably lost, and the Allies must not be misled any longer."

Characteristically, after Kornilov's failure Right-wing society at once lost its taste for the war and began to talk peace.

Nabokov writes,

> I recall that in one of my many automobile trips with Miliukov, I expressed my opinion—he was still Minister of Foreign Affairs—that one of the fundamental causes of the revolution was war fag. Miliukov disagreed decidedly. "Who knows, perhaps it is *thanks to the war that everything still hangs together somehow, and without the war it would have broken down more quickly*." Of course, mere realization that the war was breaking up Russia would not have made things any easier. But if it had been clearly realized that the war was over for Russia, and all attempts to prolong it would lead nowhere, there would have been another orientation in this fundamental question. Who knows, we might have succeeded in averting the catastrophe.

Here in brief is the key to the feeling of the entire Russian liberal bourgeoisie. Dread of the social consequences of the revolution made it cling to the war as an anchor of salvation. The war required national unity, hence, postponement of all decisive economic reforms. Then, hurrah for the war! At that time the liberal bourgeoisie claimed a monopoly of patriotism. But patriotic phrases were insufficient to shout down "the Red menace." On the contrary, the war, which cost 88,000,000 rubles a day, besides the 8,000,000 rubles of general expenses, which kept over 10,000,000 soldiers under arms while the Ministry of Supply had declared it could feed a maximum of 7,000,000, the war under such conditions strained all social bonds. They threatened to explode in a universal catastrophe. The more this realization penetrated Right-wing society, the stronger was its doubt as to the correctness of its original tactics. But a sharp change of front was difficult. So through inertia the liberal and nationalist press still boasted, and cast suspicion on all who considered it advantageous to make an international demonstration by proposing a democratic peace. But in private the ground was being prepared for yesterday's bourgeois adherents of the Entente to shift *to a Germanophil orientation.*

The Left-Center parties of Soviet democracy (in the party of Social Revolutionaries those grouped around Chernov) supported General Verkhovsky in his idea that the war was not yet lost, that sometimes a "Kutuzov" policy of retreat was more rational than a "Napoleonic" one. Russia could no longer support an army of over ten millions, and at her Allies' demand overcome German technique by mountains of human flesh. But Russia could wear down her opponent's strength by her great area. The farther the enemy advanced into the country, the greater the army he must maintain there. In a revolutionary country the occupying army is subject to an inevitable law of decay. On the other hand, the psychology of the Russian soldier when fighting on his border, in Latvian, Lithuanian, Polish, Galician territory, and his psychology when faced by the enemy in his own, genuinely Russian provinces would be very different. The occupying forces could not avoid suppressing the conquests of the revolution; the national revolution and its foreign oppressor would, for the first time, meet face to face, not in idea, but in fact. Only such conditions could set off an explosion of a spontaneous popular enthusiasm and wrath, as in France when the armies of the Duke of Brunswick invaded her soil to save the king and nobles from revolution and to "establish order."

"In any case the war will be decided not in the east but in the west," these circles felt.

> The farther the armies of the Hohenzollerns wander into Russia's depths, the more disorderly and tumultuous will be their retreat when the western front is disrupted. They will not only rush backwards; they will arrest their commanders; instead of the banner of the Empire, they will hoist the red flag of revolution, they will fraternize with the popular revolutionary Russian armies following at their heels. Those armies may have to go to Berlin, not as conquerors, but as allies of the German revolution, as assistants in securing for the new Germany an honorable peace, to which the old Germany was not entitled. That would mean a new era for Europe and for the entire world.

Of course, such historical prospects could only frighten the Russian bourgeoisie. The very idea of "admitting" German armies to the heart of Russia seemed sacrilegious to the bards of liberal nationalism. The vague prospect of a *national and revolutionary war*, which would force the upper and privileged classes under the wing of occupying armies, but in return would appeal within the enemy's camp to social and political radicalism, did not appeal to those who had represented "His Majesty's Opposition" in the Duma.

General Verkhovsky saw two possibilities: either immediate, decisive social reforms, which the moderate socialists were now vainly trying to drag through the "needle's eye" of the coalition; that meant Left-wing government, radical, popular with the masses, through energetic activity cutting the ground from under Bolshevism; or else, an attempt to come to an agreement with the Bolsheviks, to compromise with them, to make generous concessions, if at this price they would abstain from further disintegration of the army. If neither means succeeded, everything was lost, and the future could only bring complete breakdown, Bolshevism, civil war.

On September 8 General Verkhovsky explained his program to the Central Executive Committee of the Soviets. He referred to his activity in the Moscow military district as a partial test of its execution in miniature. "In that work," he declared, "I did not come into conflict with the Bolsheviks, who in Moscow gave me every necessary support even in suppressing insurrection." This calculated statement was followed by negotiation with the Bolsheviks. But under Lenin's inspiration, the Bolsheviks of Petrograd were not so pliable as those of Moscow, who were at the Right wing of their party. Verkhovsky failed to achieve an agreement with the Bolsheviks. Their program demanded establishment of the elective principle in the army from bottom to top. Their minimum demands were: (1) the privates' right to certify all their commanders, (2) their right to challenge the appointment of unsatisfactory commanders, and (3) the right of elected delegates from the privates to take part in the conduct of military operations. Verkhovsky tried in vain to convince them that if they secured power on the morrow, they would immediately have to reject all these measures as destructive of the army's unity and driving power. History soon confirmed his predictions. But the Bolsheviks could not be persuaded. Perhaps they were sincere.

One possibility, agreement with the Bolsheviks, had vanished.

One more remained: a government which was popular with the masses, was not afraid to revolutionize agrarian and industrial conditions from above, to forestall anarchic revolution from below, and which dared break with the upper classes in order to subordinate them to the "dictatorship of democracy." Verkhovsky promised to fulfil this program rapidly, if the Provisional Government would give him the necessary power.

In essence, this was not a new program; it was merely a peculiar, semidictatorial means of executing the very program which, under genuinely democratic forms, could and should have been carried out by a Tseretelli-Chernov government. It had been suggested for a moment by the course of events, but had been discarded because of indecision within the moderate parties of the Soviet.

Verkhovsky met a categorical *non possumus* from the majority in the government. Kerensky and his group, he notes with melancholy in his diary, "are not at present up to the demands of the situation." "The masses are turning to the Left, while the intelligentsia are turning Right. . . . Kerensky stands still, and beneath him an abyss is forming."

To Kerensky Russia seemed to be "repeating the story of the French Revolution." Unfortunately, he had but a superficial concept of that revolution.

Kropotkin early remarked that the true history of the fourteen months from June, 1793, to the end of July, 1794, had not yet been written; people had studied the external side of events, the reign of terror, while their profound essence lay "not in the terror, but in the extensive parceling out of landed property, the agrarian revolution." That measure, with the *uncompensated* abolition of all feudal dues, "was a complete revolution." It created the new revolutionary patriotism which flamed up in the people.[5]

In Russia the same might have been achieved by the agrarian bills proposed by Chernov and the Chief Land Committee. They were, however, resisted most of all. They were the very measures the bourgeoisie dreaded. The inert mass of the middle classes had quickly tired of revolution.

The same was true of the nationalities question. Although the fighting quality of military units was undoubtedly raised through grouping them by nationality, Kerensky accepted this principle only with great reluctance. Why? Because the military authorities feared national separatism as a new source of disintegration in the army. Indeed, "Ukrainization," "Esthonization," etc., of military units is a stick with two ends: it may strengthen or undermine the army, depending on the state of the nationalities question in the rear. Tsarist Russia had been "the prison house of peoples"; its walls had collapsed. There were now two possibilities. Either democratic Russia would preserve the imperial policy of centralization and forcible assimilation. Then the struggle against the nationalities would never end, and it would be suicidal to allow the "nationalization" of any military units. Or else the revolution would once and for all abolish the division of nationalities into ruling and subject, and without hesitation or omission proclaim new Russia the *voluntary union* of all the nationalities under its roof. Then, and only then, would it be possible to embark boldly on a thorough "nationalization" of military organization. The army's structure must correspond to that of the country. Every disharmony would be pregnant with conflict and decay.

The problem of creating a revolutionary army for the revolutionary country was thus closely bound up with a proper orientation in foreign and domestic policy. On this truth General Verkhovsky had stumbled by experience. Revolutionary policy was in a bad way, and without it purely military measures could not give the necessary results: it was not enough to appoint new commanders, or reduce the army's swollen bulk. In the Provisional Government, which no longer included Tseretelli or Chernov, or even Skobelev and Avksentiev, there was no sign of creative volition in the social or nationalities questions. Its "socialist" section now consisted either of "ex-Socialists" or colorless personalities, obedient "satellites" for the central "star," Kerensky. Kerensky's idea was simple: to continue the policy of the original censitary government, perhaps curtailing it still further, but having the work done by "Leftists," and accompanied by suitable democratic phraseology to make it palatable to the masses.

In three lectures at Paris in 1920, Kerensky no longer concealed his great satisfaction with the work of the original Provisional Government. Its members "laid the foundation of the new Russia"; they realized that they "must represent the people, the nation, not a class," and that "a state can be created only on the basis of extensive social reforms." Kerensky could discover all these virtues in a government whose inanity and helplessness disheartened all Russia.

> That first period brought extensive creative work. *All later work consisted in narrowing and restricting it. . . .* It is commonly said that first there was a bourgeois period of the revolution [till May], and then a coalition and socialist period. That is a mistake. The essence of it lay not in any change, but in the maturing of the Left to the work; *the coalition government did not enlarge the sweep of the program;* on the contrary, *it continually narrowed its bounds.*[6]

Instead of catching the revolutionary wind in its sails, the later Provisional Government finally chose the tactics of *putting on the brakes.* The country was turning to the Left, the government to the Right. The moment was coming when the ship would cease to obey the helm, and would become a plaything for the elements.

At times Kerensky realized this. At the preliminary parliament a significant phrase broke from his lips: "I know that I am doomed." Beauty of pose meant nothing for the country which he was trying to govern by methods "doomed" to failure.

In late September Verkhovsky wrote in his diary, referring, apparently, to a minister, Tretyakov: "One of our big manufacturers, a member of the Provisional Government, thinks we should abandon the struggle and *let anarchy triumph.* Then the people will see what that leads to, and will return to reason."

These tactics meant playing into the hands of Bolshevism in order to reduce social democracy to an absurdity. It was an application of the rule: the worse, the better. From this viewpoint the most important thing was not to let the moderate parties of the Soviet secure power. Let the wave sweep over them and lift on its crest the most Left of all, those who think and act "more Left than common sense."

Naturally, Verkhovsky's attempts were bound to fail before this double obstacle: Kerensky's pursuing a "Right policy with Left hands," and the blissful "the worse, the better" of the bourgeois wing in the government.

Driven to despair, Verkhovsky took two incautious steps. At a secret session of a commission of the new advisory preliminary parliament, directly braving Tereshchenko, who demanded that the true situation be colored, with truly soldierly frankness Verkhovsky painted a discouraging picture of the army's state and its inability to fight under present conditions. Then, at a session of the Provisional Government he declared that "the power granted to the Minister of War was too limited" to create conditions necessary for the army's recovery and the country's preservation from ruin.

Later, even Right-wing Cadets like Nabokov admitted that in the first question "he was, unfortunately, absolutely right." At bottom he was right in the second as well. The army could be preserved and resurrected not by this or that purely military measure, within the competence of the Minister of War, but only by a new policy carried out by the entire Provisional Government.

But Verkhovsky, who coöperated with the Soviets, and seemed to have inherited Kerensky's now evaporated popularity, had become almost as odious to the majority in the government as Chernov earlier. It was easier to besmirch him. Burtsev's *Common Cause*, in violation of cabinet secrecy, published a sensational, deliberately false report that General Verkhovsky had proposed that the government make a separate peace with Germany. From the Provisional Government came equally unfounded rumors, hinting that General Verkhovsky had offered to become dictator.

Verkhovsky's fate was sealed. He was assigned "a fortnight's rest" by the government. Kerensky exacted from him a pledge to leave Petrograd immediately. In return a dryly official communiqué was issued, denying the report that Verkhovsky had proposed a separate peace.

The one man in the Provisional Government who still tried, perhaps clumsily, to display some creative initiative had been thrown overboard.

CHAPTER NINETEEN

THE PARTY OF SOCIAL REVOLUTIONARIES

ONE striking feature of 1917 was the unprecedented growth of the Social Revolutionary party. At the first Congress of City Soviets the Social Revolutionaries and their sympathizers had over 300 votes, almost three times the number of the Bolshevist faction. In the new Petrograd Duma they were first, with 54 seats, increased to 75 by supplementary elections. In Moscow their list secured 60% of the votes and 116 seats. Social Revolutionaries became mayors of both capitals.

At the first All-Russian Congress of Peasants' Soviets the 776 delegates questioned divided as follows: Social Democrats (Bolsheviks, Mensheviks, etc.) 103, nonparty 136, Social Revolutionaries 537. When dominance of the Petrograd Soviet passed to the Bolsheviks, of the 5 seats in the presidium left to the opposition, 3 went to Social Revolutionaries and 2 to Mensheviks. At the August elections to the Petrograd City Duma the Bolsheviks almost doubled their representation, securing 67 instead of 37 seats. Despite the complete collapse of the Populist Socialists (2 instead of 17) and the Mensheviks (8 instead of 40), the Social Revolutionaries not only held their own, but gained 21 seats.

Even the October coup d'état failed to knock the Social Revolutionaries from the saddle at once. Despite a flood of enticing decrees from the new government, despite every sort of pressure exerted by the War Revolutionary Committees, the faith of the masses in the Social Revolutionary party once more gave it a brilliant victory in the elections to the Constituent Assembly. Lenin himself admitted that of 36,200,000 votes cast the Bolsheviks had received only 9,000,000, while the Russian Social Revolutionaries had 16,500,-

000, and with the Social Revolutionaries of other nationalities almost 21,000,000, or 58% of the total.

This very strength of the party was the source of its weakness. The motley, many-headed street poured resistlessly into its ranks. It was a herdlike stampede. People who yesterday had absolutely no conception of the party today vied in calling themselves Social Revolutionaries and in deciding questions of party life. The ridiculously meager cadres of old Social Revolutionaries tried in vain to cope with the varied, unformed mass which was flooding the party. For no other party was the transition from the former "skeleton" organization to full-blooded life so tumultuous. And in the preceding period of life-and-death struggle against the autocracy no party had suffered so many sacrifices or been so severely bled. Gregory Gershuni, perhaps the greatest revolutionary of all, organizer of the party's militant struggle, had died in a Tsarist prison ten years before. Michael Gots, a man of remarkable ability and untiring energy, justly called the "party's conscience," had died of a mysterious disease, aggravated by the Neapolitan prison into which he had been cast at the instance of the Imperial Government. Victor Chernov, creator of the party's "military doctrine," the theorist of the movement, felt himself cruelly alone after these losses.

His isolation was aggravated during the World War. Like all the parties of the Second International, the Social Revolutionaries were sharply divided as to whether they should make the war "their own" or regard it as "alien" to socialists. A considerable majority of the leading Social Revolutionary *émigrés* adopted an attitude like that of Scheidemann and Noske in Germany. On the other hand, Chernov welcomed the slogans of Romain Rolland and other pacifists who were trying to rise *audessus de la mêlée*, and supported the antiwar protests by Liebknecht in Germany and Friedrich Adler in Austria. He took part in the Zimmerwald antiwar socialist conference. His group, however, was weakened by the inclination of one part of it to join the so-called "Zimmerwald extreme Left," a separate faction organized by Lenin, Radek, and Platten, which proclaimed the paradoxical idea that the proletariat of each country should strive for the defeat of its own government. Chernov tried to steer the party between Scylla and Charybdis, between the slogans of "all for the war," "war to victory," and their opposite, the defeatist tendency.

"War to victory" naturally inclined its followers to coalition with the industrial bourgeoisie, which in turn refused to break with the landed aristocracy and caste of generals. To preserve such a coalition social reform had to be postponed. At the opposite wing the youth, the workers, and, in places, even the peasantry tended to the other extreme. The urge to stop the war as soon as possible brought them close to the Bolsheviks. Dissatisfied with the concept of the "labor" revolution, transitional between the classical bourgeois and integral socialist revolutions, the Left wing of the Social Revolutionary party began to dream of the bold experiment of "introducing socialism" by a single radical act.

To these party discords one more was added. In almost all socialist parties the parliamentary section is usually more Right than the central leadership. Long and stable popular government tends to smooth out this difference, but at the birth of representative institutions it was bound to be great. In the party of Social Revolutionaries there was a strong divergence between the party center, led by Chernov, and Kerensky's Duma group. The party, engaged in terrorist struggle against the government, had no legal branch in the Duma. Kerensky, who called himself a Social Revolutionary, led the Duma faction of "Laborites," a half Socialist, half petty-bourgeois group, tinged with Populism; within it he acquired the ways of a petty dictator, which he was never able to drop.

Within the Social Revolutionary party, from beginning to

end, Kerensky remained a "person in himself," a self-willed and capricious guerrilla fighter in politics. His personality, or his name, became the natural rallying point for the so-called "March Social Revolutionaries," a hybrid group, drawn to the party by herd feeling, by the fashionableness of Social Revolutionary philosophy, by the aureole of its preceding heroic struggle, or simply by careerism. These men made a living banner of Kerensky with his skill in fashioning coalitions and his dictatorial airs. They were joined by men of the party's Right wing, who, of all that Social Revolutionary meant, had kept only the name.

The All-Russian Party Congress had been convoked for May. It was to show the strength of these two centrifugal forces, and test the resistance of the party Center. Before the congress met, a part of the Right wing founded a new paper, *Volya Naroda,* in Petrograd, in competition with the official organ, *Delo Naroda.* At the congress the same group, for the first time in the party's history, attempted to organize a separate faction of members in sympathy with *Volya Naroda.* The summons was unsuccessful. But this precedent emboldened Left-wing elements to summon a separate and rather large conference of their own. The alarmed supporters of party unity could only organize a group of the "Center." In the test of strength, however, the resolutions of the party Center were carried by great majorities, and the policy formulated by Chernov was adopted. This policy was based on a striving for peace, not by one-sided dictation to the vanquished, but by applying to all the same standard of international law, and on an effort to strengthen the new revolutionary government by a constructive socialist policy of labor and agrarian legislation. In form the party's unity in support of the policy formulated by its Center was assured. Its united exertion for a democratic peace and for social advance within the country seemed guaranteed by the unanimity of the congress.

Such were the results of the Third Congress. Obviously,

the line of conduct which it outlined was not carried out between May and October, 1917. The Social Revolutionary ministers were not a united group. Chernov's efforts to carry out the party's agrarian policy isolated him within the Provisional Government, and led to his withdrawal. The leading figures in the party sacrificed Chernov's policy to the coalition. Instead of shifting the balance within the government as the forces of socialism grew within the country, the government was continually reconstructed by Kerensky so as to replace loyal party socialists by compliant nonparty "socialists." The party tolerated all this so long that the final downfall of the Provisional Government, which it had tried in vain to defend, became a catastrophe for it as well.

The party of Social Revolutionaries did not carry out *its own* policy, the policy of its Third Congress. Its line deviated far to the Right. What caused this deviation? The next party congress condemned the Central Committee for its weak leadership, for tolerating violations of party discipline, and for failure to live up to the party decrees. For the historian that is insufficient: he seeks, not "culprits," but general causes. The Fourth Congress saw one cause in the excessive variety within the Central Committee, which made it a "parliament of opinions" with an unstable, fluctuating majority. The Third Party Congress, meeting after a long hiatus, had elected a Central Committee rather blindly. In addition, many central party figures evolved rapidly during the revolution. Leaders theoretically "Left," after taking responsibility for all the complicated "kitchen" of backstage, interparty, and government agreements and combinations, turned more and more to the Right. Many, theoretically "Right" like the Samara group, when obliged to lead the peasant movement in their own provinces, adopted tactics of self-made, revolutionary, local legislation, and declared the orders of the coalition government "null and void." All this undermined the central leadership.

The triumph of centrifugal over centripetal forces, characteristic of the Russian Revolution, as of all revolutions growing out of military defeat, found a partial expression within the leading parties, through the weakening of their Center and the growth of their extreme wings. The fate of the party of Social Revolutionaries, when thus considered *sub specie æternitatis*, merely reflected the fate of the revolution.

Individuals and groups were only more or less blind tools in this historic process. Kerensky, who for a short time became the idol of the street, a living banner for the "March socialists," certainly had no intention of depriving the revolution of its firm basis, that united Social Revolutionary party which had felt the beating pulse of Russian history. If he at first conceived a hatred for Miliukov, then almost came to hate Tseretelli, and finally concentrated his hatred on Chernov, that was because he sincerely considered each of them a party sectarian, incapable of "thinking like a statesman." He considered himself misunderstood, the victim of countless envious persons. Having exhausted the ingenuity of a lawyer, the energy of a monomaniac, and the eloquence of a neurotic in trying to square the circle—to unite the bourgeois and nationalist camp with the internationalist and revolutionary one—he arrived at the conclusion, natural for him, that parties and classes with their separate interests, and especially leaders of parties and classes, were only an obstacle to the true statesman. The impossibility of securing a workable coalition of *parties* led Kerensky to the idea of replacing it by a coalition of *men*. Hence the "government of public safety," led by a "directory," a dictatorship of three or five men, from which there was but one step to the dictatorship of an individual. To that Kerensky was inwardly drawn, but outwardly resisted.

The fact that Kerensky was enrolled as a Social Revolutionary caused frightful complications for the party. Their responsibility for him was intimate, as for one of their own leaders, albeit one who had suddenly emerged as if from another planet. Yet his policy contradicted the entire Social

Revolutionary platform. To break with him was all the more difficult for the party, since that meant trying to form a relatively homogeneous government of labor democracy, with a socialist tinge. It meant breaking with the Menshevist party which resisted this idea with might and main. There was also the danger of a party split, the founding of a "national Social Revolutionary party," and desertion of the party ranks by many men with big names. A split just before the elections to the Constituent Assembly might compromise all the party's successes. The central group, led by Chernov, could not accept this lightly. It was restrained above all by the unreliability of the swollen Left wing, which showed a strong psychological "descent to Bolshevism." The Left was already talking of "All power to the Soviets," not merely in the sense of forming a government from the leaders of the Soviet parties, but of transforming the Soviets into direct organs of government. They were considering tackling the immediate realization of an integral maximal socialist program, of a dictatorship of the party of Social Revolutionaries and of a Constituent Assembly to work under the mouths of Kronstadt cannon, in a word, the Bolshevist program in Populist disguise.

The enthusiasms of the Left wing, by the law of psychological reaction, threw part of the Center elements to the Right, while the coalition mongering and capitulation tendencies of the Right threw many of the Center elements far to the Left. The extremes fed each other. The Center melted away on both sides.

These conditions made the task of the central group no easy one. It would not have been easy even if all its former kernel had been there, with Chernov, Michael Gots, and Gregory Gershuni. But there remained only Chernov, who was rather a theorist, a man of speech, literature, the writing desk and lecture platform than a professional politician. A genuinely Slav breadth of nature, a certain pliancy and adjustability were combined in him with a tendency to withdraw into the world of ideas, of social diagnosis and prognosis, of intellectual initiative and creative imagination, and to leave to others the concrete organization of current work.

Chernov trusted people more than a politician should. At first with the younger Gots he reached out to Kerensky: a young force, a tremendous popularity, that was splendid for the party. True, Kerensky's popularity was superficial, it had still to penetrate the masses. Gots and Chernov built plans: they would advance Kerensky in a new rôle, have him sign a decree to halt all dealings in land, link his name with the peasants' traditional dream of emancipating the land from private landlord ownership, with the dream of free access to the land for those who work it. Kerensky seemed to agree, then not. He was unwilling to undermine his popularity among the censitary public. Eventually these plans and hopes had to be abandoned. For long Chernov was unwilling to sacrifice the hopes he placed in Kerensky. He wrote the declaration which was to regularize Kerensky's relation to the party, without whose knowledge he had entered the bourgeois government. At the Third Congress Chernov stood up wholeheartedly for Kerensky in the Left fraction which was raging against him, and made a pacifying speech. That, however, did not protect Chernov from being suspected by Kerensky's enthusiastic worshipers of responsibility for his failure to be elected to the Central Committee. This legend was accepted by the deeply offended Kerensky the more readily since later, especially after he had elbowed Tseretelli out of the government, Chernov was cruelly disappointed in him, and after the Kornilov affair began to consider the connection with him fatal for the party.

After the withdrawal of the four Cadet members, then of Prince Lvov, from the government, Chernov concluded: if we wish to live in peace and fraternal accord with the nationalities which are under a single governmental roof with the Great Russians, we must work out a great, federal charter for the nationalities—hence we must govern without the

Cadets. If we wish to avert a Pugachev revolt, we must carry out an energetic and radical policy to facilitate the access of labor to the land—and hence, govern without the Cadets. If we wish to avoid further undermining of the war-shaken national economy by strikes or lockouts, we must immediately introduce control of production, limitation of profits, and fixing of real wages—hence, we must govern without the Cadets. If we wish to dispel the thought which is disorganizing the spirit of the army, that although Russia has renounced annexations and indemnities for herself, the army is forced to conquer the right to annexation and tribute for the Allied governments, we must exert strong pressure on the Allies to publish thoroughly democratic peace conditions—hence in international relations we must represent Russia without the Cadets. Chernov made a report to this effect at a well attended private "conference of old party members."

However, in the Central Committee of the party, elected by the Third Congress, Chernov encountered a resistance scarcely expected after the resolutions passed by that congress. The party leadership remained in this indefinite state until the Kornilov plot. Only then did the long needed change occur. In particular, Kerensky's attempt to make his administration still more irresponsible by concentrating it in the hands of a small "directory" met with sharp and universal resistance. The Central Committee of the party adopted Chernov's resolution, which declared an alliance with the Cadet party impossible.

But in the Central Committee of the Social Revolutionary party on September 4 and 12, a resolution was again passed stating the desirability of a coalition with the censitary elements, enlarged and supplemented by responsibility to the "preliminary parliament," although the decree against coalition with the Cadets remained in force. The resolution also established the principle of *unit voting* for all members of the Central Committee; only the right of "unmotivated abstention" was granted to those who disagreed. A fortnight later this decree was reënforced by the obligation for all members of the Central Committee to carry out its policy actively and by complete prohibition of "individual voting contrary to the opinion of the Central Committee."

These decrees, passed just before the opening of the Democratic Conference, bound Chernov hand and foot and weakened his position still further. If he was the most "consistent" politician of the Social Revolutionary party, his energy encountered many obstacles. Despite his steadfastness and sporadic impetuosity, despite his resourcefulness in defending his general aims, he did not always display these qualities in day-to-day politics. This would have required greater concentration of will, less tendency to scatter his forces than were possessed by his typically Russian nature. For a professional politician he was too much a democrat in all his habits and, in addition, lacked that active love of honor and power so important in the political arena. He was completely satisfied with literary and oratorical successes, which are politically imponderable. It was perhaps splendid, but it was not practical, when he tried by personal example to show how party discipline should be observed; at decisive Soviet meetings and congresses he was at times silent or abstained from voting in order not to violate some decree of the Central Committee with its unstable majority and varying decisions, while other comrades in the committee were unhampered by them. He was still living in the inertia of that period when the leaders of the party had represented a firm moral unity. Those times were far in the past.

In 1917 the upper ranks of the party were so out of touch with the lower ranks that a man of Lenin's character could have achieved much by delivering ultimatums to the leading circles, and reënforcing them by appeal to the lower ranks of the party. Critical circumstances too often demanded abrupt turns of the helm; but fear for the fate of party unity weakened Chernov's pressure. He acted less resolutely and firmly than was demanded by his own viewpoint, sometimes in order not to strain the already weakened party bonds, again in order not to mislead the local organizations by the appearance of a sharp personal struggle during his disagreements with Kerensky, sometimes in the hope that a policy of waiting and postponing the conflict would prove who was right and painlessly correct the party line. These were, perhaps, very respectable motives. But it must be acknowledged that Chernov sacrificed to the fetish of unachievable party unity the energetic defense of the very program which the party had formally adopted at his initiative.

After the Third Congress of the party, for a half year the party line was deflected to the Right. Matters went so far that a series of Chernov's warning articles was not published in the central organ of the party, even as his personal opinion. The Central Committee decided that the party was so accustomed to regard Chernov's articles as its official position that their divergence from the decisions of the Central Committee might cause general confusion. Even here Chernov submitted to discipline and patiently waited to appeal to the Fourth Party Congress. The congress met. It was unanimous in supporting Chernov's "Left-Center" resolutions. It condemned the wavering of the Central Committee and its inability to maintain party discipline. It elected a more homogeneous Central Committee. Unfortunately, the accelerated tempo of historic events had outstripped the functioning of the cumbersome party machine. While the congress was being organized and assembled, the Bolshevist overturn had taken place. The party line was corrected, but it was now too late.

CHAPTER TWENTY

THE DESCENT TO BOLSHEVISM

ONE trump remained to the majority parties of the Soviet: the Democratic Conference.

The conference opened on September 14. Kerensky made the sensational announcement that the rôle of dictator had been offered to him before Kornilov. He evaded the question, "By whom?" He assured the conference that, although he had put through the law restoring capital punishment at the front, he had not ratified a single death sentence; in other words, he had quite uselessly provoked the great storm over that law.

A heated debate now began. Two resolutions were presented. One proposed excluding from the coalition "elements in the Constitutional Democratic party [Cadets], or in other parties if implicated in the Kornilov mutiny." The second was more drastic: it declared further coalition with the Cadets impossible. Instead of putting the question as to which resolution the conference wished to adopt as a basis for its discussions, the presidium of the conference, in its struggle to save the coalition, used a trick which was clever rather than honest. It declared that before the resolutions came up, a vote of principle would be taken for or against coalition. The protests of Chernov and others that an abstract "coalition in general" did not exist, and that such a vote would be ambiguous and indefinite, were of no avail. During the roll call Chernov, bound by the resolutions of his own Central Committee, could only abstain from voting, without even the right to explain his abstention. This caused great confusion. His enemies interpreted it as a sign of irresoluteness. The delegates of the Soviets and the nationalities organizations cast more than two-thirds of their votes, the zemstvos three-quarters, the trade-unions four-fifths of their votes against the coalition; the delegates of the cities divided almost evenly; only the votes of the coöperative organizations, cast almost unanimously for the coalition, gave a majority, though a very weak one, to the abstract "principle of coalition."

Then the proposal to throw overboard those "elements" implicated in the Kornilov mutiny—a proposal which would seem beyond dispute—passed by 797 to 139, with 196 abstentions. The presidium tried to declare the voting at an end. But the members who favored excluding the entire Cadet party from the coalition protested so strongly that their resolution had to be put. It secured 595 *yeas* against 493 *nays*, with 72 abstentions.

Now the partisans of the coalition resolved on a desperate measure: the presidium, discarding all pretense of impartiality, declared that the vote on the question of principle implied approval of the main resolution while the two later ballots merely amended it; hence it proposed to vote on the "resolution as a whole." Fresh protests followed. This interpretation was declared arbitrary; a roll call for or against an abstract principle was not the same as voting a resolution; amendments to a resolution were never balloted after passage of the main resolution. The presidium carried out the roll call. Now the purpose of the maneuver was exposed. Violating all the decrees of the Central Committee of their party on unit voting, the Right-wing Social Revolutionaries declared that they would vote against the resolution as a whole. Dan announced that the Mensheviks would join them, and Berkenheim that the coöperative delegates would do the same.

That was just what the Bolsheviks wanted. They were worried by the prospect that a homogeneous labor government might be created. It might gain popularity, and bar their path to revolution. It would be much easier to snatch power from the coalition government, weakened by internal dissension, and headed by a "finished man," Kerensky. In the Bolsheviks' name Trotsky declared that, although they had voted for both concrete resolutions, now that they were linked to recognition of the abstract principle of coalition, they were obliged to reject the "resolution as a whole." The same declaration was made by the Left-wing Social Revolutionaries and Internationalists, not to be outdone in radicalism. The Right and Left thus joined forces to leave the Democratic Conference with no resolution whatever. Three affirmative ballots, three plusses, equalled one minus. It was proved that the conference could offer only a shifting majority, each time based on a fresh combination of votes. The united majority had disappeared. The two extreme wings of the conference had swollen ominously, while its Center was vanishing.

"The presidium has discussed the situation and unanimously recognized that within organized democracy there is no unity of will which can be crystallized," Tseretelli declared after an intermission. Labor democracy could not have dealt itself a more suicidal blow. Under the prevailing conditions, for democracy to sign its own act of bankruptcy was an indirect admission that the only solution was dictatorship. On that day there was but one victor, numerically the weakest faction—the Bolsheviks.

The failure of the Democratic Conference to decide the question of government meant that Kerensky had recovered his freedom of action. He made haste to paste together a new government of sorts, replacing the Petrograd Cadets by Moscow ones. He again dragged into his cabinet, practically by main force, Konovalov, who had twice resigned. He added Tretyakov, well known through his projects for a camouflaged shutdown of industry. He surrounded himself with several "pale-pink" individuals, "quasi socialists." Of course neither formal responsibility to the preliminary parliament nor fulfilment of the August program of the Moscow State Conference were possible under these conditions. Kerensky threatened to abandon power. The Central Committee of the party of Social Revolutionaries resolved "to send to Kerensky a new delegation, to try to persuade comrade Kerensky to consent to the demands of democracy" (resolution of October 1). The Bolsheviks demanded that the settlement of the question be postponed till the Second Congress of Soviets. The partisans of coalition were willing to accept any abridgment of their program and any government however motley, provided it lasted till the Constituent Assembly. Endless negotiations, bargaining and haggling went on, sometimes with dramatic turns, sometimes comic.

At one moment it seemed as if there would be no agreement, and the only alternative would be a homogeneous "labor" government. At one hasty meeting the Central Committee of the Social Revolutionary party even gave a presumptive ministerial slate to its delegates, who were negotiating with Kerensky. Tseretelli was proposed for Premier and Minister of Foreign Affairs; for Minister of Finance, V. A. Rzhevsky (a former Progressist, president of the finance commission of the Imperial Duma, who joined the Social Revolutionaries in 1917); for Commerce and Industry, the Right-wing Bolshevik, Krassin; as Minister of Labor, the Social Democrat Kolokolnikov; for Agriculture, Chernov's assistant, the well-known agronomist, P. A. Vikhlyayev; for Supply, the coöperator Berkenheim; as Minister of Home Affairs, the Social Revolutionary Timofeyev or the Social Democrat Bogdanov; for Justice, Kerensky, or, if he refused, Hendelman; for Education, Timiryazev or Bekhterev; General Verkhovsky and Admiral Verderevsky would remain as Ministers of War and Marine. Chernov preferred to remain outside the government, but was willing, if necessary, to return to the Ministry of Agriculture or head a new "Ministry of Nationalities."

However, this list was probably taken by Gots and Avksentiev only to put the screws on Kerensky by flashing before his eyes a project which could be realized without him if he were too stubborn. Even inwardly hesitant supporters of the coalition were hypnotized by the closeness of the elections to the Constituent Assembly. All new government combinations ought to be postponed till then. They must not be compromised in the short remaining interval, inevitably uncertain and troubled.

They apparently failed to understand that the question of the government would determine whether the Constituent Assembly was to exist at all, and whether the country would reach it without a fresh revolution. A revolution just prior to the Constituent Assembly would of course mean the end of it.

Here was the usual misfortune: the revolution was everywhere behindhand. The sin of delay was stamped on all its acts, on convoking the Constituent Assembly, perhaps, more than on anything else.

On March 6 Buchanan had telegraphed London: "To my question concerning the Constituent Assembly His Excellency [Miliukov] replied that a proclamation would be issued announcing its convocation at the earliest opportunity, but without setting a date."[1] In negotiating with the Soviets to organize a government the Duma representatives promised to convoke the Constituent Assembly "within a very short time." The Provisional Government gave assurance that it "by no means intended to take advantage of war conditions to delay execution of the above-mentioned reforms and measures." However, according to Miliukov, immediately after this, "among the original members of the Provisional Government the conviction arose that this could be done only during a lull in military operations, i.e., not before autumn." In other words, the delay was based actually on "war conditions." Two months of purely bourgeois government were insufficient for the "Special Conference," appointed to prepare a draft election law, to assemble and begin work. On March 13, in the "contact commission" between the Provisional Government and the delegates of the Soviet "there was a long conversation about the Constituent Assembly. The government reluctantly confirmed its promises. . . . We agreed that the Constituent Assembly should be convoked during the summer."[2]

The delegates of the Executive Committee felt that even this date was too far off, and they were right. All later revolutions from the German Revolution of 1918 to the Spanish one of 1931, show that, only if convoked immediately, can the Constituent Assembly exert a formative influence on the revolution. Otherwise, the fate of the revolution and of the Constituent Assembly will be decided prior to it and without it. In his speech of March 24 Chkheidze rightly demanded that the summoning of the Constituent Assembly be speeded. The Moscow District Conference of Soviets was correct in insisting a few days later that "the date of convocation must not in the slightest depend on when the war may end."[3]

But in April, at the All-Russian Conference of Soviets Kerensky's right-hand man, Stankevich, unexpectedly declared that "the Constituent Assembly cannot be summoned before September." In justification he invoked the calendar. The electoral lists had to be drawn up by the "proper" organs of local self-government. Yet the first Provisional Government had not bothered to issue a law for the new urban self-government, had left that to the first coalition; that in itself resulted in two months' delay. They "made haste slowly" with the electoral law for the Constituent Assembly. With the pompous advertisement that it was "to speed its convocation," the first session of the conference was set for May 25. There was so far no mention of a date for the election itself. Why could not the voters' lists for electing the Constituent Assembly have been drawn up by the same method and at the same time as those for zemstvo and municipal elections? This was an insolent question, regarded by the liberal bourgeois wing of the government and its learned commission of jurists as an insult to the eternal principles of constitutional law. Only on June 14, three and one half months after the revolution, did the Provisional Government, under pressure from Tseretelli and Chernov, at last set the election date for September 17 and the opening of the Constituent Assembly for September 30. The Cadets declared this "avowedly inexecutable."* The second coalition hastened, as Miliukov put it, "to correct the political mistake of the first, which had set the election to the Constituent Assembly for an obviously impossible date, just to please the Left-wing socialists." Despite denunciation of this "sabotage" in the press and Soviets, on August 9, with the consent of the Soviet Executive Committee, the election was postponed to November 12, and the convocation of the Assembly to November 28. During the negotiations with Kerensky for a "third coalition," suggestions came up that the election be postponed to a still later date. On September 12 the Central Committee of the Social Revolutionary party "unanimously decreed, as an ultimatum," that "the convocation of the Constituent Assembly must not be delayed." This, however, might be called "a conversation in the realm of shadow": both dates, new and old, exceeded the time limit granted to the Provisional Government by long-suffering history.

Even Chernov's plan to form a "labor government," so often rejected or shelved, was finally accepted. The Central Committee of the Social Revolutionary party passed this resolution unanimously, in Chernov's absence, without pressure by him. "It is considered necessary to form a homogeneous socialist government immediately, with representatives of all socialist parties." So read the resolution, adopted on November 14, 1917. This "immediately" was too late. It was then three weeks after the overthrow of the Provisional Government and the Bolsheviks' advent to power.

This was the chief disease of the 1917 Revolution—tardiness. It was, in a way, an echo of a certain retardedness in Russia's historical development.

The Tsar had been behindhand with his responsible ministry and with his own abdication to save the dynasty. The

* Miliukov.

Guchkovs, Krymovs, and Tereshchenkos were too late with their plan for a palace coup to forestall the people's revolution. Then the revolution, delayed in its coming, began a series of its own tardiness. It was behindhand with its coalition, again with its homogeneous government. The tardy coalition government was behindhand in the labor, peasant, and nationalities questions. There was no urgent need which it did not postpone "till the Constituent Assembly." The constant postponement of the Constituent Assembly "capped the edifice" of tardinesses. It gave the Bolsheviks one of their strongest trumps. It enabled them to assert that convocation of the Constituent Assembly was being systematically sabotaged; that the Cadets, seeing the Left parties growing and their own declining, did not want a Constituent Assembly till after a victory in the war, since they could then count on an outburst of national vainglory and of chauvinistic greed; that Kornilov had exposed these cards by promising "through victory to lead the country to the Constituent Assembly"; that the entire plan for the offensive had been dictated by a desire to create an atmosphere filled with passion for victory, or else a "white heat of military operations" which would justify a "first-class funeral" for the Constituent Assembly. If the Bolsheviks' noisy compaign must be recognized by the historian as a "great falsehood," that is not because there was no truth in their assertions, but because they themselves in their hearts had already discarded the Constituent Assembly and were accusing others of what they themselves were preparing to do.

What was occurring within the Bolshevist party? How was it preparing for the rôle which history had assigned to it?

According to a widespread opinion, from the very beginning of the revolution the internal history of Soviet democracy pivoted on a desperate struggle between Menshevism and Bolshevism. This opinion calls for substantial qualifications. Even the final breakup of Social Democracy into formally distinct parties, of which one later adopted the new name of "Communist," was not the starting point, but the result of the current of events. Trotsky has reminded the world that

in labor centers like Ekaterinburg, Perm, Tula, Nizhni-Novgorod, Sormovo, Kolomna, Yuzovka, the Bolsheviks separated from the Mensheviks only at the end of May, 1917. In Odessa, Nikolayev, Elisavetgrad, Poltava, and other centers of the Ukraine even in the middle of June the Bolsheviks had no organizations of their own. In Baku, Zlatoust, Bezhetsk, Kostroma the Bolsheviks finally separated from the Mensheviks only at the end of June.[4]

In the two capitals events moved more rapidly. However, according to a prominent Bolshevik, in the Moscow Soviet during the first half of March

all questions were decided in the Executive Committee and the plenum of the Soviet without any separation on factional lines. . . . No one organized factions; indeed, among the workers feeling was not favorable for factional work. That sentiment was strong, not only among nonparty members, but among party comrades.[5]

The question was more complicated in Petrograd, where factional divisions were sharpest. But the opposite extreme, excessive factional subdivision, led in Petrograd to practically the same result—it nullified party influence in the Soviet. And the Bolsheviks were least prepared to influence it. They still had to find themselves spiritually and politically.

The first attempts to do so left an impression of casualness, of random groping, of a "zigzag course." The Bolshevist organization at first had no "concrete answer in the question of government organization."[6] On February 28 the Central Bolshevist Committee urged the workers and soldiers to immediately "elect representatives to the Provisional Revolutionary Government, which must be established under protection of the insurgent revolutionary people and army." This vague appeal had no effect. In the Executive Committee of the

Soviet "no one even referred to a government of Soviet democracy, despite the Bolshevist manifesto of the preceding day."[7] All, even the Bolsheviks, were satisfied with their right to exclude odious individuals from the Provisional Government.

Even so firm a Bolshevik as Stalin said at the party conference on March 27:

> The Provisional Government has in fact undertaken to intrench the conquests of the revolutionary people. The Soviet of Workers' and Soldiers' Deputies mobilizes forces, supervises; the Provisional Government, albeit restively, confusedly, intrenches the conquests which the people have already won in fact. Such a situation has both negative and positive sides: at present it is not advantageous for us to force events and thus hasten the secession of the bourgeois strata which later must inevitably break with us.

Later Stalin was to be hounded by Trotsky for this. Trotsky asserted that till Lenin arrived from abroad, Stalin was only "a vulgar revolutionary democrat."

In this form Bolshevism could be only a radically tinged appendage to the Social Democratic front as a whole, and till Lenin's arrival it was just that. At the Petrograd Menshevist city conference, early in March, the question of fusion with the Bolsheviks was on the agenda. At the Bolshevist conference in March Stalin urged that they respond to Tseretelli's fusion proposals, since "to look too far ahead and anticipate disagreements was wrong"; they could be "overcome within the party." In the question of the war at first "the Bolsheviks, properly speaking, advanced no independent program." Stalin said in so many words, "The mere slogan—'Down with war!'—is absolutely useless as a practical tool." In mid-March Kamenev returned from Siberia. He and Stalin took over the leadership of the Bolshevist faction in the Soviet and the editing of its central newspaper, *Pravda*. However, this did not create a gulf between Bolshevism and the central leadership of the Soviet, but rather the contrary. *Pravda* dropped its recklessly demagogic tone. Even in the burning question of the war it asserted that "the war will go on, for the German army has not yet followed the example of the Russian army and still obeys its emperor"; under such circumstances, for the Russian soldiers "to disperse to their homes would be a policy, not of peace but of slavery, a policy which the free Russian people will reject with indignation." The newspaper defended the necessity "for replying to each bullet by a bullet and to each shell by a shell," without permitting "any disorganization of the revolution's military forces." While demanding the opening of negotiations "to find a way to end the World War," *Pravda* constantly insisted that "till then each must stick to his post."

All this was not far from the official position of the Menshevist and Social Revolutionary majority. Indeed, at about that time (late March or early April) "a joint meeting of Mensheviks and Bolsheviks was arranged, at which the question of unification was touched upon incidentally." Previously, in Moscow "at the party [Bolshevist] conference, among other matters, the question was brought up of the possibility of uniting with the Mensheviks, since in the provinces there was a rather strong urge to that."[8] The fusion negotiations dragged along till Lenin's return from abroad quickly put a stop to them. At that time Lenin remarked ironically that he knew of only two real Bolsheviks: himself and his wife.

Yet it would be wrong to attribute to Lenin personally the subsequent change in the Bolshevist course. No one man can ever effect such abrupt changes in the feeling of an entire party. Some proletarian strata of Petrograd liked the spirit of the old *Pravda*, that "incoherent, primitive, but Left" tone, as Trotsky called it, or chaotic, "demagogical, and pogromlike," according to Sukhanov.

The day the first number of the reorganized *Pravda* appeared, March 15, was one of triumph for the "defensist" groups. The entire Tauride Palace hummed with a single piece of news: the victory of the moderate, reasonable Bolsheviks over the extremists. . . . When that number of *Pravda* reached the factories, it aroused extreme perplexity among the members of our party and its sympathizers, and sarcastic delight among our opponents. Indignation in the several districts was tremendous. When the proletarians learned that *Pravda* had been seized by three of its former editors, now returned from Siberia, they demanded that they be expelled from the party.[9]

Shlyapnikov, of course, saw the "proletarians" through his own spectacles. There are proletarians and proletarians. Of that "unreformed" *Pravda* Kamenev told Sukhanov that "it was absolutely indecent in tone, unsuitable in spirit, and of bad reputation"; "even the circles of our own workers are much dissatisfied with it." Naturally there were other circles of workers, pleased by "frenzied articles, playing on unbridled instincts." The skilled workers are one type, and quite another the raw recruits of the factories, the primitive and motley crowd, living chiefly by emotional impulses.

Beside the proletarian "*demos*" there exists in all capitalist countries a proletarian "*ochlos*," the enormous mass of *déclassés*, chronic paupers, *Lumpenproletariat*, what may be termed the "capitalistically superfluous industrial reserve army." Like the proletariat, it is a product of capitalist civilization, but it reflects the destructive, not the constructive aspects of capitalism. Exploited and downtrodden, it is full of bitterness and despair, but has none of the traditions and none of the potentialities of organization, of a new consciousness, a new law, and a new culture, which distinguish the genuine, "hereditary" proletariat.

In Russia the growth of capitalism had been strongest in its destructive, predatory aspects, while its constructive achievements had lagged. It was accompanied by a catastrophic growth of the "*ochlos*," a tremendous mass of uprooted, drifting humanity. Wrongly idealized at times, as in Gorky's early works, this mob supplied the contingents for those sporadic mass outbursts, pogroms, anti-Jewish and other, for which old Russia was famous.

The war had swollen the mob of *déclassés* enormously. It brought the scourge of wholesale evacuation, carried out by the military authorities in a wanton and reckless manner. Besides the Jews, who were driven en masse from the prefrontal area on a general and unsupported suspicion of espionage and aid to the enemy, besides the government officials and voluntary refugees, there was the largest group of all, those expelled by the military in order to depopulate territories abandoned to the enemy.

> The military authorities have lost their heads completely; it is as if chaos were being created intentionally. . . . People are torn away from their native villages, and driven off to remote and unknown places. . . . Abandoned supplies and even their huts are burned before their very eyes. . . . This great mob pours back over every road in an endless torrent. . . . People die by hundreds of starvation, cold, disease. . . . The second great migration of nations, organized by Army Headquarters, will involve Russia in misfortune, revolution, and ruin.[10]

The personnel of industry had also been completely transformed by the war. The ranks of factory workers, severely depleted by indiscriminate mobilizations, were filled with whatever human material came to hand: peasants, small shopkeepers, clerks, janitors, porters, people of indeterminate trade, anyone for whom war industry was the only refuge against dispatch to the front. The genuine proletarian was submerged in a motley crowd of Lumpenproletarians and Lumpenbourgeois.

Then came the perodic breakdowns of production due to inadequate supply of fuel and raw material, internal conflict, and finally, the open use of the lockout. To the privations of unemployment and growing inflation the maddened mob of *déclassés* reacted not by organized class struggle but by clamor for a social miracle, the provision of work, "good money," and general prosperity by government ukaze.

There was also the mob of soldiers, especially from the garrisons in the rear. During the last years of the monarchy, Russia swarmed with overgrown rear garrisons. Badly trained, worse disciplined, and scantily officered, they were but huge laboratories for making unformed peasant lads into morally empty people, embittered by monotonous and idle existence amid urban temptations.

In the capitals the situation was still worse. At first the garrisons looked on in perplexity at the events of the revolution. Then they joined in, sometimes with great delay and largely through herd feeling. They all became "heroes of the struggle for liberty." The Soviets solemnly guaranteed them the "revolutionary" privilege of not being transferred to the front. True, the formation of front-line battalions from reserve regiments went on. But the more successful this was, the more the best elements were drained from the garrisons, the more unreliable the remaining troops became. "Natural selection" in many barracks created a picture of shameless self-seeking, of lazy indulgence in the sport of crunching sunflower seeds, card playing, drunken debauch, idling about the streets from one street meeting to another. Among this ignorant and backward mass were a few groups opposed to the war on principle; their speeches were echoed by the masses, for whom they were a convenient camouflage for laziness and slacking. Gradually these states of mind were transmitted to the front through recently recruited troops.

Lastly there was the very essence of all *déclassé* types, the deserter. According to official record, deserters from the front even prior to the revolution amounted to over 195,000 men, and on August 1, 1917, to 365,000. Together with slackers, hidden in hollows, forests, and various dives (the "greens") they totaled about 1,500,000 before the revolution, according to Rodzianko's figures, and by October 1, 1917, about 2,000,000. Finally, in a gesture of magnanimity, more beautiful than practical, the revolution almost everywhere opened the prison gates, even for criminals.

These were the chief sources of the formless mob. As victim rather than culprit of its social position, it experienced the universal enthusiasm of the revolution. But this cheerful holiday spirit could not outlast the "honeymoon" of the new order. The stern prose of life exacted its due. The more primitive these elements, the sooner they fell prey to objectless bitterness. All these elements formed a daily crowd, continually holding meetings. In the big cities, on boulevards, squares, markets, street corners, these street meetings assembled, with illiterate but fiery orators. The "street" lived its own noisy political life. In Petrograd a permanent meeting was held before the Kseshinsky Palace, now occupied by the Bolsheviks. Here the Bolshevist agitators learned to adapt themselves to a very definite stratum of the urban population, not the proletarians, but the unemployed paupers. Hence a change in the arsenal of Bolshevist phraseology. Fiery revolutionary appeals were now addressed to a social category never favored by Marxism, the "urban and village poor." The popular paper of the party soon took the title of *The Poor* (*Bednota*). The class basis of Bolshevism shifted from the proletariat to the Lumpenproletariat—Bolshevism committed the sin of which it had always accused the *anarchists*.

Lenin's first address delivered before a Marxist and Social Democratic élite, members of the recent All-Russian Conference of Soviets, had aroused general stupefaction. Down with the Provisional Government! Down with the petty-bourgeois Soviets; no bourgeois democracy, no parliamentary republic, no government except direct government by the Soviets of the poorer classes, a government conquered by the proletariat. Down with the Social Democratic party; instead, long live the new Communist party! Down with the socialist international peace congress at Stockholm; long live peace through fraternization at the front, hurrah for negotiations by the revolution effected on both sides, in each squad and battalion! Long live civil war, which would end the imperialist war! After this speech an old Bolshevik, Goldenberg, took the floor to declare: "Lenin has presented his candidacy for a throne in Europe vacant these thirty years: Bakunin's throne. Lenin's new words tell the same old story of primitive anarchism. Lenin the Social Democrat, Lenin the Marxist, Lenin the leader of our militant Social Democracy is no more!" Another Bolshevik, of the Left-wing, *Forward* (*Vpered*) faction, Bogdanov (Malinovksy), beside himself, shouted that Lenin's speech was the raving of a madman; pale with rage and contempt, he showered blame on those who had applauded: "One should be ashamed to applaud this rubbish, you cover yourselves with shame! And you are Marxists!"

Despite the challenge of Lenin's speech, plainly intended to disrupt the negotiations already in progress for a fusion of Mensheviks and Bolsheviks, its first result was the opposite. In the universal outcry provoked by his speech, Lenin left the meeting. Shortly, about fifteen Bolsheviks left in protest against the hostile reception of their apostle. The rest recognized almost unanimously the need for a congress to unite all Russian Social Democrats, and even chose a committee for that purpose, including Bolshevist representatives. "Even Lenin's closest comrades, men who had worked with him for decades, began to oppose him. . . . Disputes, especially in the *Pravda* editorial offices, were extremely bitter."[11]

Many writers are inclined to attribute entirely to Lenin's personality his ultimate victory over his own followers. It would be very superficial to imagine that Lenin, a typical paranoiac, exchanged all the concepts of the Left wing of a once united Russian Social Democracy for anarchist revolt merely because of the capricious deviations of his individual thought. On the contrary, for Lenin, from youth fanatically confirmed in the dogmas of Marxism, it was no light matter to abandon the path of Marx for that of Bakunin, and to shift his main center of support from the socially mature industrial proletariat to the *déclassé* mobs of "poor people," "lower classes," of sailors and soldiers—the variegated and unreliable "street." He had his moments of doubt and attempted to hold the movement within reasonable limits. But the mob was impatient of restraint. To abandon it and concentrate on the proletarian *demos* would have condemned him to an unending and practically hopeless struggle against the Mensheviks with their strong hold over the skilled workers.

Lenin's hesitations were reflected in his party's decrees. The All-Russian Conference of Bolsheviks in April decreed —thus condemning the future Bolshevist program of action: "The proletariat of Russia, acting in one of the most backward countries of Europe, amid the masses of petty peasant population, cannot strive for immediate socialist reconstruction." It resolved that "this war could not be ended through refusal of the soldiers of only one side to go on fighting, through cessation of military action by one of the warring sides." The accusation that the Bolsheviks were inclined to a separate peace with Germany it denounced as "base slander." Mass fraternization it declared the means, not to separate peace, but to simultaneous workers' revolution on both sides of the front. In April the Bolshevist Central Committee opposed the slogan, "All power to the Soviets." After the "Miliukov crisis" Lenin, in a special article, attacked "overhasty individuals." "The crisis could not be solved by the violence of individuals, by partial actions of small armed groups, by Blanquist attempts to seize power, to arrest the Provisional Government, etc."[12]

But Lenin had to cope not only with "Leftist individuals" in his own party, quick to respond to the ultrarevolutionary platform which had astounded his most intimate comrades immediately after his return to Russia. Behind these "Leftist individuals" was the elemental force of the *déclassés*. They had felt a certain disappointment at the conduct of the Bolsheviks during the April days. Now they sought other leaders. Their searchings met with response among certain anarchist elements.

The All-Russian Congress of Soviets had just opened when a sensation occurred in Petrograd. Over the semi-anonymous signature of an "Executive Committee for liquidating the newspaper *Russkaya Volya*," a proclamation was issued to justify the arbitrary seizure by an armed group of the Berezin printing plant. This group explained rather incoherently that the seizure was not an attack on freedom of the press, but was merely "to return its property to the people" and combat an abnormal situation which left many friends of the people without money or means of publication. The confiscated plant was surrounded by a hostile crowd. Two battalions of soldiers were also brought to the scene of action. The leaders of the congress wished at any price to avoid staining the opening days of the congress by bloodshed. Yet they insisted that revolutionary order forbade arbitrary acts, that the requisitioning of buildings for the needs of the various revolutionary organizations was subject to authorization by a special commissar of the Provisional Government and the approval of the Soviet, in which all revolutionary trends, including the anarchists, were represented. The Berezin plant must be vacated. A Soviet delegation, including a Right-wing Bolshevik, Kamenev, forestalled a fight. The investigation led the authorities to the Durnovo summer villa, seized just as arbitrarily, and transformed into the headquarters from which forays were being made, again under the anarchist flag. The attempt of the authorities to evacuate this villa met with armed resistance. At several factories in the Vyborg ward a protest strike was declared against the government's "counterrevolutionary" action. Now the Petrograd Soviet interfered. It had the Durnovo park opened to the workers, and the palace to the trade-unions. It ordered the workers of the Vyborg ward to end their strike. It concurred in the necessity for removing from the Durnovo Palace that insurgent group which, camouflaged under anarchist slogans, had collected ignorant, semi-criminal elements, and openly expressed its intention of seizing the printing plants of the *Novoye Vremya, Russkaya Volya,* and Cadet *Rech,* and transferring them to anarchist and socialist organizations known only to itself. The congress approved the action of the Petrograd Soviet by an overwhelming majority. Yet Kamenev, for the Bolsheviks, and Lunacharsky, for the "United Internationalists," declared that their factions, while not approving the anarchists' conduct, could not assent to the resolution. Some of them voted against approving the action of the Petrograd Soviet, some abstained, despite general excitement, despite shouts from the majority benches of "Hypocrites!"

All this occurred on June 8. Immediately after, it was discovered that, taking advantage of the continued excitement over the affair of the Durnovo summer palace, the Bolshevist Central Committee had set June 10 for a demonstration with the slogans, "Down with the capitalist ministers!" and "All power to the Soviets!" The Congress of Soviets raised the alarm. For the first time a Soviet party was trying to influence the Soviet's decisions from the street. The question had become acute: either the Bolsheviks would recognize the "unity of the labor front" created by the Soviet, and submit to common revolutionary discipline, or else they would be expelled from the Soviet. In the stormy debates on this question the Bolsheviks twice left the hall of the congress in protest, but returned and finally called off their demonstration. In return they issued an inflammatory appeal, complaining that the people were being deprived of their most elementary and legal right: that of expressing their political feelings by a peaceful street demonstration.

The Petrograd Soviet decided to remove all ground for complaint. After waiting for tranquillity to be restored, it not only permitted, but organized a great demonstration, with full liberty to choose slogans. The Bolshevist organization used this opportunity most zealously. People joked that the Bolsheviks had more banners than demonstrators. But they attained their aim. The abundance of placards demanding that the "ten capitalist ministers" be expelled from the government made a strong impression. In this the Bolsheviks had easy game: participation of bourgeois ministers in the government bound it hand and foot in every urgent question. The Bolshevist demonstrators, who had demanded liberty for themselves, immediately attacked other people's liberty by starting a fist fight and tearing up a placard demanding "Confidence in the Provisional Government." But there were almost no placards of this kind. The majority in the Soviet was defending the coalition with the bourgeoisie under great strain, like a heavy cross laid upon it. Though the Bolsheviks had secured partial revenge for their previous defeat, they had to be more cautious. The spirit of rebellion was too strong. There was too much inflammable material lying about. On the other hand, they were in danger of being expelled from the Soviets, and of succumbing to the blows of the government, with no protection from revolutionary democracy.

On July 1 the Bolshevist Petrograd City Conference met. Reviewing its forces—32,000 organized members, 2,000 of them armed and enrolled in military organizations, 4,000 organized "sympathizers," and about 160,000 votes at the elections to the ward duma—its spirit rose. On its third day the conference heard sensational news: the four Cadet ministers had left the Provisional Government, the government had broken up, negotiations were in progress to reëstablish the coalition with the Cadets. In a word, "the cause of the revolution was in danger." Then two representatives came from the regiment of machine gunners. They reported excitement, fear of being cashiered, determination to act. One of the leaders at the conference, Volodarsky, declared that "the party had determined not to act, and the party members in their regiment must submit to that decision." The representatives of the regiment left, protesting. At 4 P. M. the Central Committee met. Telegrams were arriving from the front about the offensive now begun, and the committee feared lest street fighting in Petrograd furnish an excuse to blame the Bolsheviks for its possible failure. It seemed preferable to wait till the offensive was over and their hands freed. It was so decreed. Stalin warned the bureau of the Central Executive Committee of the Soviets of the step taken by the machine-gun regiment, and of its delegates' dispersal among the factories to start a demonstration. Thus the Bolsheviks acted with the majority and in accord with the Soviet's previous decisions. At 5 P. M. the Bolshevist City Conference decided to suspend its labors and to dispatch its delegates throughout the city to restrain the workers. From the beginning, however, the movement was rather one of soldiers than of workers. According to *Pravda*, "Workers were asking: who is summoning us on to the street? No one could give a plain answer."[13] But local feeling had already swept over the Bolsheviks' heads. At the Putilov Factory the Bolshevist workers "expressed dissatisfaction with the Central Committee for its slowness to act." In the Moscow Regiment, "a Bolshevik who spoke against the demonstration was called a 'liquidator' and not allowed to speak." At 7 P. M. the Kseshinsky Palace was approached by two demonstrating detachments. The members of the Bolshevist military organization, Lashevich and Kurayev tried to dissuade them, but met with shouts of "Down with them!" Similar scenes occurred as a demonstration of workers approached the palace.[14] Podvoisky, Sverdlov, Nevsky, and others urged the machine gunners to be satisfied with sending a special delegation to the Soviet demanding that it take power into its own hands, and to return to their barracks. But the "attitude to the speakers was so hostile that many machine gunners, to show their feeling, held their guns cocked."[15] "All efforts of the Military Organization," reported Podvoisky, "were in vain. Evidently there were other forces at work."

What were those mysterious forces? No doubt, the anarchists were carrying on a powerful agitation in the regiment of machine gunners. These were the same elements which had tried to seize Berezin's plant and the Durnovo villa. From it they had been driven by military force, after armed resistance, and several persons were arrested, among them the Kronstadt sailor, Zhelezniak, an anarchist, later famous through his service to the Bolsheviks in dispersing the Constituent Assembly. Among the Kronstadt sailors the rumor of their comrades' arrest and "bloody mistreatment" aroused great excitement. Certain sinister elements now urged them to seek the person responsible for the raid on the Durnovo villa, the Minister of Justice, Pereverzev, and lynch him. If he could not be found, other ministers should be seized as "hostages." Before the building of the Soviet an attempt was made to seize Tseretelli, but he succeeded in escaping. Relying on his popularity, the Minister of Agriculture, Chernov, went out to assuage them; the same sinister elements, with the aid of a group of sailors, seized him and tried to carry him away in an automobile; they were unable to do so because of the dense concourse of people. The Bolshevik, Ryazanov, and the Left-wing Social Revolutionary, Kamkov, who tried to secure Chernov's release, were manhandled. At the demand of the Soviet Trotsky was sent, and obtained Chernov's freedom. Later Trotsky accidentally encountered in prison several of the men who had seized Chernov; he asserts they were ordinary criminals. But in Stalin's report to the Sixth Congress of Bolsheviks the demonstration was painted in idyllic tints, with the remarkable reservation: "Unless we include the escapades of gangs of hooligans and criminals."

Criminal elements alone could not have overcome among the masses all the appeals of the Soviet and even of the Bolsheviks. Later, to facilitate Kornilov's plot, an adventurer, the ataman of the Cossacks, Dutov, and his tools tried to improvise a "Bolshevist" demonstration. Evidently, there was something like this here too. The *Izvestia* of the Soviet, even before the first Bolshevist demonstration, had published a warning: "Ominous rumors have long filled Petrograd of a

Black Hundreds demonstration that is being prepared. In inns, teahouses, markets, talk has been heard of people anxious to set a pogrom for April 23, the name day of the ex-Empress, now under arrest. In public squares and courtyards money has been distributed to more pliable people."[16] Later the Bolsheviks tried to prove that this Black Hundreds element had used the April 21 demonstrations for and against Miliukov for their own provocative purposes.[17] No doubt, German agents, too, were bound to try to provoke and exasperate all internal disturbances and disorders.

In all these demonstrations no small rôle was played by sudden and provocative shots, mysteriously discharged. To them the excited and unorganized mob of soldiers replied by panicky and random salvos. Podvoisky's report shows that even within the ranks of the Bolshevist demonstrators things almost came to a massacre. In his report Stalin praised the discipline of the grenadier regiment, "particularly those battalions which through their organization were closest to us [Bolsheviks]." He relates: "When the machine gunners yielded to provocation and opened fire, the grenadiers declared that they would fire on them unless they stopped."

All this is typical of the movements of the *déclassé* mob, the "*ochlos*": elemental force, violence, excesses, hooligans, criminal elements, provocation—finally mysterious, hidden, directing forces of a very sinister character, difficult to identify, but clearly felt. Two newspapers were then appearing, the *Little Gazette* and the *Living Word*, militant, even insolent, audacious, talented, with purely Bolshevist methods of polemic, cloaking themselves in socialism, but with an undercurrent of passionate nationalism. At first they flattered Kerensky, tempting him to become a revolutionary dictator. Later, they denounced him roundly and urged Admiral Kolchak as "Russia's savior." A kind of Russian "Hitlerism" was trying to make its way, a demagogical, thoroughly false and adventurous "national socialism." Bolshevism (and in part, anarchism) had to compete with it for influence over the rebellious mob, which in its sporadic outbursts could easily overwhelm the capital's proletarian kernel, now psychologically unstable and diluted by the flood of alien elements.

The July movement had taken the Bolsheviks by surprise. Besides, Lenin was away from Petrograd. Distraught, unable to halt the movement, the Bolsheviks now rushed headlong with the torrent of events. First, there was a private conference of the Petrograd Bolshevist Committee, then a joint meeting of the Central Committee, All-City Conference, and deputies from the regiments and wards, and finally a meeting of the workers' section of the Soviet, or, rather, of its Bolshevist part, after the demonstrative withdrawal of the Mensheviks and Social Revolutionaries. All these bodies decided to reopen the question and to lead the movement which now threatened to pass under other leadership. After his return Lenin approved this decision. But in the workers' districts a psychological reaction was already maturing. The soldiers, having rioted without object and fired at random, returned to their barracks depressed. The regiments which had remained neutral—the Semenovsky, Preobrazhensky and Izmailovsky Regiments—went to defend the Soviet. Meanwhile, a composite military unit, commanded by a socialist lieutenant, Mazurenko, was on its way from the front to Petrograd to restore order. The Bolsheviks could only announce that the magnificent Petrograd demonstration had attained its goal, had loudly proclaimed the will of the proletariat and revolutionary army, and therefore the strike was declared at an end, and the soldiers summoned to return to their barracks.

The disorderly course of the strike, its excesses, the wantonly shed blood of bystanders at first seemed to have dealt a tremendous blow to the Bolsheviks' popularity. During July at factory meetings Bolshevist orators were often shouted down. The reorganization of the more turbulent troops was progressing and great hoards of weapons confiscated in Bolshevist districts. The investigation of the conspiracy began. Lenin and Zinoviev hid to avoid arrest and trial.

At that time it would not have been difficult to suppress the Bolshevist organization completely. Nevertheless, the Soviet did not go so far. It did not even expel the Bolsheviks. Why? Because to take such strong steps against the Left while continuing to compromise with the Right, when General Kornilov was beginning his political demonstrations, meant breaking forever with democracy and openly joining the counterrevolution. To disarm the Bolsheviks and their sympathizers completely was possible only for a government which could win the sympathy of the toiling masses by far-reaching social reforms, by a firm policy in the question of war and peace and by creating radically new conditions for nationalities in Russia. But the government was paralyzed by its alliance with the bourgeois nationalists. It had to counterbalance its concessions to them by equal tolerance of Left-wing extremism. In other words it had to be weak on both fronts.

The withdrawal of the four Cadets from the government over the Ukrainian question and Prince Lvov's resignation over agrarian policy seemed to have set the Soviet majority on a firm course. Even Tseretelli and Dan, albeit reluctantly, now had to consider in earnest forming a new government minus the Cadets. Chernov saw no other way out. And far-sighted Cadets like Miliukov saw clearly that "the coalition was a compromise which paralyzed the government from within, as it had previously been paralyzed from without." On July 2 the Cadet Central Committee declared: "A strong and united government can be created either by making it more homogeneous or else by so reorganizing it that all its component elements can decide fundamental matters of state, not by numerical majority, but by mutual agreement, directed to the fulfilment of common national tasks." Only the first "horn of the dilemma" could be considered. The second possibility meant legalizing that very "paralysis" of the government "from within."

Left circles likewise favored "increasing the homogeneity" of the Provisional Government, not to the Right, but to the *Left.* The July events, however, almost destroyed the will to execute this reorganization. To begin it now seemed to many leaders a surrender to the pressure of the turbulent, motley, unstable street. It meant yielding, not to the people, not to the organized workers, but to the rabble of the public square. It meant creating a new prætorian guard to make and unmake governments by fist right and rifle butts. The Soviet was unwilling to offer this unstable support to a new government. It shrank from the thought of a more homogeneous government, to which experience had been leading it. The Soviet was readier to appeal against rebellious, Bolshevized Petrograd to the rest of the country, upon which that Petrograd wished to force its will, at bottom the will of a majority of the disintegrated Petrograd garrison.

Instead of profiting by the Bolshevist failure in July, the majority in the Soviet returned to its point of departure. It began all over again the same old story, trying to reëstablish the hopelessly decayed coalition. Rather, Kerensky had never desisted from that attempt, while the majority in the Soviet now inclined to the tactic of *laissez faire, laissez passer.*

Bolshevism had lost considerable ground by being partially disarmed and deprived of its leaders, who went underground. It forfeited its recent prestige by its "zigzag course" during the July attempt and by its ultimate failure. But its will to fight had not been broken. At best this was a small-scale rehearsal. The experiment was encouraging: despite complete lack of organization, despite the chaos of the movement, it had controlled Petrograd for two days, leaving the government a helpless spectator.

Even for the Bolsheviks, and especially for those who had heard the thunderous "Down with them!" resound in the mob, and seen rifles cocked, a problem arose: if they tried seriously to lead this mob, would they not become its slave rather than its master?

Lenin's great significance for the Bolshevist party was shown in that difficult moment of moral and political decision. To those who were frightened by the adventurousness of such tactics, he opposed his headlong determination, his remarkable will power, and his fixed idea. For him the July days were an unpremeditated crossing of the Rubicon. After hesitating as to whether Lenin and Zinoviev should appear before the investigators and judges or hide, the Bolshevist Central Committee chose the second solution. The path of legality was barred. The path of illegality had to be traveled to its end. A single goal had to be attained: insurrection, overthrow of the Provisional Government, seizure of power.

Lenin realized perfectly that Bolshevism was not so strong in the rest of Russia as in Petrograd and Moscow. But he reckoned that it might be no less effective in the provinces; even there it could set in motion masses of people relatively as great. Everywhere there was plenty of inflammable material. Failure of the Left to utilize that material merely abandoned it to adventurers, to petty local dictators. Or it blazed up of itself and burned out in senseless local conflagrations.

The population was tired of revolutionary storms and eager for strong government. This longing was the key to the appearance of those absurd little republics with absolute authority vested in casual dictators. For Lenin All-Russian power had to be seized from the Left without delay. Otherwise it might be seized from the Right, by the army, with hidden intent to restore monarchy. The ability of reactionary demagogues and of casual individuals to master the ignorant, disorganized mob became in Lenin's hands an argument to compel his Bolsheviks to be even more skilful and reckless demagogues, to excel in simplifying slogans to the level of the most primitive minds, as, for example, in his famous cry of "Plunder the plunderers."

In this process Lenin, of course, did not lose all he had acquired in the school of Marxism. He realized that the mob was unstable, friable, changeable; it was useful as a force, but required a strong and concentrated center. This he sought in the proletariat. Had Russia, like prewar France, had a strong anarchist-syndicalist movement, Lenin would have found what he needed in alliance with it; although Russian anarchism of the capitals was motley and scattered, he would not have hesitated at an alliance between the "Red Guard" of the Bolsheviks and the "Black Guard" of the more demagogical anarchists. But Russian anarchism had no influence among the trade-unions. The Mensheviks dominated them, and had the support of the Social Revolutionaries.

Lenin's inventive mind found a solution even here. Against the trade-unions he started the Factory Committee movement. It was supported by the unskilled workers, and urged direct, immediate, and decentralized control of production by the workers. The older Bolshevist leaders like Ryazanov were horror stricken: for them the Factory Committees were merely to serve as local organs of the trade-unions; their emancipation from the trade-unions seemed an open, unpardonable disorganization of the unions. Lenin was unconcerned. He needed to break down the Mensheviks' trade-union strongholds. "The insurrection of the Factory Committees" against the central trade-union bodies was to him a magnificent idea. Later, after the destruction of Menshevism, the trade-union central bodies could be seized; then, with firm hand, everything could be reversed, and the Factory Committees subjected to the trade-unions. Lenin was, above all, a skilful tactician. He dealt with trade-union principles as he saw fit, in accord with his immediate advantage. The idea was already forming in his mind that an All-Russian Congress of Factory Committees should be convoked and made the basis for national economic life after the Bolshevist seizure of power. As a constructive idea for the future, this was, like most of Lenin's ideas, empty of real content. As a tactical maneuver with "pragmatic" value for the moment, it was magnificent. It aroused ambition. It strengthened the collective "organized patriotism" of the pioneers of the Factory Committee movement. It threatened to uproot the Menshevist trade-unions by destroying their direct hold on the factory.

The first Conference of Factory Committees, which opened on May 30, received little attention from the Mensheviks and Social Revolutionaries. This was due to their rejection of the very idea of making this movement "self-sufficient." The Bolsheviks on the other hand put up several of their strongest men, with Lenin, Sverdlov and Zinoviev. Probably the greatest service to the Bolsheviks was a speech by the Minister of Labor, Skobelev. He took an officially optimistic tone and asserted, contrary to fact, that "at present there is no occasion to speak of unemployment"; where it existed, "it is a result of uneven distribution in the labor supply." The rest of his speech developed the idea that "we are in the bourgeois stage of the revolution's development"; it "would not be aided" by transferring the factories to the workers; "Russian capitalism was too young" and military expenditures too great for its resources to suffice for that.[18] This was all to the Bolsheviks' advantage. Zinoviev's resolution was adopted by 297 to 21, with 44 abstentions. Bolshevism had taken a new and important step in wooing the mass of workers from Menshevism.

Lenin realized perfectly that no matter how much he advertised the Factory Committees, with their slogan of state control of capital by labor from below, as "a new form of the labor movement," as a purely Russian and uniquely revolutionary form, still their significance was doubtful. For him the main thing was the Bolshevist party itself, reorganized as an ultracentralized party, under military discipline—not a democratic self-governing party, open to all, on the Western European style, but rather like a medieval order of "knightly monks." This was necessary not only to win the fight for power but still more to hold and use that power.

The July days had shown that the coalition government, "paralyzed from within," was no stronger than the preceding government of the liberal bourgeoisie, which had been "paralyzed from without." Petrograd could be mastered even by a completely unorganized mob. Lenin had to dispel the doubts of his own followers: if they seized power, "could the Bolsheviks hold it?" He gave a brief and radical answer.

> After the 1905 Revolution Russia was governed by 130,000 landowners; it was governed with endless violence against 150,000,000 people, by subjecting the tremendous majority to prison-like labor and semistarvation.
>
> Russia, they say, cannot be governed by the 240,000 members of the Bolshevist party, cannot be governed in the interest of the poor against the rich. These 240,000 now have on their side at least 1,000,000 votes among the adult population; such a proportion to party membership is set by European and Russian experience; for example, in the August elections to the Petrograd Duma. Thus we already have a government apparatus of 1,000,000 people, devoted to socialist government.

That was bold. To make his own party, with its immediate periphery, the direct apparatus to administer the country—such a plan had no precedent in history, except perhaps the Jesuit communist government in Paraguay.

Yes, that was bold, insolent, yet practical, even prosaic. Russia, for centuries an absolutist régime, was attempting to become a modern democracy of the European type, but one which would solve the social problem in the spirit of the most advanced ideals of the century. It was attempting this, shut in by the fiery ring of war, while rapid economic breakdown was causing outbursts among the ignorant, discontented, systematically pauperized population.

Democrats like Kerensky, people "on a small scale," were

in despair and exclaimed pathetically: "Who are you, a free people, or formless mobs of rebellious slaves?"

The captains of Russian industry had reluctantly accepted political democracy, but were horrified at the idea that it might be supplemented by "industrial democracy," that the rights of property and capital might be subordinated to the rights of labor. They were ready to flee abroad with their capital or support anyone who, with a strong hand, would "stop the revolution."

Strong-willed generals, like Kornilov, in response to this "social command," reached for power, camouflaging their old-régime essence by solemn promises to lead Russia "through victory over the foreign foe to the Constituent Assembly."

The majority parties in the Soviet, united in their ambition to expand democracy, both political and economic, disagreed hopelessly in their estimate of the possible. Faced by tumultuous, elemental force, they feared that too great daring might turn against them the country's educated upper strata, which could not abandon censitary Russia and support the revolutionary government.

Warnings that this excessive caution was the greatest risk in the face of an aroused country, that the irresolution of labor democracy in carrying through its *own* program, and its constant reluctance to abandon fruitless and empty alliances and compromises would most effectively disillusion the masses and throw them into the embraces of Bolshevism, were "like a voice crying in the wilderness."

At one blow the Bolshevist party had greatly simplified its task. To a country which had lived under absolutism for centuries, it did not offer rebirth and reëducation into its opposite, democracy. Instead, it offered to let it come under the rule of a new, beneficent, enlightened absolutism, friendly to the workers, and under its leadership to complete the "revolution from above." It offered economic equality and general prosperity at the price of an illusory freedom, alienated to a dictatorial government under the high sounding title of the "dictatorship of the proletariat."

The lure of these slogans, contrasted with the permanent fruitlessness of the Provisional Government, predetermined the victory of Bolshevism.

EPILOGUE

THE SPIRIT OF THE RUSSIAN REVOLUTION

THE spirit of the Russian Revolution is the spirit of Maximalism which has often been called the root of all evil, defeating all efforts at sound reconstruction. Its inspirations and instigators have been sought. It has been identified with Bolshevism. Or the converse: Bolshevism has been described as the *reductio ad absurdum* of the spirit of the Russian Revolution and of the Russian intelligentsia.

But there was another Maximalism: the Maximalism of Russian counterrevolution, a *Bolshevism of the Right*. It was no less demanding, no less entranced with its bright dream, but it turned to the past, not to the future.

These are two faces of the Maximalism of Russian life and history.

Where extreme historical backwardness persists, where centuries have heaped up unsolved problems, nature, which supposedly makes no leaps, often has but one means of movement, the most reckless *salto mortale*.

Irresistible repulsion to the past makes men hack in two the Gordian knots of political and economic life even when they might simply be untied.

This is our strength, and our weakness. Strength because in the sphere of the spirit, in the sphere of pure thought there is no place for compromise. Minds and hearts can be moved only by an idea which marches fearlessly to its logical conclusion. Weakness, because in practical application the design alone is nothing, just as the architect's sketch is nothing without a knowledge of the environment, soil, quality of materials, total capital, and labor resources available.

The spiritual history of the Russian intelligentsia teems with unreconciled contradictions. The intelligentsia were often reproached for breaking with the country's ancient historical traditions, for having no "spiritual fatherland." They were accused of egotistic self-sufficiency, bordering on an insanity of pride.

There is some truth in this charge. The Russian intelligentsia did experience most intensely a complete spiritual rupture with the older cultivated group. The older Russian culture was one of the nobility. When it came into touch with the intellectual life of the West, it responded to all its currents, even its most advanced tendencies [which were far ahead of the time in the West and even more so in Russia]. Russia of the nobility produced Pushkin and Lermontov, Turgenev and Leo Tolstoy, Alexander Herzen and Michael Bakunin. It was the nobility, even the titled aristocracy, which furnished the precursors of the revolution, the Decembrists.

But in its boldest moments the nobility never cut the cord which bound even its vanguard to the social class which gave it birth. There long remained a slender spiritual bond which made reconciliation seem possible even after the most bitter conflicts. The appearance of a new plebeian class of intelligentsia marked the irrevocable separation "to opposite sides of the barricade." The period of revolutionary Populism completed this separation.

Socialism became for the Populists a lay religion. But every religious wave is inevitably Maximalist during its rise. In the name of austere, æsthetically revolutionary plebeianism Pisarev repudiated Pushkin's Epicurean poetry as beautiful but superfluous. Because of the upper-class subjects of his novels, Pisarev's followers denounced the future apostle of the simple life, Leo Tolstoy.

To the spiritual children of the older culture the new intelligentsia were apostles of pure destruction.

Their typical characteristic was once called "Nihilism," although it was not a Russian but a German, Max Stirner, who applied its broadest formula to the movement:

Ich habe mein' Sach' auf Nichts gestellt,
Und mir gehört die ganze Welt.

And the theory of the "permanent revolution" was created, not by a Russian, but a Frenchman, Auguste Blanqui. But only in Russia could it survive till our day. Only in Russia could revolutionary thought accept nothing less, even when disciplined by the prosaic economics of the Marxist school.

Across these teachings falls the mighty shadow of Michael Bakunin. When he proclaimed that the spirit of destruction was the creative spirit, when he said that the organization of revolution was a contradiction in terms, for it deadened and killed the very soul of revolution, the enthusiasm of free annihilation of the old and free assertion of the new; when he called on people to "trust the eternal Spirit, which destroys all only because it holds impenetrably in itself the eternally active spring of life and creativeness," the obsession of freedom spoke in him. Freedom in capitals, Freedom the absolute, which arises only in a country of absolutism, the negation of freedom.

In this absolutism the Russian intelligentsia and the Russian Revolution were profoundly national. The Maximalism of the intelligentsia was flesh of the flesh and bone of the bone with the people's Maximalism.

The history of rough-hewn popular thought, long shackled by the iron bonds of religious forms, the history of religious free thought and sectarianism among the common people, furnish tragic examples of "audacity," rivaling those of the intelligentsia.

The people, the common people, transformed the comedy of the church schism over the two-finger or three-finger sign of the cross and the writing of "Jesus" or "Isus" into an heroic epic. Under the icy crust of Old Russia's revolt against Peter's reforms there boiled up a popular rebellion against the growing burdens imposed by the reforged, aggressive state. In Russian history there was inscribed a chapter of mass searchings for "wild freedom" beyond the protective barrier of primeval forests and swamps, in the "retreats" of the dissenters.

Popular sectarianism in the 1870's and 1880's produced a sect of spontaneous religious anarchists and individualists, called "Not Ours." They pronounced all bases of modern life "alien," "not ours": family, state, school, court, taxes, property. They renounced them in word and deed. They refused all contact, however remote or superficial, with that discarded world. No matter what persecutions menaced them, they regarded as their most sacred duty the daily, incessant preaching of their faith, a demonstrative contempt for everything "not ours," a passive, but unyielding nonobedience to its requirements, even in insignificant details.

At the dawn of the present century popular sectarianism in the Urals gave birth to a new sect, the "Jehovists." Contrary to the "Not Ours," the Jehovists urged active resistance. For them the entire world was divided into two camps, Jehovists and Satanists, the Russian paraphrase of the eternal struggle between Ormuzd and Ahriman. The clergy of the state church, the officials of civil and military government, the possessors of land and money, were all "Satanists" and must be destroyed. Dynamite for mining purposes was unhesitatingly used by the Jehovists against the pillars of the modern state and church.

Russian Dukhobors brought this inexorable thirst for spiritual revolt even to peaceful Canada. The new sect of "Sons of Freedom" confronted the astonished Canadian state with its Maximalist "all or nothing": "either let us live according to the inner tenet of our hearts, or take from us everything, and leave us naked on the naked earth."

In "questions of this earth" it was the same as in "questions of heaven." It was no accident that during the World War the Russian revolutionaries echoed so loudly the summons to break with the war and to withdraw to the Aventine hill of Zimmerwald and Kienthal; no wonder the Tolstoyan idea of nonresistance to evil was developed with such implacable logic in Russia. Naturally, its opposite also existed in Russia: terrorism as a system, as an organized method of struggle against autocracy. Moral repulsion, unconquerable hate for every kind of violence were expressed in a sharply contradictory form—the struggle by revolver and bomb. The psychology of the revolutionary terrorist was a consecration enthusiastically accepted for the people's sake, poisoned with the consciousness that what is politically imperative is morally unjustifiable: no person, no state has the right to take what it cannot restore—life. It was no accident that Russia gave the world three of its greatest anarchists: the religious anarchist, Leo Tolstoy, the philosophical anarchist, Peter Kropotkin, and the political anarchist, Michael Bakunin.

Is it surprising if all possible forms of Maximalism cropped out in the revolution? There was the pacifist Maximalism of the soldier, eager to thrust his bayonet into the ground and embrace his late enemy. There was proletarian Maximalism, which demanded that its Soviets stop sparing the bourgeois—"Let there be no more bourgeoisie." And nationalist Maximalism, ready, no matter what the consequences, to break up Russia, only yesterday the "prison house of peoples." There was the naïve agrarian Maximalism of the muzhik, ready in a homely way, without waiting for a complicated government land reform, to divide up the landlords' fields among the neighboring villages and households. And each of these Maximalisms was opposed by a corresponding "counter-Maximalism," on the other side of the barricade.

All Russian history is marked by two curves of development. The first is the curve of the state's defensive enlargement. Open to migration and invasion by successive nomad hordes from the East and to the pressure of more civilized and politically organized peoples to the West, caught between civilization and barbarism, Russia was compelled to force the development of her own statehood in spite of her inward barbarism. The burden of her governmental "superstructure" was too heavy for her primitive economic and social foundation. Since it had not grown organically from below through the development of social bonds among the population itself, Russian statehood seemed to the people a network cast over the country from above, so completely "external" to the people that folk tradition embodied this estrangement between state and people in the myth of the summoning of the Varangians. Historical criticism later questioned this origin of Russian statehood, but even if it were a mere legend, it would be all the more symptomatic of an ancient dualism between state and people in Russian history.

The second tendency is the growth of Russian settlement on the Eastern European plain. The direct routes to Siberia and Central Asia first opened for the East the thoroughfare across Russia to the West, but with the strengthening of Russia's defensive power they unlocked her road to the East.

Historians define Russia's past as a "history of colonization." But that colonization was provoked not so much by scarcity of land as by government pressure. The unbearable burden of serfdom drove the people along the line of least resistance to the north and east. There they found a short breathing spell and could straighten their backs bowed by forced labor. But step by step the state followed the "Russian land wanderers" like an ineluctable black shadow, and they tried vainly to escape this, their own shadow. The irrepressible quest for liberty rolled on to the mountain ranges of Tibet and Mongolia, to the great Chinese Wall and the shores of the Pacific. It could go no farther. It then turned upon itself and at last swept away the walls of absolutism and the partitions of the nobles' landed property. The "black partition" is bound up with the most profound traits of Russian history.

In Central and Western Europe the growing density of population led slowly but surely to a concentration of human life in a given area. The peasant learned to put into the same area an increasing expenditure of labor and capital. The population capacity of the territory grew correspondingly. The development of industry and urban life contributed most powerfully to the tendency by creating a demand for the most valuable products of the soil.

Russia, on the other hand, remained a country of extensive agriculture.

When people spoke of the Russian state as a colossus on clay feet, consciously or unconsciously they meant that the grandiose character of Russia's state superstructure was in startling contradiction to its primitive economic base.

The cost of maintaining that superstructure was disproportionate to the national income.[1] The burden of taxation, added to every kind of private exploitation, did not permit capital accumulation in their peasant economy, and without it there could be no transition to higher organization and technique. Escape through colonization in the East intensified the trend toward extensive rather than intensive agriculture. The enormous open areas were the safety canals through which the chief increase in population splashed away. But for this the state would long before have had to reflect that a decisive transition must be made to more intensive farming and therefore it was impossible always to take from the village without compensating it in any way for the damage thus done to its economy.

Realization of the burden imposed on the stagnant village by the state superstructure, and the second superstructure—the hothouse capitalist industry nursed by the government—and fear lest the peasantry grasp this situation and draw dangerous political conclusions, led the state intentionally to keep the village ignorant, illiterate, and culturally backward, with a single window in its dark kingdom of pitiless toil, the saloon, which, as a state liquor monopoly, was merely an additional means for extracting every extra penny from the muzhik's pocket.

For the village every path to a higher level of agriculture

was definitely closed. Progressive exhaustion of the soil in many of the original black-soil provinces turned the subsistence allotment into a ruin allotment.

The peasant's customary love for his fields was crushed in a feeling of hopelessness. He did not cease loving the land and striving for it with all his soul. But the land which he adored was not his own meager allotment. The magnet was the nobles' land, which, within the memory of his fathers and grandfathers, had slipped from his grasp, and been left to the master at the abolition of serfdom. That injustice was felt almost physically by the peasantry. "We belong to you, but the land belongs to us," the peasants said to the nobles. The village refused to separate property in land from the right to the peasants' labor; they had existed in an indissoluble unity under serfdom and must be buried together.

Since the peasants owned communal lands, which they redistributed among individual households at definite intervals, either in accord with the number of adult workers or of mouths in the family, the idea of remedying the injury inflicted by the nobles' unjust possession gradually became more and more definite. The peasants demanded a redistribution of the land. The entire country must be transformed into one great all-Russian land community with equal labor rights to the land for those alone who watered the land with their sweat.

To the obsession of liberty was added the obsession of a leveling down of landed property. A better future for the peasant was not pictured as the result of technical development and increased productivity. The problem of productivity was completely overshadowed by that of the equal distribution of the land. From its solution miracles were expected; people regarded it as a magical means for achieving the peasant's happiness and prosperity.

Revolution conquered the village with the double slogan of "Land and Liberty." This slogan in itself was not socialistic. It was because only a socialist party (the party of Social Revolutionaries) resolutely propagated it that it became the mistress of the thoughts and hopes of the village.

It was not merely undernourishment, poverty, the beggarly satisfaction of its needs that stirred the village to consciousness. Need is highly relative. Scantiness of needs corresponds to low cultural level. The happiness of the savage lies in the absence of needs. The true mobile force in social movements is not so much an unsatisfactory standard of living, not so much direct exploitation, as it is the greatness of social contrasts which strikes the imagination of the masses. The atmosphere of revolution was created less by any rational realization of material, economic class interest, than by an irrational feeling that the situation was intolerable. To the masses revolution seemed the right hand of an impersonal, lay god, the god of vengeance and justice, hurling thunder and lightning on the heads of mankind's enemies here on earth, leading the downtrodden and injured into paradise and casting the oppressors and outragers into fiery Gehenna.

One can understand the feeling of isolation and helplessness which paralyzed the landowners.

The enormous Eurasian prairie was not a plain in the geographical sense only. Its class structure was peculiar; it was a social prairie.

> Instead of a lofty, narrow, many-storied, complicated class structure, in the Western European style, we find a peculiar pyramid with a low, broad, over-wide base of the peasantry, above it weak layers of the middle and upper classes, and the lofty and burdensome cupola of absolutism at the summit.*

The collapse of that cupola was bound to bring down the middle layers. The "social prairie" threatened to swallow up almost everything that had succeeded in rising above it. During the revolution there was a time when even the indus-

* K. Kocharovsky.

trial proletariat, which had risen least above the social prairie of agrarian Russia, began to flee from the silent, paralyzed factories to be absorbed by the village, to turn peasant again.

Across the plains blizzards and storms are free to move and rage.

The storm of revolution revealed the genuine "color and aroma" of the people's soul, in its brilliant strength and opaque weakness, with all the best features of the national character, and all the savage passions and vices implanted by its history.

Idealizers of the revolution see only the first half of this truth. The heralds of revolutionary Maximalism paid joyful reverence to the irrational factor in the revolution, "that unknown which no bookkeeper can count, no political apothecary weigh, no political chemist analyze." Revolution enticed them by its play of seething passions, which turns the wise men of this world into madmen and makes madness the sovereign of the spirit. These romantics sensed in the people's spirit the fermentation, the breathing of the "genius of revolution." It was enough to bring the crowd to a state of "revolutionary ecstasy," spread by mass contagion, and all else would take care of itself. A dangerous conception, from which a "treacherous declivity" leads to unbridled demagogy.

During the first Russian Revolution, in 1905, the writings and speeches of the Maximalists described eloquently how, in an atmosphere of revolution, the impressionability of the masses increases, how new feelings and impulses spread in them with epidemic force, how faith in their own strength, unaccustomed and all the more intoxicating, driving them on to all audacities, is born in them. "*De l'audace, encore de l'audace, toujours de l'audace*"—Danton's old slogan is always resurrected during the convulsive shudders of the national organism. Those who are gripped by it are in their way right. The masses, thrown out of the routine of everyday existence, shaken by the thunder of events, eagerly drink in the evangel of the new teaching. The fewer its refinements and reservations, the simpler, the more categorical, the more straightforward it is, the more eagerly they drink. This is one of the secrets of the success of Bolshevism. The masses want their obscurely realized interests, their vague feelings and yearnings suddenly presented to them in well-rounded formulæ, with the halo of an authoritative "scientific" character, half understood but impressive. They suddenly believe in these formulæ fanatically, hypnotically. This is an enormous advantage for achieving the immediate aims of the revolution. But what aims? Naturally, its negative ones. However, revolution has positive aims. And those characteristics of the masses which are needed for their achievement do not grow from the revolutionary hurricane.

The creative forces, habits of organization, capacity for economic self-administration, for responsible leadership in production, for economic construction, are not essential for a victorious explosion. They are vital if the revolution is to be utilized to the full. They are developed in "organic," not in "critical" moments of history. They are a slowly accumulating capital. "Intensity," "receptivity," "impressionability," "electric charges of will power," have very little influence here, and that not always positive. When the working class rises to a comprehension of its special historic "mission," it builds its collective life quite differently. Its class organizations are not only its apparatus of defense and attack, its fortified camp, its trenches and bastions. No, it sees in them something greater: the embryo of a new economic order. Around its class organizations there grow up all kinds of institutions, in which a new way of life, a new working-class law, a new working-class culture are elaborated. This is the significance of the new, constructive tendency in the working-class movement, which demands for tasks of social construction priority over destructive ones.

In Russia the embryo of the new order had not matured. The revulsion against the old order, however, was tremendous.

This was due to powerful factors in Russia's history.

By the time Russia approached her revolution, most European countries had passed through a series of revolutions. They had varied in content, in historic function. Most of them had been, as it were, revolutions with a single element: revolution against the Church, or Reformation; peasant, agrarian, antifeudal revolution, such as Wat Tyler's rebellion in England, the *Jacqueries* in France, the Peasants' War in Germany, the Pugachev rebellion in Russia; the bourgeois, antifeudal revolution of the Third Estate; democratic revolution, bringing political emancipation from absolutism; revolution of national emancipation; antibourgeois, anticapitalist revolution, such as the insurrection of the Paris proletariat of June, 1848, or that of the Paris Commune.

The Great French Revolution stands out as a revolution universal in type, at once antimonarchic, anticlerical, antifeudal, bourgeois, and peasant agrarian, with the embryo of proletarian revolt expressed in Babeuf's Conspiracy of Equals.

This universal character is stamped in still greater degree on the Great Russian Revolution.

Potential revolutionary forces and passions, denied an outlet in partial revolutionary achievement, were piled on one another. All the unsolved problems were heaped up, twisted and confused, together with all forms of evil, disaster, oppression, and exploitation.

The country's prerevolutionary history ended as it had begun, with the maximal conflict between liberty and authority. The government took under its wing every privilege and monopoly. Under the flag of liberty was grouped everything ignored, downtrodden, oppressed, exploited.

This maximal concentration of directly antagonistic forces nourished and brought to a state of paroxysm the two Maximalisms of absolutely opposite social and political feeling: the Maximalism of the Right and the Maximalism of the Left.

They grew in a soil made ready by all preceding history. They completed its work.

NOTES

CHAPTER ONE

1. *Krasnyĭ Arkhiv* (1923), Vol. II.
2. S. I. Witte, *Vospominania,* I, 245.
3. *Krasnyĭ Arkhiv,* XXXXVIIII, 102.
4. Lloyd George, *War Memories,* III, 469.

CHAPTER TWO

1. I. V. Semennikov, *Romanovy i germanskie vliyania, 1914–1917* (1929).
2. The text of this proclamation, referred to by Paléologue, was found in the personal papers of the late Tsar and reproduced in Semennikov, *op. cit.,* pp. 37–38.
3. A. I. Denikin, *Ocherki russkoĭ smuty,* Vol. I, Pt. 1, p. 17.
4. Semennikov, *Politika Romanovykh nakanune revoliutsii* (1927) pp. 12-19.
5. Cf. Durnovo's reactionary-pacifist memorandum, *Byloye,* No. 19 (1922), 161–176.
6. B. Lemke, *Dvesti shestdesyat dneĭ v tsarskoĭ Stavke* (Petrograd, 1920).

CHAPTER THREE

1. M. V. Rodzianko, "Gosudarstvennaya Duma i fevral'skaya revoliutsia," *Arkhiv Russkoĭ Revoliutsii,* VI, 13–14.
2. V. Shulgin, *Dni* (Belgrade, 1925), pp. 133–134.
3. Report of the director of the Moscow department of the secret police, August 1, 1916, *Sbornik Politseĭskikh Dokumentov,* Tsentroarkhiv, pp. 81, 82, 83.
4. *Ibid.,* pp. 62–63.
5. *Ibid.,* p. 76.
6. *Ibid.,* pp. 147–148. The "summaries" and "reports" of the *gendarmerie* and secret Okhrana, in general, are extremely one-sided. Where they found repulsion to revolution among persons "observed" and "suspected," their evidence has undoubted value.
7. "Zapiska," *Arkhiv Russkoĭ Revoliutsii,* V, 339.
8. The protocol notes of the secret meetings of the Council of Ministers of July 16 to Sept. 2, 1915, made by the vice director of the secretariat, Yakhontov, *Arkhiv Russkoĭ Revoliutsii,* XVIII, 114–115.
9. *Ibid.,* pp. 59, 63, 74, 77, 91.
10. Avdeyev, *Revoliutsia 1917 g. Khronika sobytĭi,* I (Moscow, 1923), 18, 23, 25.
11. *Sbornik,* Tsentroarkhiv, p. 186.
12. Shulgin, *op. cit.,* p. 148.
13. P. N. Miliukov, *Istoria vtoroĭ russkoĭ revoliutsii,* Vol. I, Pt. 1, pp. 35–36.

14. A. Blok, "Poslednie dni starogo rezhima," *Arkhiv Russkoĭ Revoliutsii,* IV, 22.
15. Denikin, *Ocherki russkoĭ smuty,* Vol. I, Pt. 1, pp. 37–39.

CHAPTER FOUR

1. Shulgin, *Dni,* pp. 158, 163, 184.
2. N. Sukhanov, *Zapiski o revoliutsii,* I, 244.
3. Y. V. Lomonosov, *Vospominania o martovskoĭ revoliutsii 1917 goda* (Stockholm-Berlin, 1921), p. 56.
4. "Semeĭnaya perepiska Romanovykh," *Krasnyĭ Arkhiv,* IV (1925), 215–220.
5. Shulgin, *op. cit.,* p. 271.
6. Denikin, *Ocherki,* Vol. I, Pt. 1, p. 54.
7. Sukhanov, *op. cit.,* I, 278–279.
8. Miliukov, *Istoria,* Vol. I, Pt. 1, p. 52.
9. *Ibid.,* p. 54.
10. Shulgin, *op. cit.,* pp. 297–298.
11. Rodzianko, *Gosudarstvennaya Duma i fevral'skaya revoliutsia,* pp. 61–62.
12. Shulgin, *op. cit.,* p. 305.
13. Lomonosov, *op. cit.,* p. 63.

CHAPTER FIVE

1. *Sbornik,* Tsentroarkhiv, pp. 130–131.
2. Sukhanov, *Zapiski o revoliutsii,* I, 19.
3. *Ibid.,* II, 279.
4. G. Shvittau, *Revoliutsia i narodnoye hozyaĭstvo.*
5. Sukhanov, *op. cit.,* II, 278; the Marinsky Palace was the residence of the Provisional Government.

CHAPTER SIX

1. See the systematic development of this conception, in V. M. Chernov, *Konstruktivnyĭ Sotsialism* (Prague, 1925), Vol. I.
2. This theory received a final and more profound formulation in Trotsky's pamphlet, *Permanentnaya revoliutsia.*
3. Shulgin, *Dni,* p. 147.
4. Sukhanov, *Zapiski o revoliutsii,* I, 234, 235, 261.
5. Shulgin, *op. cit.,* p. 124.
6. Report of three lectures by Kerensky, published in the periodical, *Rodina,* which is close to him politically, in No. 5, reported by I. N. Kovarsky, his intimate.
7. Miliukov, *Istoria,* Vol. I, Bk. 1, pp. 91–92.
8. Report published in the periodical, *Dni,* edited by Kerensky, No. 118 (December 7, 1930), 9.

CHAPTER SEVEN

1. Article by V. Storozhev, "Pravovye osnovy osobogo soveshchaniya," in No. 27 (August 30).

2. Sukhanov, *Zapiski o revoliutsii,* II, 306–307.

CHAPTER EIGHT

1. *1917 g. v derevne,* Gosizdat, p. 301.

2. Newspaper, *Zemlya i Volya,* No. 3, 1917.

3. *1917 g. v derevne,* p. 40.

4. *Ibid.,* p. 64.

CHAPTER NINE

1. A. S. Lukomsky, *Vospominania,* I, 53. General Y. N. Danilov is franker: "In beginning mobilization disorders among the conscripts swept like a broad wave through a number of places in Russia . . . To suppress them strong measures had to be taken, including armed force." (*Rossia v mirovoĭ voĭne,* 1924, p. 111.) "Patriotic demonstrations and outbursts of enthusiasm evidently formed merely a cheap façade . . . The Russian people was unprepared for war. Its chief mass, the peasantry, scarcely realized why they were being summoned to war . . . They went because they were accustomed to do everything the government demanded: patiently, but passively they bore their cross." (*Ibid.,* p. 112.)

2. N. Maximov, "V gody voĭny," *Letopis' revoliutsii,* I, 243–246.

3. V. B. Stankevich, *Vospominania, 1914–1919 gg.* (Berlin), p. 18.

4. Danilov, *op. cit.*

5. N. N. Golovin, *Iz istorii kampanii 1914 g. na russkom fronte,* pp. 141, 143, 152, 155, 378.

6. K. Hesse, *Der Feldherr-Psychologos; Der grosse Krieg, 1914–1918,* herausgegeben von M. Schwarte; General François, *Marneschlacht und Tannenberg.*

7. Golovin, *op. cit.,* p. 79.

8. *Ibid.,* pp. 33, 36–37.

9. *Ibid.,* pp. 207, 215, 226, and 255.

10. Lukomsky, *op. cit.,* I, 36, 37, 58, 84.

11. *Ibid.,* I, 106.

12. The figures have been borrowed from the book of General A. Verkhovsky, *Rossia na Golgofe.*

13. Denikin, *Ocherki,* Vol. I, Pt. 1, p. 30.

14. Verkhovsky, *op. cit.,* p. 36. General Danilov in *Rossia v mirovoĭ voĭne* likewise remarks how unjust it would be to blame the soldiers because "the technical superiority of the enemy naturally struck the imagination of our troops and depressed the buoyance of their spirits."

15. M. V. Rodzianko, "Krushenie imperii, zapiski," *Arkhiv Russkoĭ Revoliutsii.*

16. Verkhovsky, *op. cit.,* p. 60.

CHAPTER TEN

1. Miliukov, *Istoria vtoroĭ russkoĭ revoliutsii,* I, 73.
2. "Zemel'noĭ vopros v deyatel'nosti Vremennogo Pravitel'stva," *Zapiski Instituta Izucheniya Rossii,* II, 346.
3. A. V. Peshekhonov, "O predotvrashchenii anarkhii v sfere zemel'nykh otnosheniĭ," *Delo Naroda,* March 23, 1917.
4. *Sel'skiĭ Vestnik,* March 3, 1917.
5. *Nash golos,* paper of the Samara organization of the Russian Social Democratic Workers' party, June 2.
6. Miliukov, *op. cit.,* Vol. I, Pt. 1, p. 65.

CHAPTER ELEVEN

1. Miliukov, *Istoria,* Vol. I, Pt. 1, p. 84. How Miliukov sometimes "emphasized pacifist aims" is illustrated by his newspaper interview of March 22, in which he attacked "peace without annexations" as a "German formula which people are trying to palm off on the international Socialists."
2. *Ibid.,* I, 86.
3. *Ibid.,* I, 87.
4. S. I. Shidlovsky, *Vospominania,* II, 129.
5. Miliukov, *op. cit.,* Vol. I, Pt. 2, p. 112.

CHAPTER TWELVE

1. V. A. Auerbach, "Revoliutsionnoye Obshchestvo po lichnym vospominaniam," *Arkhiv Russkoĭ Revoliutsii,* XIV, 13–14.
2. *Rabochee dvizhenie v 1917 g.,* Gosizdat, 1926.
3. A. Pankratova, *Fabzavkomy Rossii,* Glavpolitprosvet, 1923, p. 202.
4. *Arkhiv Russkoĭ Revoliutsii,* XVIII, 66.
5. Auerbach, "Revoliutsionnoye Obshchestvo po lichnym vospominaniam," *Arkhiv Russkoĭ Revoliutsii,* XIV, 34–35.

CHAPTER THIRTEEN

1. See *Trudy vtoroĭ sessii Glavnago Zemel'nago Komiteta* (Petrograd, 1917).
2. L. Lutokhin, "Zemel'nyĭ vopros v deyatel'nosti Vremennago Pravitel'stva," *Zapiski Instituta Izucheniya Rossii,* II, 355.
3. A. Alaverdova, "Ocherk agrarnoĭ politiki Vremennago Pravitel'stva," *Sotsialisticheskoye Hozyaĭstvo,* II, 163, 1925.
4. Telegram from Balashovsky District Land Committee (Archives of the Provisional Government).
5. See his articles in the Paris *Zhizn'* and Geneva *Mysl',* collected in *Deĭstvitel'nye i mnimye porazhentsy.*
6. Lutokhin, *op. cit.,* II, 360.
7. *Ibid.,* p. 361.
8. V. I. Lenin, "A New Deception of the Peasants by the Social Revolu-

tionary Party," *Collected Works* (New York, 1932), Vol. XXI, Bk. II, p. 141.

9. Z. S. Katzenellenbaum, "Finansovaya storona zemel'noĭ reformy," *Russkie Vedomosti*, Nos. 123 and 130, 1917.

10. *1917 g. v derevne*, pp. 193–194.

11. From materials of the Ministry of Agriculture, first published in the newspaper, *Delo Naroda*, in August, 1917.

12. Newspaper, *Zemlya i Volya*, 1917, October 5; *ibid.*, April 14.

13. *Krasnyĭ Arkhiv*, XIV, 205.

14. Shidlovsky, *Vospominania*, II, 122–123.

15. *1917 g. v derevne*, pp. 70–71.

16. *Ibid.*, p. 185.

17. *Ibid.*, p. 174.

CHAPTER FOURTEEN

1. *1917 g. na Kievshchine, Khronika sobytiĭ*, ed. V. Manilov, pub. Kievskiĭ Istpart, p. 26.

2. V. Maklakov, "Iz proshlago," *Sovremennye Zapiski*, XLIV, 442.

CHAPTER FIFTEEN

1. K. D. Nabokov, *Ispytania diplomata* (Stockholm, 1921), pp. 98–99.

2. Miliukov, *Istoria*, Vol. I, Pt. 1, p. 178.

3. Conversation with Buchanan, reported by Carlotta to Sonnino, *Krasnyĭ Arkhiv*, V (XXIV), 155–156.

4. Miliukov, *op. cit.*, Vol. I, Pt. 1, p. 167.

5. *Third Congress of the Party of Social Revolutionaries*, stenographic report (Petrograd, 1917), p. 194.

6. Stankevich, *Vospominania*, p. 146.

7. Denikin, *Ocherki*, Vol. I, Pt. 2, p. 160.

8. *Delo Kornilova*, p. 15.

9. Stankevich *op. cit.*, p. 160.

10. Lukomsky, *Vospominania*, I, 225.

CHAPTER SIXTEEN

1. Denikin, *Ocherki*, Vol. I, Pt. 1, pp. 73, 77.

2. Denikin, *op. cit.*, Vol. I, Pt. 1, pp. 11, 15–16.

3. Stankevich, *Vospominania, 1914–1919 gg.*, pp. 178, 182.

CHAPTER SEVENTEEN

1. A. I. Verkhovsky, *Rossia na Golgofe*, p. 108.

2. Stankevich, *Vospominania*, p. 224.

3. Denikin, *Ocherki*, Vol. I, Pt. 1, p. 77; Vol. I, Pt. 2, pp. 189–190.

4. B. V. Savinkov, *K delu Kornilova* (Paris, 1919), p. 5.

5. A. Kerensky, "Iz vospominaniĭ," *Sovremennye Zapiski*, XXXIX, 232.

6. Denikin, *op. cit.,* Vol. I, Pt. 2, p. 192.

7. Brusilov, *Moi vospominania,* p. 215; Denikin, *op. cit.,* Vol. I, Pt. 1, p. 174; Lukomsky, "Iz vospominanii," *Arkhiv Russkoĭ Revoliutsii,* II, pp. 42–43; "Iz dnevnika generala Alekseeva," *Russkiĭ Istoricheskiĭ Arkhiv,* I, 35.

8. Kerensky, "Iz vospominanii," *ibid.,* pp. 232–234.

9. F. Vinberg's *V plenu u obezyan: Zapiski kontr-revoliutsionera* cannot be located, and is known only by the excerpts which P. N. Miliukov made from it in Kiev.

10. Lukomsky, *Vospominania,* I, 232.

11. O. Chaadaeva, *Kornilovshchina* (Moscow, 1930), pp. 30–31.

12. Denikin, *op. cit.,* II, 27.

13. Shidlovsky, *Vospominania,* II, 141.

14. Miliukov, *Istoria,* Vol. I, Pt. 2, p. 113.

15. Denikin, *op. cit.,* II, 31. Miliukov, hinted at here, asserts, on the contrary, that during a long interview with Kornilov he warned him of the inopportunity of a decisive struggle against Kerensky, and met with no strong objections from him. Which is right, Maklakov or Miliukov, might be settled by Kornilov, were he not silenced forever. Regarding this, Denikin writes: "In such a delicate question documentary traces are seldom left; but they will turn up with time."

16. Savinkov, *op. cit.,* p. 18.

17. *Ibid.*

18. V. D. Nabokov, "Vremennoye Pravitel'stvo," *Arkhiv Russkoĭ Revoliutsii,* I, 46.

19. "Inostrannye diplomaty o revoliutsii 1917 g.," *Krasnyĭ Arkhiv,* V (XXIV), 152–154.

20. Telegram No. 396: "It would be beneficial for Alexis Aladin, member of the Second Duma, who has lived a long time in England, to come here. He could be consulted concerning the departure of others."

21. Chaadaeva, *op. cit.,* p. 65.

22. Sir George Buchanan, *My Mission to Russia and Other Diplomatic Memories* (Boston, 1923), II, 175, 182, 185.

23. Denikin, *op. cit.,* II, 63.

24. Miliukov, *op. cit.,* Vol. I, Pt. 2, pp. 116, 126, 148.

25. Chaadaeva, *op. cit.,* pp. 51–54.

CHAPTER EIGHTEEN

1. Preface by Maklakov to *La chute du Tsarisme* (Paris, 1927).

2. Lukomsky, *Vospominania,* I, 259.

3. *Ibid.,* I, 261.

4. *1917 g. v materialakh i dokumentakh: Razlozhenie armii,* edited by N. Kakurin, documents Nos. 146–149.

5. P. Kropotkin, *Sochinenia* (Moscow, 1919), II, 407, 421, 290, 465.

6. Kerensky in periodical, *Rodina,* No. 5 (1920).

CHAPTER TWENTY

1. "Inostrannye diplomaty o revoliutsii 1917 g.," *Krasnyĭ Arkhiv,* V (XXIV) (1927), 114.

2. Sukhanov, *Zapiski o revoliutsii,* II, 209; *also* N. Andreyev, *Revoliutsia 1917 g. Khronika sobytĭi.*

3. Andreyev, *op. cit.,* pp. 119, 130.

4. "Blok levykh i pravykh," *Biulleten' oppozitsii,* No. 17–18 (Nov.–Dec., 1930), p. 24.

5. E. Ignatov, *Moskovskĭi Sovet Rabochikh Deputatov v 1917 g.* (1925), pp. 29–30.

6. Sukhanov, *op. cit.,* I, 93–95.

7. *Ibid.,* p. 255.

8. Ignatov, *op. cit.,* pp. 85, 89.

9. That is, Kamenev, Stalin, and Muranov; *see* Shlyapnikov, *Semnadtsatyĭ god* (1925), Vol. II.

10. "Tyazhelye dni: Sekretnye zasedania soveta ministrov po zapisyam upravdela A. Yakhontova," *Arkhiv Russkoĭ Revoliutsii,* XVIII, 32–33, 37.

11. V. Bonch-Bruyevich, *Na boyevykh postakh fevral'skoĭ i oktyabr'skoĭ revoliutsii,* p. 83.

12. Lenin, "Uroki Krizisa," *Pravda,* April 23, 1917.

13. *Pravda,* No. 99 (July 5, 1917).

14. Stalin's report at the Sixth Congress of the Bolshevist party; *also* Shelavin, *1917 god. Ocherki russkoĭ revoliutsii* (1923), I, 140.

15. Report of N. Podvoisky, July 16, 1917, at the Second All-City Conference of Petrograd Bolsheviks.

16. *Izvestia Soveta Rabochikh i Soldatskikh Deputatov,* No. 47 (1917).

17. Shelavin, *op. cit.,* p. 56.

18. *Pervaya rabochaya konferentsia fabrichno-zavodskikh komitetov* (1917), p. 14.

EPILOGUE

1. In a very important work of V. I. Pokrovsky (*K voprosu ob uspekhakh aktivnogo balansa russkoĭ vneshneĭ torgovli*) the national income per person, in 1894, was reckoned at 73 rubles annually. Mulhall, *Industry and Wealth of Nations* (1896), placed it at 74 rubles, for Germany at 184, France 233, Great Britain 273, United States 346, Australia 374 rubles.

INDEX

DUE

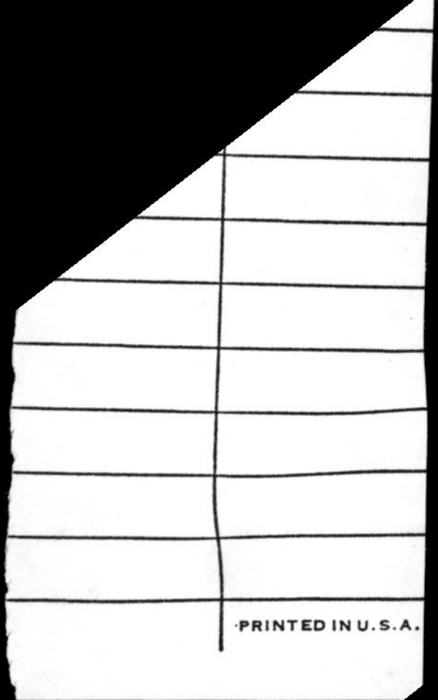
PRINTED IN U.S.A.